GETTING TO KNOW CATALONIA

COL·LECCIÓ SOM I SEREM, 3

GETTING TO KNOW CATALONIA

Josep-Maria Puigjaner

Generalitat de Catalunya

Biblioteca de Catalunya. Dades CIP:

Puigjaner, Josep Maria
Getting to know Catalonia. -- 4th ed.
Bibliografia
ISBN 84-393-3854-6
I. Catalunya. Generalitat II. Títol III. Col·lecció
1. Cultura catalana 2. Catalunya -- Descripcions i viatges
008(467.1)
914.671

First edition November 1990
Second edition November 1991
Third edition September 1992
Fourth edition March 1996
Circulation 500 copies

Cover and graphics Connecta RBP
Translation of the original Catalan text Toni Strubell

ISBN 84-393-3854-6
Legal deposit B-11.125-1996

Coordination of the edition and photo-composition Entitat Autònoma del Diari Oficial i de Publicacions
Printing T. G. Hostench, SA

CONTENTS

PRESENTATION

Aquest llibre és una invitació a conèixer Catalunya, un poble europeu que ja ha celebrat mil anys d'història. Les seves pàgines, en les quals la imatge ocupa un amplíssim espai, tenen com a objectiu presentar els trets essencials de la realitat col·lectiva catalana: la que constitueix el llegat de la seva història, la que ha cristal·litzat en el perfil del moment present i la que ja està continguda en els seus projectes de futur.

En una visió panoràmica del país, aquesta obra descriu els trets d'identitat de Catalunya, aquells que l'estructuren com a poble diferenciat, com a comunitat humana amb personalitat nacional. És a dir, la llengua, la cultura, el dret, la història, les institucions pròpies. Aquests són els trets singulars que mostren que Catalunya és una nació. Ja ho era embrionàriament abans de l'any 1000. I ho va ser en plenitud a mitjan segle XV. Avui és una nació sense estat propi que gaudeix de competències exclusives d'autogovern, en determinats àmbits, en una Espanya estructurada en territoris autònoms.

El segon aspecte que el llibre posa en relleu és el ritme vital d'aquest país. El 1992 —l'any olímpic de Barcelona, capital de la nació—, Catalunya ha d'haver aconseguit el nivell de competitivitat suficient per no cedir terreny no només en l'àmbit espanyol, sinó també en el marc europeu i mundial. Aquest és el repte fonamental amb què s'enfronten les diverses facetes de la vida catalana: des de l'ensenyament universitari o la formació professional fins a la comercialització dels seus productes industrials, des de les noves tecnologies fins a la creació d'un model social just i atractiu, des de la cultura fins al món de la comunicació. La implantació del Mercat Únic europeu comporta un alt desafiament per al desenvolupament de l'economia, però també obliga a posar a punt les activitats de tot el conjunt de la societat. No tinc cap dubte que la societat civil catalana serà capaç de donar una resposta positiva a tots aquests reptes de futur, ja que ha estat ella la que fins al dia d'avui ha assumit sempre aquesta responsabilitat.

En la concepció i en la realització de Conèixer Catalunya *hi ha, finalment, un tercer objectiu, el de la projecció cap a l'exterior. Catalunya, per situació geogràfica i per tarannà col·lectiu, ha estat sempre un país de portes obertes, tant per comunicar-se com per assimilar els missatges que li han vingut de fora. Ara, en aquesta circumstància de vinculació formal a l'Europa comunitària —en esperit, Catalunya ha sentit sempre la seva condició europea—, ha arribat el moment d'ampliar les seves transmissions als altres en la seva pròpia longitud d'ona. Modestament, però amb tota la convicció i amb tota la il·lusió, haig de dir que el nostre poble vol afegir el seu haver al conjunt de valors que constitueixen el patrimoni —no només material, sinó moral i espiritual— d'aquest vell continent, suma de pobles, nacions i estats, que és Europa.*

Jordi Pujol
President de la Generalitat de Catalunya

This book is an invitation for you to get to know Catalonia, a European country which has already celebrated a thousand years of history. Its pages, which are largely made up of illustrations, aim to offer the reader the basic features of Catalan society. This account covers not only the elements that make up the country's historical legacy, but also those that have crystallized out into the present reality and those already forming part of the country's future projects.

By way of a panoramic view of the country, this work describes those main features of Catalonia which help to make it a distinct country, a human community with a national character. That is to say: the country's language, culture, law, history, and particular institutions. These are the individual factors which prove that Catalonia is a nation. It already was a developing nation before the year 1000 AD, and a fully-fledged one in the mid-15th century. Today Catalonia is a stateless nation with full rights and competences for self-government in certain areas. It forms part of a State which is divided up into autonomous territories.

The second aspect the book stresses is the vital rhythm of this country. By 1992 (the Olympic year of Barcelona, the nation's capital) Catalonia will have become sufficiently competitive to avoid losing ground within the Spanish, European and World contexts. This is the basic challenge facing the different areas of Catalan life: from university teaching or professional training to the commercialization of industrial products; from new technologies to the creation of a socially just and attractive social model; from culture to the world of communication. The establishment of the European Single Market not only implies a great challenge for the development of the economy, but also calls for the modernization of all aspects of society. I have no doubt that Catalan civil society will be able to face all the different aspects of this challenge because, so far, it has always accepted that responsibility.

Lastly, a third aspect behind the conception and construction of *Getting to know Catalonia* is the projection of the country's image abroad. The geographical situation and the social character of Catalonia has always made it an open country, both as regards communication and the assimilation of foreign influence. In this present period of formal attachment to the European Community (in spirit, Catalonia has always felt its European condition), the time has come for the country to extend its communication with the rest of Europe, on the same wavelength. In all modesty, but with all conviction and enthusiasm, it can be said that our country wishes to make its contribution to the joint values that make up the heritage (not only material but moral and spiritual too) of the countries, nations and States that make up this old continent called Europe.

Jordi Pujol
President of the Generalitat of Catalonia

CHAPTER I

A COUNTRY WITH ROOTS IN THE DISTANT PAST

GEOGRAPHY, TERRITORY AND PEOPLE

Catalonia is a Mediterranean country. This statement holds true for her situation, her climate, her vegetation, her history and the character of her people. The country has a surface area of 31,895 square kilometres, slightly larger than that of Belgium. The inland perimeter is 707 km long, and there are 508 km of Mediterranean coastline.

The most outstanding physical feature about this Mediterranean country are her mountains. Catalonia is straddled by four mountain ranges: the Pyrenees, with peaks ranging from 2,500 metres to 3,143 metres high (Pica d'Estats); the Transversal mountain system, with peaks from 1,300 to 1,500 metres; the Prelitoral (precoastal) mountain system, which Montserrat (1,236 metres) and Montseny (1,712 metres) form part of; and the coastal range, with peaks about 500 metres above sea level.

The coastline offers a wealth of variety. To the north is the Costa Brava, which combines dramatic sea-battered cliffs with the peace and quiet of small sandy coves. Heading southwards, the coast takes on the name of Costa del Maresme, and long beaches and tourist resorts become predominant. The city of Barcelona, the capital of Catalonia — open to the sea and commerce thanks to its magnificent port — is the nerve centre of this section of coast. Further south, the coastline becomes more varied once again, and alternate stretches of sand and rocky cliffs lie side by side in an area known as the Costa Daurada (Golden Coast), of which Tarragona is the principal city.

The river system may be divided into two groups: those rivers that flow in an easterly direction and run directly into the sea (Ter, Fluvià, Tordera, Besòs, Llobregat, Francolí); and those that flow westwards as tributaries of the Ebre (Noguera Pallaresa, Segre,

Noguera Ribagorçana, Valira, etc.). Lakes are not abundant in Catalonia. However, there are small glacial lakes in the Pyrenees above the 2,000 metre mark, as well as Banyoles lake, which has a surface area of over a hundred hectares.

Rainfall varies in different areas of the country: there is a humid part of Catalonia (Pyrenees and Transversal mountain range), and a dry part (coastal and low-lying inland counties). Annual average temperatures also vary considerably: 3.4° centigrade in certain parts of the Pyrenees over the 2,000 metre mark, to 16.6° centigrade in the Ebre Delta. This means that temperatures, except in moments of exceptional atmospheric conditions, are not extreme either in winter or in summer.

Catalonia is a country which is divided into *comarques* or counties. The *comarca* is a unit established on the basis of geographical, economical and commercial criteria. Each *comarca* has its own identity, and a strong sense of internal cohesion. Nowadays there are 41 *comarques*, in accordance with the distribution laid down by the Catalan Parliament in 1987. However, the system of provinces (Barcelona, Tarragona, Lleida — Lérida — and Girona — Gerona) established throughout Spain in 1833 still stands.

The population of Catalonia is approximately six million, which is 16% of the total population of the Spanish State. Approximately 68% of the population is concentrated in Barcelona and its neighbouring *comarques*, where the main industrial centres are to be found. It is interesting to note that in 1857 Catalonia had 1,650,000 inhabitants in order to get an idea of the demographical development there has been. The most remarkable population booms have occurred this century as successive waves of immigrants arrived from other areas in Spain, especially in the twenties, the forties, the fifties and the sixties. Citizens born outside Catalonia, along with their offspring (many of whom are Catalans by birth), now make up 40% of the country's total population. Immigration has exerted — and still exerts — a powerful influence on aspects associated with politics, education, language and culture. Despite a series of social problems associated with this kind of phenomenon the world over, these newcomers have contributed significantly to the economic prosperity of Catalonia.

HISTORY

From the dawn of history to medieval times

Archaeological remains inform us that the Catalan lands were settled during the Early Paleolithic period. There are excellent samples of the artistic work of settlers in the Later Paleolithic period at several sites (Cogul, Tivissa). There are also examples of the more recent art of the Neolithic Age man (such as dolmens or tribal graves of the period) throughout Catalonia. The Ibers were a race endowed with a distinct cultural character. They had their own (hitherto indecipherable) alphabet and also left remarkable samples of their art, inhabiting our land in the period that leads up to the arrival of the Greeks, the Phoenicians and the Etruscans, in the 8th century BC.

The Greeks founded Empúries on the Alt Empordà coast in approximately the year 600 BC.

It was a city given over to commerce and the production of pottery, and it exerted an enormous influence on the rest of the territory. At a later stage, when the Carthaginians were at war with the Romans (the Punic Wars) in the year 218 BC, Romanization began, and in the 2nd century BC, Roman culture and art were introduced on a large scale throughout the Catalan lands. Empúries, Girona, Barcelona, and above all, Tarragona, are the cities which conserve most of the legacy left by this nation of jurists, builders and soldiers.

The progressive decline of the Roman Empire opened up the field to other European tribes — the so-called "barbarians" — who at this period began to spread across Europe. The Visigoths settled on Catalan soil and continued to develop the Roman tradition. But the Visigoth kingdom collapsed at the very beginning of the

8th century. The Moors crossed the Strait of Gibraltar, invaded the whole Peninsula and went as far north as Poitiers. The arrival of Charlemagne marked the beginning of a new period: the Arabs were expelled from the counties in the north of the country (Urgell, Empordà, Cerdanya, Besalú) and a frontier was established with the territories under Arab domination (known as the *"Spanish March"*). At a later stage, the Arabs tried to recover lost ground, and destroyed Barcelona in 985. Three years later, in 988, the Count of Barcelona, Borrell II, broke off ties of vassalage with the French King Hugh Capet. He proclaimed the sovereignty of his county and drew closer bonds of solidarity with neighbouring counties. It is for this reason that we celebrated the Millennium of the political birth of Catalonia in 1988.

The Church took on extraordinary importance in the 10th and 11th centuries, especially as a body associated with the patronage and promotion of culture. In 1032 Ripoll Monastery was founded, and over the course of the century, the monasteries of Montserrat, Sant Martí del Canigó, Sant Miquel de Cuixà, Sant Joan de les Abadesses and Sant Pere de Roda were built. All these monasteries are outstanding examples of Romanesque architecture.

In the 12th century, in the year 1137 to be precise, the Catalan-Aragonese Confederation was established as a result of the marriage of the Count of Barcelona, Raymond Berenguer IV, with Petronila of Aragon. This marriage did not in any way affect the juridical and political entity of either country. The main bond was limited to the figure of the monarch, who took on the title of King in Aragon, and Count of Barcelona in Catalonia.

As a result of the Treaty of Corbeil (1258), the frontiers with France were established. Catalonia still maintained her sovereignty over the Rosselló (Roussillon) and Cerdanya territories on the northern side of the Pyrenees, up until 1659.

Catalonia, a Mediterranean power

During the reign of James I (1213-1276) Catalonia became more and more powerful in the Mediterranean area. Commercial links built up by Catalan traders, especially with the Italian maritime republics, though also with countries on the north African coast and in the East, brought great prosperity to Barcelona, and, coincidentally, to all of Catalonia. These traders often became organized in groups, and even promoted the creation of the post of Consul, an official who was to represent common interests before the local authorities at each foreign port and who acted on behalf of the sea consulate (consolat de mar).

The commercial expansion was so great that it called for an appreciable juridical set-up as well as for the development of navigational techniques. Over the course of the 13th century, several maritime codes appeared, which were collected two centuries later in the *Llibre del Consolat de Mar* (Book of the Sea Consulate), published in 1484. In this work, the ship's working order, the rights and duties of the captain and crew, the problems associated with different types of merchandise, breakdowns, the relations between shipowners are all dealt with other questions. It is not surprising that cartography developed swiftly and at an earlier stage than it did at Pisa. The first Catalan Atlas was drawn up in 1375 by the Majorcan Jew, Cresques Abraham.

Commercial expansion grew hand in glove with the urge to conquer new territories. The Catalan-Aragonese Confederation soon annexed the island of Majorca (1229), as well as Sicily (1282), naples (1284), Corsica and Sardinia (1295). At the outset of the 14th century, Catalan expeditions arrived as far away as Greece. The duchies of Athens and Neopatria came under the rule of the Catalan-Aragonese Crown until 1387. These conquests were made possible by the operations of the *Companyia Catalana* of the *Almogàvers*, a select Confederation army corps.

An empire of this size inevitably called for a complementary form of political organization. A liberal, moderate and decentralized formula was chosen: each annexed territory was to conserve its own autonomy as well as its own institutions, leaving sovereignty over questions of law and order and affairs of general interest in the hands of the Catalan-Aragonese monarch.

As early as the 13th century, in the reign of James I, the assemblies at which the monarch sought advice and suggestions from his subjects were institutionalized. They were given the name of "Corts" and a formula for the representation of the three estates (the nobility, the church and urban or popular estate) was established. The Diputació del General or Generalitat was set up during the reign of Peter III, and operated as a body subsidiary to the Corts. As from the 15th century, it carried out executive activity in the political, financial and judicial areas. The model of political organization which the Catalan Corts (one of the first Parliaments in Europe) adopted in 1359 was maintained for centuries until the beginning of the 18th century. It was the working basis for the Confederation's states — Valencia (València), Balearic Islands, Aragon and Catalonia — as well as for the other confederated Mediterranean kingdoms — Sicily, Naples, Athens and Neopatria.

Decline and attempts at recovery

It was as if the country had become exhausted with the effort made in the Mediterranean campaign. Indeed, Catalonia only managed to "limp" into the new historical period we refer to as the modern era, — an era which begins with the fall of Constantinople to the Turks in 1453.

As a result of the so-called War of the Serfs *(guerra dels Remences)* (1462-1472), a period of dramatic decline was triggered off. The situation was aggravated by two further factors. Firstly, the marriage in 1469 of the "Catholic Monarchs", Isabella of Castile and Ferdinand of Aragon. This was the first step towards the union of Castile and Catalonia-Aragon, although both kingdoms continued to be governed by their own laws and administrations. The second factor was the discovery of America, which shifted the core of commercial activity away from the Mediterranean towards the Atlantic and newly-discovered lands. The Catalan people would be left out of the financial and economic operations associated with the birth of capitalism, which took place at that time.

Although the depression was profound and drawn out, it would be a historical error to believe that Catalonia had been written off as a nation. At the end of the 15th century, and throughout the 16th century, the Generalitat made a persistent effort to maintain the political prerogatives that would permit it to govern the

Principality. It was the fancy of the Hapsburg dynasty to fight endless wars of occupation in different European lands. Catalonia, however, only contributed to them with the levy of the *servei* or war tax, subject to the consent of the Corts, and with troops if Catalan soil was to be defended. At the end of the 16th century, in 1599, the Catalan Corts sessions were interrupted. Regal absenteeism had now become common practice, and a viceroy was appointed for Catalonia. This office represented the authority of the king throughout the territory of the Principality.

From a political point of view, relations with the royal authority became more and more strained over the course of the 17th century. In 1640, things came to a head, and the *revolta dels Segadors* (Reapers' Revolt) broke out. It was the first episode of a war which was to last twelve years and which ended up indecisively. Although the Catalan people, aided by the troops of Louis XIII of France, had revolted against him, Philip IV once again swore to respect the Catalan Constitutions.

However, not long afterwards, the Spanish Crown signed the Treaty of the Pyrenees with the French Crown (1659). This treaty laid down that the Rosselló (Roussillon) and part of the Cerdanya were to come under French Administration, disregarding the fact that the unity of territories with a close historical association was being overridden. Dynastic interests and so-called "reasons of State" prevailed over human, social, cultural and linguistic links and over the need to conserve the unity of the Catalan lands.

In this period, Catalonia was immersed in a deep economic crisis which led to social strife, struggles amongst the nobility and widespread poverty. Furthermore, it was forbidden for Catalans to try their luck at making a fortune in the new lands of the American continent. Nevertheless, there were manufacturers and merchants who did their best to see the country through the worst of the crisis. This was especially true after the publication of *Fénix de Cataluña* (The Phoenix of Catalonia), a book by Narcís Feliu de la Penya which was to provide great moral encouragement. Various operations concerning cloth production were carried out, and a group of Catalan specialists was sent to European countries to receive training and learn new techniques.

There was also a great increase in commercial and maritime activity. It can be said that the last third of the 17th century was a time for the reconstruction of the country.

The Catalan nation under the heel of the centralist State

On the death of Charles II, in 1700, Philip of Anjou, a member of the French Bourbon dynasty, was proclaimed King of Spain, with the style of Philip V. Some European powers, such as England and Austria, opposed this proclamation, and defended the right of Archduke Charles of Austria to succeed Charles II on the throne. The Catalan people supported the Archduke, who was proclaimed King of the Catalans in Barcelona in November 1705. From this moment onwards, a full-scale war — known as the War of Succession — broke out between England, Holland and Austria on the one hand, and France and Spain on the other. After several concessions and mutual compensations had been made, the two sides decided to sign the Treaty of Rastatt, bringing the war in Europe to an end. In this way, Philip V received international recognition.

Nevertheless, Catalonia decided to continue the war against Philip V, seeing in him a clear exponent of the kind of absolutist and centralist monarchy that she at all costs wanted to avoid. Catalonia, deprived of foreign aid, kept battling on in what can only be considered to have been a war of national survival. Despite the unfavourable course of the war, the Generalitat decided to run the risk of staking all on the defence of Barcelona. The city resisted heroically with only 10,000 men against 40,000 fully-armed assailants, but after Rafael Casanova, the head Councillor of the Council of the Hundred (Consell de Cent), had been wounded, the city was forced to surrender to the Duke of Berwick, commander-in-chief of the joint French and Spanish forces, on the 11th September 1714. As a result of this defeat, Catalonia lost her sovereignty to the Spanish Crown. Indeed, two years later, in 1716, the *Nueva Planta* decree (a series of repressive acts that were to define the new organization of the Principality) came into force. By the terms of the decree, the age-

old institutions of the country — the Corts or Parliament, the Generalitat, the Council of the Hundred and other town councils — were all swept away. These acts did away with the very juridical, judicial and administrative structure of Catalonia. But this was not all. Severe repression was brought to bear against the Catalan language, and at the same time provisions were made for the introduction of the Spanish language in the courts of law, in local administration and in schools.

Recovery in the 19th century

The increase in population that took place in Catalonia in the 18th century, (during which the number of inhabitants doubled), parallel with marked economic growth that was only temporarily affected by the War of Succession, paved the way for the period of the 19th century that was to prove decisive for the life of Catalonia. Another important factor was the permitting of Catalan ports to trade with America, an activity that had previously been forbidden.

The outset of the 19th century was unsettled for the Principality. The Peninsular War (1808-1814), fought against the armies of Napoleon, set back the recovery which had been initiated in the previous century. Many factories were destroyed, and industrial and commercial development suffered the consequences. The war did nothing for agricultural development either.

With the new century under way, industry was thoroughly modernized, and this predictably led to important changes in the financial and commercial situation. The steam engine was introduced into industry, and, in 1848, the first railway line was inaugurated. Despite the fact that industrialization was only a partial phenomenon, affecting only the textile and capital goods trades, Catalonia became the most advanced of the State's territories, and the whole of the Spanish economy came to depend on her.

In contrast with the backward, agrarian and shabby image of Spain, a country run by despots, Catalonia had an altogether different air about her which was modern, active, industrial and

set on progress. This vitality was largely due to the existence of a broad-based middle class capable of taking the initiative in the economic field. Industrial activity and the subsequent conurbations it led to, brought in a new set of problems: those raised by the proletariat, which at this time was beginning to organize trade unions in order to better working and living conditions.

The last third of the century is a period of great political activity. New ideas calling for State organization along federal lines were gaining support, and on the 8th March 1873, Catalonia declared her independence from Spain. This proclamation, however, did not take effect as a result of bilateral negotiations and a promise by the central Government to reorganize the State on a federal basis, once it had been converted into a democratic Republic. From this moment onwards, Catalanism began to take shape as a political movement with its different wings and factions. Catalonia once again proclaimed her national status. More on this subject later.

The major events of the 20th century

The loss of the last Spanish colonies in America (1898), the demands of the working class and the coming of age of political Catalanism are the three phenomena which mark the turn of the century. With the beginning of the 20th century, social and economic events evolved swiftly.

In 1914, the four provincial councils agreed to join together and constitute the Mancomunitat de Catalunya, a form of joint government for the four Catalan provinces (1914); presided over by that extraordinary statesman, Prat de la Riba, the Mancomunitat stood for the revival of the Catalan language and culture. However, the homogenizing and uncompromising spirit life in Spain once again brought the boot down on Catalonia with the military Dictatorship which lasted from 1923 until 1930. In Catalonia, the Mancomunitat was abolished.

With the fall of Primo de Rivera's Dictatorship, and amidst great enthusiasm and nationalist jubilation, Francesc Macià proclaimed the Catalan Republic, as a member State of the Iberian Federation.

This decision, which went beyond what had been agreed with the different political groups opposed to the monarchy at the 1930 Pact of Saint Sebastian, came as a surprise to the provisional Spanish Republican Government. After a great deal of haggling and negotiating with the representatives of the central authorities, a decision was taken to abandon the idea of a Catalan Republic in favour of the creation of an autonomous national authority within the Spanish Republican State. This institution was to take on the historical name of Generalitat de Catalunya (1932). The following institutions were to form part of the Generalitat: the Cabinet or Government: the Parliament or congress of elected members of Parliament, and the Tribunal de Cassació or Supreme Court of Appeal. Francesc Macià was the first President of the Generalitat. On his death in 1933, he was substituted by Lluís Companys, who, on the 6th October 1934, declared his opposition to the Madrid Government and proclaimed the Catalan State within the Spanish Federal Republic. Military reaction was immediate and the Catalan Government and several members of Parliament were imprisoned. The Statute of Autonomy was revoked until February 1936. In July of that same year the Spanish Civil War broke out. It lasted until 1939 and was won by General Franco. The totalitarian coup prevailed throughout the Spanish territory, leading to the systematic throttling of anything that smacked of Catalonia (especially her native tongue, Catalan) and her national identity. However, not everyone bowed down to the will of the dictator. Sectors of the intelligentsia, liberal professions, clergy, craftsmen and workers never turned their back to their own language and culture. Resistance to the Franco regime, though timid at first, became stronger and more deeply felt. In 1971, all the forces of opposition joined together to form the Catalan Assembly or Assemblea de Catalunya.

Forty years were to pass, though, since 1939, before Catalonia recovered her institutions for self-government. Four years after the death of the dictator (1975), the Catalan people voted in favour of the Statute of Autonomy (1979), and in April 1980, the first elections to the Catalan Parliament were held.

From an economic and social point of view, Catalonia entered the 20th century with the same nerve that had led to the

industrialization and modernization process initiated in the mid 19th century. Foreign capital and know-how poured in to back local initiative, which was especially active in the textile field. The First World War years (1914-1918) gave ample opportunities for exporting to the countries which were at war. This period was followed by years of recession and economic crisis, which were further aggravated by the bitter struggle of the workers' organizations for their demands. Despite the brief period of recovery afforded by the International Trade Fair of Barcelona (1929), the Republican years failed to show any signs of economic recovery. It goes without saying that the Civil War years (1936-1939) brought nothing but misery and the situation of the country did not improve until the sixties. The twenty years that span the period 1960-1980 have been marked by the intense modernization of the means of production and by a steady rate of economic growth.

The recent incorporation of Spain into the Common Market is a new challenge for Catalonia, in so far as she is a developed country. We shall deal with this subject at a later stage.

THE IDENTITY OF THE CATALAN PEOPLE OVER THE COURSE OF TIME

The Catalan language — a key factor

Catalan is a Romance language (as are French, Spanish and Italian, for instance) and is a product of the evolution of the Latin language brought by the Romans to the territory which is today equivalent on the map to the area covered by the Catalan language. Catalan is a language which came of age in the 10th and 11th centuries. As from 1150, the use of Catalan became normal practice in written documents, despite the fact that Latin continued to have the status of a language of universal culture.

Catalan is spoken in the Principality of Catalonia, in Valencia, in the Balearic Islands, in the Principality of Andorra, in a narrow strip of Aragon, in several counties in southern France, and in L'Alguer — a town on the island of Sardinia. The inhabitants of all these territories comprise about ten and a half million people. Of these, about six million speak the language. These figures indicate that Catalan is not one of the "great" languages in the world, but it is certainly not one of the "minor" ones either. As regards the number of Catalan speakers, it stands alongside Danish, Swedish and Norwegian.

It must be added that Catalan, as in the case of other languages, has different variants or dialects, as may be perceived in the pronunciation. This situation sometimes leads to comprehensible denomination conflicts. No objections are to be raised to the use of the terms "Valencian", "Majorcan", "Minorcan" or "Algueròs" in referring to the language used in those communities, as long as there is no doubt that they are all variants of the same language: Catalan.

Strange as it may seem, the Catalan language, over the course of its eight centuries of existence, has had to put up with difficult situations and has endlessly suffered attacks. Luckily we can say that it has held its own. In the 16th and 17th centuries no political pressure was brought to bear against the use of the Catalan language. The *Virreis* or viceroys — representatives of the Spanish monarch in Catalonia — published orders and decrees in Catalan. However, in the 18th century, King Philip V attempted to erase the national character of Catalonia, making every effort to snuff out the Catalan language by introducing Spanish in all Catalan-speaking countries under his sovereignty. In this century, there have been further attempts to eradicate Catalan. The most serious of these occurred after the Spanish Civil War. The Franco Dictatorship not only abolished the official status of Catalan, but also completely forbade its use in public.

At the turn of the century, an exceptional figure was to appear on the scene: Pompeu Fabra. He was to become the mastermind behind the standardization of the Catalan language. He wrote a Catalan Grammar and a General Dictionary of Catalan Language that were to be key works in the defence of the language against the attacks it was receiving, and would receive in the future.

At present, with the new democratic regime in Spain, the Catalan language has embarked on a process of normalization and full reinstatement in all walks of public life. It would seem that the language is no longer in danger of extinction, but a long period of convalescence is foreseen.

Cultural exponents

We could define Catalan culture as the spiritual wealth accumulated over the course of history that identifies the Catalan people and distinguishes them from their neighbours, within the context of the Iberian Peninsula and Europe.

The foundations of this culture are the country's language, Catalan, and hence the literature, as well as the art, specific laws, festivals, traditions and other signs of group identity.

Catalonia has benefited from a long succession of eminent writers who bear out the vitality and the creative resources of her language. A few of the more famous ones can be mentioned as examples. Ramon Llull (Raymond Lully), from Majorca (13th century), whose works are to be found in the more important libraries in the world. In València we must mention Arnau de Vilanova (14th century), a world-famous doctor and writer, who drew his inspiration from the scientific, psychological and theological knowledge of his time. The nobleman, Joanot Martorell, another Valencian (15th century), author of an extraordinary novel of adventures called *Tirant lo Blanc*, which Miguel de Cervantes called "the best book in the world". Another Valencian, Ausiàs Marc, raised the prestige of Catalan poetry to a very high level. In more recent times, the following authors stand out in the 19th century: Jacint Verdaguer for his poetry, the dramatist Àngel Guimerà, and Narcís Oller for his prose. Joan Maragall is the figure who marks the passage from the 19th to the 20th century. In the first third of this century, the list of outstanding writers is considerable: Carles Riba, Josep-Maria de Sagarra, Josep Pla, Llorenç Villalonga, "Gaziel", Marià Manent, Josep Carner, J. V. Foix, Josep-Sebastià Pons, J. Puig i Ferreter, "Guerau de Liost" etc.

In the area of historical and literary scholarship, we find important names such as Lluís Nicolau i d'Olwer, Agustí Duran i Sanpere, Jordi Rubió i Balaguer, Ramon d'Abadal i de Vinyals. As occurs in all countries, art is perhaps the expression of the human soul which throws most light on what a particular nation has been and is. Before Catalonia existed, the art of the primitive inhabitants of our territory had already left its mark on the rock faces of the caves. If we leap forward in time, we still conserve today samples of the fine taste of the Greeks in the art of making mosaics (Ampurias), and we may still contemplate the mastery of the Romans in civil and military architecture at Tarragona.

Nothing short of an extensive chapter would suffice to cover the Romanesque period. This was the art form which appeared at the time the Catalan national identity was being forged. Samples of this form of art are to be found in all the *comarques*. It is invidious to make a short list of monuments, but let us settle for the monasteries of Santa Maria de Ripoll, Sant Pere de Roda and the cathedral of La Seu d'Urgell or the cloister of Girona cathedral. A visit to the Catalan Art Museum is essential if one

wishes to see the best collection of Romanesque painting in the world. The boom in the world of commerce and the dynamics of city life brought about the development of the refined Gothic style, which flowered fully in Barcelona, as is evidenced by the civil palaces of the Barri Gòtic, the Cathedral, and the basilica of Santa Maria del Mar. During the 15th century, Catalan Gothic painting reached extraordinary standards of quality, with significant names such as the Bassas, the Serras and Lluís Borrassà, among others. In the 17th and 18th centuries, during the Baroque period, there were important Catalan sculptors (Agustí Pujol, Lluís Bonifaç) and painters (Viladomat, Tramulles). In the 19th century, Francesc Pla "el Vigatà", and Joaquim Vayreda stood out as painters; and the Vallmitjana brothers in sculpture. But the main 19th century figure was Marià Fortuny, a painter of impecable technique, a master of light effects in a way that recalls the nascent impressionism of the period.

Increasing industrialization made the 19th century a time of feverish architectural and town planning activity. Architect Ildefons Cerdà's project for the rational layout of the modern city of Barcelona is such an example. After neoclassical architecture had fizzled out in Catalonia, English "Modern Style" found its specific echo there (especially in the city of Barcelona) under the name of "*Modernisme*". The architect Antoni Gaudí, who built the spires of the Sagrada Família, the major architectural wonder of Barcelona, stands out at the beginning of the 20th century as a genius of unlimited imagination. In the field of the plastic arts, the panorama is illuminated by three artists of universal fame: Joan Miró, Salvador Dalí and Pablo Picasso. A visit to the Miró Foundation in Barcelona suggests that Miró must have painted under the influence of some form of magical spell. The works on show at the Dalí Museum in Figueres dispel any doubts about the possibility that Dalí's work did not go hand in glove with a mastery of technique. Pablo Picasso, who was born in Malaga, was educated in Barcelona and bequeathed a very significant part of his work to the city of Barcelona. It is to be admired in the museum that bears his name. In the field of music, the 19th century may boast the exceptional figure of Josep Ferran Sorts, the maximum exponent of Catalan musical romanticism. Later on, the composers

Isaac Albéniz and Enric Granados were also to stand out. In the 20th century, it is the figure of Pau Casals, the exceptional cellist and conductor, as well as soloists such as Maria Barrientos and Conxita Badia, who are outstanding.

A brief look at the world of science

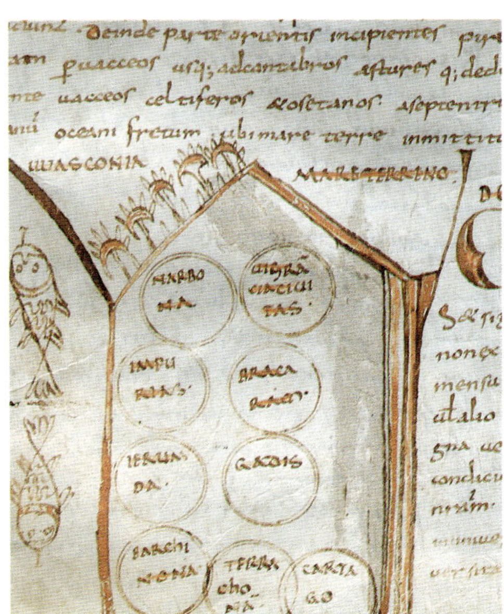

It is not surprising that Catalonia's geographical position should have made her an area of mixed scientific influences, and acted as a conveyer belt of knowledge during the late Middle Ages. The cultural and scientific activity carried out at Ripoll monastery was a reference point for all European centres of culture in the 11th and 12th centuries. Numerous Ripoll manuscripts were responsible for transmitting Arabic scientific knowledge — especially matters associated with astronomy — to western Christendom.

With the ever-strengthening consolidation and the blossoming of the Catalan nation, a truly autochthonous strain of scientific learning took root. Once again it can be appreciated that full political power and economic prosperity tend to be conducive to a strong scientific tradition. In the 13th century, a splendid period began for Catalan science. Once the classical and Arabic traditions had been assimilated, the Catalans of the period — both Christians and Jews — carried out creative and original works. It must be remembered that Ramon Llull, in his *Ars magna*, tried to concentrate all his knowledge into a set of basic principles to enable all kinds of problems to be worked out on a mathematical basis. To Arnau de Vilanova we owe the writing of general tracts and the compilation of documents on the medical knowledge of the period. The reign of Peter III, which saw the culmination of Catalan supremacy in the Mediterranean area, coincided with the most brilliant moment of Catalan scientific culture in the Middle Ages. In the medical field, besides the translation of the *Llibre de la figura de l'ull* (Book of the figure of the eye), an ophthalmological tract by the writer from Toledo called Alcoatí, translated by Joan Jaume, we find the *Regiment de preservació a epidèmia o pestilència e mortaldats* (Book of instructions for prevention of epidemics, plagues and mortal diseases), by Jaume d'Agramunt, a professor at the *Estudi de Lleida* or Lleida University, founded in 1300. The so-called Catalan Atlas *Atles català* of 1375, with its comprehensive cosmographic

and astronomical appendices, is world-famous. It is generally attributed to the Jewish Majorcan, Cresques Abraham (1325-1387).

During the 15th century, the scientific and cultural centre shifted from the Principality to Valencia, which also became the financial centre not only of the Catalan-Aragonese Confederation, but of the monarchy. In the last twenty-five years of the 17th century, when Spain was under the effects of a deep depression, Valencia was also to be the city where the progressive *Novator* Movement took a foothold, channelling the beneficial influence of the new European scientific tradition into the Peninsula, by way of intellectual circles and Academies. At the end of the 17th century Catalonia began to come to life again; Catalan scientists had not lost contact with Europe, especially as regards the exchange of ideas and knowledge with their French colleagues. As from the second half of the 18th century, there had appeared a solid bourgeoisie in the Principality which aspired to political and economic power. A series of scientific institutions were founded (Academy of Practical Medicine, Academy of Sciences and Arts, etc.), which helped to bring the country up to the European level. However, the trauma brought about by the Peninsular War (1808-1814) and the subsequent restoration of an absolutist monarchy opposed to novelty and innovation of any kind led to the paralysation of progress and the suppression of scientific activities all over Spain. Nevertheless, the years between 1833 and 1898 were put to good use in Catalonia. Both the Catalan *Renaixença* (Catalan renaissance movement) and industrialization paved the way for a new period of ebullience for the local scientific spirit that will make itself felt in the period known as *Noucentisme*, once the new century had got under way.

There is not enough space here to deal with the development of the different scientific disciplines, during the period running up to the Civil War. We also lack the overall picture that would permit us to summarize the period from 1939 to the present-day with a sufficient degree of accuracy and objectivity. However, no one questions the extraordinary professional prestige and international renown acquired by Dr. Ignasi Barraquer — who founded an Ophthalmological Institute in Barcelona — in this medical speciality, and by Dr. Josep Trueta in orthopaedic surgery, amongst others.

Historical and political Catalanism

In the second half of the 19th century a movement which stood for the recovery of the political entity of Catalonia grew up alongside the cultural movement known as the *Renaixença.* The most pronounced moment of change came in 1873 when a proposal for a Catalan State was included in the draft for a Spanish Federal Republican Constitution. It was not only the Republican Catalans who dared to back projects which clashed with the monolithic image of Spain. Liberal sectors of the bourgeoisie were also becoming increasingly won over by moderate Catalanism. Nevertheless, the need to give vent to the profound convictions of a wider range of society called for a more precise definition of political Catalanism.

Valentí Almirall tried to introduce a social, democratic, progressive and republican brand of Catalanism. In other social strata, however, a more conservative and traditional form of Catalanism was taking shape, inspired by the ideas of Bishop Torras i Bages. A key year for the development of political Catalanism was 1892. The *"Bases de Manresa",* a foundational document for the Catalan Regional Constitution, was drawn up. Two years later, in 1894, Prat de la Riba made his contribution to the debate and clarified matters by substituting "nation" for "region" in defining Catalonia. In the same period, the industrial bourgeoisie, exasperated by the economic policy of the Madrid Government, demanded administrative decentralization and a special economic statute for Catalonia. This state of opinion led to the victory of the allied Catalan candidatures over the centralist ones at the elections to the Madrid Parliament in 1901. The most outstanding event concerned with the progressive growth of Catalan nationalism was the electoral alliance of all Catalan political factions (excluding the pro-Spanish followers of Lerroux) under the banner of the Solidaritat Catalana (Catalan Solidarity), which carried out a brilliant victory at the 1907 Spanish general elections.

After this followed the Mancomunitat de Catalunya, the dictatorship of Primo de Rivera and the Republican period Generalitat, which we have already considered.

Costa Brava: the might of her rocks and the peacefulness of her coves. The Catalan coast is varied and beautiful. In the north, the sea clashes against the stony mass of the Costa Brava, which abounds in abrupt cliffs where the Mediterranean waves break and white horses occasionally rear up, as at Tossa in the photograph. Close at hand, however, the peaceful haven of the small sandy coves is to be found. They have a variety of characteristic semi-circular shapes, as can be seen in the bird's eye view of Aiguablava, Fornells and Platja Fonda.

The Sant Maurici Lake and Aigüestortes National Park. Lakes are not plentiful in Catalonia. In the Pyrenees, however, there are a wealth of small glacial lakes, such as Sant Maurici — in the photograph — calm and isolated, only disturbed by gentle ripples in the slight breeze. The lake forms part of the 1,900-metre high Encantats lake district in the Central Pyrenees, in the municipality of Espot. On its way down from the lake, the water seeps through a plain of dense and — in places — wild mountain vegetation, called the Aigüestortes National Park.

Tossa de Mar and Lloret: beaches and bathers. On the lower reaches of the Costa Brava and along the Maresme Coast there are plenty of beaches. In summer they attract Catalans and tourists from all over Europe, as in this view of Lloret de Mar, with its modern castle in the background. The impression of human density is even more acute on Tossa de Mar beach in full summer season. It forms a delightful bay which is girdled by pines that sway in the Mediterranean breeze. The stretches of bare sand in winter are quite another story!

The rocky Montserrat massif. At the intersection point of three counties (El Bages, L'Anoia and Baix Llobregat) is the impressive rocky Montserrat massif, which is 10 kilometres long and 5 kilometres wide. The highest point (1,224 m) is Sant Jeroni. The southern slope is made up of vast crags, some of which are fully 300 metres high.

Montserrat: spiritual haven and cradle of culture. In the heart of the rocky massif, there is a monastery, the existence of which goes back to the origin of Catalonia as a country. In the year 875, Montserrat mountain, after it was won over from the Moors, was granted to Ripoll monastery, who established a priory there in 1023, at the orders of Abbot Oliba. In 1409, Pope Benedict XIII raised the priory to the category of abbey. Montserrat, from the architectural point of view, is made up today of a series of irregular constructions: the remains of a Gothic cloister and the modern façade of the Monastery give way to the basilica's cloister porch, which was consecrated in 1592. In its interior there is a primitive Romanesque façade. Nevertheless the most important feature about Montserrat is the role it plays as a spiritual centre and its contribution to Catalan culture. It has a marvellous library, with plentiful incunabula and ancient manuscripts, among which is the famous 1392 *Llibre Vermell* (Red Book).

Banyoles, a natural lake with plenty of water sports. Banyoles is a natural lake of a tectonic and karstic origin. It is situated outside the Pyrenean area. It is 2,080 metres long, and its width varies from 235 to 730 metres. The deepest water areas are 62 metres deep. The lake is fed by subterranean sources which supply water at a rate of 600 litres per second. The landscape is pleasant and picturesque, and there is plenty of waterside vegetation on the lake's banks. Sunsets here give the lake an intriguing charm. In the last few decades, Banyoles has become a dynamic centre for the practice of water sports: swimming, sailing, rowing and water skiing. Angling is also a popular activity here. The lake has been chosen as the site for various competitions at the 1992 Olympic Games.

The Ebre Delta, an area of agricultural and ecological interest. This sunny panorama features the place where the Ebre ends its meander across the delta, in search of the sea. It provides us with a clear image of the alluvial nature of the ground. The Ebre Delta is 320 km^2, and is intensively cultivated, largely thanks to two irrigation canals. The principal crops are rice, on the lower ground, and vegetables on the higher ground. The delta is being studied in depth by geographers and ecologists to conserve its authoctonous wildlife: turtles, frogs and birds, the latter of which migrate through the area in large numbers.

The river Ter on its way through Camprodon. Camprodon's Pont Nou (New Bridge) has watched the waters of this river passing under its arch since the 16th century. It is the 167-kilometre-long Ter, one of the country's major rivers. It is born near Setcases in the eastern Pyrenees. It crosses towns and cities, which over the course of the centuries, and largely thanks to the river, have become dynamic industrial complexes: Torelló, Manlleu, Roda. Further on, the Ter turns east and flows down into the Guilleries. In this century, the river has here been damed at several points, and becomes a source of electric power by way of the hydoelectric power stations at Sau and El Pasteral. The Ter is not merely a watercourse, but a source of energy that has contributed to Catalonia's development.

A Roman mosaic at Empúries. A mosaic from a Roman house at Empúries, a city founded by the Greeks in 600 BC. This city was protected by its ally Rome during the second Punic War. Later on, Empúries continued to be an important city on the Mediterranean coast because of its privileged geographical condition and its commercial and industrial activity. In the times of the Roman Empire, it covered an area of 50 acres. It had a complete wall about it, and contained luxurious villas, as well as a forum, an amphitheatre and an arena. Excavations — which have facilitated the discovery of archaeological treasures accumulated over the years — were initiated in 1907 by Josep Puig i Cadafalch.

The Roman amphitheatre at Tarragona. Tarraco, as from the 3rd century BC, played a major role in the Romanization of the Iberian Peninsula's way of life and social structure. After the period of Augustus, Tarraco became capital of one of the Empire's provinces, known as "Tarraconense", and put all the advantages of Romanization to full use. Thus, in the 3rd century BC, the city had an amphitheatre, beside the sea, and an aqueduct, the Berà Arch and the Tower of the Scipios near the city.

Berà Arch, a monument in honour of a Roman general. The Berà Arch is a genuine exponent of the triumphal arches built by the Roman Empire throughout the province. It is situated on the Roman road known as the Via Augusta. The monument has a single arch which is 10.14 m high and 4.87 m wide. There are two Corinthian columns on either side which sustain the entablature and are supported by a socle. The engraving tells us that it was built on the orders of Lucius Licinius Sura, whose memory it was to honour. He was a general in Emperor Trajan's army, towards the end of the first century AD.

Roman sculptures in Tarragona. The Archaeological Museum of Tarragona has a wealth of examples of Roman art which excavations have recovered for us to admire. The God Dionysius — a Roman copy of an original of the Greek god Praxiteles — and a 2nd century BC. Venus, are two of the most remarkable pieces of Roman sculpture on show in the museum, which is to be found on the very site of the necropolis. It contains the most important collection of Roman archaeological pieces in Catalonia.

The aqueduct, a Roman monument in the Tarragona area. The Roman aqueduct is one of the finest architectural monuments within the Tarragona city limits. It would appear that this feat of engineering was constructed in the 1st century AD to bring water from the river Francolí to the city of Tarragona. The aqueduct is made of stone blocks of various sizes, arranged to form pilasters and arches, with eleven arches on the lower level and twenty-five above. It is 217 metres long and 17 metres high.

Romanesque door at Ripoll monastery. Ripoll monastery church's 12th century door, with high relief sculpture work. It is one of the finest works of Romanesque sculpture and architecture in Catalonia. The monastery, which was founded in about 879 by the powerful Wifred the Hirsute — a count who ruled over five counties —, immediately became one of the most influential centres in medieval Europe, both in a religious and in a cultural and economic sense, especially during the period it was presided over by abbot Oliba. The church, which was founded in the 10th century, has been restored in modern days. It has a transcept with 7 apses and an adjoining 12th century cloister.

The bell-tower and cloister of Sant Miquel de Cuixà. The bell-tower is one of the basic elements in the Romanesque style monastery of Sant Miquel de Cuixà. The 12th century cloister is also remarkable, although only half of it remains on the site. Cuixà is the only old monastery on the northern slopes of the Pyrenees to be found in the Conflent county, which today lies within the French State. Since 1965 there has been a Catalan Benedictine community — from Montserrat — residing in the monastery.

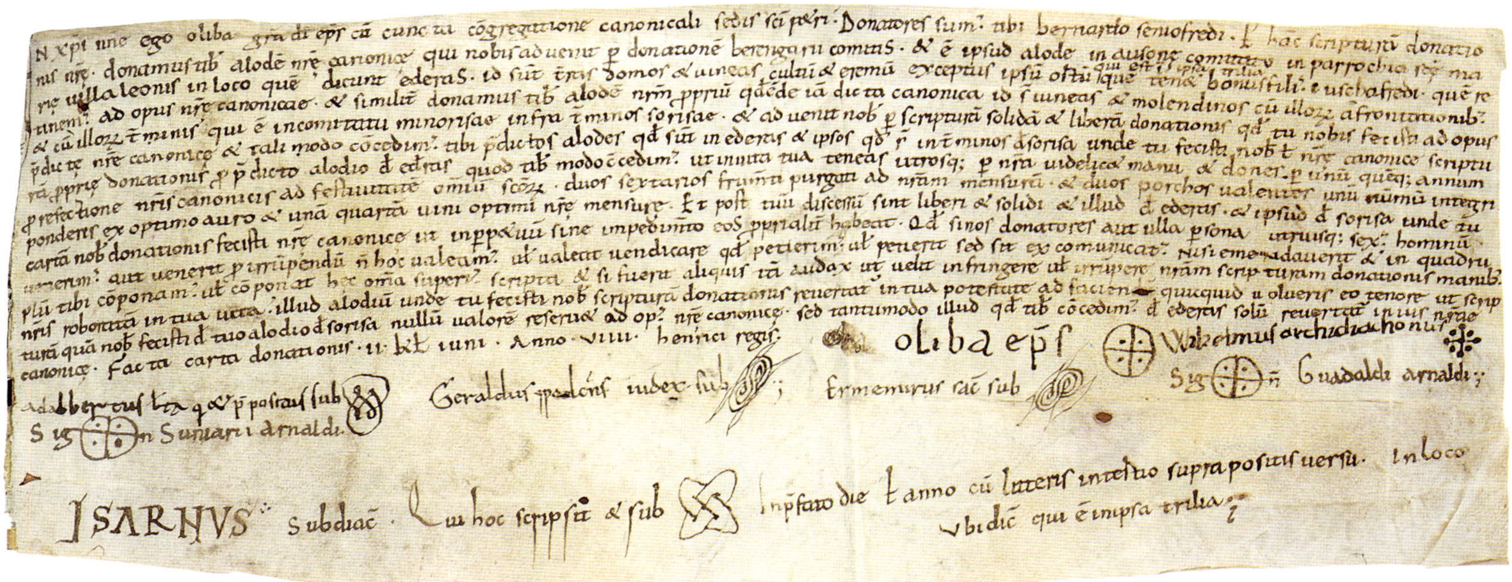

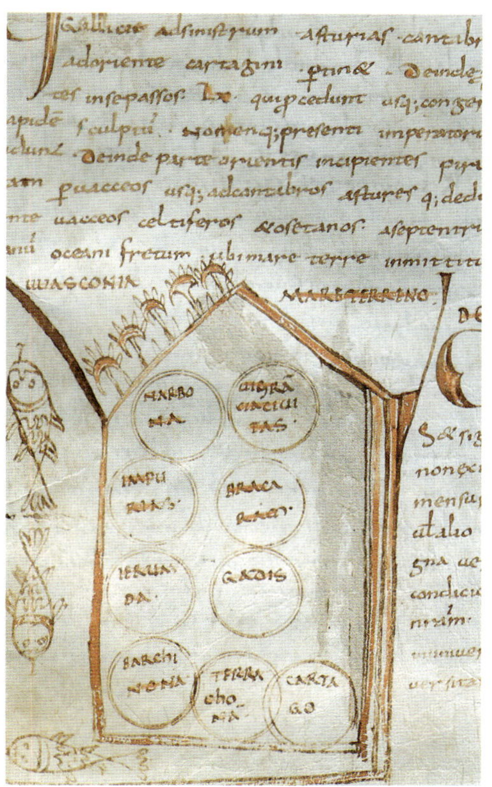

Fragment of the Ripoll *Còdex Miscel·lani*. An 140-page fragment of the *Còdex Miscel·lani patrístic, poètic i científic de Ripoll*, a manuscript which contains the written works of several patristic authors, poetic works, astronomical charts, and mathematical treatises. The whole work is illustrated with abundant coloured drawings. According to the palaeographer and medievalist Anscari M. Mundó, "the most interesting illustration is a rudimentary map of the Iberian Peninsula (the oldest on record)". As regards this manuscript, it must be remebered that Ripoll was the most important centre for Romanesque miniatures. In about the year 1000, the two most important bibles in the world were illustrated here: the *Ripoll Bible* (Vatican Library) and the *Sant Pere de Roda Bible* (Paris National Library).

Document featuring bishop and abbot Oliba's signature. The parchment of this document, dated in 1040, bears the signature of Oliba, bishop of Vic as well as abbot of Ripoll and Cuixà. Eminent medievalist, Manuel Mundó, described Oliba as "a key character in the late 10th and early 11th century, responsible for the formation of the patriotic spirit in primitive Catalonia. In his writings and activities, one may perceive the idea of the territotial context which he and his contemporaries referred to as 'fatherland', which included almost all medieval Catalonia, from the Rosselló (Roussillon), Conflent and Cerdanya, counties in the north, and from the Urgell and the westernmost counties as far south as Tarragona and the Ebre counties, all united under the mantle of the Church". Oliba is also a leading character in the promotion and dissemination of the period's culture throughout the Catalan counties.

The *Creation Tapestry* (12th century). The *Creation Tapestry* is one of the oldest artistic tapestries conserved in the Catalan Countries. It is woven in linen, and is quite large (3.65m × 4.70m). It consists of two concentric circles: the smaller one contains an image of the Pantocrator God, and the larger one is a representation of first two chapters of the book of Genesis. The tapestry is on view at Girona cathedral.

Virgin and Child: Romanesque sculpture. Polychrome sculptures are very representative of Catalan Romanesque art, especially in the 12th century. They are normally frontal and quite rigid in form, often representing the Virgin and Child Jesus, like this one which is on show at the Diocesan Museum in La Seu d'Urgell. Its director, Albert Vives, describes this splendid piece as follows: "The delicate and serene expression on the faces is quite striking, as is the fine structure of the body contours. This proves that the sculpture belongs to the late Romanesque period, although its features announce the mystical realism of the Gothic period".

The *Beatus* of La Seu d'Urgell. This painting on parchment is one of 90 illustrations contained in the manuscript known as the *Beatus* of La Seu d'Urgell, which is the "Commentary of the Apocalypsis of the Pious Man of Liébana", written in minuscule Visigothic script, although it is of uncertain chronology. Experts are not unanimous about its origin, but reckon that it was in La Seu d'Urgell at the beginning of the 12th century. There is no doubt, however, that, after the 10th century, the art of illustrating manuscripts achieved splendid results from the point of view of colour and figurative composition.

11th century apse of Santa Cecília de Montserrat. Santa Cecília is on the eastern side of Montserrat mountain. It had been a monastery, founded in the year 945 in the county of Manresa. In the 14th century, the monastery entered a period of decline and soon became a hostel. The 11th century Romanesque church has been conserved to our day. It has three naves of different sizes and three apses, which have blind arcatures on the outside and an original bell gable.

Pre-Romanesque arches of Sant Miquel de Cuixà. Elongated Pre-Romanesque arches at Sant Miquel de Cuixà church (Conflent), which was consecrated in the year 974 and subsequently added to in later periods. Abbot Oliba completed the construction with Romanesque-style additions, about the year 1045. In the days of Oliba, the monastery exerted a considerable degree of cultural, artistic and religious influence throughout Europe. It was at that period that its scriptorium, one of the most active in all Europe, was at its peak. The church is part of the Romanesque ensemble of Sant Miquel de Cuixà, a benedictine monastery at the foot of the Canigó mountain, in the heart of the Pyrenees.

A Romanesque capital at Santa Maria de Lluçà. This magnificent capital of the Ripoll school of sculpture (12th century), with decorations featuring animals, belongs to the small cloitser of Santa Maria de Lluçà monastery (Osona). It is a rectangular cloister made up of twenty-two columns which support semicircular arches. Beside the cloister is the mid 12th century church, which is also Romanesque. To these attractive constructions one may add another discovered of late (in 1954) beneath the heart of the church: a remarkable set of Gothic wall paintings, with scenes from the life of Jesus Christ and the Virgin, a large Pantacrator and scenes from the life of Saint Augustine.

Illustration from the *Llibre Vermell* (Red Book) at Montserrat. The library at Montserrat conserves a manuscript on parchment, writen in 1392, with texts in Latin and Catalan, basically from the 14th century which is given the name *Llibre Vermell* because it is bound in red Morocco leather. This manuscript is interesting at many levels: historical, lithurgical, homilethical, geographical (because of the maps it contains), astronomical, literary and musical. The choreographical documentation regarding five "*balls rodons*" (round dances) in the book is of great importance for the history of religious dancing.

Sant Pere de Roda, the masterpiece of Catalan Romanesque architecture. The blue backdrop of the sea gives the setting one of Catalonia's finest Romanesque constructions deserves: Sant Pere de Roda monastery, founded in 944, has a Lombard bellfry, which is balanced by the parallel line of the magnificent main tower. The cloister has been badly damaged. The abbatial church's foundation date is uncertain, but it is of an unusual height for the Romanesque period. It has an ambulatory and a fine crypt beneath the presbitery. The church has three naves separated by pilasters with adjoining columns. Some of the capitals are of Arabic and others of Carolingian inspiration.

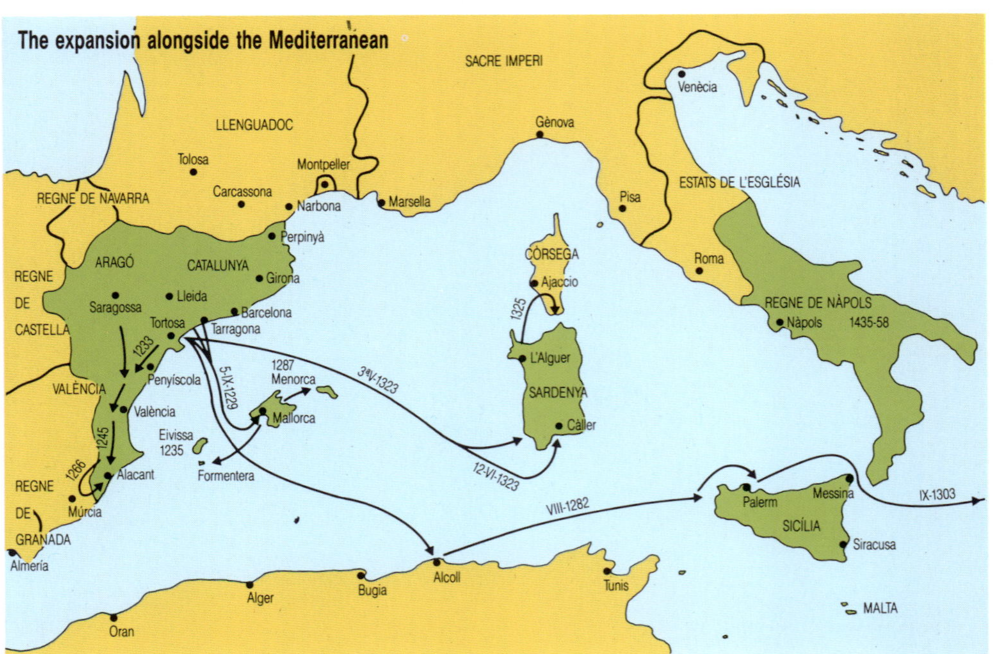

Territorial dominions of the Catalan-Aragonese Confederation. The mid 14th century was the moment of maximum splendour for the Catalan-Aragonese Confederation. It was a period of political dominion and commercial possibilities. Apart from the territory now covered by the Principality of Catalonia, the dominion of the Confederation spread as far as the Rosselló (Roussillon — at present under French rule), the Kingdom of Majorca and the rest of the Balearic Islands, the Kingdom of València, the island of Sicily, the island of Sardinia, the Kingdom of Naples and the Greek duchies of Athens and Neopatria. Strangely enough, the peak of this period of expansion coincided with a serious demographic crisis, which the country did not recover from until one hundred and fifty years later.

Libreappellat
Conſolat de mar. Nouament eſtam
pat e corregit. Affegits los capitls
e ordinacions dels drets del Gene/
ral. E del dret del pes del Senyor
Rey. Ab altres coſes neceſſaries:
les quals fins al preſent no erẽ eſta-
des eſtampades.

The *Llibre del Consolat de Mar* (Book of the Sea Consulate), printed in 1518. Catalan commercial influence throughout the Mediterranean area was so important that juridical organization was called for. In the 13th century, different sets of rules came out, and these were gathered together in the *Llibre del Consolat de Mar* two centuries later. They were first published in 1484 in a book which grouped together the norms applied by the Sea Consulate Court in Barcelona. The book covers different fields: internal organization of the ship, rights and duties of the captain and the crew, problems arising from merchandise, the relationship between shipowners, among other subjects. The page we have before us is from the Johan Rosembach edition, printed in Barcelona in 1518.

The Drassanes, Gothic civil architecture in Barcelona. The Drassanes or ship-building and repair yards are situated by the sea near the harbour, and evolved alongside the use of materials and the development of technology. In Catalonia the most primitive ones, built in the 11th century, were in Barcelona. Today's Drassanes were built in the 14th century. Their construction was initiated by King James I, and Andreu Febrer was responsible for directing the works. The building is considered to be one of the most magnificent exponents of Catalan Gothic civil architecture.

King James' campaign in Majorca (1229). The scene shows a camp of Catalan soldiers during the conquest of Majorca. In the centre, a group of officers are conversing with King James at his campaign tent. The soldiers of the light infantry, the fearful *Almogàvers*, participated in the great expeditions which achieved the conquest of Valencia and other Mediterranean victories (Majorca, Sicily, Greece, etc.). In the picture is a fragment of a wall painting in the Art Museum of Catalonia (Barcelona).

The Cresques Abraham Atlas, produced in 1375. The Majorcan Jew, Cresques Abraham, was the author of one of the most important cartographical works of the 14th century. It was called the *Atles català* (Catalan Atlas), a superb example of Majorcan cartography, which at that time was considered to be one of the finest in the Mediterranean area. Cresques Abraham, with the aid of his son, drew this seven-coloured world map on six parchment pages in 1375. It also includes explanations and legends in Catalan. The other pages contain four maps which, when placed side by side, cover the world as it was then known: Europe, Asia and Africa; the original version of this world map is in the National Library in Paris.

The Generalitat's foundational document, dated in 1359. In the second half of the 14th century, during the reign of Peter III the Ceremonious (1336-1387), Castile began to take on the air of an emergent power, managed to overcome the general economic crisis and tried to obtain a hegemonic position in the Iberian Peninsula. There were military operations which demanded great expense of the Catalan-Aragonese Crown. This circumstance obliged the Catalan Parliament (Corts catalanes), held at Cervera in 1359, to institutionalize a permanent body — as can be seen in the document conserved — which would see to the raising and administration of funds. This body was to be called the Diputació del General. It depended on the Parliament, later took on the name of Generalitat and became the effective representation of the Parliament in the period between sessions. After the 15th century, the Generalitat took on executive, governing, political, financial and judicial functions.

The Gothic gallery in the Generalitat Palace courtyard. The gallery in the Generalitat Palace's Gothic cloister is supported by slender columns made of Tortosa red marble. The work was planned in the 15th century by the master architect Marc Safont. This Palace is the most important medieval civil building in the city of Barcelona. This is so not only for architectural and artistic reasons, but for political ones too: it is one of the few medieval buildings in Europe to have been built as the seat of a particular political institution, and which is still used as such. Therefore, the history of this flammiferous gallery, and that of the whole Palace, may be considered to be the very history of the Generalitat itself.

Incunabulum page with an illustration of the Catalan Corts (15th century). This minutely illustrated page from the 15th century *Constitucions i altres drets de Catalunya* (Constitutions and other rights of Catalonia), represents the Catalan Parliament. In the Catalan-Aragonese Confederation, the Parliament (Corts) was the assembly summoned and presided over by the king, with the participation of the different estates or arms (nobles, clergy and bourgeoisie). Its essential objective was to reach agreements and pass laws. The king summoned the Parliament in each of the territories that made up the kingdom, and each territory's identity was respected. Thus, in words of historian Pierre Vilar, the Aragonese Crown became a sort of Commonwealth, based on a flexible form of institutional articulation, in the framework of a federal political conception. This Parliament, which started in the 13th century, met until the 18th century.

Saint George fighting against the dragon, **a 15th century Gothic sculpture.** During the first half of the 15th century, the Generalitat Palace's architecture was greatly added to. In 1416, the deputies agreed to build the wall and the Carrer del Bisbe (Bishop's Street) entrance. Above it, we find the elegant medallion of Saint George, by Pere Joan, a famous artist who also worked in Tarragona, Zaragoza and even in Naples. According to the art historian, Joan Ainaud, Pere Joan is not only responsible for the medallion, but also for the frame about it and the ornamental gargoyles that project out of the façade, especially the ones on either side of the medallion.

The St. Eulàlia and St. Clara altarpiece. Serenity and delicacy are perhaps the foremost features emanating from the human qualities of these two figures (St. Eulàlia and St. Clara) in the central part of Pere Serra's altarpiece. The balanced use of colour and the harmonious and symmetrical position of the figures show the skill of this artist, who lived and worked in Barcelona at the beginning of the 15th century, at the same time as other illustrious artists such as the Bassas, Bernat Martorell and Lluís Borrassà. The attributes they hold clearly identify the figures in the altarpiece: St. Eulalia with the palm of martyrdom, and St. Clara with the book of Franciscan Rules and the abbess's crozier.

The Lieutenant's Palace in the Aragonese Crown Archives. During the reigns of the monarchs of the House of Austria, the figure of the lieutenant or viceroy acquired great significance. The *"virrei"* (viceroy) was the representative of the monarch's power in Catalonia, a post almost always taken up by Castilian aristocrats. This Renaissance-style building in Barcelona — today seat of the General Archives of the Aragonese Crown — was built by Antoni Carbonell and finished in 1557. It was constructed as a result of an agreement of the Monzón Parliament session in 1547. The palace, as its name suggests, was the residence of the viceroys in Catalonia. Inside the present building, which shows signs of restoration work over the centuries, there is a panelled ceiling which, according to historian Martínez Ferrando, was built towards the end of the 16th century.

***The battle of Lepanto* (1571), by Antoni de Brugada.** The Hispanic monarchy, the Pontifical States and Venice formed an alliance known as the Holy League because of the expansion of the Turks in the eastern Mediterranean. The fleet, under the command of the young John of Austria — a command that was more symbolic than real — engaged the Turkish fleet in the Gulf of Lepanto. The Turkish fleet was defeated. This battle has been the subject of special attention in Catalonia because of the significant participation of ships and seamen from the Catalan Countries. John of Austria's lieutenant was the Catalan noble, Lluís de Requesens, who was to be the real commander of the fleet and responsible for the victory. The Catalan painter, Antoni de Brugada, gave vent to his imagination in this painting of the fierce combat between two rival ships, tossed by the waves.

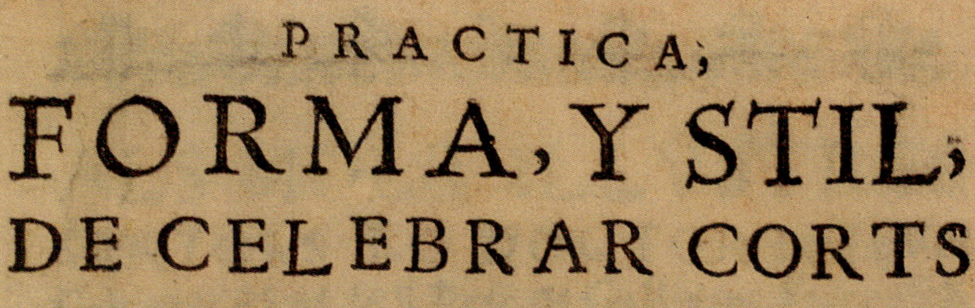

PRACTICA;
FORMA, Y STIL,
DE CELEBRAR CORTS
GENERALS EN CATALVNYA,
y materias incidents en aquellas.

Diuidida en tres Parts.

Per lo nobleDon Luys de Peguera del Consell de sa Magestat en la Real Audientia de Catalunya.

De manament dels Senyors Deputats de Catalunya,
En Barcelona, per Gerony Margarit, any 1632.

The cover of a 17th century treatise on Catalan constitutional law. *Pràctica, forma, y stil de celebrar corts generals en Catalunya* (Practice, form and style for the celebration of General Parliament sessions in Catalonia), is one of the main works of the judicial official, Lluís de Peguera, attorney at the Royal Court of Catalonia and consultant to the lieutenancy of the Principality. This work was printed in Barcelona in 1632 during the reign of Philip IV. Despite the fact that Conde Duque de Olivares aspired to subdue all kingdoms in the reign "to the style and laws of Castile", Catalonia continued to maintain her constitutions — which Philip IV had sworn — and exercise her right to home rule. Catalonia was tied to the Spanish Empire, but clung — opposing submission — to her juridical doctrine, that involved pacts and agreements, and her own political style of self-government. Both characteristics were upheld until 1714.

CONSTITVTIONS
Y
ALTRES DRETS
DE
CATHALVNYA,
COMPILATS EN VIRTVT
DEL CAPITOL DE CORT LXXXII.
DE LAS CORTS PER LA S.C. Y R. MAJESTAT
DEL REY D'ON PHILIP IV. NOSTRE SENYOR
CELEBRADAS EN LA CIVTAT DE BARCELONA
ANY M.DCCII.

VOLVM PRIMER.

BARCELONA: En Caſa de Joan Pau Marti, y Joſeph Llopis Eſtampers, Any 1704.

Constitutions y altres drets de Cathalunya **(Constitutions and other rights of Catalonia), 1588.** The continual enactment of successive legislative ordinances by the public powers (King and Parliament), in the course of time, especially in the Modern Era, called for the up-dating of the Constitutions and Parliamentary Stipulations of Catalonia. At the 1585 Monzón Parliamentary session, a decision was made regarding the need to produce another compilation. The job basically involved up-dating the first collection of documents (1495), adding subsequent legislation and doing away with any sections that had become out-dated. The work was published in three volumes in Barcelona. Later on there was a third compilation in 1704, three years after King Philip V himself had sworn them, and shortly before the War of Spanish Succession broke out, a war in which the Catalans opted for another monarch.

A Catalan soldier in the Reapers' War (*guerra dels Segadors*, 1640). This soldier, called Salvador Darder — a member of the silversmiths' guild — joined up in the Bandera de Santa Eulàlia regiment. He participated along with Catalan and French troops in the glorious battle of Montjuïc against Philip IV in 1641. It was a time of great political upheaval and continual military campaigns. The repeated shortcomings of the king as regards his oath of loyalty to the rights and freedom of the Catalans made Catalonia cut her ties with the Spanish monarchy. The Generalitat's deputies, in the Junta de Braços (Estates Assembly) session of 16th January 1641, suggested that Catalonia become a Republic under the protection of France. The proposal was accepted, and the Council of the Hundred (Consell de Cent), the government of the city of Barcelona, voted its approval. The new regime did not take root, though. There were not enough financial resources nor military forces to successfully take on the powerful Castilian army.

The territory of Catalonia after the Treaty of the Pyrenees (1659). The 1659 peace agreement between Louis XIV of France and Philip IV of Castile and Catalonia-Aragon, known as the Treaty of the Pyrenees, put an end to a war that had started in 1635. The Spanish Crown exchanged several European territories for the Rosselló (Roussillon) and part of the Cerdanya (Cerdagne) counties, which were handed over to the French. This treaty did not take into account the linguistic, cultural, social and economic unity of territories closely associated by a common historical trajectory. The fact is that the people of the Rosselló of that period — and for many decades after — considered themselves to be Catalans and regarded the term "French" or "Catalan French" as an insult.

Pau Claris "defender and liberator of the fatherland". The Generalitat of Catalonia's Diary describes Pau Claris as the "great restorer of our fatherland and mother Catalonia, defender and liberator of our nation". Pau Claris, who was born in Barcelona in 1586, was elected president of the Generalitat for the 1638-41 three-year period. Claris challenged the royal authority of Philip IV and his representatives in Catalonia, among other reasons for the increasingly burdensome taxes the Catalans had to pay to the Crown. The confrontation ended up in the declaration of war on the part of the Generalitat against the Conde Duque de Olivares, a war that did not cease until 1652, and which had its most significant episode in the "Bloody Corpus Day" (*Corpus de Sang*) in 1640.

Dos llibres de Pedro Seraphin, de Poesia vulgar, en lengua Cathalana.

EN BARCELONA
En casa de Claudes Bornat.
1565.

Ab priuilegi Real per deu anys.

Pere Serafí, painter and poet, a follower of Petrarch. Pere Serafí (1505-1567) was the most prominent of that period's Catalan writers to have followed in Petrarch's footsteps. Almost surely from Italy, he settled in Barcelona, where he developed his taste for painting in several altarpieces and on the organ doors at Barcelona and Tarragona cathedrals. In 1565 he published the work *Dos llibres* (Two books), which contains 170 poems, distributed in two parts: one on lay subject matter and another on spiritual subjects. Apart from following Petrarch, Pere Serafí also took inspiration from Ausiàs Marc and Joan Boscà. Catalan literary production slumped considerably in the 16th and 17th centuries; Pere Serafí is one of the few authors with works of any great standing.

Pottery frieze illustrated with mercantile activity (17th century). While the Castilian economy was undergoing a major monetary crisis and suffering uncontrolled inflation, the territories of the Crown of Aragon (Catalonia, Valencia, and Aragon itself) had entered a period of recovery. Barcelona port participated actively in the boom of agricultural production, especially wine growing. Barcelona is the commercial centre that receives imported wheat from Italy and France, and exports wine and brandy to England, Germany and Holland. The economic activity and leading role played by maritime transport at the end of the 17th century is what is reflected on this pottery frieze in the Pottery Museum of Barcelona.

Archduke Charles of Austria lands in Barcelona. The print shows a schematic view of the walled city of Barcelona. Outside the port, in formation, are the ships which accompanied archduke Charles of Austria to the Catalan capital, where he was received as triumphant king. At that moment, a war had already broken out throughout Europe (Spain and France against England, Holland and Austria), called the War of Spanish Succession. It was a dynastic war over the succession to the Spanish throne. But Catalonia, a country which joined forces with the enemies of Spain, only sought the preservation of her national rights. The alliance signed with England in exchange for guaranteeing the Catalan institutions, whatever the result of the war might be, proved worthless. The war ended in 1713 with the Treaty of Utrecht, ratified one year later at the Treaty of Rastatt, where Catalonia was abandoned to her fate. One year later, in 1714, the armies of Philip V, aided by the French, defeated the Catalans at the heroic siege of Barcelona.

CANÇO NOVA

VIva, Viva, Carlos viva,
puix nos dona llibertat:
vagen fora los Franceſos,
ja que tant nos han offeſos,
en lo noſtre Principat.
Guerra, Guerra, per la terra,
Cridan tots los Cathalans:
ſie Carlos Rey de Eſpanya,
y poſemnos en campanya,
ſi volem ſer triumfants.
Ja que França, tant nos cauſa,
vage fora, promptament:
à las Armas Valeroſos,
que ſerem victorioſos,
ſi perſeguim à tal gent.
Ea, Carlos, alcanſarlos,
fins que ſien retirats,
à la part de tremontana
per ſert vna gent Villana
que tant nos han maltratats.
Fortazela, ſens vileza,
Valeroſos Vigatans:
ja que Carlos vos demana,
y en voſtres mans encomana,
las coſas mes Importants.
Se retiran, y ſuſpiran,
los Gabaigs del Empurda,
per eſtar plens de malicia,
quant veuhen que de juſticia,
lo Rey Carlos Regnara.
Gran empreza, gran proeza,
los de Vich, han començat,
ſens tenir temor de França.
tenint molta confiança,
en lo Princep Darmeſtad.
Aſſegura, gran Ventura,
à la noſtra nacio,
del Rey Carlos la vinguda
per la qual havem tinguda,
molt gran conſolacio.
Se Refian, y Confian,
que tindran molts Valedors,
los que del Rey murmuraven,
y con Juſel lo tractaven,
à manera de traydors.
Fou gran Xaſco, per Velaſco,
no poderſe retirar,
ab la gent dintre Gerona
quant ſou rendit Barcelona
per volerſe mes venjar.
Mes mal homa, que mahoma,
fou contra los Cathalans,
perque de la ſanch dels preſos,
y de molts altres offeſſos,
ſe volgue rentar las mans.
Tots clamaven y cridaven,
muyra lo Virey Traydor,
que cauſa tanta maranyà,
y viſca lo Rey de Eſpanya,
Carlos Tercer gran Señor.

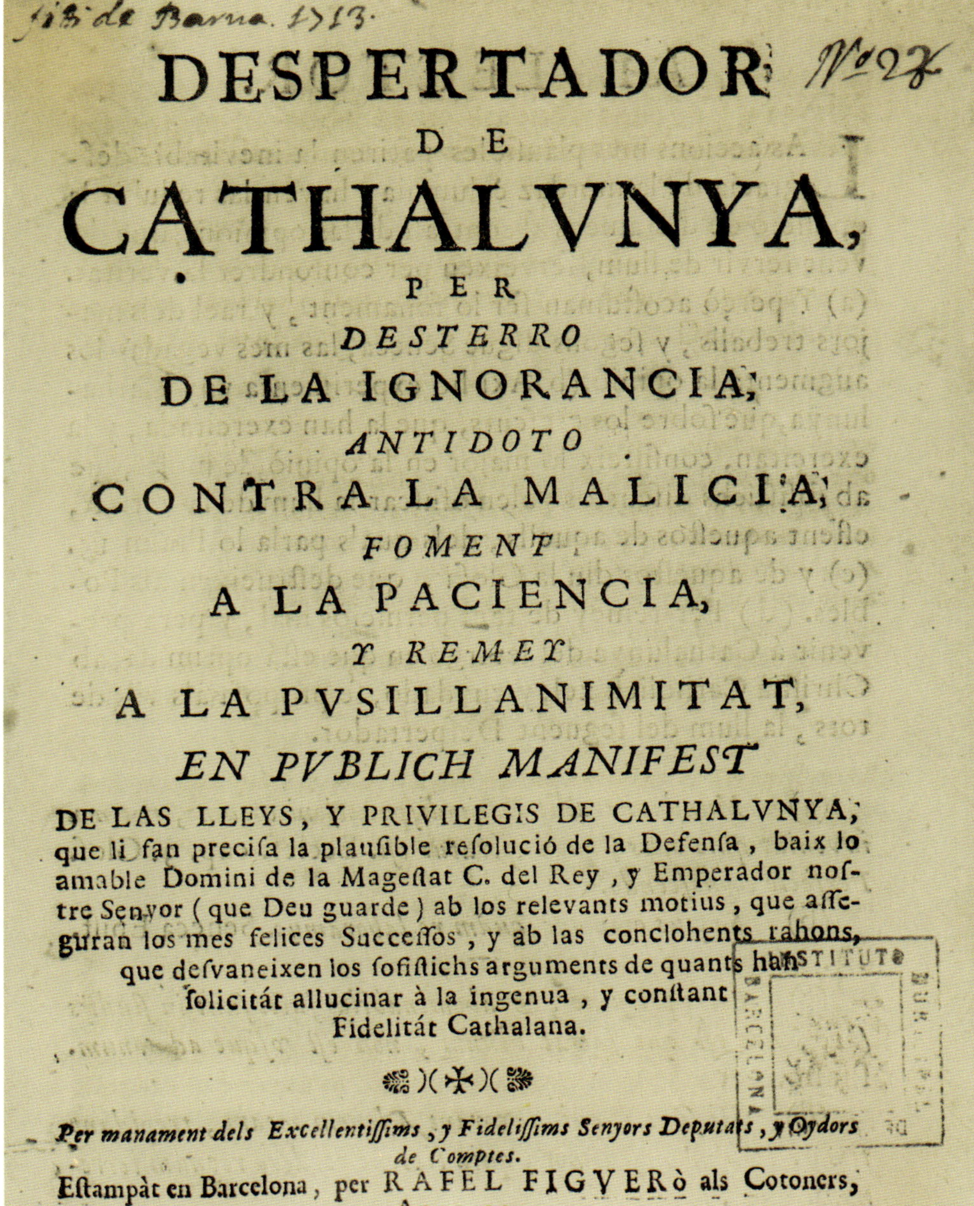

DESPERTADOR
DE
CATHALVNYA,
PER
DESTERRO
DE LA IGNORANCIA;
ANTIDOTO
CONTRA LA MALICIA;
FOMENT
A LA PACIENCIA,
Y REMEY
A LA PVSILLANIMITAT,
EN PVBLICH MANIFEST
DE LAS LLEYS, Y PRIVILEGIS DE CATHALVNYA;
que li fan preciſa la plauſible reſolució de la Defenſa, baix lo amable Domini de la Mageſtat C. del Rey, y Emperador noſtre Senyor (que Deu guarde) ab los relevants motius, que aſſeguran los mes felices Succeſſos, y ab las conclohents rahons, que deſvaneixen los ſofiſtichs arguments de quants han ſolicitát allucinar à la ingenua, y conſtant Fidelitát Cathalana.

Per manament dels Excellentiſſims, y Fideliſſims Senyors Deputats, y Oydors de Comptes.
Eſtampàt en Barcelona, per RAFEL FIGVERò als Cotoners, Any 1713.

A popular tract favourable to the dynastic rights of archduke Charles of Austria. This tract, which is known as the *Despertador de Cathalunya* (The knocker-up of Catalonia) is another clue to the political atmosphere presiding the Principality during the period the succession to the Spanish throne was disputed, at the death of Charles II, in 1700. It is a political tract, based on juridical and religious reasons, and published with a view to justifying the rights of archduke Charles of Austria to the Spanish throne. It was published in Barcelona in 1713 at the request of the deputies and official accountants, who, in effect, were responsible for Catalan politics at the time. They considered the archduke to be the candidate offering a guarantee for the conservation of Catalan institutions and self-government.

Print featuring the military siege of Barcelona in 1714. Both the Generalitat, through its Estates Assembly, and the Council of the Hundred (City Council), decided to base the defence of the national rights of Catalonia on one strategy: the defence of Barcelona. This print, which was drawn by a Catalan from the Rosselló county working at the French court of Louis XIV, shows the position taken up by the attacking French and Spanish forces, under the command of the Duke of Berwick. The siege had lasted over a year. In the background, within the walls, all the Catalans were determined to resist as long as possible, though numbered four to one. The Head Councillor, Rafael Casanova, was wounded during the final assault. The city's Governing Junta finally decided to call for negotiations and, in the end, had to surrender.

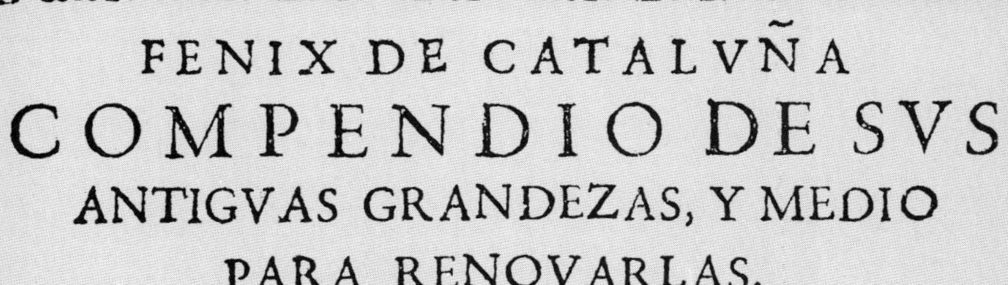

FENIX DE CATALVÑA
COMPENDIO DE SVS
ANTIGVAS GRANDEZAS, Y MEDIO
PARA RENOVARLAS.

A LA SACRA, Y
CATHOLICA MAGESTAD
DE NVESTRO GRAN MONARCA
Carlos Segundo (que Dios guarde) Rey de
las Efpañas, y Emperador del
Nuevo Mundo.

*CONSAGRALE MARTIN PILES MERCADER
de Lienços de la Congregacion de San Iuliàn,vezino defta
Nobiliffima Ciudad de Barcelona,natural de
la Ciudad de Vique.*

CON PRIVILEGIO.

En Barcelona : En la Imprenta de Rafael Figuerò , á los
Algodoneros. Año de 1683.

The *Fénix de Cataluña* (Phoenix of Catalonia) marks the recovery process of the 17th century. As from 1680, a new current of thought, associated with practical interests, appears in Catalonia. Its objective is to promote commercial activities. Within the context of this movement, which was made up by a group of contemporary industrialists, Narcís Feliu de la Penya — a historian and man of action — publishes his *Fénix de Cataluña*, a book which proposes the recovery of the country and which became the symbol of the activity of a group of patriots. They were determined to rid the Principality of the prevailing ills of Spanish 17th century decadence. Historian Joan Reglà has compared the role of Feliu de la Penya with that of Joan Maragall in the face of Spain's crisis in 1898. However, De la Penya was not only an ideologist and lawyer, but was also fully conversant with the problems of the Catalan economy, for which he proposed viable solutions.

Painting of the Reapers' Revolt in 1640. This painting by Antoni Estruch represents the Reapers' Revolt, also referred to as the Bloody Corpus Day, which took place in Barcelona on June 7th 1640. It was the first episode of a war that lasted twelve years. The war became the first attempt at the secession of Catalonia from the hispanic Crown of the House of Austria. The Catalans refused to participate in the foreign wars of King Philip IV of Castile. The declaration of war between France and the Spanish Crown in 1635 had indeed led to the entry of mercenary troops into Catalonia. This turned out to be an excessive load (lodging, taxes, etc.) on the Catalan people. Ill-feeling led to a popular uprising in 1640. After several vicissitudes, motivated by political conveniences, France and Spain signed the Treaty of the Pyrenees (1659) which broke up the age-old unity of the Catalan countries.

NVEVA PLANTA
DE LA
REAL AVDIENCIA
DEL
PRINCIPADO
DE
CATALVÑA,
ESTABLECIDA POR
SV MAGESTAD,
CON DECRETO DE DIEZ Y SEIS DE
Enero de mil ſetecientos y diez y ſeis.

En Barcelona: Por IOSEPH TEXIDÒ, Impreſſor del Rey N. S.
Se hallarà en ſu caſa en la Calle de S. Domingo.

Bust of heroic general Josep Moragues. Despite the surrender of Barcelona, Catalonia continued resisting the invasion of the French and Castilian forces with guerilla warfare. One of the leading figures behind this resistance movement was General Josep Moragues, who had already won renown in the first actions of the War of Succession. Indeed, his forces beat the "Filipistes" (Bourbon troops) at the Battle of El Congost, where he himself captured the commander of the enemy. General Moragues was finally captured at Montjuïc in 1715. He suffered torture of every description; he was quartered and they hung his head in a cage at the Portal de Mar in Barcelona, where it remained for twelve years, as a warning to the Catalan people.

Royal Decree of *Nueva Planta* (New Constitution): 16th January, 1716. Once the Catalan forces had been disarmed and defeated, after the fall of Barcelona (11th September 1714), the Generalitat and Council of the Hundred were abolished, the Mint closed, and the University of Barcelona and General Faculties of the Principality supressed. The new regime was established on the basis of the Decree of *Nueva Planta*, which confided the government of the Principality to a military officer, the Captain General, who was to be assisted by the Real Audiencia. The juridical, judicial and administrative structure of Catalonia was done away with. Catalonia was deprived of her condition as a self-governing nation.

General Bellver with Barcelona's Governing Junta, eleventh of September, 1714. During the siege of Barcelona, and a few hours before the final surrender, the city's Governing Junta, assembled at the Portal de Sant Antoni, was still discussing the possibility of resisting further. This Junta decided that, before calling for negotiation with the enemy, the citizens were to hear a proclamation. The document was read by General Bellver and was a kind of political will of Catalonia before her military defeat. It stated that slavery would without doubt be the lot of the Catalans, and protested about the harm, ruin and distress the afflicted fatherland would be suffering, taking it for granted that the honours and privileges of Catalonia would be done away with.

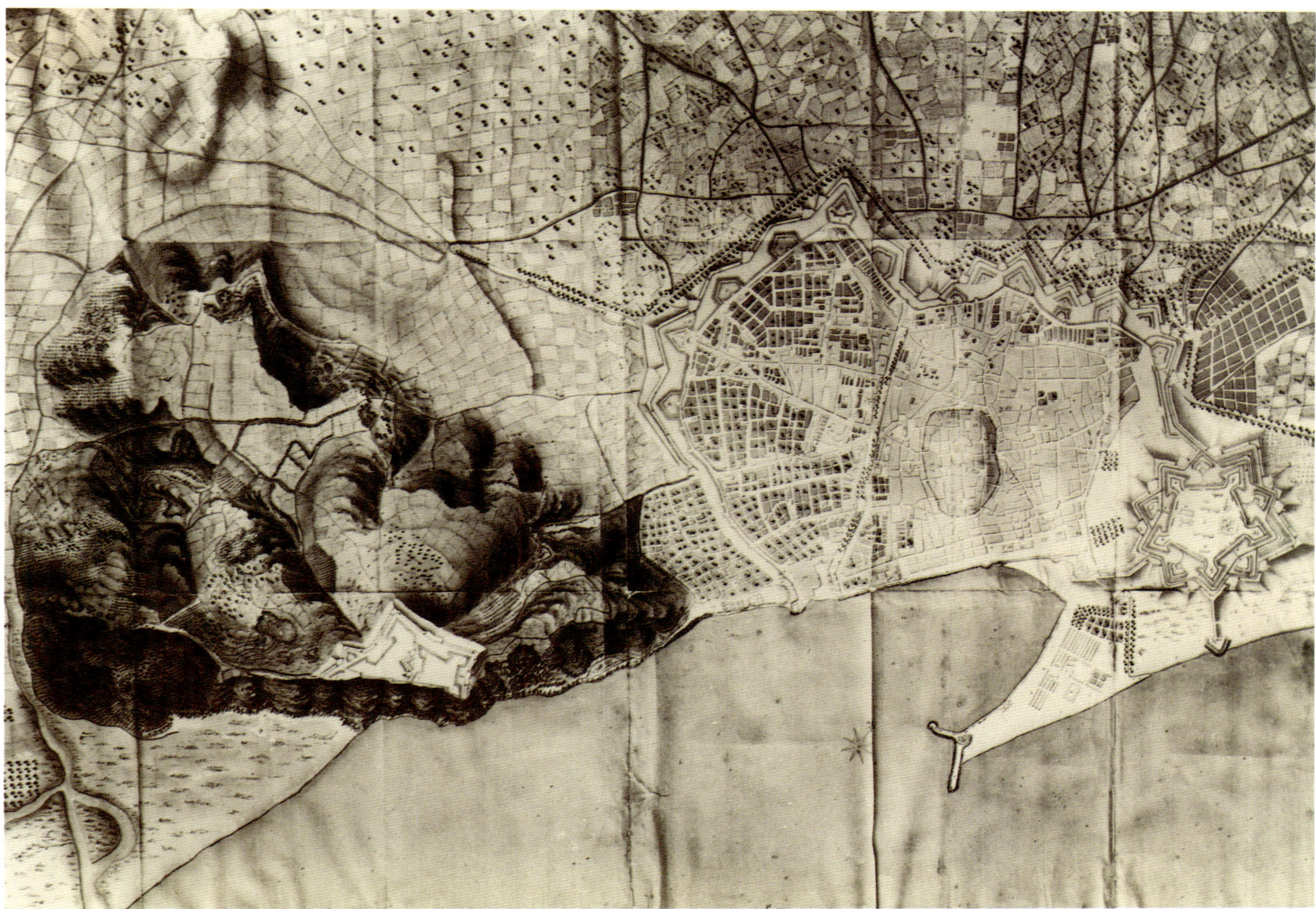

Despite oppression, Barcelona is a dynamic city at the end of the 18th century. This is the look Barcelona had at the end of the 18th century, as portrayed in a contemporary plan. On the right-hand side of the walled city, one can clearly see the Ciutadella (city fortress), a star-shaped fortification which Philip V had had built in 1716 to watch over the city that had been hostile to him. Once the war wounds had slowly healed, in the second half of the 18th century, Catalonia began to develop. The "real country" was stronger than the "legal country", which remained under the boot of the *Nueva Planta* decree. Insofar as the country's capital is concerned, the creation of the Junta de Comerç (Commerce Board), in 1758, would revitalize (in the words of contemporary historian, Joan Mercader) the commercial and industrial sap of the new Barcelona.

The Barcelona Exchange (Llotja de Barcelona), with its orthodox neoclassical façade. This is the present aspect of the Barcelona Exchange (Llotja de Barcelona), a building with a neoclassical façade, which was added during the modernization works architect Joan Soler carried out in 1772. Inside there is a great Gothic hall, which was finished in 1392 by Pere Arvei, and a large section of the Consular Hall (Sala dels Cònsols). After the aforementioned restoration works, there have been further works, particularly those undertaken in 1902. Over the course of time, the building has served various functions: Chemistry and Surgery School, Nautical and Noble Arts School. At present it is the seat of the Barcelona Exchange and the Saint George Fine Arts Academy (Acadèmia de Belles Arts de Sant Jordi).

Print of a Royal Trading Company deed. This Barcelona Royal Trading Company (Reial Companyia de Comerç) nominal deed, dated in 1758, proves that "de facto", Catalonia already traded with America before the "de iure" authorization granted by King Charles III, twenty years later. This company enjoyed the privilege of trading with Puerto Rico, Santo Domingo, Honduras, Guatemala, Margarita and Venezuela, and obtained considerable profits.

Nº 1136.

ACCION DE LA REAL COMP.ª DE COMERCIO ESTABLECIDA EN BARCELONA

Interesa: Christoval Gironella Comerciante Vecino de Barcelona en la Rl. Compª con esta Accion por doscientos y cinquenta pesos de â ciento y veinte y ocho quartos cada uno, que ha puesto en su Thesoreria; y en los repartos de utilidades que se hizieren en el modo y tiempos que se acordaren, se entregarà al dueño de la Accion, ô â su apoderado, lo que por ella le corresponda: De este instrumento tomarà razon el Contador, le refrendarà el Secretario, y sellarà con el sello dela Rl. Compañia. Barcelona treinta de Agosto de mil setecientos cinquenta y ocho.

Tomó razón

Por acuerdo de los Sres. Directores.

A scene of hand to hand fighting during the Peninsular War. This violent scene corresponds to the Peninsular War, a war in which Catalonia became involved as a result of the French Convention's declaration of war against the Spanish king, Charles IV. From an ideological point of view, it was a "popular" war for Catalonia, because the people saw the chance of avenging former political defeats and recovering the Rosselló and Cerdanya counties in France; the chance of annulling the Treaty of the Pyrenees (1659). Nevertheless, Charles IV's government played a relatively passive role and failed to provide Catalonia's captain general with the necessary resources to maintain a war with any possibility of victory.

REAL DECRETO
EN QUE S. M. HA RESUELTO ampliar la Concesion del Comercio libre, contenida en Decreto de 16. de Octubre de 1765. Instruccion de la misma fecha, y demás Resoluciones posteriores, que solo comprehendieron las Islas de Barlovento, y Provincias de Campeche, Santa Marta, y Rio del Hacha, incluiendo ahora la de Buenos-Aires, con internacion por ella à las demás de la América Meridional, y extension à los Puertos habilitados en las Costas de Chile, y el Perú, &c.
Expedido en 2. de Febrero de 1778.

Royal Decree of Charles III, authorizing free trade with America. In 1778, King Charles III granted all his subjects in Spain the right to trade with all Spanish American countries. Catalonia benefitted from this right. Charles III carried out a more favourable policy towards Catalonia, and, on the economic front, he favoured Catalan interests and enterprises. This positive side did not, however, exonerate him from another negative aspect: his decrees against the use of the Catalan language, ordering primary and secondary education to be carried out in Spanish, and even forbidding the use of Catalan for the teaching of divinity.

"El timbaler del Bruc" **("The El Bruc drummer", a symbol of resistance in the Peninsula War.** Sculptor Frederic Marès placed his monument to the *"timbaler del Bruc"* against the background of Montserrat mountain and beside the main road. According to legend, an army composed of nothing but Catalan townsfolk, with few weapons and no military training, defeated a French column of 3,800 men, commanded by Brigadier Schwartz. The confusion created by the frantic and constant beating of a drum by a young lad is said to have made the French believe that they were being attacked by a large force. It would seem, though, that things did not really occur in that way. Although there was civilian participation in the action, involving the militia from Manresa, Igualada and other towns, the victory on June 6th 1808 was achieved by popular guerilla forces alongside Swiss infantry and a brigade of Walloon guards.

Ballad against the Count of Spain, during the First Carlist War. In 1838, Carles d'Espanya, a Languedocian who had already been captain general of Catalonia (1827-1832), was appointed captain general of the Carlist zone in the Principality. The Count of Spain was an extravagant and cruel character, with a paranoic temperament. He committed unspeakable attrocities in Catalonia in the First Carlist War: he ordered the burning of Olvan, Gironella and Berga. It is for this reason that ballads were published, expressing popular feelings of hatred towards him. Here he is referred to as a vicious tiger. His own fellow Carlist partisans ordered his execution.

Cataluña libre del tigre feroz, Conde de España.

Dialogo de despido entre Cataluña y el Conde de España con motivo de haber tenido que abandonar este Principado de resultas de las ocurrencias de Berga originadas por la fuga del pretendiente y convenio de Vergara.

CATALUÑA.

Conde España, Conde España,
Tú me abandonas por fin;
Y gracias á Dios me libras,
De la fiera mas ruin.

ESPAÑA.

Me voy triste Cataluña,
Bien [illegible] puedes alegrar;
Que á quedarme aqui mas tiempo,
Hasta habrias de llorar.
No presumas que de Carlos
Siguiese el partido yo,
Por creer en sus derechos;
No era este mi intento; no.
Lo mismo á mi se me daba
De Carlos que de Cristina;
Lo que yo queria solo,
Era lograr tu ruina.

The Carlist War, seen by Joaquim Vayreda. Painter Joaquim Vayreda (1843-1894) painted a scene from the Third Carlist War on Catalan soil. The Carlist movement was strongly rooted in the rural counties of Catalonia's hinterland — especially in the Solsonès, Berguedà and Osona counties —, where peasants and craftsmen were not benefitting from the industrialization and capitalist development policy the Liberals were advocating. In the Third Carlist War, there was also an important Catalanist component. The Carlist pretender, Charles VII, promised to bring back the "*fueros*" (national rights) to the countries of the Aragonese Crown, and stood for a return to the situation prior to the Decree of *Nueva Planta* (1716).

The *"patuleia"*, in a painting by J. Arrau i Barba. The *"patuleia"* was the name given to the poor and idle people's brigades which took part in the First Carlist War. These brigades took advantage of revolutionary situations to loot, destroy monuments and quarrel with citizens from other social strata, who were opposed to their cause. The painting, of remarkable plastic qualities, brings us closer to an understanding of the *patuleia* in the street.

The Sedó textile factory, at Esparreguera. Since the mid 19th century, the valleys of the rivers Ter and Llobregat were an ideal site for the establishment of the textile industry. One of the oldest and most important ones is Can Sedó, on the right-hand side of the river Llobregat, in the Cairat gorge, where there is a dam the factory uses for electric power. Apart from the industrial workshops, there is a colony for workers, with a school and parish church. It is in the Esparreguera municipality.

Centenario del Ferrocarril en España - Línea de Barcelona a Mataró

1848 - 1948

The first railway in Catalonia. 1848. In 1765 James Watt invented the steam engine. Not long after, it replaced animal traction as a means of transport. The first steam engine began operating in England in 1804. The new machine quickly spread to other European countries. Catalonia inaugurated her first regular railway on 28th October 1848, covering the line between Barcelona and Mataró. The invention of the railway was vital as a catalyst of the industrial revolution throughout Europe and in the United States of America. Initially, the railway was only used for the transport of heavy goods. Later short distance passenger transport was brought in. Finally, towards the end of the century, the economic resources of different countries were invested in the transformation of the railway into a means of long distance transport.

General Gaminde is christened "General Boom-Boom" by *La Campana de Gràcia* magazine. Gràcia, a town with its own corporation, was one of the most active urban districts in the federal and workers' movements of the mid 19th century. In 1870, the town of Gràcia, under the leadership of the Federal Republican Centre, protested against the reintroduction of military conscription. A fully-fledged popular rebellion flared up which was put down by the Captain General of Catalonia, Eugenio de Gaminde, who bombarded Gràcia on the morning of April 5th 1870. *La Campana de Gràcia*, a satirical political magazine, christened Gaminde "General Boom-Boom".

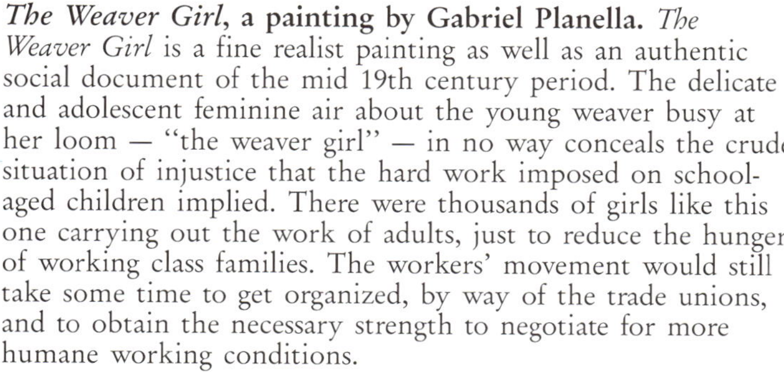

***The Weaver Girl*, a painting by Gabriel Planella.** *The Weaver Girl* is a fine realist painting as well as an authentic social document of the mid 19th century period. The delicate and adolescent feminine air about the young weaver busy at her loom — "the weaver girl" — in no way conceals the crude situation of injustice that the hard work imposed on school-aged children implied. There were thousands of girls like this one carrying out the work of adults, just to reduce the hunger of working class families. The workers' movement would still take some time to get organized, by way of the trade unions, and to obtain the necessary strength to negotiate for more humane working conditions.

El Born market, in Barcelona, in the second half of the 19th century. This photograph shows us the Born Market as it was in the second half of this century — a fruit and vegetable distribution centre supplying the city of Barcelona. El Born is a huge metal building which still stands in the old Ribera district. It is similar to others of its period — and was constructed in mid-19th century. The building, which has been carefully restored, is now used for cultural events.

Proclamation of the First Republic in Barcelona. The so-called "September Revolution", in 1868, heralded a period of great political activity. On February 11th 1873, after the abdication of King Amadeus I, the Spanish Parliament proclaimed the Republic. This scene — in Sant Jaume square, in front of the disused Generalitat building — portrays civilians and soldiers celebrating together. It also shows the popular enthusiasm the new — though short-lived — regime was received with. The Barcelona Provincial Council (Diputació) became Government of Catalonia overnight. Amidst an atmosphere of confusion and anarchy, the Catalan Federal State was proclaimed on 8th March 1873. The first Spanish Republic came to an end on January 3rd 1874 when General Pavía dissolved the Parliament.

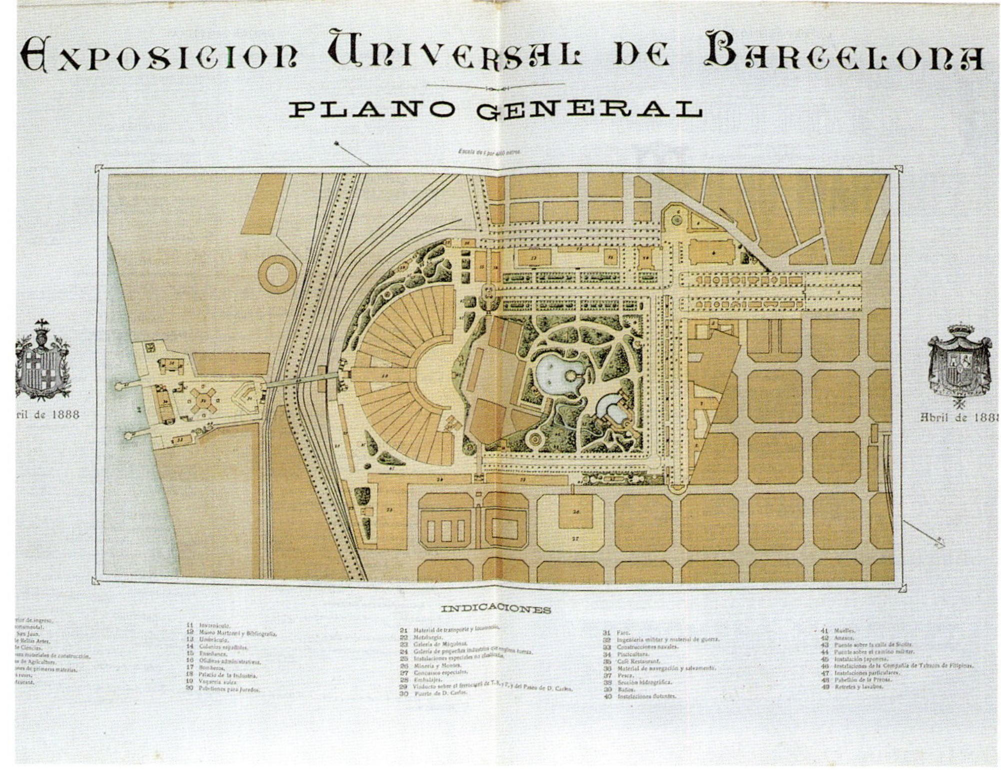

The festival poster for the 1888 Universal Exhibition. The poster announcing the festival shows the kind of popular participation Barcelona's Universal Exhibition had. The variety of the ceremonies here announced shows the imagination and ambition of the organizing board — the city Town Council: regattas, "kermesses", horse races, cavalcades, choir competitions, etc. The poster also shows that the recovery of the Catalan language had yet to come about, for the Barcelona Town Council failed to use it for official public use. For that to occur, a few years more had to pass.

The Barcelona Universal Exhibition of 1888. The 1888 Universal Exhibition was an exponent of the industrial verve of Barcelona and in Catalonia generally. In contrast with Spain, a country which in the words of contemporary poet Joan Maragall was "sad, and badly administered by bureaucrats", Catalonia strove to fend for herself as any other nation. The general plan of the Exhibition shows how this fine Baroque building — the current seat of the Catalan Parliament — was adapted for use, and how important new works were constructed: the Arch of Triumph, the monumental cascade with sculptures by Nobas and Vallmitjana, the so-called "Castell dels Tres Dragons" ("castle of the Three Dragons") — designed by Domènech i Montaner, a pioneer of Modernist architecture — and the "Hivernacle" or Greenhouse, among others.

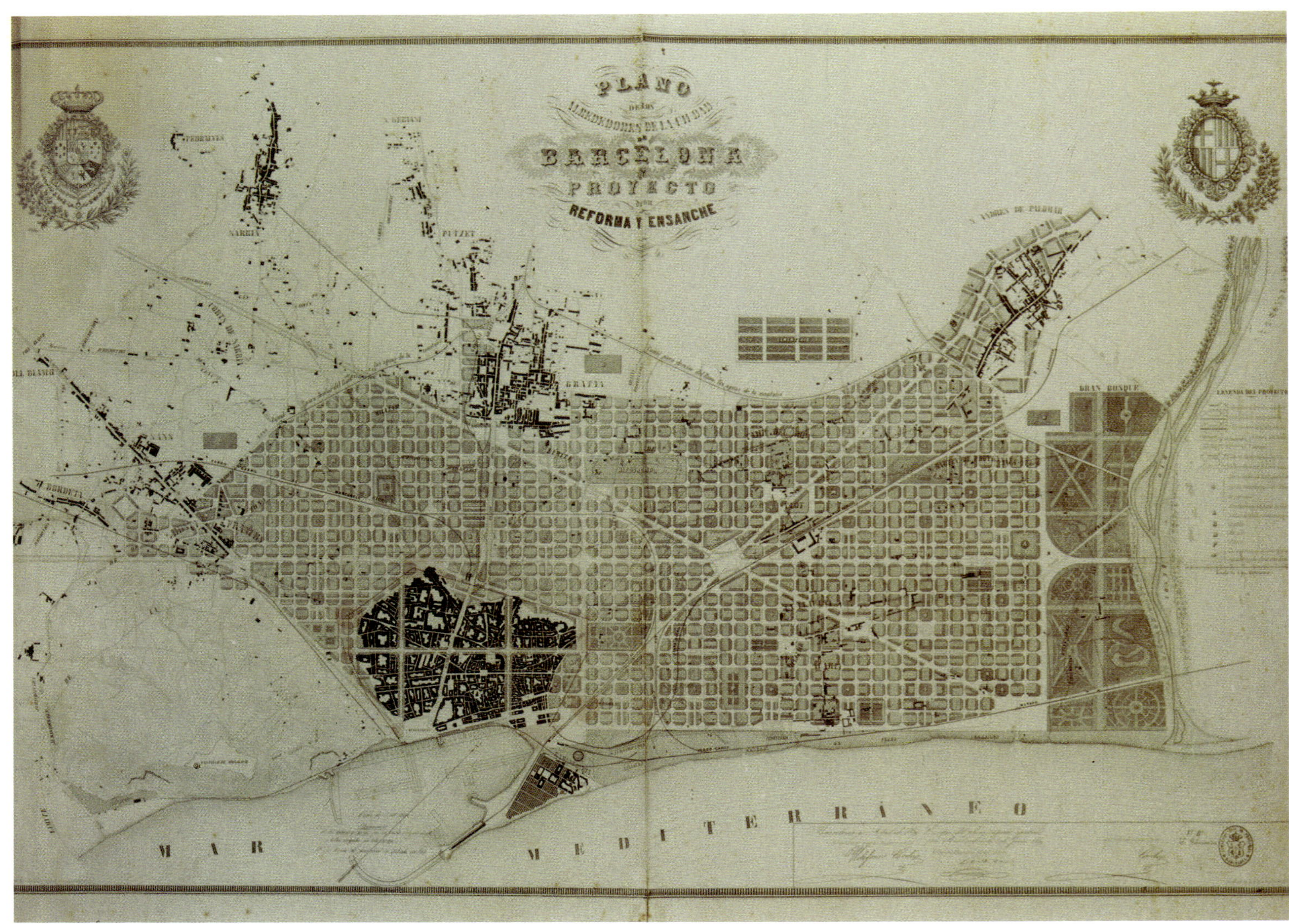

1859 Plan of Barcelona's Eixample. In the same year the *Jocs Florals* were brought back (they were to be the important Catalan literary competition which flourished during the *Renaixença* or the Catalan literary Renaissance), the works of the Reform and Extension Project of Barcelona were initiated. The plan had been drawn up by engineer, town planner and politician Ildefons Cerdà. The Cerdà Plan was a rational planning model for a city that in 1854 did away with the restrictions imposed on it by the old medieval walls. The Plan had the following technical characteristics: social infrastructure organically distributed on an open road network; an attempt to harmonize with nature, maintaining each block open on one of its sides; the lack of the concept of "centre"; and the creation of nuclei that would generate further districts. However, over the long course of the Plan's development (1860-1930), it suffered several modifications as a result of current political circumstances.

A bird's-eye view of Barcelona's Eixample. This is a bird's-eye view of the Eixample, planned by Ildefons Cerdà, as it is today. The rational nature of a project planned in mid-19th century clashes first with the irrationality of not having respected the original plan to make it efficient. It also comes up against the irrational speculation of forty years of urban anarchy during a dictatorial regime, which have converted the Eixample into a buzzing mass of cars madly trying to make their way through swarms of pedestrians.

Troops embarking for the Cuba War in 1896. The war in defence of the last colonies, including the island of Cuba, is one of the events that left a mark on the turn of the century throughout Spain, a country that was fighting to retain the remains of her glorious empire. Meanwhile, her intellectuals pointed to the fact that Restoration Spain had no solid base, and that Spanish society had fallen into a state of despondency. The people of Barcelona saw war ships sail from her harbour to the Cuban war, but their interests were elsewhere, the whole affair being contemplated from another point of view. Catalan society was more industrialized and took a more active part in public life, and public concerns were quite different: conservative regionalism, republican politics and revolutionary workers' movements.

Guns against the 1917 strikers. This photograph was published by the magazine *La Ilustració Catalana*, and shows the repressive role played by the army during the general strike in 1917. On the 27th March of that year, the CNT, "Confederació Nacional del Treball" (Anarchist Union), and the UGT "Unió General de Treballadors" (Socialist union), issued a joint proclamation threatening to call an indefinite general strike if "fundamental changes in the system, guaranteeing basic living conditions for the people, and the possibility of carrying out activities that would lead to their emancipation" were not undertaken. It was a revolutionary alliance which one must see in the context of the international upheaval caused by the soviet revolution, and which failed to achieve its objectives of justice for the working class.

Ferrer i Guàrdia, republican, pedagogue and freemason. Francesc Ferrer i Guàrdia was one of the legends arising from the period of political repression suffered by the left (republican, freethinkers, anarchists, socialists) in Catalonia in 1909. He was a pedagogue, thinker, republican and freemason. He created the "Modern School", which was based on laicism, rationalism and not on the State. His execution on Montjuïc brought about a strong wave of international protest. It may be seen as an exemplary punishment against the anarchist movement, which had then become very strong in Catalonia and was taking root in Spain. However, as a pedagogue Ferrer i Guàrdia did not stand out as a Catalanist: "rather than Catalan, I prefer Esperanto", was one of his more unfortunate statements.

Prat de la Riba, *"seny ordenador"* (rational director) of Catalonia. Enric Prat de la Riba received the honorary title of *"seny ordenador"* (rational director) of Catalonia, and deservedly so, because he was a fine theoretician in his political writings, and this became especially clear on the publication of *La nacionalitat catalana* (The Catalan Nationality), where he defines nationality as the united will of people who speak the same language, express the same convictions and have the same feeling for laws which have their bases in customs. This was also so on the practical front, because he created cultural, pedagogical, scientific and artistic institutions, without ever turning away the cooperation of people from other persuasions who were willing to make a contribution to the country's progress.

Salvador Seguí, a pacifist and Catalanist anarchist. Salvador Seguí was a workers' leader of great prestige. He was known as "*El Noi del Sucre*" (the "Sugar Lad"). He was an authentic anarchist — pragmatic, pacifist and Catalanist. In 1910 he waged for the union of all the Peninsula's workers. In 1916 he was the principal promoter of an alliance agreement between the two major unions, CNT and UGT, an initiative that was to serve to bring pressure to bear against the constant rise in the cost of living and the incompetence of the government to control it. As secretary general of the anarchist union CNT, he led various important strikes — La Canadiense, the Gas and Electricity Companies —, achieved the 8-hour working day and the 48-hour week for all guilds.

SALVADOR SEGUÍ («NOY DEL SUCRE»)
La figura más eminente que ha tenido el movimiento obrerista catalán. Murió asesinado

Francesc Macià, tried in Paris after the Prats de Molló affair. In September 1923, Miguel Primo de Rivera, Captain General of Catalonia, headed a coup d'état and established a military dictatorship throughout the Spanish State. Francesc Macià was forced into exile in Perpinyà (Perpignan). After 1923, the political situation entered a period of crisis, and there was even an attempt to bring about a military coup on June 23rd 1926, with the participation of liberal officers, republicans, anarchists and Catalan separatists — a coup which was not successful. Macià then considered the possibility of attempting an invasion from French territory across the Pyrenees. He recruited Italian anti-fascists and Catalan anarchists, but the plot failed because of the intervention of the Gendarmerie, and Macià was arrested at Prats de Molló. At the subsequent trial in Paris, Macià was accused of illegally possessing weapons and expelled from France. He then went into exile in Belgium.

A hospital exemplifying *"noucentista"* architecture. The four years Prat de la Riba presided over the Mancomunitat were very productive insofar as cultural, educational and service infrastructure of every kind was concerned. A major effort was made to modernize the country: roads were built, the grid was extended to several rural areas, and telephone lines were installed in over 400 villages and towns. The health service was greatly developed and improved. One exponent of this activity is the Santa Coloma de Gramenet mental home, a building that reflects the new aesthetic line of Noucentisme, a cultural movement of a political origin that started up in Catalonia in the early 20th century.

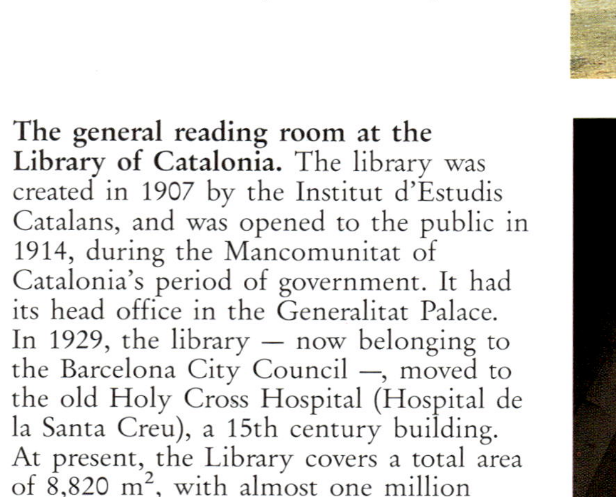

The general reading room at the Library of Catalonia. The library was created in 1907 by the Institut d'Estudis Catalans, and was opened to the public in 1914, during the Mancomunitat of Catalonia's period of government. It had its head office in the Generalitat Palace. In 1929, the library — now belonging to the Barcelona City Council —, moved to the old Holy Cross Hospital (Hospital de la Santa Creu), a 15th century building. At present, the Library covers a total area of 8,820 m^2, with almost one million books. It also owns 620 incunabula, 3,163 manuscripts and 7,686 titles of a collection on Miguel de Cervantes.

Barcelona International Exhibition, 1929. At the foot of Montjuïc, a hill that rises 173 metres above sea level, a whole series of enormous pavillions were built for the Barcelona International Exhibition in 1929. This exhibition was an exponent of the economic power of the country and, above all, of the country's outward going nature. Puig i Cadafalch was made responsible for the overall architectural plan, and the garden project was carried out by the Frenchman Forestier. Carles Buïgas' spectacular multi-coloured and ever-changing fountains, with their luminous spouts, can be seen at the far end of the central avenue. The National Palace, with its crown of splayed out light beams, looms up behind. The Palace is now seat of the Art Museum of Catalonia.

The crowd before the Generalitat Palace, 1932. On April 24th 1932, the Catalan people turned out for a demonstration, demanding a Statute of Autonomy that would permit the country to be self-governing. It was called the Núria Statute, and had already been voted in by a huge majority just a few months before (August 1931). It defined Catalonia as an "Autonomous State within the Spanish Republic". Finally, after bitter negotiations with the Madrid government, Catalonia achieved the approval of a rather more moderate Statute of Autonomy which defined her as an "autonomous region within the Spanish State". This occurred on 9th September 1932. With that Statute, Catalonia recovered the power to legislate, although in a limited way, and the possibility of organizing her own Justice Administration.

Francesc Macià proclaims the Catalan Republic, 1931. The Town Council elections of 12th April 1931 were won by republican parties throughout the State. On 14th April, Francesc Macià — the undisputed leader of Esquerra Republicana de Catalunya (The Catalan Republican Left party) — displayed great daring and, convinced that all Catalans would follow him, proclaimed the Catalan Republic, a sovereign State within the Iberian Confederation. From the balcony, the new President proclaimed: "I have taken possession of the Government of Catalonia in the name of the people of Catalonia. The country has voted for us so that we may rule the city, and I, in the name of Catalonia, take full responsibility for her government and inform you all that we are determined to defend her freedom. I trust that the people of Catalonia will follow suit. To expell us from here, they will have to pass over our dead bodies. I must also tell you that we must make ourselves worthy of the freedom we have just conquered, and I hope the Catalan people, if need be, will give up their lives like us, to defend that freedom".

The constitution ceremony of the First Autonomous Parliament in the second Republic period. After the Statute of Autonomy had been approved by the Spanish Parliament the first Autonomous Parliament of Catalonia was constituted on 13th December 1932. Esquerra Republicana de Catalunya (Catalan Republican Left party) had the majority, having defeated the ambiguous middle of the line position of Acció Catalana (Catalan Action), the Lliga Regionalista (Regionalist League) and Lerroux's discredited Partit Radical (Radical Party). Francesc Macià was ratified in his short-lived post as President of Catalonia. He died one year later, on Christmas night 1933.

The President of the Generalitat, Macià, with the President of the provisional Government of the Spanish Republic. On 26th April 1931, Alcalá Zamora, President of the provisional government of the Spanish Republic, which had been declared twelve days before, visited Francesc Macià, President of the Generalitat. This picture shows the official party accompanying him to Barcelona's Pedralbes Palace. The relationship between President Macià and the leading figures of the Republic was based on a spirit of equality and clarity. A few days later Macià made the following statement to the press: "My political beliefs are the same as ever... All my efforts pursue the creation of a Federal Republic which, in its very essence and constitution, is the only form of government that will satisfy our thirst for social justice and the will of the people".

President Macià takes the Statute of Autonomy to Madrid. A spontaneous demostration took place at the Estació de França (Barcelona Railway Station) when Francesc Macià, President of the Generalitat, was about to leave for Madrid to deliver the so-called "Núria" Statute of Autonomy — which had been ratified at the polls — to the provisional Republican government in Madrid. It was the 14th August 1931. Macià was going to Madrid with the spirit of a charismatic leader of Catalonia, a country which, as he had proclaimed twelve days before, from the Generalitat balcony, was now free. However, he also added that: "it is now that I most wish to open my arms to embrace the other lands of the Iberian Peninsula, to help them to achieve the freedom that we already have. They will now see that our cordiality was, and is, sincere".

President Macià, accompanied by the Catalan MPs at the Madrid Parliament. The brilliant, sharp and persuasive speeches of Manuel Azaña, head of the Republican government in Madrid, were decisive at the Parliamentary sessions on the Catalan Statute of Autonomy, which was finally approved on 9th September 1932. This photograph shows us the Catalan MPs shortly after their return from Madrid, the day after the Statute was approved. It was taken at the Generalitat Palace, where the MPs and President Macià had arrived surrounded by an enthusiastic crowd, which had accompanied them from the Passeig de Gràcia station.

The Supreme Court of Appeal of Catalonia: constitution ceremony. On 2nd March 1934, after assuming executive and legislative powers conferred to her by the Statute of Autonomy, Catalonia also assumed judicial competences by way of the creation of the Supreme Court of Appeal. The Court was made up of a President and twelve magistrates, and had two courtrooms: a civil one, and another for litigation and administrative affairs. This judicial institution was short-lived. It suspended its activities in 1938 because of the civil war. In this photograph of the constitution ceremony, Estanislau Duran i Reynals, Joan Casanovas, Lluís Companys — who at that time had already been appointed President of the Generalitat — and Santiago Gubern, President of the Supreme Court of Appeal.

President Macià, at the Eleventh of September celebration in 1933. The celebration of the Onze de Setembre (11th September), Catalan National Day (*Diada*), was especially joyful and triumphant in 1933. Two days before, the Spanish Parliament had approved the Catalan Statute of Autonomy. Macià presided over the official *Diada* ceremonies with a steadfast expression. That day's newspapers published the President's speech, made before an enthusiastic crowd in Plaça de la República (Square of the Republic) the day before. In the speech, he declared: "I at all times believed that Catalonia would be granted her freedom because the Catalans were determined to obtain that freedom".

The Spanish army quickly put down the revolutionary uprising of 6th October 1934. In April 1934, the Catalan Parliament, with the decisive action of the majority — Esquerra Republicana — approved the Law of Cultivation Contracts, which aimed to facilitate land ownership to tenant farmers, tax farmers and special crop contract holders. This step stirred up unrest among many rural land owners and an appeal was presented before the Republican Constitutional Guarantee Court. This high Spanish Judiciary body annulled the bill on grounds of unconstitutionality. "This factor," in the opinion of Joan Reglà "occurring during a period of increasing radicalization, helps to explain why the Generalitat government joined the revolutionary movement which demanded independence from the central government". The photograph shows a group of soldiers resting after a night's fighting (6th-7th October).

A crowd gathered before the Generalitat, 6th October 1934. Over the course of 1934, the Generalitat's moderate and progressive policy began to clash with the Madrid Republican government's policy, which was run by right-wing parties that had won the November 1933 elections. The most powerful of these Spanish right-wing organizations was the Confederación Española de Derechas Autónomas (CEDA) (Spanish Confederation of Autonomous Right-Wing parties), which had come to power in October 1934. Internal revolutionary pressure and the rebellious atmosphere in other parts of the Iberian Peninsula (especially in Asturias) brought pressue to bear on the Generalitat Government to proclaim the "Catalan State of the Spanish Federal Republic". This is what President Lluís Companys effectively did before the enthusiastic crowd in the Plaça de la República, on the evening of 6th October 1934.

An enthusiastic popular reception awaited President Companys on his return to Catalonia. The victory throughout the State of the left-wing parties at the February 1936 general elections led to amnesty for the President of the Generalitat and the other members of the Government who had been emprisoned for proclaiming the Catalan State on October 6th 1934. The photographs featuring the return of the President, show indescribable joy: not only was the freeing of men unjustly emprisoned being celebrated, but also the recovery of the Generalitat. After that moment, the Catalan Government tried to maintain an atmosphere of democratic harmony and difficult social stability. However, the military coup of 18th July 1936 broke the peaceful state of Catalan society.

President Companys and other members of the Catalan Government in prison, 1934. As a result of the 6th October affair, Catalan autonomy was suspended de facto, as a "preventive and transitory" measure. The members of the Catalan Government were taken to Barcelona's Model prison, and a large number of left-wing democratic politicians were removed from office. An army officer was appointed Barcelona city mayor, and another officer provisionally took charge of the Generalitat. The whole Catalan Government was tried, condemned and emprisoned. President Companys was sentenced to thirty years in prison. He served the first year of prison in Cartagena and Puerto de Santa María jails, but was freed in February 1936.

President Companys at a meeting in Barcelona's *Monumental* Bullring (1936). The military uprising that led to the Civil War did not catch the Catalan Government by surprise. As the Generalitat then had powers and responsibilities over public order, the Catalan Government tried to lead the popular reaction against the fascist military uprising, and accepted the creation of new organizations which were associated — on paper at least — with the Generalitat, such as the Anti-fascist Militia Committee or the Catalan Economy Council. "Under the political leadership of Lluís Companys" says historian Joan Villarroya, "the Generalitat gradually managed to impose its authority on the anarchists and took steps to put the actions of uncontrolled elements into check, although acts of extreme violence were still committed". Once the war had got under way, President Companys became personally involved, and often visited the front line and campaign hospitals.

Wartime Catalan National Day Poster. *"Catalans!"* is the evocative word on this poster commemorating the 11th September *Diada* (Catalan National Day). In September 1938, the Spanish Civil War was now in its final stages, and everyone knew that Franco's victory would not only be a defeat for Catalonia as a nation, but would also unleash the most gruesome form of repression. As from April that year, Franco's forces had been advancing through Catalan territory, and the fascist Burgos government abolished Catalonia's Statute of Autonomy. The significance of September 11th was conjured up by the call *"Catalans!"* uttered by a woman holding the Catalan flag in the shade of a soldier.

The undeniable connivance between nazis and Franco regime. The head of the German nazi youth organizations was invited to Spain by Franco's fascist regime. On his arrival at Barcelona, he reviewed the University Militia sergeants in front of the Provincial Prefecture. Only a small fraction of Catalonia's youth of that period were captivated by nazism and fascism. In general, and despite the traumatic experience of the war, those young people who had not fought were not tempted by foreign ideologies that clashed with the character of a country that, despite the complete lack of freedom, had a solid basis.

The nazis display propaganda in Barcelona University. A revealing photograph showing nazi presence in Barcelona University in the first years after the Civil War, during the Second World War. It features a book exhibition in the centre of the University central hall, aimed at promoting German National Socialist doctrine. Indeed, the Spanish dictatorship put into practice a rather more mitigated form of National Socialism, with a totalitarian state run by an unchallenged and unified authority, whose policies were decided by a supreme dictator.

Exaltation of the Virgin of Montserrat, 1947. The Catalan language was first used in public after the Civil War (1936-1939) at Montserrat. This occurred on the occasion of the enthronement of the Virgin of Montserrat, on April 27th 1947, when the multitudinarious ceremony ended up as a demonstration of Catalan national identity. During the forties, harsh political, cultural and linguistic repression exerted by General Franco's regime against Catalonia was. Despite strict police control, a huge Catalan flag was unfolded at the top of one of Montserrat's rounded peaks by the National Resistance Groups. The country was half suffocated, but far from dead.

The Galinsoga case, a coordinated action by the Catalan resistance. One of the finest concerted actions carried out by the Catalan resistance, in the face of the humiliation and despotism generated by the dictatorial regime of General Franco, was the so-called Galinsoga case. On leaving a church on 21st June 1959, Mr. Luís Martínez de Galinsoga, director of the newspaper *La Vanguardia Española* had insulted all Catalans because the mass had been said in Catalan. Galinsoga angrily uttered the phrase: "All Catalans are shit". The reaction of the Catalan people was impressive: thousands of leaflets were distributed informing about the incident. At the end of the year, the newsaper had lost 15,000 subscribers and a good deal of its publicity contracts, and direct sales at the news stands had gone down considerably. The campaign ended up with the victory of Catalan society and the recovery of her offended dignity: Mr. Galinsoga was dismissed from his post on 5th February 1960.

DIGNITAT CONTRA XULERIA

El Sr. Galinsoga és un enticatalà furiós, fins el punt que durant la guerra civil va arribar a escriure **que calia destruir Catalunya.** Durant tot aquest temps que l'hem hagut de suportar com a director d'un diari de tanta importància com "La Vanguardia" les expressions injurioses i les xuleries han estat la seva norma. Finalment, fa poc —el dia 21 de juny d'aquest any— s'ha permès pronunciar en plena parròquia de St. Ildefons de Barcelona (Travessera de Gràcia, 55), després d'altres expressions insultants, aquesta frase altament ofensiva: **"¡Todos los catalanes son una mierda!"**

Ha arribat l'hora de demostrar al Sr. Galinsoga i a la gent com ell que **a Catalunya encara hi ha dignitat.** Per tant, considerant que és una vergonya que un diari de la importància de "La Vangurrdia", editat a Barcelona, tingui de director un home d'aquesta mena, ens dirigim públicament al Comte de Godó, propietari del diari, amb el prec de que el Sr. Galinsoga sigui substituït per una persona de més dignitat i més respectuosa envers Catalunya.

Mentres aquesta substitució no es produeixi **cal que les persones que estan subscrites a "La Vanguardia" se'n donguin de baixa i que els qui el compren en els quioscos deixin de comprar-lo.**

Ja són moltes les persones que s'han donat de baixa o que han deixat de comprar aquest diari. Però cal que això s'intensifiqui a fi que ens sigui donada la satisfacció a que tenim dret.

CATALANS:

HEM DE DEMOSTRAR QUE NO SE'NS POT INSULTAR IMPUNEMENT

EL CORREO CATALAN

BARCELONA al DIA

PARA HOY

Se estudia y trabaja en una reorganización a fondo de los transportes urbanos

• El gobernador civil formula importantes declaraciones sobre los últimos incidentes

ADVIERTE QUE MANTENDRA EL ORDEN PUBLICO DE FORMA DECIDIDA Y CON LOS MEDIOS QUE FUERAN PRECISOS

El cupón de los ciegos

¡NOVIOS! Compren sus alfombras en CASA PRESAS CUCURULLA, 9

MILITARES

ABASTECIMIENTOS

MARITIMAS

POLICIA

All Barcelona supported the 1951 tram strike. On March 1st 1951, the citizens of Barcelona started a mass boycott of the tram service — the most widely used form of public transport — because of the rise in fares decreed by the government. The boycott was the first multitudinarious demonstration of opposition to the Franco regime, and turned out to be a major success. The most active clandestine political and trade union groups, brought all their resources together for this action and managed to gain the support of the population at large. The authorities, using the typical terminology of the period, detected the origin of the popular strike, and exposed it in the following words of Barcelona's civil governor, Eduardo Baeza Alegría: "I can categorically prove that professional agents in the service of political ideologies of sad memory, have taken advantage of the social situation". But the strike was a success and the government had to withdraw the decree ruling the rise in fare of tram tickets.

Abbot Escarré, accusation and exile, 1963. In November 1963, the world's leading newspapers spoke of the statement made to *Le Monde* by Aureli Maria Escarré, abbot of Montserrat Monastery, the spiritual and cultural centre of Catalonia, a refuge in times of repression against Catalan nationalism. Abbot Escarré had declared: "The regime of general Franco calls itself Christian, but fails to obey the basic principles of Christianity. Catalans have a right to their own culture, history and customs — all of which have their own personality within the context of Spain". "The first rebellion in Spain is that of its government." This was one of the statements that led him into exile.

VINGTIÈME ANNÉE — N° 5856 20 PAGES — DERNIÈRE ÉDITION JEUDI 14 NOVEMBRE 1963

Le Monde

In una intervista al «Monde»

Il priore di Montserrat critica il regime di Franco

RABAT : M. Guedira remplace M... aux affaires étrangèr...

ALGER : M. Ben Bella conclu... avec le colonel Mohar...

Spanischer Abt kritisiert Franco-Regime

Prophetenwort wurde zitiert

Aus Südvietnam

...ime espagnol se dit chrétien mais n'obéit pas ...x principes de base du christianisme »

déclare au « Monde » l'abbé de Montserrat

De notre envoyé spécial J.-A. NOVAIS

Le peuple doit pouvoir choisir son gouvernement

POLEMICA SUL SEPARATISMO CATALANO

CRITICHE A FRANCO dell'abate di Montserrat

Dura deplorazione di un organo governativo - Insorge in difesa del regime un altro benedettino, l'abate del monastero della «Valle de Los Caidos»

10 Part I—MON., JAN. 27, 1964 Los Angeles Times

Catalonia Nationalists Fear Drive by Franco

Criticism of Madrid Regime by Liberal Elements Brings Threats of Reprisals

Unique Position

Questions Regime

Publish Books

RAYMOND ARON

Le Grand Débat

initiation à la stratégie atomique

CALMANN-LÉVY

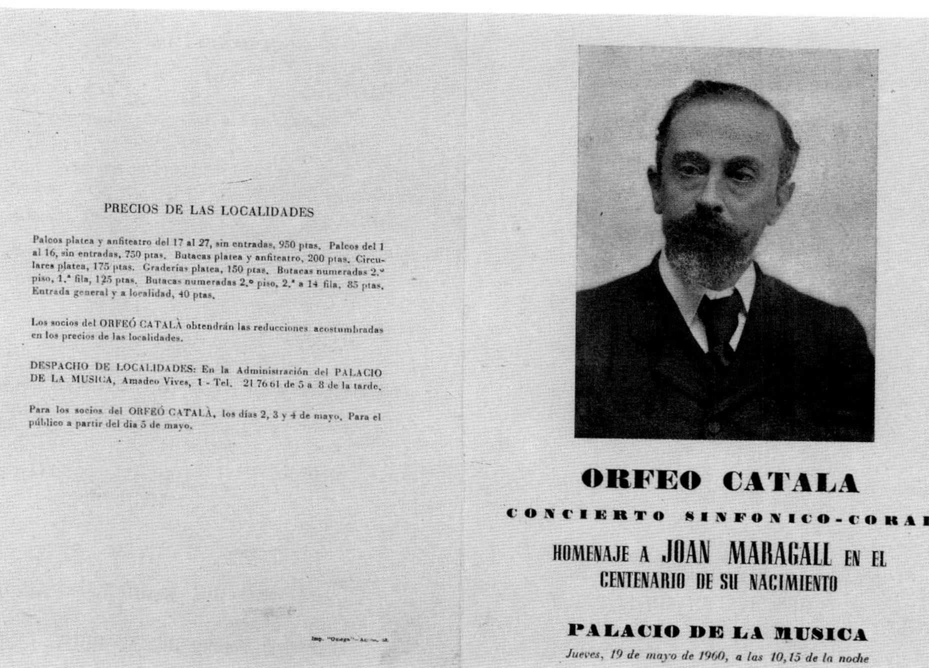

PRECIOS DE LAS LOCALIDADES

Palcos platea y anfiteatro del 17 al 27, sin entradas, 950 ptas. Palcos del 1 al 16, sin entradas, 750 ptas. Butacas platea y anfiteatro, 200 ptas. Circulares platea, 175 ptas. Graderías platea, 150 ptas. Butacas numeradas 2.º piso, 1.ª fila, 125 ptas. Butacas numeradas 2.º piso, 2.ª a 14 fila, 85 ptas. Entrada general y a localidad, 40 ptas.

Los socios del ORFEÓ CATALÀ obtendrán las reducciones acostumbradas en los precios de las localidades.

DESPACHO DE LOCALIDADES: En la Administración del PALACIO DE LA MUSICA, Amadeo Vives, 1 - Tel. 21 76 61 de 5 a 8 de la tarde.

Para los socios del ORFEÓ CATALÀ, los días 2, 3 y 4 de mayo. Para el público a partir del día 5 de mayo.

ORFEO CATALA

CONCIERTO SINFONICO-CORAL

HOMENAJE A JOAN MARAGALL EN EL CENTENARIO DE SU NACIMIENTO

PALACIO DE LA MUSICA

Jueves, 19 de mayo de 1960, a las 10,15 de la noche

ORFEO CATALA

AUDICION CML

Director: MTRO. LUIS M.ª MILLET

Subdirectores:

Mtros. J. Tomàs y J. J. Llongueres

Jacqueline Brumaire

soprano

Anna Ricci

mezzo soprano

Orquesta Sinfónica

92 profesores

Orfeó Català

DIRECCION

MTRO. LUIS M.ª MILLET

PROGRAMA

I

STABAT MATER . . . . F. POULENC

para soprano solo, coro mixto y orquesta

Jacqueline Brumaire - Orfeó Català - Orquesta

II

TRES ASPECTOS MUSICALES DE LA PLEGARIA

AVE VERUM . . . . W. A. MOZART

Orfeó Català y Orquesta de cuerda

PREGÀRIA A LA VERGE DEL REMEI . . . L. MILLET

Sección femenina del Orfeó Català y Orquesta

"*DIALOGUES DES CARMELITES*" . . . F. POULENC

(2.º cuadro del 2.º acto)

(1.ª audición en concierto)

Jacqueline Brumaire — *La nouvelle Prieure*

Anna Ricci — *Mère Marie de l'Incarnation*

Sección femenina del Orfeó Català — *Les Carmelites*

Orquesta Sinfónica

III

HOMENAJE A JOAN MARAGALL EN EL CENTENARIO DE SU NACIMIENTO

EL CANT DE LA SENYERA . . MARAGALL - L. MILLET

Escrito expresamente para la bendición de la «Senyera» del Orfeó Català

ORFEÓ CATALÀ

CANT ESPIRITUAL . . . MARAGALL - MONTSALVATGE

(2.ª audición)

para coro y Orquesta «Premi Lluís Millet» del cincuentenario del «Palau de la Música Catalana»

CANT DE MAIG, CANT D'ALEGRIA . MARAGALL - PUJOL

(estreno de la versión de coro y Orquesta)

Pequeño poema original para coro y tres coblas — Versión orquestal de RICARDO LAMOTE DE GRIGNON

ORFEÓ CATALÀ - ORQUESTA

Dirección: Maestro LUIS M.ª MILLET

The 1960 "Palau de la Música Catalana Affair". General Franco did not often visit the city of Barcelona during his dictatorship years, perhaps because he felt the opposition of a large proportion of Catalan society. In May 1960, soon after the "Galinsoga case", Franco visited Barcelona. His visit was a good occasion for the opposition to try and set public opinion against the dictatorship. The crowning moment in the campaign was the so-called "Palau de la Música affair". The Catalan Choral Society (Orfeó Català) was offering a concert on the occasion of the centenary of the birth of poet Joan Maragall. At the precise moment indicated for it on the programme — despite the prohibition of the governor — one part of the public began to sing the *Cant de la Senyera*, a hymn which acted as a substitute for the *Cant dels Segadors* — the true National Anthem of Catalonia, which at that time was completely forbidden. The police arrested many Catalans in the Palau — among them Jordi Pujol i Soley, the current President of the Generalitat of Catalonia. The photograph shows the cover of the programme of the Catalan Choral Society concert for that day.

A unitary democratic organization against the Franco regime: The Catalan Assembly. During the last few years of the Franco regime, democratic opposition forces were able to find efficient ways of struggling against the dictatorship which progressively received more and more popular support. In November 1971, the joint effort of the democratic forces crystallized out into a unitary organization called the Assemblea de Catalunya (Catalan Assembly). The Assemblea was open to all institutions, groups and personalities from the various political and ideological tendencies, and managed to unite them in support of a programme containing four points, the foremost of which was the demand for Catalan self-government and the right to self-determination of the Catalan people. The photograph shows one of the meetings of the Standing Committee. Different figures from the current public life of the country are clearly visible.

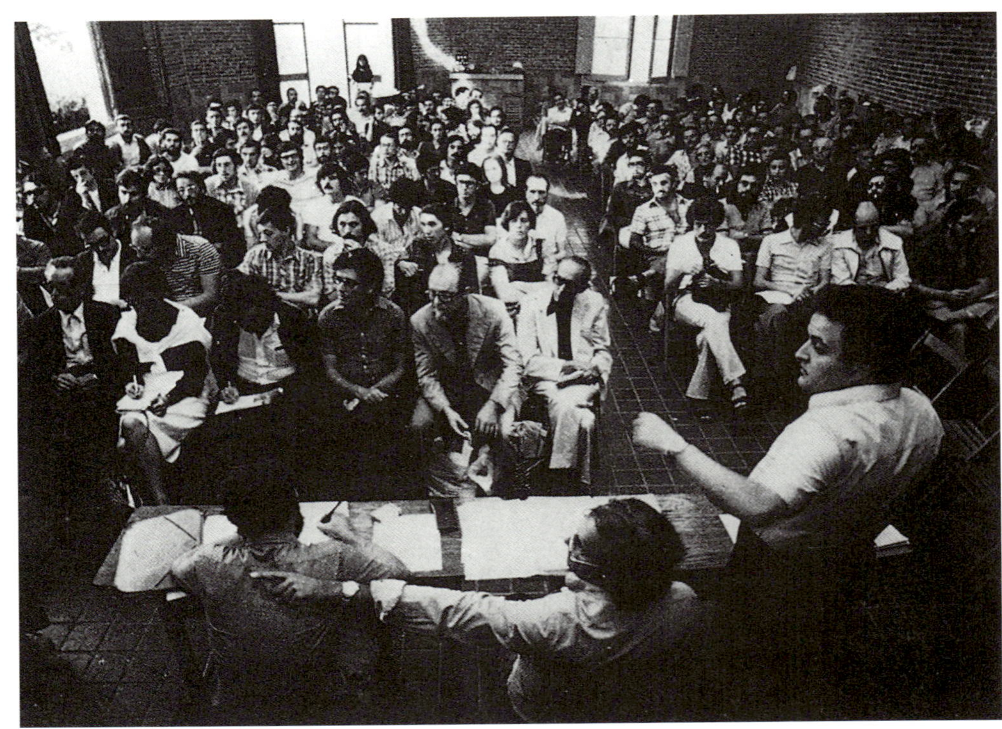

The Congress of Catalan Culture, a review of 40 years. The most important popular initiative of the Catalan people during the Franco regime was certainly the creation, in January 1975, of the Congress of Catalan Culture. The initiative immediatley received the backing of professional schools, popular organizations, personalities from the culture world, and also met with great popular support. The Congress was organized throughout the Catalan Countries (Principality, Valencia, North Catalonia — in the French State — and Andorra). The Congress's work was organized in different activity areas, and was to serve as a review of the state of culture in the Catalan Countries between 1936 and the time of the Congress. The closing ceremony — as can be seen in the photograph — took place in November 1977, and was presided over by Josep Tarradellas, who by then had been appointed President of the Generalitat of Catalonia.

A million people show their support for the Statute of Autonomy. The largest demonstration in the history of Catalonia was held in Barcelona on September 11th 1977. Over a million citizens from all over Catalonia — belonging to a wide range of political tendencies — demonstrated in favour of a Statute of Autonomy which would mean the effective recovery of the historical institutions of self-government. Parallel to the recovery of a democratic regime in the State, the political representatives of the Catalan people drew up the text of a Statute which was approved in a referendum on 25th October 1979. On 1st January 1980, Josep Tarradellas, President of the provisional Generalitat, called the first Catalan Parliament elections. After the elections, the Parliament elected Jordi Pujol i Soley first President of the new Generalitat, and 115th in the history of Catalonia's Government.

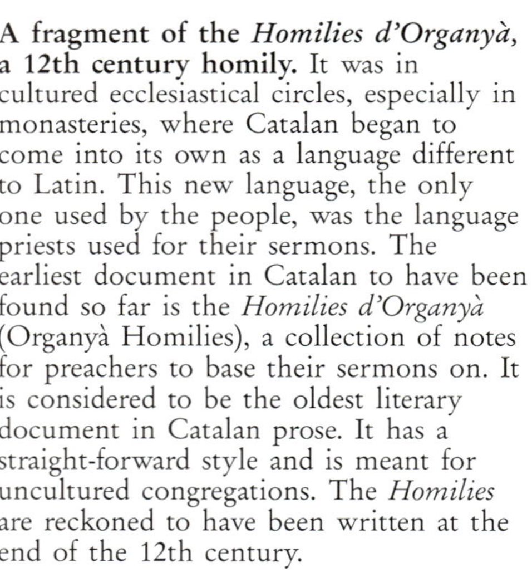

A fragment of the *Homilies d'Organyà*, a 12th century homily. It was in cultured ecclesiastical circles, especially in monasteries, where Catalan began to come into its own as a language different to Latin. This new language, the only one used by the people, was the language priests used for their sermons. The earliest document in Catalan to have been found so far is the *Homilies d'Organyà* (Organyà Homilies), a collection of notes for preachers to base their sermons on. It is considered to be the oldest literary document in Catalan prose. It has a straight-forward style and is meant for uncultured congregations. The *Homilies* are reckoned to have been written at the end of the 12th century.

A poem that praises the fatherland and the language. This poem — *La Pàtria* (the Fatherland) — by Bonaventura Carles Aribau, is taken as a chronological reference point associated with the rebirth of the literary and cultural movement in Catalonia — a movement known as *La Renaixença* —. The poem was written by Aribau in Madrid in 1833, and was published in the newspaper called *El Vapor*. It has the melancholic and nostalgic air of the Romantic period, but was not artificial nor uncouth. Other than the inspiration and fine literary execution the poem displays, it is also remarkably efficient, in a civic sense, because it contributes to making a whole country enthuse once again with the idea of the fatherland and the possibility of using her language for cultural activities.

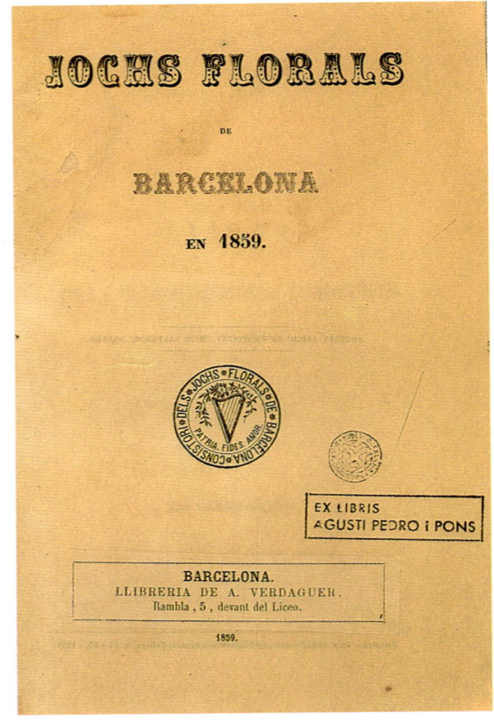

The *Jocs Florals*, an institution for the cultivation of the Catalan language. This cover belongs to a book published in 1859 in Barcelona, containing the poems that had received prizes at the Barcelona *Jocs Florals* (poetry competition). 1859 was the year this literary competition had been brought back during the Renaixença (Renaissance) of Catalan literature. The *Jocs Florals* were presided over by Manuel Milà i Fontanals. The Board which was created for the organization and promotion of the *Jocs Florals* laid down that its aim was to bring back and popularize an institution which had been founded by the old kings of Catalonia-Aragon in the 14th century, and encourage young people to cultivate the Catalan language and its literature. Joaquim Rubió i Ors thought up the motto *"Patria, Fides, Amor"* (Fatherland, faith and love), the three subjects which competing poets had to keep to.

THE AREA COVERED BY THE CATALAN LANGUAGE

Map of the area in which the Catalan language is spoken. This map covers the area in which the Catalan language is at present spoken. It is easy to observe that linguists, on the grounds of phonetics, distinguish two major branches of the language: Eastern Catalan and Western Catalan. Each one of these branches incorporates different dialects which tend to take on the name of the area where they are spoken: Valencià, Mallorquí, Eivissenc, Alguerès, Rossellonès, etc., all of which supply the language with a remarkable degree of richness and give rise to great beauty of literary and oral expression. It must be remembered, though, that these are dialects of one sole language with a remarkable degree of lexical, semantic, phonetic, morphological and, above all, syntactical cohesion. It is this level of cohesion that explains the fact that the existence of the different dialects does not make comprehension difficult among Catalan-speakers throughout the area.

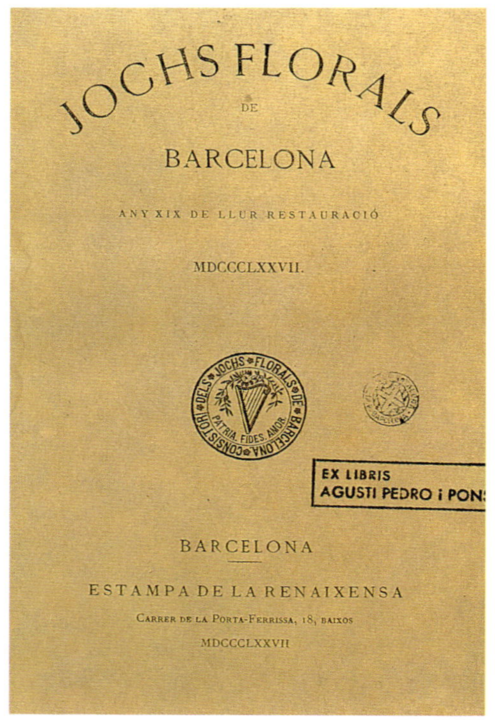

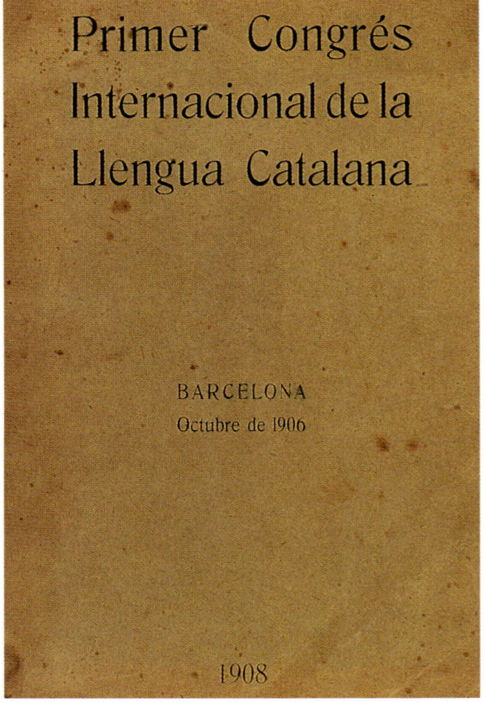

1877: three prizes for one poet alone. The cover of this book shows the continuity of the *Jocs Florals* after their restoration in 1859. This literary competition encouraged many young writers and acted as a show case for the literary skills of poets who had to use a language that was live, but which lacked any kind of official support and suffered some gramatical lackings. 1877 was the year of the extraordinary emergence of Àngel Guimerà, who won the three ordinary prizes in one fell swoop: the natural flower, the violet and the eglantine. Two years later, Guimerà embarked on his prolific works as a playwright, a carrer that was to bring him great fame.

Book commemorating the First International Congress on the Catalan Language (1906). The First International Congress on the Catalan Language took place in October 1906 on the initiative of Antoni Maria Alcover, who presided over the Congress. Three study sections were set up in the following fields: philology and history, literature, and society and law. The three sections were presided over by Alcover, Rubió i Lluch and Ramon d'Abadal, respectively. Foreign Romance language philology specialists participated as well as representatives of all the language's dialect areas. In the words of Francesc de B. Moll, "The Congress was tremendously important, not only on a scientific plain, but also promoting the linguistic and literary renaissance of the Catalan Countries".

The Catalan Language *Jocs Florals* during the long exile period. At the end of the Spanish Civil War (1936-1939), the Catalan Language *Jocs Florals* were to be held in exile. After their prohibition by the Franco dictatorship, the *Jocs Florals* were held in different European and American cities: Buenos Aires (1941 and 1960), Mexico City (1942, 1957 and 1973), Montpellier (1946), London (1947), Paris (1948, 1959 and 1965), Tübingen (1970), Brussels (1971), Geneva (1972), Amsterdam (1974), and Caracas (1975) — in the photograph —. This age-old literary competition was introduced by King John I in 1393 under the name of *Gaia Ciència*. The competition was interrupted in the 15th century, but was brought back in 1859 under the name of *Jocs Florals de Barcelona*, the city where it had often been held.

5

5 Las Cauſas en la Real Audiencia ſe ſubſtanciaràn en lengua Caſtellana, y para que por la mayor ſatisfaccion de las Partes, los incidentes de las Cauſas ſe traten con mayor deliberacion; mando, que todas las Peticiones, preſentaciones de Inſtrumentos, y lo demàs, que ſe ofreciere, ſe haga en las Salas. Para lo corriente, y pùblico, ſe tenga Audiencia pùblica Lunes, Miercoles, y Viernes de cada ſemana en una de ellas, por turno de meſes.

6 Pero las Peticiones, y preſentaciones de Inſtrumentos, ſe podràn hazer en otros dias ante los Eſcrivanos, y ſe darà cuenta en Audiencia pùblica, para que no ſe paſſen los tèrminos de las Cauſas, ſi los huviere ſeñalados.

7 Y porque puede la malicia de los Litigantes procurar la dilacion de los Pleytos; mando, que los tèrminos de prueba, y otros, puedan limitarſe, ò ceñirſe ſegun cada una de las Salas juzgàre ſer juſto; porque ſu fin ha de ſer evitar las calumnias, y adminiſtrar juſticia con la mayor brevedad, y la ſatisfaccion de las Partes.

8 Por embarazar mucho à los Miniſtros la relacion de los Pleytos, para el mas pronto expediente de las Cauſas, aunque las Partes, por lo paſſado, tenian la ſatisfaccion de verſe, y relatarſe por uno de los que havian de votar; para ocurrir à uno, y otro, he reſuelto, que para cada Sala haya dos Relatores Letrados, Graduados de Doctores, ò Licenciados en Univerſidad aprobada, y que hayan practicado quatro años con Abogado, ò ſino Aſſeſſores de algun Juez Ordinario; los quales hayan de tener el primer aſſiento en el Banco de Abogados, y hazer la relacion, preſentes las Partes; y como antes ſe pagava el derecho de Sentencia, que ſe aplicava à los Miniſtros, aora deverà aplicarſe à los Relatores, y ſe cobrarà de la manera que antes, para que no reciban coſa alguna de mano de las Partes, y dichos derechos de Sentencia ſe reduciràn à cantidad, que poco mas, ò menos tenga al año ſeiſcientas libras de vellon de Cathaluña cada Relator; y eſtos han de entregar Sumarios, ò

A 3 Me-

King Philip V and his family. This magnificent oil-painting of Philip V and the royal family by Van Loo can be contemplated in the Prado Museum in Madrid. This Bourbon king did away with the age-old self-governing institutions of Catalonia by way of the famous Decree of *Nueva Planta* in 1714. From that period onwards, the Catalan language would find it very hard to maintain its place in public life. However, despite decrees, prohibitions, and obstacles of every kind, the Catalan people have remained faithful to their own language.

Justice administration is forbidden in Catalan. "Cases in the Royal Court will be followed in the Spanish language". This is one of the reiterative "ordinances" emerging from the Castilian Court of King Philip V after 1714. In it, the complete elimination of the Catalan language from the Justice Administration becomes evident. The Bourbon king transformed the victory of the Eleventh of September 1714 into linguistic repression, and, indeed, into the national oppression of Catalonia.

General Primo de Rivera takes the offensive against the "regions". In 1923, General Primo de Rivera, in fine dictatorial style, began to issue decrees and ordinances throughout the State. On October 22nd 1925 he passed judgement on the future of Catalonia and other peninsular nations with these abusive remarks: "Not one more word about the 'Region'. Just twenty-five years of silence regarding this word, generally a euphemism for separatism or a brand of nationalism that disguises it, even promoting it in good faith, and Spain will have got rid of one of her worst dangers". The regime of restrictions and limitations for our country and her language was to last as long as 1930.

The Catalan language is even prohibitted in churches. As a result of the Franco government law, enacted on April 5th 1938 — coinciding with the occupation of the city of Lleida — abolishing the Catalan Statute of Autonomy, approved by the Parliament of the Spanish Second Republic, the Catalan language ceased to be official in Catalonia. Some months later, the Lleida newspaper *La Mañana* published the following information: "With the recent introduction of a resolution, the use of Catalan as second official language in the Catalan provinces, has been banned. From now on, only the Spanish language will be accepted as the official language in the Catalan provinces". This resolution meant the elimination of the use of Catalan in any public activity, even in churches, as is shown in the document we reproduce here. The language was to be restricted to family life. The posters on view in Barcelona after the invasion by Franco's forces read: "If you are Spanish, speak the language of the Empire".

BANDO

USO DEL IDIOMA OFICIAL
en todos los Servicios públicos

D. ______________________ Alcalde

Presidente del Ayuntamiento de ______________

HAGO SABER: Que por el Excmo. Sr. Gobernador Civil de esta provincia se ha dictado con fecha 28 de julio de 1940 (B. O. del 31 id.) una circular cuya parte dispositiva dice así:

«PRIMERO.— A partir del día 1.º de agosto próximo, todos los funcionarios interinos de las Corporaciones provinciales y municipales de esta provincia, cualesquiera que sea su categoría, que en acto de servicio, dentro o fuera de los edificios oficiales, se expresen en otro idioma que no sea el oficial del Estado, quedarán «ipso facto» destituídos, sin ulterior recurso.

SEGUNDO.— Si se tratase de funcionarios de plantilla, titulares o propietarios en tales corporaciones, y se hallaran pendientes de depuración, dicha falta determinará la conclusión del expediente en el estado en que se hallare y la inmediata destitución del transgresor sin ulterior recurso.

Si se tratase de funcionarios ya depurados y readmitidos incondicional o condicionalmente, se reabrirá su expediente de depuración, y puesto que toda depuración hasta ahora realizada es revisable, se estimará esa falta como nuevo cargo adicional al capítulo correspondiente, y, en consecuencia, se propondrá sanción o se agravará la ya aplicada, pudiendo, en ambos casos, llegarse a la destitución.

TERCERO.— Los mismos criterios se aplicarán con respecto a los funcionarios interinos y propietarios o titulares adscritos a cualquiera de los servicios públicos civiles de la provincia, especialmente los que sean maestros y profesores del Estado, así como inspectores municipales de Sanidad. Por lo que se refiere a maestros y profesores privados, autorizados para la enseñanza, los infractores quedarán personalmente incapacitados para el ejercicio de la función docente.

CUARTO.— Ningún expediente de información — cuando proceda instruirlo con arreglo a lo anteriormente dispuesto — será sobreseído por falta de pruebas; pudiendo bastar la de indicios, y, en todo momento, la espontánea conciencia que del caso se forme el instructor y que este expresará en sus conclusiones, cualquiera que sea el resultado de la prueba practicada.

QUINTO.—Todos los agentes de Inspección y Vigilancia, fuerza de Policía armada y Guardia Civil, tanto de la capital como de la provincia, extremarán el celo y la vigilancia para el más exacto cumplimiento de esta disposición y elevarán las denuncias juntamente con el atestado, en el que se recomienda la práctica de información testifical.

La autoridad espera de los señores presidentes de Corporaciones y servicios públicos civiles de toda especie, la más asidua, abnegada y patriótica colaboración a fin de lograr, rápida y eficazmente, el restablecimiento del uso exclusivo del idioma nacional en todos los actos y relaciones de la vida pública en esta provincia.»

Lo que hago público, para general conocimiento y cumplimiento.

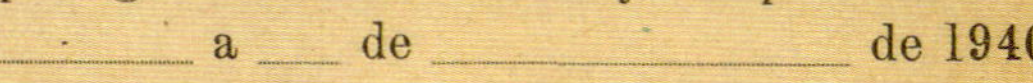

______________ a ___ de ______________ de 1940.

El Alcalde,

The picture Joan Miró dedicated to the first issue of the newspaper *Avui*. The 23rd April 1976 — the Day of Saint George, patron saint of Catalonia — was a significant and joyful day for the recovery of the public usage of the Catalan language, in an area which until then had met with a solid wall of regime prohibitions. The first edition of *Avui* came out, the first newspaper to be published in Catalan since the end of the civil war in 1939. In the last few years of democracy, other Catalan newspapers have sprung up around the country: *El Punt, Diari de Barcelona* — previously in Spanish — *Diari de Lleida, Regió 7*, and *El 9 Nou*. Painter Joan Miró dedicated a painting to this event, and shortly after, it was converted into a poster which was widely distributed in the country.

A delightful mystical treatise by Ramon Llull (14th century). The Majorca Theological Studies Centre director and Ramon Llull (Raymond Lully) specialist defines the *Arbre de Filosofia d'Amor* (Tree of the Philosophy of Love) as a "delightful mystical treatise that contains novel-format fragments of great literary value". It represents the culmination of Llull's love doctrine, in which Amic and Amat are the two main characters. Llull wrote it in Paris in 1293, and dedicated it to the King and Queen of France, Philip IV and Jeanne. This book contains the famous *Cant de Ramon* (Ramon's Song), a piece of immense literary force and perfection of form; and also a third section called *Llibre del gentil e dels tres savis* (Book of the heathen and the three wise men), which is an ecumenical dialogue between a pagan and three experts representing the most important monotheistic religions: a Jew, a Christian and a Muslim. The parchment we reproduce belongs to the *Llibre del Gentil* and contains well-conserved blue and red initial letters, section marks and headings.

***Llibre dels Àngels* (Book of the Angels), by Francesc Eiximenis, a scholar from Girona.** Francesc Eiximenis, a scholar and writer born in Girona, is one of the leading figures of the late Middle Ages. He participated in the intellectual life of Paris, Cambridge, Oxford, Cologne and Rome universities. His chief work was the thirteen volumes of *Lo Crestià* (The Christian), of which only three have come down to us. It was an encyclopaedia of medieval life. The revolutionary invention of the press led to the dissemination of this and other Catalan writers' work abroad. This particular work was translated into Latin, French, Flemish and Spanish. One intriguing thing about Eiximenis' work is the fact that the first book to be published in Granada in 1496, was a Spanish version of the *Vida de Jesucrist* (Life of Jesus Christ), another of his works. The picture here shows a miniature from another work, called *Llibre dels Àngels*, the French translation of which was also the first book to be printed in Geneva, in 1478.

Santa Maria del Mar, Gothic 14th century basilica. Gothic was the style that was predominant throughout Europe in the 13th, 14th and 15th centuries. In the context of the typical form Gothic architecture was taking on in the Mediterranean countries, Gothic architecture left its mark throughout the Catalan countries, both in rural and urban areas. One of the most magnificent Gothic monuments in Barcelona is the Basilica of Santa Maria del Mar. Although quite simple, from a structural point of view, it is imposing for its extraordinarily graceful lines and for the sensation of width given by its wide spaces. The tombstone of constable Peter of Portugal is conserved in the basilica.

Religious and civil constructions in Barcelona's "Gothic" quarter. In the 13th century, Barcelona became the capital of the Catalan-Aragonese Confederation, and the habitual residence of the kings and oligarchy made up of honourable citizens and merchants. The great presence of Gothic architecture in the city may be explained by the fact that Barcelona became the centre of operations of considerable political and economical weight, being predominant in most of the Mediterranean area. Palaces, churches, lavish residences, hospitals, ship-building yards, city walls — all are the product of a particularly dynamic period of this nation's history —. Catalonia maintained her power and dominions during the 14th and 15th centuries. The Dalmases Palace, in the photograph, is a significant example of Barcelona's Gothic architecture.

A page from *Les Quatre Grans Cròniques* (Four Great Chronicles) (15th century). The page reproduced here belongs to a parchment and paper manuscript containing two of the four Great 15th century Chronicles of Catalonia. The *Llibre dels feits* (Book of Events), or Chronicle of King James I, and the Chronicle of Bernat Desclot, also called the *Llibre del Rei en Pere* (King Peter's book), on the reign of Peter the Great. The two other chronicles are ones associated with Ramon Muntaner and Peter the Ceremonious. This series of chronicles, despite concessions made to anecdotes and legends, enable us to get to know the background of several reigns — from James I to Peter the Ceremonious — which cover Catalonia's greatest period, characterized by commercial expansion, the harmony attained by the institutions within the feudal framework, and the development of all aspects of culture.

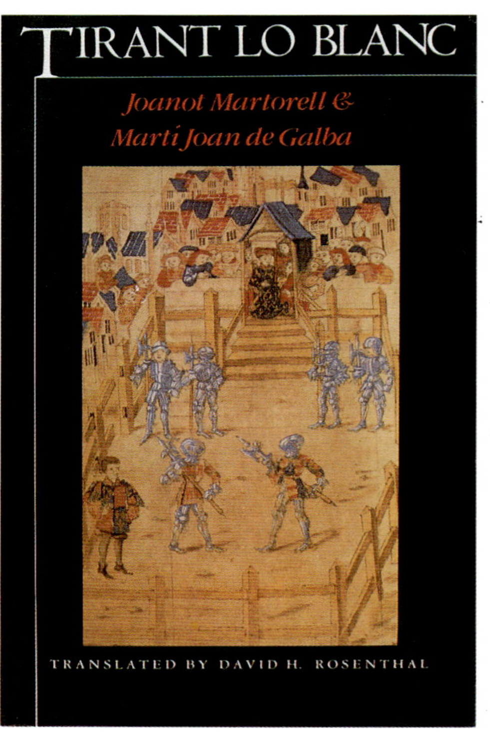

***Tirant lo Blanc*, a novel of chivalry translated into several languages.** It is a well-known fact that Miguel de Cervantes defined Joanot Martorell's novel — which was first printed in Valencia in 1490 — with these words: "This is the best book in the world". It is not clear whether Cervantes said this because Martorell had managed to avoid the clichés associated with contemporary chivalrous novels, giving his work a realistic, humourous and natural air. A factor that is not so well-known, however, is that this Catalan medieval novel has lately become a best-seller: editions have been published in English, Italian, Dutch, Finnish, as can be seen from the book covers. By the 16th century, editions had already been made in Spanish and Italian, and in the 18th century, in French. It is no exaggeration to state that *Tirant lo Blanc* is one of the finest works of European literature.

Jacint Verdaguer, National Poet of Catalonia. Jacint Verdaguer i Santaló has been referred to as the "National Poet of Catalonia". It is not a gratuitous claim, if only for the clear and emotive consciousness he had of his homeland, which he conceived as a combination of language, tradition, history and landscape. It must be remembered that *Canigó* is an impressive historical poem which he dedicated to his nation. The poem's action takes place in the Pyrenees. Beside this facet as an epic poet, Verdaguer was also an extraordinarily gifted lyrical poet, his strong points being sensitivity, tenderness, emotion and an eye for simple details. After a few years, several of Verdaguer's works, especially the epic poems *Canigó* and *L'Atlàntida* (Atlantis), were translated into the majority of the world's cultured languages. The monument by architect Pericas i Morros and sculptor Borrell i Nicolau, erected in Barcelona's Diagonal Avenue in the twenties, justly extols the exceptional literary and linguistic genius of Verdaguer.

Àngel Guimerà, a dramatist of international fame. If there is one dramatist who has entered into the spirit of the people, it must surely be Àngel Guimerà, who is here seen in a cartoon on top of a good many of his works. The popularity of works such as *Maria Rosa, Terra Baixa* (The Lowlands) or *Mossèn Joanot* (Reverend Joanot), aroused the interest of some of the most prestigious of the Spanish-language stage companies, such as the María Guerrero company, which staged versions of his work. The first two of the plays mentioned were soon translated into English and staged in the United States. He also staged *Scivolando sulla terra* in Italian prior to its staging in Catalan. This was to be a real international novelty. The Generalitat Drama Centre has recently staged *Maria Rosa*, as can be seen in the photograph.

Narcís Oller, leading *Renaixença* novelist. Narcís Oller was the first writer to have managed to rid himself of subservience to Romantic aesthetics and from slavery to literature understood as a tool of history. He was able to dedicate all his efforts to producing fine literary works: portraying his characters in depth or describing the social environment they lived in. After *La papallona* (The Butterfly), which was published in France by Émile Zola, he wrote *La febre d'or* (The Gold Fever), *L'escanyapobres* (The Usurer) and other novels and short stories. The peak of his career was marked by the publication in 1906 of *Pilar Prim*, which the English Catalanophile, Alan Yates, professor at Sheffield University, has described as "a mature work, in which the psychological depth and the cultivation of a more refined style indicate the adoption of post-naturalist tendencies and procedures". Bewteen 1913 and 1918 he wrote his *Memòries literàries* (Literary Memoirs), which were published many years later, in 1962. He was also the translator of works by Dumas, Turguenev, Tolstoy, and Flaubert, among others.

Salvador Espriu or the assumption of an inevitable task. When discussing Salvador Espriu, and forgetting for one moment his extraordinary quality as a poet, it must be remembered that the bulk of his work appeared during the bitter years of oppression the Franco dictatorship brought to bear against the Catalan language. In this sense, two lines of his poetry jump to mind. They became an emblem, project and oath for a whole literary career: "But we have lived to save our words,/ to return the name for every object to you".

German and French translations of Espriu's work. Salvador Espriu is perhaps the contemporary Catalan author whose name is most familiar even to people who are not very widely read. He was also a poet whose influence went beyond the Catalan-speaking lands. He was terribly self-demanding, always searching for a kind of formal beauty which was dense in content, and which, apart from producing pleasing aesthetic results, challenges us with its ethical demands. In the future, forthcoming generations will find it hard to forget the powerful exposure of the senselessness and evil of the Spanish Civil war — "A war among brothers", he says — in *La pell de brau* (translated into German in 1985, and into English in 1987). In the book *Llibre de Sinera* (Book of Sinera), the poet shows a deep sense of allegiance to his fellow countrymen and to his country, Catalonia. Here is a photograph of the French version. It must be added that, in the last few years, many translations have been made of Espriu's other works. All his prose work has been published in Spanish.

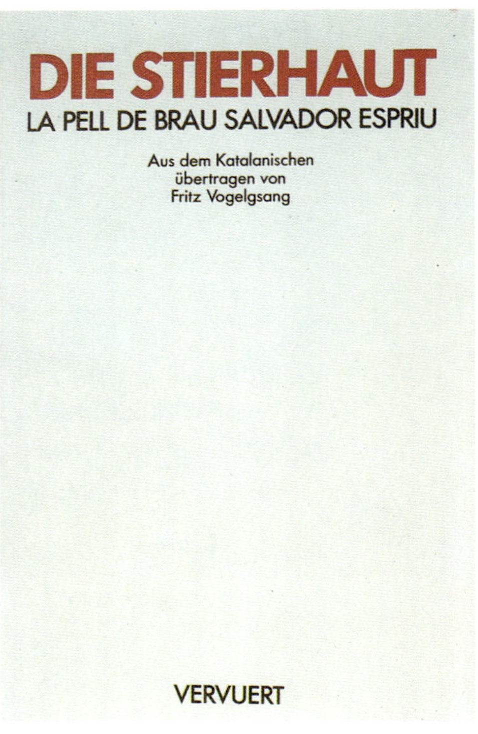

Mercè Rodoreda: what lies behind the sparkle in her eyes? In this photograph of Mercè Rodoreda in the last few years of her life, her sparkling eyes show all the distinction, intelligence and sensitivity of a writer who has made an undisputed name for herself not only in the context of Catalan literature, but also in European literary history. This has been made possible by the many translations there have been of her works. The literary critic, Carme Arnau, points to the following constant features of her production: "The essentially feminine subject matter, with young girls as the central characters, and action centred on love affairs which are expressed in a poetic and symbolic fashion". In her last works, and especially in *Mirall trencat* (Broken mirror) (1974), Rodoreda introduces the mythical element: the main characters become immortal. There is no doubt about the fact that the film and television versions of *La plaça del Diamant* (The time of the doves) made a major contribution to further popularizing the late Mercè Rodoreda, herself a mythical figure.

***La plaça del Diamant*, translated into 17 languages.** These two elegant book covers belong to the Greek and Bulgarian editions of Mercè Rodoreda's most widely read novel: *La plaça del Diamant.* This book has been translated into seventeen foreign languages. But not only this novel has received attention. Other works of hers have recently interested publishers and readers, especially in Europe. *Mirall trencat* (Broken mirror), *Viatges i flors* (Journeys and flowers), and *La meva Cristina i altres contes* (My Cristina and other short stories), for example, have all been translated into German between 1981 and 1988.

Marià Manent: poet and translator of English poetry. Marià Manent has been one of the most solid literary figures of the 20th century. He was a poet of the *Noucentista* movement, and dedicated his activity to creative work, translations and adaptations of Chinese and English poetry, as well as prose work and literary criticism. In the photograph is the book *El gran vent i les heures* (The big wind and the ivy), a second edition — forty years later — following the first one commissioned by Bartomeu Rosselló-Pòrcel. It is a free anthology offering a wide range of first-rate British and North American poets, especially contemporary ones. These fine translations thoroughly enrich the poetic expression of the Catalan language.

Carles Riba, eminent poet and brilliant translator. Carles Riba, one of this centuries finest poets, was obliged to publish the most important of his literary works, *Elegies de Bierville* (Bierville Elegies), in Argentina in 1942. Postwar repression against the Catalan culture was relentless in the forties. By then, Riba had already published his first and second book of *Estances* (Stanze) and was an undisputed master. In time, a further series of books appeared, among which the following were particularly significant: *Salvatge cor* (Wild heart) and *Esbós de tres oratoris* (Outline of three oratorios). As his poetry developes, the influence of the following become apparent: Hölderlin, Rilke, Guillén, Valéry and Mallarmé. Riba also stood out as a translator: Sophocles, Aeschilus, Plutarch, Hölderin, Kavafis, etc. His most important work in this field was the translation in verse of Homer's *Odyssey*.

Pere Calders, a narrator who never ceases to surprise. Behind the ambiguous expression of this apparently serious and static look lies the rich literary personality of Pere Calders, the epitomy of fantasy, exoticism, irony and sensitivity. These are the most outstanding and tangible ingredients that the author invests in balanced proportions in one of his best works: *Cròniques de la veritat oculta* (Tales of the hidden truth). After many years of exile after the Spanish civil war, and with the baggage of a lifetime of experiences behind him (as seen through the eyes of a true humanist), Calders offers a large corpus of prose works which have their most outstanding exponent in *L'ombra de l'atzavara* (The shade of the agave cactus). This novel won the Sant Jordi Prize — the most important novel prize in Catalan — in 1964. Pere Calders has been translated into English, French, Spanish, Czech and German. He is also a journalist and drawer.

The Tinell Hall, in the Main Royal Palace. Simple beauty and harmonious proportions are the characteristics which stand out, at first glance, in the Tinell Hall (also known as "Sala dels Paraments"). It was constructed in the 14th century by master builder Guillem Carbonell. It is 17m wide and 33.5 m long. Although there are 11th century architectural features to be seen, the present arrangement owes much to King Peter III, who used the hall as a Parliament, banquet and ceremonial hall. Ferdinand II of Aragon and Isabella of Castile received Christopher Columbus here when he returned from his first voyage to America. Nowadays, exhibitions and a variety of cultural events are held in this marvellous Gothic hall.

From ship-building yard to maritime museum. The interior part of the Barcelona Drassanes, a Gothic-style building for the construction of ships (that already existed in the 14th century), is today a maritime cultural museum. Visitors can see an attractive visual display on the history of sailing, ships, war ships, merchant ships, fishing boats, sports and pleasure craft. There are also tools and documents associated with nautical astronomy, naval archaeology, arms and antiquities, with art and other human activities related with this vast medium — the sea. It is a museum where we can contemplate and conjure up memories of the maritime feats of the Catalan-Aragonese Confederation, although it also covers aspects related to Spanish and universal maritime culture.

Balsareny Castle, a relic from the first Millennium. Balsareny Castle is a striking building because of its symmetrical proportions and stony elegance. The first records of this castle go back to the year 990. It is made up of an elongated rectangle, with large Gothic windows and, up above, a crown of multiple embattlements, witnessing the additions made in the 14th century. Beside the castle is the Mare de Déu del Castell Chapel, which is the enlargement of a 12th century Romanesque church.

A Gothic cloister and a Romanesque church, at Sant Joan de les Abadesses. At Sant Joan de les Abadesses, a town in the foothills of the Pyrenees, there are fine examples of medieval architecture. One exponent ifs the Romanesque church of Sant Joan. It has five apses — three that used to form part of an old ambulatory, and one on either side of the transept. They are decorated, both on the inside and the outside, with arcatures and small columns. The major apse contains a marvellous ensemble of sculptures called the *Descent from the Cross* or *Holy Mystery* which is also Romanesque, dating back to 1251. However, the cloister — as can be seen in the photograph — is Gothic and was begun in 1442, although it contains a few arches from the old Romanesque cloister. The static harmony of the columns — a gift handed down to us by past generations — is a delight to observe.

Jaume Huguet, the painter of natural expression. Jaume Huguet is the name of the 15th century artist who painted this painting known as *Saint Abdó and Saint Senén altarpiece*. It is painted on wood, and it to be found in the side chapel of Sant Pere's church in Terrassa. In words of art historian Joan Ainaud de Lasarte, this altarpiece "is a mature work, with a serene and expressive natural quality. Huguet and his artistic group stand out in Catalan late 15th century painting, developing the brand of naturalism that had been introduced by Lluís Dalmau and other artists who were acquainted with contemporary currents in Flemish painting. Huguet adapted this new style to harmonize with the country's best tradition. In his painting, golden backgrounds are still to be seen, but in a fine harmonious way that shows an acquaintance with the work of Italian artists".

The Mestre de la Seu d'Urgell announces the Renaissance. This work, a prodigy of colourism and detailed observation, emerged from the exceptional career of the so-called Mestre de la Seu d'Urgell. The theme is that of the Annunciation of the Angel to the Virgin Mary and dates from the last third of the 15th century. During this period, together with the naturalism of Dalmau and Huguet, some Catalan artists, such as the Mestre de la Seu d'Urgell, cultivated the Flemish Gothic style, formally dominated by great technique in the treatment of colour, perspective and realistic forms, already announcing the Renaissance. In the picture above, a fragment of the main altarpiece of Saint Mary on polychrome wood and with a hint of Italian trends, preserved in the cathedral at Tortosa.

The Odalisque **by Marià Fortuny**. Marià Fortuny was the most remarkable nineteenth century Catalan painter. He had outstanding technique and was capable of creating light effects recalling the nascent art of the impressionist of the period. He was a restless spirit and keen to discover new styles and techniques, often travelling to Paris, London, Florence, and working for long periods in Rome, where he painted *The Odalisque* — the painting reproduced here — in 1859. He was later to produc two very well known works: *The Battle of Tetouan*, which he also painted in Rome between 1862 and 1864, and *The Vicarage*, which he finished in Paris in 1869. "In his day" says critic Francesc Fontbona, "he was considered to be one of the greatest painters of all times".

A landscape by Joaquim Vayreda. The painter Joaquim Vayreda was one of the most outstanding artists of the 19th century. Until 1870 he tended towards genre paintings, religious works and landscapes, in which browns, greens and ochres stand out, with obvious aesthetic influence from Marià Fortuny and the romantic realism of J.F. Millet. He was also interested in politics, and presided over the first Catalanist Assembly at Manresa, where the famous *Bases de la Constitució Regional Catalana* (a political declaration for national rights) were approved. But he was above all concerned with the cultural development of his country and his city, Olot, where he founded the famous Olot School, which produced some fine landscape artists.

The bold stroke of Francesc Pla, "El Vigatà". One of the outstanding painters of the Catalan 18th century was, without doubt, Francesc Pla, who was better known by his nickname, "El Vigatà". He was an impulsive and sometimes impetuous artist who decorated the Bishop's Palace in Barcelona, at the time of Bishop Gabino Valladares. He also stands out for the set works that are gathered in the Moja Palace, in Barcelona's Rambla. The overall decoration of this palace's hall, which is equivalent in height to three floors, is particularly fine, and shows El Vigatà's splendid fresco and tempera technique, this latter system being used especially on the polychromatic sections. Santiago Alcolea, Barcelona University professor, says that Francesc Pla is an artist "of great boldness of stroke and economy of means".

Perfect execution in the work of the Vallmitjana brothers. The Vallmitjana brothers (Venanci and Agapit) must be placed among the finest representatives of Catalan sculpture of their time. Their style betrays romantic reminiscences and marked naturalism and realism in the details. They worked together on several works and sculpture ensembles at Manchester, Valencia, Paris, but above all, in Barcelona. Several of their works of fine execution are on show in the Ciutadella park. It would seem that the sculpture shown here — Queen Isabella II and her son Alphonse — is also the joint work of both brothers, being made at the request of the Queen of Spain herself.

Pau Casals, cellist, conductor, composer of the *Hymn of Peace*. Pau Casals was without doubt one of the world's greatest cellists, a wonderful conductor and first class composer. On October 24th 1971, when he was 94, he personally conducted the first audition of the *Hymn of Peace* — work he had been commissioned with — in the United Nations building. On that occasion, the secretary general of the United Nations Organization, U Thant, awarded him a medal, and, in his speech, he recalled that Pau Casals, as a man and as an artist, had dedicated his life to the cause of truth, beauty and peace. Casals later answered with the following words: "Peace has always been my major concern. Furthermore, I am a Catalan. And Catalonia had the first democratic parliament, long before England. It was in my country that the first United Nations sessions were held... Back in the 11th century, they were already getting together to speak of peace, because the Catalans of that period were already opposed to war. For this reason, everything related to peace goes straight to my heart".

Salvador Dalí: a painter of universal standing. Salvador Dalí is one of the universal Catalans of this century. As a young man he was very active, not only as an avant-garde painter, but also as a lecturer, writer of press articles, and "illustrator of truth", in a phrase coined by Daniel Giralt-Miracle. His style has been called superrealistic as it uses reality as a starting point to move into the realm of fantasy. Abstraction is never his aim, for Dalí was a great opponent of abstraction. The artistic personality of Salvador Dalí was most versatile. Apart from painting, he also cultivated drawing, stage, ballet and film set design, poster design, sculpture, jewellry design, poetry and even novel writing. Although he was a universal artist, he never turned his back on his homeland and the place where he had been born. It is for this reason that Empordà scenery is present throughout his works, as a setting for his characters and objects.

A representative painting by Joan Miró. This painting, which the photographer chose as a backdrop to his face, is typical of the naïve and fantastic style of Joan Miró, an artist given over to the exaltation of bright colours. Miró is another Catalan artist to be acclaimed throughout the world. He began as a cubist in the twenties, and later took up superrealism, although it has never been possible to adscribe him to any one school of painting. Miró was also an engraver, mural and tapestry designer, although his most important artistic facet — along with painting — is that of sculptor. Many of his works are on display at the Miró Foundation in Barcelona, a centre which he himself created in 1971. In the last few years of his life, he produced various monumental sculptures.

Young Picasso as seen by Ricard Opisso. Ricard Opisso, Catalan painter and drawer, saw his friend and contemporary — Pablo Picasso — in this way. Picasso had been born in Malaga in 1881, although, throughout his life, he always professed a great feeling of identification with the Catalan spirit. Picasso was as much of a painter as a drawer, engraver, sculptor and potter, for artistic creation of every description streamed from his hands, creating shapes and styles inspired by the exuberance of his creative genius. In 1901 he began his blue period, followed by the pink period, cubism and abstraction. But his artistic restlessness knew no limits as his art developed into giantism, Dionysian paroxysm and superrealism. The quality and magnitude of his artistic work has won Picasso universal fame. Picasso repeatedly professed his allegiance to Catalonia, and indeed the *Encyclopaedia Britannica* defines him as a "Catalan painter, born in Malaga".

"La Pedrera" or Casa Milà, a house designed by Antoni Gaudí. The Pedrera — also known as the Casa Milà (for Gaudí designed it for Pere Milà i Camps) — is one of the buildings that symbolize Barcelona. It is on Passeig de Gràcia, one of the city's main avenues. It is made up of two residential blocks. Gaudí's originality is fully expressed in its conception: the flats' distribution plan is absolutely free, no two rooms being alike. There are no straight lines involved. In contrast with Gaudí's other work, there are no decorative elements on the stone façade, except for forged metal work on doors and balcony railings. The façade is made up of a capriciously undulating surface which stimulates the fantasy of the observer and here inspires the photographer.

Gaudí's Sagrada Família: the Nativity Façade. The towering spires of the Sagrada Família temple have become the symbol, visiting card and major architectural wonder of Barcelona. The Sagrada Família is the genuine and amazing expression of a unique personality in the world of architecture: Antoni Gaudí. Exuberant, imaginative, implausible in his artistic discoveries and as intuitive as unrepeatable in terms of technical solutions (which were without doubt way ahead of their time), Gaudí materialized his skills as an architectural genius in this temple, inspired by his innermost faith as a Christian.

Arnau de Vilanova, doctor, leading scientist and religious reformer. Scholars still lack information regarding the birthplace of this wise man called Arnau de Vilanova, who has been described as "fantastic, intellectually restless and versatile". What we do know is that he attended the court of King James II and that he was a professor at Montpellier University, where he became an undisputed scientist and intellectual at the turn of the 15th century. Doctor to popes and kings, he was also concerned with progressive thought — especially in a social and religious context — and with the need to develop medicine as much as possible, using all the resources that were available at the time. His works have been studied in depth by Luis García Ballester and by North American Michael McVaugh, from North Carolina University. Between them, they have gathered over one thousand two hundred previously unknown manuscripts. Most of these documents have not surprisingly been found in the lands of the old Catalan-Aragonese Confederation: Catalonia, Valencia, Aragon and Majorca.

bonificatũ bonificare sũt equales p ẽntiã ꝛ sic de intellectu ꝛ voluntate/et etiã de igne itate ꝛc. suo modo põt dici. Et sic de equalitate accñtiũ causaliũ ꝛ moraliũ. Per ipsas quidem tres species intellectus ascendit et descendit vt ṽitates rerũ attingere possit qº ad genꝰ maioritatis equalitatis ꝛ minoritatis. ꝛ etiã quoad genꝰ substãtiale ꝛ accñtale. Et iste ascensus ꝛ descẽsus est valde artificialis ad adquirendum scientias. ¶ Diximus de secunda figura: que instrumentuz ẽ intellectui: cũ quo agit ĩ prima figura. qm̃ p ~~bonitatem~~ distinguit inter bonitatem et magnitudinem ꝛc. et cũ concordantia concordat. ꝛ sic de alijs suo modo. Item distiguit cũ differentia in essentia bonitatis per bonificantem bonificatum et bonificare. et cũ concordantia quidem concordat qꝫ sint idem p essentiam naturaliter. moraliter vo nõ. qm̃ differentia nõ est innata. sed adquisita. eo quia occasione sunt principia.

De tertia figura.

BC	CD	DE	EF	FG	GH	HI	IK
BD	CE	DF	EG	FH	GI	HK	
BE	CF	DG	EH	FI	GK		
BF	CG	DH	EI	FK			
BG	CH	DI	EK				
BH	CI	DK					
BI	CK						
BK							

Tertia figura ẽ cõposita ex prima et secũda. que habet. xxxvi. cameras. vt ĩ ipsa aꝫ. In q̃lꝫ camera sunt due littere. ĩ prima. b. c. ĩ secunda. b. d. et sic de alijs. Et dicitur composita ex duabus figuris. quia suum. b. valet. b. quod est ĩ prima figura/ꝛ. b. quod est ĩ secũda. Et sic de c. quod valet. c. quod ẽ ĩ prima/ et. c. quod est ĩ secunda. et sic de alijs. ¶ Intentio quare hec figura in hac arte ẽ posita: ẽ ad significandum: vt cũ vno principio homo applicet vel associet aliud pricipiũ. sicut ad. b applicãtur. c. et. d. vsqꝫ ad. b. k. Et hoc: vt cũ. c. d. notitia habeat de. b. e. et secũdũ illã notitiam de quocũqꝫ. b. queratur. Et sic diximus de. b. ita intelligendũ est de. c. sic respicere. c. cũ. b. et postmodũ cuꝫ. d. et sic dein ceps vsqꝫ ad camerã. c. k. et sic de alijs camris per ordinem vsqꝫ ad cameraꝫ de. i. k. et hoc ad placitum. secundũ qꝫ homo multiplicare voluerit rationes ad cãdem cõclusionem. Et hoc respiciendo significata camerarum/ꝛ applicando ad propositũ. Hec figura docet descendere de vniuersali ad particulare gradatĩ quattuor modis. Primo sic dicendo per camerã de. b. c. bonitas hẽt magnã differẽtiam ꝛ concordantiam. Secundo quando intellectus cõsiderat angulum de d'a: descẽdit ab vniuersali ad particulare/intelligendo differentiam et concordantiaꝫ esse inter sensuale ꝛ sensuale ꝛc. vt dictum est in secunda figura. Tertio descẽdit plus: quando considerat: qꝫ differentia et concordantia bone sunt inter ignem et aerem. qui concordant in caliditate. Quarto modo descendit intelligẽdo: qꝫ bona differentia et concordantia sunt inter bonificatiuum ꝛc. que sunt de essentia bonitatis. Et sicut diximus de. b. c. ita potest dici de alijs cameris huius figure.

De quarta figura.

Quarta figura tres hẽt circulos. vt in ipsa apparet. et comprehẽdit primã figuram secundam et tertiam. et in ipsa colliguntur illa principia: ex quibus tabula ẽ composita. quoniam camera de. b. c. d. facit columnam in tabula de. b. c. d. compositam. et camera. b. c. e. facit columnam compositam de. b. c. e. ¶ Intentio quare hec figura in hac arte ẽ posita: ẽ: vt ex ipã fiat ta/

Llull's *Ars magna*, a compendium to discover the truth. This edition of one of Ramon Llull's major works, the *Ars magna* — written between 1305 and 1308 — is kept in the Catalan National Library, or Library of Catalonia. The aim of this work, which combined several of the "arts" he had already exposed in previous works, was to put forward a series of very general principles which could be applied to all sciences, and which would be of service in order to discover the truth and to solve various scientific problems. This systematic method of searching for the truth had a religious intention: that of converting Moslems and Jews to Christianity.

The Barcelona Botanical Institute and the Salvador Family. The Barcelona Botanical Institute, in Montjuïc Park, has a section to honour the memory of the Salvadors, a family of illustrious botanists and pharmacists who lived in Barcelona in the late 17th and 18th centuries. The most outstanding member of this family was perhaps Jaume Salvador i Pedrol, who read natural science at Montpellier, and accompanied the Frenchman Tournefort on his first botanical expeditions in the Iberian Peninsula. With his sons, he founded the first botanical gardens in Catalonia at Sant Joan Despí in 1723.

Dr. Josep Trueta, an eminent surgeon of world-wide repute. Dr. Josep Trueta is one of the Catalans who most deservedly obtained the title of "Universal Catalan". As a surgeon trained in Barcelona, he developed a system for the treatment of open wounds, which he described in his work: *El tractament actual de les fractures de guerra* (Current treatment of war wounds). This important contribution to traumatology was immediately translated into English, and his treatment was adopted — "not without reserves at first", as Dr. Oriol Casassas points out — by the allied forces. At the time his work was becoming known, Dr. Trueta took up residence in Oxford, where he was to live in exile after 1939. With the economic cooperation of Lord Nuffield, he founded the first orthopaedic hospital, a pioneer research centre. His studies on kidney circulation, poliomyelitis, scoliosis etc. were particularly significant. He was also an active Catalan nationalist, and wrote *The spirit of Catalonia*, a book that was to inform the English-speaking world about the plight of Catalonia. He also helped to found the Anglo-Catalan Society.

The *Ictíneo*, the submarine invented by Monturiol. This is the experimental submarine that Narcís Monturiol invented and called *Ictíneo*. It was first tested in Barcelona port in 1859. Monturiol was an idealist, a romantic and pacific revolutionary and a humanist. The idea of constructing a submarine occurred to him during a period of political confinement at Cadaqués (Costa Brava), as he sat on a rock at Cap de Creus and watched the sufferings of red coral divers. His invention served no warlike purpose, and was intended for discoveries and deep-sea investigation. He manned the craft himself, with the aid of some friends. It stood up to several test runs and proved that it was possible to remain submerged in the sea. The only problem he was unable to solve was that of propulsion. He tried to apply a steam engine to the *Ictíneo*, but to no avail. Electricity, the only solution to submarine navigation, would not be applied until a few years later.

Ictíneo Monturiol

The Barraquers, a family of famous ophthalmologists. The Barraquers are a family of doctors who have specialized in ophthalmology and neurology. Josep Antoni Barraquer i Roviralta, who may be considered to be the patriarch of the family tradition, was one of the fathers of Catalan modern ophthalmology, and founded a surgery for this purpose in the Santa Creu Hospital in 1879. His son, Ignasi Barraquer i Barraquer carried out thousands of operations on patients from the five continents. In 1947 he founded the Barraquer Institute in Barcelona, for the study, research and training of ophthalmology. It is considered to be one of the best in the world. He invented a new technique and a new instrument for the extraction of the crystalline lens. Josep-Ignasi Barraquer i Moner is Ignasi's Barraquer's son, and is responsible for the creation of a new clinical technique for the correction of cornea curving.

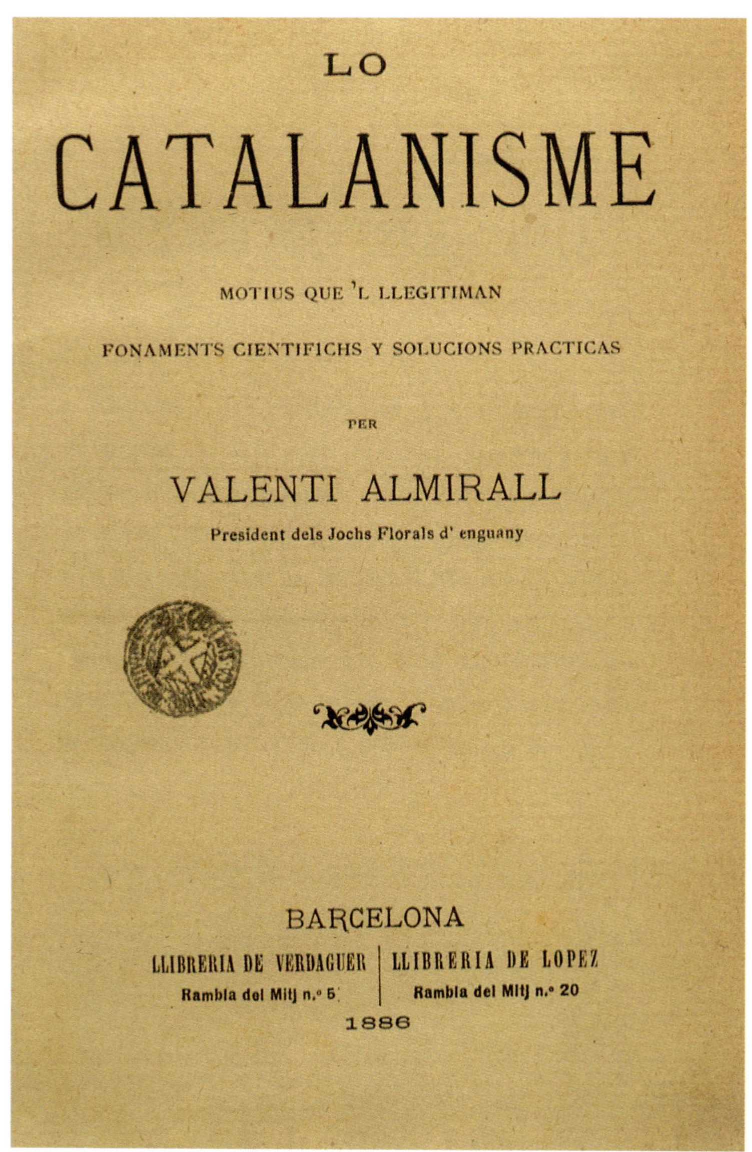
LO

CATALANISME

MOTIUS QUE 'L LLEGITIMAN

FONAMENTS CIENTIFICHS Y SOLUCIONS PRACTICAS

PER

VALENTI ALMIRALL

President dels Jochs Florals d' enguany

BARCELONA

LLIBRERIA DE VERDAGUER | LLIBRERIA DE LOPEZ

Rambla del Mitj n.º 5 | Rambla del Mitj n.º 20

1886

Valentí Almirall, Catalanist, republican, federalist. This print from the *La Ilustració Catalana* shows Valentí Almirall as chairman of the *Jocs Florals* (literary competitions) in 1886, a year of full political activity for this outstanding figure of Catalanism, who was a progressive republican, federalist and promoter of various political and cultural initiatives. In fact, 1886 was the year in which *Lo Catalanisme* (Catalanism) and *España tal cual es* (Spain as it is) were published. According to Josep-Maria Figueres, specialist in his work, Almirall is described as "the politician who was able to give the Catalanist movement, at that time related to literature and associationism, a new social and political dimension, which moved into the high cultural world and into science, thus going beyond the narrow field of action to which cultural Catalanism was confined".

Lo Catalanisme **(Catalanism), synthesis of Almirall's Catalanist political thought.** The work synthesizing the political theory of Valentí Almirall is *Lo Catalanisme* (1886), in which he exposed for the first time its reasons, scientific foundations and practical solutions". Almirall's objective was the construction of a more equitable and solidary Spanish State. Rather than aspire to the secession from Spain he energically rejected the castilianization of Catalonia and was an advocate of Catalonia's distinct profile. His constant desire was to free Catalonia from a uniform view of the state, and then unite it with the rest of the regions "establishing links based on brotherhood and mutual interest".

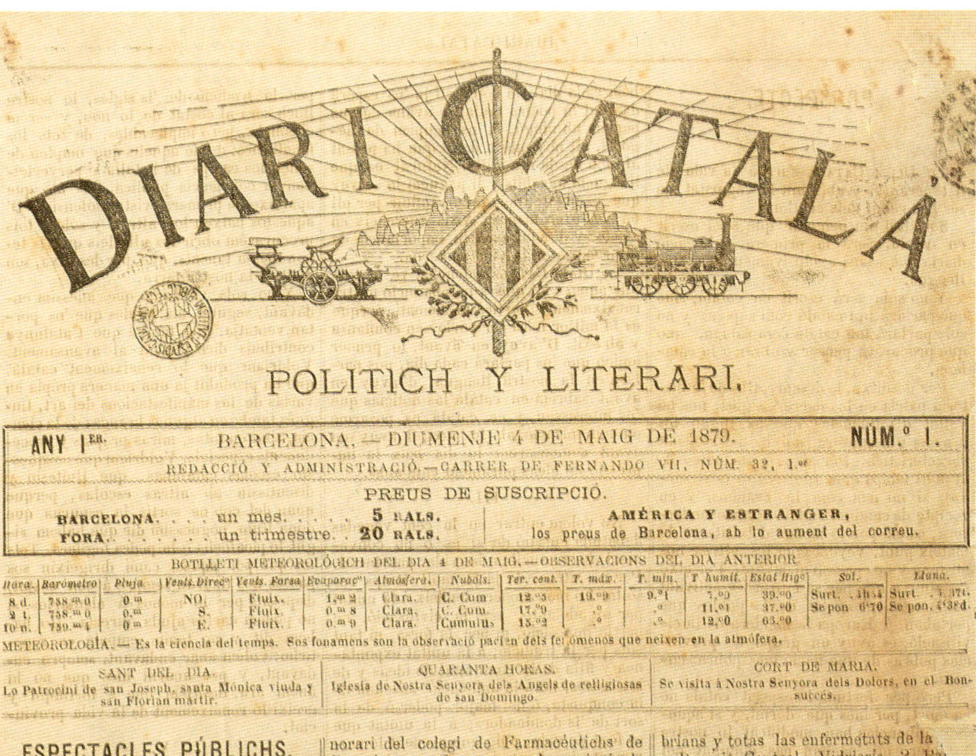

DIARI CATALÀ

POLITICH Y LITERARI.

ANY 1ER. BARCELONA. — DIUMENJE 4 DE MAIG DE 1879. NÚM.º 1.

REDACCIÓ Y ADMINISTRACIÓ.—CARRER DE FERNANDO VII, NÚM. 32, 1.er

PREUS DE SUSCRIPCIÓ.

BARCELONA. . . . un mes. . . . . 5 RALS.
FORA. . . . . . . un trimestre. . 20 RALS.

AMÉRICA Y ESTRANGER, los preus de Barcelona, ab lo aument del correu.

BOTLLETI METEOROLÓGICH DEL DIA 4 DE MAIG.—OBSERVACIONS DEL DIA ANTERIOR

Hora.	Barometro	Pluja.	Vents. Direcº	Vents. Forsa	Evaporacº	Atmósfera.	Nubols.	Ter. cent.	T. máx.	T. mín.	T. humit.	Estat Higº	Sol.	Lluna.
8 d.	758.m0	0.m	NO.	Fluix.	1.m2	Clara.	C. Cum	12.º5	19.º9	9.º1	7.º0	39.º0	Surt. .4h54	Surt. .4.37t.
2 t.	758.m0	0.m	S.	Fluix.	0.m8	Clara.	C. Cum.	17.º9	.º	.º	11.º1	37.º0	Se pon 6'70	Se pon. 4'38d.
10 n.	759.m4	0.m	E.	Fluix.	0.m9	Clara.	Cumulus	15.º2	.º	.º	12.º0	63.º0		

METEOROLOGÍA.—Es la ciencia del temps. Sos fonamens son la observació pacien dels fenómenos que neixen en la atmófera.

SANT DEL DIA. Lo Patrocini de san Joseph, santa Mónica viuda y san Florian mártir.

QUARANTA HORAS. Iglesia de Nostra Senyora dels Angels de relligiosas de san Domingo.

CORT DE MARIA. Se visita á Nostra Senyora dels Dolors, en el Bonsuccés.

ESPECTACLES PÚBLICHS.

TEATRO DEL CIRCO.—Diumenje 4.—Tarde.—*El barberillo de Lavapiés* y *La voz pública*.—Nit. *Los diamantes de la corona* y *El hombre es débil*.

TEATRO ROMEA.—Diumenje 4.—Tarde.—*O locura ó santidad* y *Mentir con suerte*.—Nit.—*Cofis y mofis* y *La nena*.

TEATRO DEL ODEON.—Diumenje 4.—Tarde.—*El nudo gordiano*; *La catedral de Sevilla* y *Cuatre soldats y un cabo*.—Nit.—*La voz del remordimiento ó El negro y el negrero* y *Gat y gos*.

TEATRO DE NOVETATS.—Diumenje 4.—Tarde.—*Ricardo III* y *Peró...*—Nit.—Societat Malibran.—*Flor de un dia* y *Espinas de una flor*.

TEATRO DEL TIVOLI.—Diumenje 4.—Tarde. *Las campanas de Carrion* y *Tres ruinas artísticas*.—Nit.—*La Guardiola* y *Tres ruinas artísticas*.

PRAT CATALÁ.—Diumenje 4.—Tarde.—*Urganda la desconocida*.

TEATRO ESPAÑOL.—Diumenje 4.—Tarde.—*Don Juan de Serrallonga* y presentació del Hércules italià signor Nàpoli.—Nit.—*La muerte civil* y *Moltas claus*.

TEATRO DE LOS CAMPS ELISEOS.—Diumenje 4.—Tarde.—*El inmortal sitio de Zaragoza*.

TEATRO DEL BON RETIRO.—Diumenje 4.—Tarde.—*La gallina ciega*, y *Para una modista un sastre* y *Primer jo*.

ESPECTACLES PARTICULARS

VELOZ-CLUB.—Funcions de 3 á 5 de la tarde y de 8 á 10 de la nit.

TIRO ALS COLOMS.—De la associació de aficionats á la cassa.—Tindrá lloch á las 8 del matí en lo local situat al extrem del carrer del Bruch.

Kramerina.—Elixir y pasta de J. MEIFREN, Professor dentista, soci honorari del colegi de Farmacéutichs de Barcelona.—Se ven en las principals perfumerías, quincallerías y droguerías d' Espanya, América y Portugal.—Depósit central, en casa de l' inventor, Fernando VII, 16, Barcelona.

¡Per l' insignificant preu de 20 duros! rellotjes Remontoires, d' or de lley, ab un estuig molt elegant, garantits per lo rellotjer Joan Feliu y Codina.—PASSATJE DE LAS COLUMNAS, Plassa del Angel, 4 y 5, cantonada á la Boria, botiga de joguinas y quincalla.

Lostau, sombrerer.—7, Pasatje de Bacardi, 7.—Gran assortit de sombreros y gorras per la próxima estació.—Preus modichs de veritat.

NOTA.—Los géneros no son del no nat Garnier de Paris ni tampoch del ilusori Ortoff de Lóndres.

Los encarrechs se fan ab lo mes esquisit bon gust y promptitut.

Los millors cuberts coneguts son los de **Nikel** (metall blanch pur), forts y elegants, llisos ó trevallats á 10 rals un.—Culleretas, safatas, palmatorias y altres articles del mateix metall. Unich despatx; casa Meneses, 19, Fernando VII, 19.—Barcelona.

Licor quitrá Vehil. Es lo verdader y mes eficaz medicament recomenat per los metjes mes eminents per la curació del catarro crónich de vejiga y demés afeccions del aparato génito-urinari; catarro pulmonar y demés del aparato respiratori, malas digestions, escorbuts, cólich, reumatismes, gota, escrófulas, brians y totas las enfermetats de la —Depósit Central, Vidriería, 2, Barcelona.

Avis.—Lo Corredor real de Comers D. Aniceto Espinach y Martorell participa á sos clients y al públich en general, haber obert son nou despatx en la Baxada de San Miquel, n.º 1, entresuelo, ahont reb tota classe d' órdres de compra y venda de valors del Estad y dels locals, cupons, etc., etc.

Máquinas de cusir.—Las millors y mes lleugeras son las del fabricant Miquel Escudér. Fábrica en la Barceloneta. Sucursal de la casa ab preus de fábrica, carrer de l' Hospital num. 6.—Enseyansa de franch á domicili.—Se venen á plassos desde 10 rals semanals.

Cuchs.—Lo millor específich per destruirlos rapidament es lo LOMBRICIDO-FORMIGUERA, premiat en varias Exposicions nacionals y estrangeras. Es sumament agradable, fa tenir gana, regenera y fortaleix á las criaturas.—Depósit Central, Dr. Formiguera, Fernando VII, núm. 7—Barcelona.

Gran noticia.—La Companyía Fabril Singer ha vengut en 1878, TRES-CENTAS CINQUANTA SIS MIL QUATRE-CENTS TRENTA DOS ó siga 73.620 mes que en 1877: aceptació universal. Venta á plassos totas las classes. 10 rals semanals, carrer de Fernando VII, 38, Barcelona.

***Diari Català*, a newspaper for progress.** *Diari Català*, the first newspaper ever written in Catalan, first appeared on Sunday, May 4, 1879 with a headline designed by the famous draftsman Josep Lluís Pellicer, who at that time resided in Paris. If we look closely, the symbolic Catalanist elements — the rocky Montserrat mountains and the national coat of arms with its four bars — combine with elements which represent progress such as the railroad, the telegraph, industrial machinery, to form an amalgamation synthesizing all avant-garde ideology. The *Diari Català* was born with an objective: "We want to advance in every field, absolutely every one: science, religion, art and politics. As far as advancement is concerned nothing will deter us".

***La tradició catalana* (The Catalan tradition), the other column of Catalanism in the 19th century.** In 1892, *La tradició catalana* (The Catalan Tradition) written by Josep Torras i Bages — who later on would become bishop of Vic —, was edited. This was the same year in which the celebration of the assembly of Catalanist movements, which wanted a regional constitution for Catalonia and which were known as *Bases de Manresa*, took place. The work of Torras i Bages, which exercised a notorious influence on the assembly, was the ideological counterbalance of Almirall's *Lo Catalanisme*. He also wanted to promote Catalonia's identity, but from a traditional and Christian conservative fundamentalist viewpoint. This book had a remarkable echo and later exercised influence among catholic Catalanists.

LA

TRADICIÓ CATALANA

ESTUDI

DEL VALOR ÉTICH Y RACIONAL

DEL

REGIONALISME CATALÁ

per

Joseph Torras y Bages.

PREVERE

Attendite ad petram unde excissi estis. (Isai. LI. I.)
Penseu en la pedrera d'hont haveu sigut tallats. —*(Traducció)*

Ab llicencia eclesiástica.

BARCELONA
Estampa «La Ilustración», á c. de F. Giró
Passeig de Sant Joan, 168.
1892

The *Bases de Manresa*, moving force of Catalanism at the end of the 19th century. The last decade of the 19th century is characterized by a growing Catalanist political movement. In 1882, Almirall founded the Centre Català, an institution embracing members of diverse political tendencies. In 1887 the Lliga de Catalunya was founded by the most conservative members of the Centre Català. These two associations were the promoters of a 1889 campaign which defended Catalan Civil Law. In 1891 the Lliga de Catalunya created a federation of entities known as Unió Catalanista to pursue Catalan objectives. This new dynamic force of the Catalanist movement organized a meeting in Manresa — that can be seen here in a print of that time. It was responsible for drawing up the so called *Bases per a la Constitució Regional Catalana*, that is, a program for the political institutionalization of the country. This document was basically conservative, with its roots in tradition, and was ideologically very close to the thought of Bishop Torras i Bages.

CHAPTER II

CATALONIA TODAY

A PEOPLE WITH A NATIONAL CHARACTER

In 1971 the Catalan Assembly or Assemblea de Catalunya, a body which brought together political forces opposed to Franco, demanded the acknowledgement of the national status of the Catalan people, and consequently the right to freely decide its political future, be it as part of the Spanish State or not. In practice, the policy of the major political parties led the affair to be solved through negotiation. This resulted in the provisional restoration of the Generalitat, the return from exile of President Tarradellas in 1977 and a formula of autonomous self-government. This formula was made applicable to other areas of the State by virtue of the Spanish Constitution, and the Autonomous Community was adopted as its basic organizational unit.

The institutions for Catalan self-government: The Generalitat of Catalonia

The Statute of Autonomy of Catalonia is the Constitutional Law which defines the political institutions on which self-government of the Catalan nation is to be based. It also lays down their powers and governs their relationship with the State. The various political institutions defined in the Statute of Autonomy make up the Generalitat of Catalonia. It must be remembered, however, that the Generalitat is by no means a recent institution, having been founded in 1359 as a subsidiary body of the Catalan Corts Generals or Parliament.

The Generalitat is made up of: the Parliament, the Presidency and the Cabinet or Consell Executiu. The Catalan Parliament, which has 135 members, legislates, votes the annual budget, and monitors the Government's activity. The President of the

Generalitat is elected by Parliament, and is responsible for the Cabinet or Government's activity. He occupies the highest political post in the Generalitat. The President is also the senior representative of the State in Catalonia. As in all democratic countries, he is politically responsible before Parliament.

The Consell Executiu or Cabinet —made up of *consellers* or ministers from the different *conselleries* or ministries —is the governing body responsible for all executive and administrative functions. The number of *conselleries* or ministries varies according to the necessities of the periods of government, which last four years. There are usually about 12 *departaments.*

There are also other important bodies: the Advisory Board (Consell Consultiu), the National Audit Office (Sindicatura de Comptes), the Síndic de Greuges or Ombudsman.

The effective powers conferred by the Statute of Autonomy

The Statute of Autonomy ensures that the Generalitat of Catalonia has exclusive powers, both legislative and executive, in a wide range of areas, among which feature the following:

Organization of the institutions for self-government.

Catalan civil law.

Culture.

The historical, artistic, monumental, architectural, archaeological and scientific heritage.

Archives, libraries and museums.

Local administration.

Town planning, public works, roads, railways, ports and airports.

Tourism.

The exploitation of hydraulic resources.

Chambers of Commerce, Industry and Shipping and Property.

Social welfare and health.

Youth.

Women's rights.

Sports, leisure activities and entertainment.

Control in some of these areas, as may be expected, is limited by the Spanish Constitution. There is a second block of important powers made up of those areas in which the Generalitat carries out legislative and executive activity. One may mention, for example, education, the regulation of credit, banking and insurance, mining and energy, and the protection of the environment.

The Generalitat of Catalonia must also see to the correct execution of international agreements and covenants in those areas for which it is responsible. Furthermore, the Generalitat may sign agreements with other autonomous communities within the State in those areas in which it has exclusive powers. One may conclude, though, that while Catalonia has indeed got a certain degree of real power, this is well below the desired level of self-government befitting her national condition and vocation.

Funding for the Generalitat and its budget

The largest proportion of Generalitat funding is made up by tax revenue transferred by the Spanish State. Nevertheless, there are other sources of funds: taxes and duties established by the Generalitat, the issue of bonds and recourse to credit, etc.

The State guarantees the funding of services which have been transferred to the Generalitat in line with effective cost of the service at the time it was transferred. Nevertheless, it is obvious that the essential conditions of a full financial autonomy are lacking, and self-government, as such, suffers the consequences.

The budgeted assets under Generalitat public sector control are now quite considerable. In 1991, the Generalitat budget was well over the billion peseta mark. This means that the regional public sector is equivalent to about 10% of the Gross Domestic Product of Catalonia. This is a respectable volume of resources, and allows the Generalitat to carry out specific activities in the areas in which it has powers and responsibilities. The most important quotas of this budget are predictably laid aside for Health and Social Security, Education and local corporations.

It is therefore possible to wield a considerable degree of power in the execution of Government action in Catalonia. Priorities can be established and alternative projects chosen. It is necessary to add, however, that the present system of funding has brought about a

good many shortcomings and limitations. If we are to compare the system applied in our country with other systems in force (for example, the yearly economic agreement), the balance is unfavourable: the degree of financial dependence is very high and subsidies subject to conditions form too great a part of it. Furthermore, tax revenue is limited and the funding of the health service is based on unnecessarily specific procedures.

If we bear in mind that the standard of living in Catalonia is higher than the Spanish average, it can be seen that the country makes a higher percentatge contribution to the overall State treasury than would be expected from the point of view of population. This leads to a situation in which the country is unable to solve important economic and social problems.

A guide to the political parties and trade unions

In Catalonia, the nationalist factor or the demand for Catalonia's national rights — which may have a more or less radical stance — is an added component to the habitual ideological differences existing between parties in any democratic country. It is probably this element that explains the fact that in Catalonia, the governing coalition is different to the party governing in Spain.

The Catalan Parliament is made up of MPs from nine different parties, of which only three are present throughout the State, although there are four more with representation in the State Parliament. The parties are as follows:

Convergència Democràtica de Catalunya (CDC), a party founded in 1974 and led by Jordi Pujol, the current President of the Generalitat. Convergència Democràtica is a Catalan nationalist party, support for which may not be ascribed to any one class. It is backed by people from very diverse social backgrounds. It has triumphed in all three election campaigns (1980, 1984, 1988) in coalition with Unió Democràtica de Catalunya.

Unió Democràtica de Catalunya (UDC) (Democratic Union of Catalonia), is a Christian Democrat party founded in 1931. It is Catalan nationalist and clearly draws inspiration from a branch of pragmatic humanism in its quest for social justice. It forms a coalition with Convergència Democràtica in the Catalan Parliament elections, and has formed part of the cabinets in all three periods of post-Franco autonomous government.

Partit dels Socialistes de Catalunya (PSC-PSOE) (Socialist Party of Catalonia). This party was formed when three different branches of clandestine socialism in Catalonia (during the Franco regime) came together. It is at present the second political party in terms of votes and Catalan Parliament MPs. It was founded in 1978.

Partit Socialista Unificat de Catalunya (PSUC), is the principal Communist party in Catalonia. It was founded in 1936, and was very active during the years of opposition to Franco. At the last elections the PSUC formed a coalition with two other left-wing parties (Partit dels Comunistes de Catalunya and Entesa dels Nacionalistes d'Esquerra) under the name of Iniciativa per Catalunya (IC).

Partido Popular (PP), formerly Alianza Popular (AP), the principal Spanish right-wing party. It was founded in Madrid in October 1976.

Esquerra Republicana de Catalunya (ERC), is also a historic party founded in 1931 by the legendary President of Catalonia, Francesc Macià. It was the major party during the Republican Generalitat period before the Civil War, (1936-1939).

Centro Democrático y Social (CDS), a middle-of-the-road party founded by Adolfo Suárez, head of the first democratic Government in Spain after Franco. It was founded in Madrid in 1982.

The two principal workers' organizations are local branches of trade unions which are active throughout Spain: Comissions Obreres, Worker's Committee linked to the Communist party; and Unió General de Treballadors, in which the Socialist party is predominant. There are trade unions of strict Catalan allegiance, such as the Confederació Sindical de Catalunya, although their membership is not so high.

The Foment del Treball Nacional stands out amongst the employers' organizations. It was founded in 1889 and tolerated during the Franco Dictatorship under the disguise of a study centre. It must be pointed out that this organization was the promoter of the Confederación Española de Organizaciones Empresariales (CEOE), the main current Spanish employers' organization.

The Catalan Parliament

The Catalan Parliament, because of its elective and democratic character, represents all the citizens of Catalonia: it is elected by the people and acts in the name of the people. The Parliament, which is renewed every four years, is made up of one single Chamber of members, who are elected by universal, free, equal, direct and secret suffrage. The electoral system established by the Statute of Autonomy is proportional and ensures adequate representation for all the different areas of the Catalan territory.

The Parliament carries out several functions. The first is legislative, giving powers to make laws, which are enacted in the name of the King of Spain by the President of the Generalitat. These laws have the same rank as those enacted by the central State Parliament, but are only applicable within the territory of Catalonia. The Parliament also has the right to take legislative initiative before the State Congress, and is entitled to present a proposition that may thereafter become law.

The Parliament is responsible for forming and controlling the Generalitat Government. The President of the Generalitat is elected from its members, and approves the programme the President draws up at the beginning of the legislature.

The Parliament must also appoint the senators representing the Generalitat of Catalonia in the Senate — the Chamber representing the nationalities and regions that make up the Spanish State.

There is another function of the Parliament associated with the economic and financial side of the Generalitat. The yearly budget, which is drawn up by the Cabinet, must be examined and approved by the Parliament. Lastly, it must also be remembered that the Parliament can raise — as can the autonomous Government — appeals on grounds of unconstitutionality before the Constitutional Court whenever it considers that a State law harms or invades the competence area of Catalan self-government.

The political parties with parliamentary representation, in order of the votes they receive (1992), are as follows: Convergència i Unió (CiU) (CDC in coalition with UDC); Partit dels Socialistes de Catalunya (PSC-PSOE); Esquerra Republicana de Catalunya (ERC); Iniciativa per Catalunya (IC), a coalition made up of the following parties: Partit Socialista Unificat de Catalunya and Entesa dels Nacionalistes d'Esquerra; and Partido Popular (PP). The governing Catalan nationalist coalition, Convergència i Unió, has the absolute majority since 1988.

ECONOMY AND SOCIETY

An evaluation of the Catalan economy

The geographical situation of Catalonia has made her a country open to ideas and cultural movements, as well as to commercial exchange and tourism.

Despite a lack of mining and energy resources, Catalonia (a country that covers 6.3% of the total area of Spain and accommodates 16% of the State population) supplied 19.3% (1989) of the Gross Domestic product and accounts for 16.7% (1990) of the total work force.

It is noteworthy that the Catalan economy has a greater turnover than Portugal or Ireland, and one almost equalling that of Greece. The healthy and dynamic economic situation of Catalonia has often led to speculation regarding the viability of its economic independence, as a first step towards full political sovereignty.

These considerations must be carried out, however, in the light of Spain's incorporation into the Common Market. It is no secret that the Catalan economy is closely associated with the economy of the regions of Spain, taken as a whole. But Spain's incorporation into the European Economic Community is changing the nature of the association that has existed up until now. Catalan products are beginning to find a much larger market in Europe, and are also coming into competition with EEC products in Spain.

The different economic areas

The structure of production in Catalonia is very similar to the European model. Only 3.8% (1990) of the work force is involved in agriculture. Industry and constuction work occupies 44% (1990) of the work force, and the services sector employs the remaining 52.2% (1990).

In the agricultural sector in Catalonia, 8.8% is dedicated to cereals and 8.4% to pod vegetables. The cultivation of vineyards and olive groves is on an important scale, resulting in significant quantities of wine and *cava* (with seven origin certification names) as well as excellent quality olive oil. As regards livestock, the principal sectors are poultry, pig and cattle rearing. Poultry alone accounts for 14.5% of agricultural production.

The industrial sector has always been very well-developed and has been the real motor behind the Catalan economy. It supplies jobs for one million people, almost half the active population.

Furthermore, Catalonia has 25% of Spain's industry — mainly centred on Barcelona and its neighbouring cities. Although Catalan industry is certainly diverse, the metallurgical, chemical and textile sectors are particularly strong, accounting for 51.3% of the Gross Domestic Product. To these three sectors one may add the foodstuff industry which has developed rapidly over the last few years.

Despite the fact that Catalonia was a leader in the construction of thermal and nuclear power stations in Spain, it is not self-sufficient: Catalonia depends on external sources for 55% of her total primary energy consumption.

The services sector has undergone the same kind of modification as it has in Europe. In the area of finance, the role of the savings banks is fundamental. The Caixa d'Estalvis i de Pensions de Barcelona, for example, is the leading savings bank in the Spanish State in terms of the volume of its deposits. Banks, on the other hand, are dominated by non-Catalan and foreign institutions. Incidentally, it must also be remembered that Barcelona has a stock exchange.

The activity of the Catalan economy is greatly enhanced by the existence of a good motorway and road network, and quite an extensive railway system. Barcelona port, which has undergone

successive extensions recently, with over 330 hectares of land surface area, is making a vital contribution to the country's economic growth. In terms of freight handled, Barcelona is the eleventh port in the European rating. A few kilometres to the south there is the port of Tarragona, which is undergoing an important boom, making it one of the principal ports in the Mediterranean. Airborne transport depends largely on Barcelona's El Prat Airport which was considerably extended to cope with the increase in traffic caused by the 1992 Olympics.

External trade links

The fact that 75% of Catalonia's exports are to the rest of Spain and only 25% go abroad may be explained by the unity of the Spanish market.

Catalonia imports iron and steel, chemical, agricultural, mineral and textile products. The countries from which Catalonia imports most of these products are France, Italy, Germany, USA and Great Britain. Import figures for Catalonia account for 28.4% (1989) of the GDP, and represent 30.4% (1990) of the overall Spanish export figures.

Catalonia also exports iron and steel, chemical, agricultural and textile products. Topping the list of countries receiving goods from Catalonia are — once again — France, Italy, Germany, Great Britain and USA. Export figures, which in relation to the GDP account for 13.3% (1989), represent 23.8% (1990) of the overall Spanish figures.

The figures for both exports and imports have grown sharply in the last few years, and this has further accentuated the outward-looking character of the Catalan economy.

Liberal legislation for foreign capital investment has led to an increase in the internationalization of the Catalan economy. Industry has clearly benefited from this situation.

The principal sources of investment are Germany, Switzerland, France and Japan. Shortly after Spain joined the EEC, foreign investment in various enterprises and commercial establishments was stepped up. In 1990, almost a third of the overall foreign investment in Spain was in Catalan firms, some of which were already established and some in the process. Investment rose to 547,857 million pesetas. It was mainly directed towards the graphic arts, the hotel business, chemical industries and financial institutions, among others. The principal sources of investment were the European Economic Community countries, the USA and Japan.

Tourism

Tourism calls for special attention. The last three decades have led to spectacular growth in this sector. At present, it accounts for over 15% of the Gross Domestic Product, and provides jobs for 12.5% of the working population.

This increase in tourism in Catalonia is partly due to the excellent geographical situation of the country, on one of the key land corridors linking the Iberian Peninsula with the rest of Europe. The increase is also due to the volume, variety and high standards of the tourist offer available, both in the summer and winter seasons.

Catalonia has a large hotel capacity with almost 213,000 beds to which a further 294,830 camping site places must be added. If to these places we add the offer of several thousand appartments which are exclusively set aside for tourism, we may confirm that Catalonia is one of the most important tourist areas in Europe. In the last few years, however, quantity has ceased to be a basic priority, and the Government of Catalonia, in accordance with the business sector, is adapting its offer towards quality, a key factor to attract an increasingly demanding tourist market.

A ever-evolving society

One of the principal characteristics of Catalan society is the desire to face up to each new period of evolution. This dynamic attitude has a remote origin. Catalonia, at the time of the industrial revolution, was the "factory" of Spain, and was therefore the most advanced area in the Spanish State.

Despite occasional disasters, recessions and other critical moments (not all has been success in the last century and a half) Catalonia has always been a centre of progress.

Today's worldwide economic recovery has made itself felt in the country. All economic indicators seem to point to the fact that the crisis is coming to an end, and that there are encouraging prospects for the future. For instance inflation has decreased considerably and unemployment figures have also fallen in a more pronounced fashion in Catalonia than in Spain taken as a whole.

In Catalonia, one must always take into account the indefatigable vitality of her capital, Barcelona, a city which may be seen as a giant test laboratory for social and cultural experiments of all kinds.

Barcelona has been a cosmopolitan metropolis since time immemorial and this makes it difficult to foresee how she will evolve in the future. The same may be said for all the other great dynamic cities of Europe: Milan, Amsterdam, Paris, London... Barcelona is a European city in situation and vocation. The forms of urban culture that appear there are not essentially different from those that appear in the north of Europe, although they always have a specifically Catalan hallmark. It is, above all, a Mediterranean culture, based on musical and artistic rather than on conceptual or philosophical precepts. Barcelona transmits this European spirit throughout Catalonia because she is her capital city.

THE CULTURAL FIELD

Basic facts regarding Catalan culture

Having examined the historical panorama of Catalan culture, a look at the present moment is called for. Catalan culture forms part of that group of cultures which are associated with the industrialized countries of the western world. These countries are now going through a critical period, a moment of change, meditation and redefinition of their own identity.

Faced with a new situation of enormous fluidity (marked by the worldwide influence exerted by news, life-style, values, social customs and habits and behavioural patterns), each culture must strengthen its specific identity and must make full use of its capacity for adaptation.

Alongside these problems raised by the period we live in, Catalan culture must also face up to two further problems: one of a generic and structural nature that is shared with other cultures; and another of a specific and unnatural kind.

The first problem stems from the country's situation within the geopolitical context of Europe, where different cultures — some of which exert a tremendous influence — mingle together. The second, more than a servitude, is a question of the subordination which results from coexistence, in the same territory, with Castilian culture. It must be remembered that Catalan culture is the culture of a nation which lost its full sovereignty in the 18th century.

Despite a situation marked by subordination and a lack of independence, Catalan culture persistently struggles on in its attempts to avoid disintegration, to survive and project itself into the future. In order to achieve this, from now on it will have to obtain (and this will depend on a political victory) the capacity to select and monitor the cultural services and products which are made available by the great mass media. It will have to adapt them to the necessities of a national identity which is undergoing a process of reconstruction.

Aspects concerning the cultural dynamics of the country

The brevity of this text makes it impossible for me to offer a more complete view of the cultural dynamics of Catalonia today. We are aware of the fact that to offer a comprehensive panorama of the whole cultural scene in Catalonia, we would have to refer to those activities — of which there is, incidentally, no shortage — that are displaying a remarkable degree of creative verve.

Literature

In reviewing the past, we have mentioned some of the most renowned figures involved in Catalan literary production over the course of time. After the 1936-1939 Civil War, literary figures such as Salvador Espriu, Mercè Rodoreda, Pere Calders, Manuel de Pedrolo, Xavier Benguerel, Joan Vinyoli, Josep M. Llompart, Jordi-Pere Cerdà, Tomàs Garcés, Joan Teixidor, Joan Oliver, Joan Fuster and Agustí Bartra have all produced serious literary work, which has been worthy of several versions in the most important publishing languages in the world. Their works have been translated into the leading publishing languages of the world. Apart from prose writers and poets, the authors of essays and works of historical, linguistic and literary scholarship are also to be taken into account: Jaume Vicens Vives, Josep Ferrater Móra, Miquel Batllori, Josep Benet, Miquel Tarradell, Pau Vila, Miquel Coll i Alentorn, Maurici Serrahima, Joan Triadú, Joaquim Molas, Josep-Maria Castellet, Antoni M. Badia i Margarit, Joan Coromines, Albert Manent, Francesc Vallverdú, and Martí de Riquer, to mention but a few.

Although there is always the danger of being unjust or neglectful when producing a work of synthesis, we will try and list some of the writers who form part of our present-day cultural scene.

This would be the case of Josep-Maria Espinàs, Jordi Sarsanedas,

Joan Perucho, Teresa Pàmies, Estanislau Torres, Ramon Folch i Camarasa, Baltasar Porcel, Josep Vallverdú, Emili Teixidor, Maria-Aurèlia Capmany, Feliu Formosa and Miquel Àngel Riera.

In their footsteps, and under the almost fully-accepted label of the so-called "Generation of the seventies" (being writers who appeared on the scene in that decade), we can mention the following names: Pere Gimferrer, Montserrat Roig, Robert Saladrigas, Jaume Fuster, Maria Antònia Oliver, Isidre Grau, Isabel-Clara Simó, Carme Riera, Oriol Pi de Cabanyes, Joaquim Soler, Gabriel Janer i Manila, Joaquim Carbó, Josep Albanell, Joan Rendé, Josep Piera, Marta Pessarrodona, Xavier Bru de Sala, Oriol Vergés, Francesc Parcerisas, Narcís Comadira, Joan Margarit, etc.

There has been no specific recognition of a generation after that of the seventies, but a further list of authors who have come to light in the eighties can indeed be drawn up. Jesús Moncada, Josep Lozano, Valentí Puig, Olga Xirinacs, Pere Verdaguer, Gerard Vergés, Quim Monzó, Vicenç Villatoro, Jaume Cabré, Valerià Pujol, Àlex Susanna, Ferran Torrent, Gemma Lienas, Mercè Canela are some of the exponents of a flourishing literature. These names, and others that we have not mentioned, are writers who have sprung up not only in Catalonia, but in all those lands where the Catalan language is spoken.

In Catalonia there are a series of outstanding authors whose literary production has been mainly in Spanish. Among these authors, the following must be mentioned: M. Vázquez Montalbán, Luis Goytisolo, Eduardo Mendoza, Juan Marsé, Juan Goytisolo, Jaime Gil de Biedma, Félix de Azúa, Francesc Candel, Carlos Barral, José Agustín Goytisolo and Josep M. Carandell.

The mass media

The mass media — principally press and radio — were thwarted by the cultural and linguistic repression that followed in the wake of the Spanish Civil War. The dictatorship suppressed the twenty-two newspapers and one thousand two hundred periodical publications that were being produced in the Catalan lands in 1936.

It is difficult to estimate the magnitude of the effects of the policy which aimed to annihilate the culture and language

of Catalonia. However, two conclusions may be made. The first is that Catalonia suffered very severely and emerged from the four decades of cultural strangulation in a very weakened condition. The second is that, against all odds, there then followed a period of recovery which was made possible by the country's determination to survive as a nation with an identity of its own.

Press written in Catalan appeared once again after the reestablishment of democracy. The country now has several newspapers in Catalan: *Avui*, *Diari de Barcelona*, *El Nou Diari*, *El Punt*, *Diari de Lleida*, and *Diari de Girona*. *Regió 7* and *El 9 Nou* can also be considered as newspapers because they come out almost every day. To these one must add the weekly magazine *El Temps,* published in València, and several monthly magazines among which one must mention *Serra d'Or*.

In the field of broadcasting, the reestablishment of self-government has enabled the country to create its own radio stations, of which Catalunya Ràdio and Ràdio Associació are two examples with remarkably large audiences. The former station has a daily audience of 924,000 listeners throughout the Catalan lands. Alongside these stations, we must also mention the radio stations belonging to Cadena Nova. The programmes of Ràdio 4, one of the radio stations run by the Spanish Government, are also in Catalan.

When the new democratic period began, one of the fundamental instruments for the linguistic normalization of Catalonia was without doubt the creation of Televisió de Catalunya, TV3 in 1983, as well as the fact that almost simultaneously, Spanish Television (TVE) began to broadcast some of its programmes in Catalan on the second channel (TV2). More recently, in September 1989, Canal 33, a new television channel for the promotion of language and communication in the Catalan nation, started to broadcast.

All things considered, it must be concluded that the situation of the mass media — insofar as the Catalan language is concerned — is not at the level that average European cultural standards would require and call for.

Catalonia has an important daily press production in Spanish. It is edited in Barcelona and is distributed throughout the country.

The following newspapers must be mentioned: *La Vanguardia*, a century-old newspaper, *El Periódico de Catalunya* and *El Observador*. Dozens of Spanish language weekly publications are published in Catalonia. Some Spanish language radio stations also broadcast specific programmes in Catalan. Others only broadcast in the Spanish language.

Publishing output

It is necessary to refer briefly to the recent history of Catalan publishing output to get an overall picture of the present-day situation.

As a result of the *Renaixença*, a cultural movement which once again set Catalan culture back on its feet after a long period of deterioration and loss of self-confidence, publishing output in Catalan began to recover once again. In 1874, 80 books were published. The establishment of the Mancomunitat (that united the four provincial councils of Catalonia) with Prat de la Riba as its president led to a period of increased cultural development. In 1923 the output figure was 400 books and ten years later, in 1933, about 750 books were published.

The determination of the fascist regime to wipe out Catalan culture was also evident in this particular field. Until 1947, publishing in Catalan was a clandestine activity. Information on the fifties and sixties is unclear, but in no case were more than 200 books published. The year 1962 was an important milestone because it marks a certain degree of liberalization in the policies of General Franco as well as the initiation of a progressive cultural offensive launched by Catalan society. There is a progression from the 270 books published in 1962 to the 611 published in 1975. From this latter date onwards, the growth in Catalan publishing activity is truly spectacular. The question that arises is whether the figure of 4,838 books achieved in 1990 will be the maximum peak. What is important, however, is not to know if the full yearly publishing potential has been exhausted, but to encourage both effective and potential readers (including the children and young people who now have access to Catalan at school) to contribute in this way (as citizens of Catalonia) to the full normalization of their language.

Although Catalan is the country's rightful language, Catalonia has lead the field as regards the production of books in Spanish since the first days of printing. This factor may be put down to the country's extraordinary cultural vitality. Barcelona currently produces over 30% of the books appearing on the market in this language.

Drama

In the last twenty-five years, drama has also been able to recover the high standards lost in the years immediately after the Civil War. When judging the overall situation, it would seem reasonable to claim that drama today in Catalonia is thoroughly up to date and to highly professional standards. It has shaken off the sham and vulgar characteristics of commercial drama. Peak moments have been reached over the last ten years with the consolidation of companies such as Els Comediants, Els Joglars and Dagoll Dagom — which have performed all over Europe — or the formation of the Teatre Lliure, a model repertory theatre company which has introduced audiences to drama of an experimental and aesthetically perfectionist kind. The country has also benefited greatly from the "repatriation", of leading actor Josep Maria Flotats. Before his return (from the Comédie Française) however, Catalan drama had already been reaping the results of the work of directors such as Lluís Pasqual, set designers such as Fabià Puigserver, and actors and actresses such as Juanjo Puigcorbé or Anna Lizarán. The impetus of current Catalan drama is largely due to the progress there has been over the last ten years, although it also owes much to the effort made, under the most adverse conditions (1950-1960), by the Agrupació Dramàtica de Barcelona or the Escola d'Art Dramàtic Adrià Gual.

The Generalitat Drama Centre, which produces plays and draws up seasonal programmes, has been created recently. A project for the National Theatre of Catalonia is also well under way.

Cinema

In these recent years of democracy and self-government, cinema in Catalan has emerged from the dark shadows the post-War years had cast on it. The Catalan Film Institute was set up in 1975 in the very year the dictatorship ended. In 1981, State powers and responsibilities in the field of §cinematography were transferred to the Generalitat of Catalonia and the Audio-visual Archives of the Generalitat of Catalonia were set up.

A brief summary of the recent history and present situation of the Catalan film industry would call for a list of the titles of the more significant films and their respective directors: *La plaça del Diamant* (The time of the doves) (Betriu), *La ciutat cremada* (The burnt city) (Ribas), *Companys: procés a Catalunya* (Companys: Catalonia on trial) (Forn), *Bilbao* (Bigas Luna), *La senyora* (Cadena). The names of Coromina, Duran and Pere Portabella stand out among the producers and promoters of films in Catalan. If cinema produced in Spanish in Catalonia is also to be taken into account here, the work of three directors is also worthy of mention: Camino, Aranda and Rovira Beleta.

The modern strain of film production in Catalonia is firmly rooted in a tradition that goes back to the early days of cinematography. If its origin is to be briefly traced, it would seem unjust not to mention the avant-garde movement known as the Barcelona School which sprang up in the sixties. But the cinema trade in Catalonia has already flourished over the course of two glorious periods; 1901-1914, when production reached a remarkably high standard; and 1914-18, when Barcelona was the headquarters for most of the production companies in the Spanish State. Going back even farther in time, one comes across the key figure of Fructuós Gelabert, founder of the Catalan film industry (he directed several films) and one of the world's cinematographic production pioneers.

Music

Symphony music is well represented in Catalonia by the Orquestra Ciutat de Barcelona (Barcelona City Orchestra) and the Orquestra del Liceu (Liceu Orchestra). New orchestras have recently appeared: Orquestra Simfònica del Vallès (Vallès Symphony Orchestra) and the Orquestra del Teatre Lliure (Teatre Lliure Orchestra). In the chamber music field, the Solistes de Catalunya ensemble must be mentioned. The names of Frederic Mompou, Manuel Blancafort, Robert Gerhard and Xavier Benguerel stand out among composers, and Alícia de Larrocha (piano), Claudi Arimany (flute) and Gonçal Comellas (violin) among performers.

Catalonia has always been a country with a strong choral music tradition, especially as from 1845 when Josep Anselm Clavé founded his first choir. Subsequently, hundreds of choirs and choral societies sprang up around the country, one of which was the famous Catalan Choral Society (Orfeó Català) founded in 1891 by Lluís Millet and Amadeu Vives. This tradition is still thriving in present-day Catalonia, where the Sant Jordi and Càrmina choirs stand out among two hundred and fifty odd choirs.

The sardana, the country's national dance, the basic form of which was laid down by Pep Ventura with later refinement by musician Vicenç Bou, was cultivated by Juli Garreta and Joaquim Serra, and has the *cobla* — a unique instrumental ensemble — as its leading musical feature. There are over a hundred such ensembles in Catalonia, of which the Cobla Principal de la Bisbal, founded in 1888, stands out. It has recently been appointed official Generalitat of Catalonia *cobla*.

Catalonia, we have said, is a country with a strong European tradition and vocation. European music is popular and is very swiftly accepted. This permeability has an obvious effect on Catalan music itself. It may be easily observed in three different musical genres: the *cançó* (mainly modern ballad singers), jazz and opera. Modern ballad-type music — the *nova cançó* as it was initially called — a genre with obvious points in common with the contemporary French movement of the sixties (Brassens, Moustaki etc.), has developed greatly. It started off as a weapon in the political struggle against Franco and is now a normal genre for aesthetic and musical communication. As can be expected, the *cançó* now competes alongside all world production of its kind. However, it cannot be said that it has fallen behind for lack of quality; nor can it be said to have been disqualified for lacking any of the requirements dictated by technical and artistic progress. A host of professionals proves otherwise: Joan Manuel Serrat, Lluís Llach, Raimon, Marina Rossell, Núria Feliu, and M. del Mar Bonet, to mention but a few.

Another original feature concerning jazz in our country is the amazing number of young musicians who attend jazz schools. In Catalonia, both the composition and playing of jazz music have a long tradition which is proud to count Tete Montoliu amongst its greatest exponents.

Opera in Catalonia, performed at the Liceu theatre in Barcelona, would deserve a chapter to itself. Since the mid-19th century, opera has been very popular in the country. There have also been great Catalan opera singers, both in the time of the tenor Viñas, and in our day, with Josep Carreras, Montserrat Caballé, or Victòria dels Àngels.

Architecture

Experts go as far as to say that in Catalonia there is a collective subconscious feeling for architecture with a long and powerful tradition which encourages continual innovation. In the 19th century, without going farther back in time, one encounters the figure of Elies Rogent, who was responsible for the construction of several public buildings. In the 20th century, intensive activity in the field of architecture led to the creation of the Catalan Group of Architects and Technicians for the Progress of Contemporary Architecture (Grup d'Arquitectes i Tècnics Catalans per al Progrés de l'Arquitectura Contemporània, GATCPAC), which was active promoting the most advanced architectural movements in the world. Particularly significant among those architects in this group was Josep-Lluís Sert, who has worked in countries throughout the world. The period between 1940 and the present day provides us with a remarkable list of professionals: Moragas, Coderch, Solà-Morales, Bohigas, Martorell, among others. It must not be forgotten that Barcelona is to be host city to the Olympic Games in 1992, and this will bring on a major advance in the quality of architecture in Catalonia. A team of architects from Catalonia (Correa, Milà, Buxadé, Margarit, Bofill), Italy (Gregotti) and Japan (Isozaki) is busy finding functional and aesthetic solutions to a giant project which will be a cornerstone in the future evolution of the city.

Plastic arts

In the section on the history of Catalan culture we mentioned the names of the three major Catalan painters (Picasso, Miró, Dalí, Juli González and Pau Gargallo), who loomed large in the first few decades of this century. Following in their footsteps, however, are a multitude of artists who bear witness to the quality of the plastic arts of this country. Their work swings with an intriguing and surprising pendulous movement between the two psychological poles which are said to form the axis of the Catalan psyche — "*seny*" (practical good sense) and "*rauxa*" (eccentric passion bordering on madness). Tàpies, Guinovart, Ponç, Clavé, Ràfols Casamada, Tharrats, Hernàndez Pijuan, Montserrat Gudiol, to mention but a few. Other than the painters, there are other admired. Such is the case of J. M. Subirachs the sculptor, Llorens Artigas the potter or Grau Garriga the tapestry maker. To this list of figures can be added a numerous group of young artists who guarantee the continuity of the creative spirit: Barceló, Garcia Sevilla, Perejaume, Zush, Amat, in painting; Susana Solano, Abat, Plensa, Carr, in sculpture; and Miralda, Torres and Muntades in installations.

Design

In the field of design, Barcelona is a leading name in the international panorama. Apart from the attention the arts and crafts have paid to the aesthetic aide, the finished product and fine detail, designers have now incorporated new materials, technical resources and a functional and practical sense, both for home and public environments.

Along with the Barcelona Design Centre (Barcelona Centre de Disseny, BCD), the professional organizations centering their activity on the promotion and projection of design are ADIFAD, in the industrial design field, ADGFAD, in the graphic design field and INFAD, in interior design.

The leading generation of the fifties (Moragas, Ricard, Milà, Giralt Miracle, Blanch, Correa, Cirici...) have been joined by the younger generation (Tusquets, Amat, Mariscal, Pensi, Lluscà, Arribas, Satué, Pla Narbona...).

Fashion

Barcelona is also the main fashion centre in Catalonia, and as from the sixties has made its mark very successfully around the world (Pertegaz, Balenciaga, Pedro Rodríguez, Assumpció Bastida). In international circles, the work of fashion designers Andrés Andreu and Toni Miró is now taken very much into account in this area of creative production. The following words of Toni Miró define the dynamic period the world of fashion in our country is going through: "Barcelona has embarked upon an exhilarating conquest of the world of fashion: experiments are abundant, needs are increasing, supply and demand are balancing out, fashion schools are improving, and institutional concern for this field has grown intensely".

Current socio-linguistic problems

Catalonia faces a problem which is not only linguistic, but cultural and social, derived from the confluence of two basic factors. Firstly, one must mention the colonizing effect of the Spanish or Castilian language — and culture — which are dominant in the Spanish State. This offensive took on an especially hostile form during the forty years of the Franco dictatorship, when the language completely disappeared from official use. The second factor has been the arrival in Catalonia of successive waves of immigrants from various areas of the State over the course of the century. The newcomers neither knew the Catalan language, nor benefited from the sociological, psychological and practical conditions needed for learning the language.

Once democracy had returned to Spain, and following what was laid down in the Spanish Constitution (1978), Catalonia set out on a process to recover her language, which is described as *pròpia* ("Catalonia's rightful language") in the Statute of Autonomy (1979). The Statute merely seeks to provide equitable juridical treatment and a conventional official standing for a natural and undeniable situation. Subsequently, in 1983, the Catalan Parliament drew up and enacted the Law of Linguistic Normalization. This Law reflects

the will of the Catalan people to see the use of their language return once more to cover all those areas from which it had been violently uprooted: Schools, Public Administration, the Mass Media, etc. It must also be remembered, albeit in passing, that the Law itself states that Catalan is today in a situation which is precarious and fails to offer a full guarantee of its survival.

This alarming statement is producing the degree of concern that would be expected. Indeed, it is not easy to find any citizens who regard the future of the Catalan language with indifference. Data giving us an exact picture of the current sociolinguistic situation in the Principality is available. It is provided by the Language Census published by the Information and Documentation Consortium of Catalonia (Consorci d'Informació i Documentació de Catalunya), and takes the resident population of Catalonia in 1986 as a basis. The survey carried out by this institution produced figures for the knowledge of Catalan of all the country's citizens. The overall figures were as follows: 90.4% understand Catalan; 64% can speak it; 60.5% can read it; and 31.5% can write it. These figures indicate a clear improvement on those of recent years. Now the issue, as regards the language, would seem to centre not so much on the knowledge and learning of the language — factors which are guaranteed — but on its real, everyday use in all fields of communication.

Linguistic objectives to be attained

In the light of the information we have just supplied, Catalonia would now appear to be undergoing a process of consolidation of her language, which is legally supported by the text of the Constitution and further fortified by the Statute of Autonomy, and especially by the Law of Linguistic Normalization. This process is taking place in three fields principally: Schools, Public Administration and the Mass Media.

In schools, the objective is to ensure that all the children of Catalonia, regardless of the language they habitually used at the outset of their education, should be able to use both Catalan and Spanish with the required degree of correctness by the end of their primary education period.

In the field of administration, the aim is to ensure that any citizen of Catalonia may exert the right the law confers on him/her to communicate with all public institutions in whichever of the two official languages he/she may freely choose.

The mass media, both written and audio-visual, are as yet deficient, if we consider the massive use there is of the Spanish language — a situation which is largely due to the forty year ban on Catalan imposed by the Franco dictatorship. The objective is to ensure that, in the not too distant future, the mass media live up to the expectations of the citizens, who will know both the official languages.

One of the remaining areas that would call for a full-scale effort as regards the full use of the Catalan language is the commercial and industrial field.

A path leading to the full normalization of the Catalan language has yet to be marked out. In this sense, the personal attitude of the *catalans vells* — native Catalans with roots in the country — and the *catalans nous* — those who have only been in Catalonia for a few years or decades — is fundamental. The former must make all possible facilities available to enable not only the language to be learnt, but for there to be a sense of identification with it. The latter — the newcomers — must adapt to the reality of a country which has its own age-old language. Thanks to the good sense of both of these groups, there is a relaxed and tolerant social atmosphere in matters concerning the language. Furthermore, the legal resolutions taken by the Catalan Parliament and the practical application of regulations carried out by the Government have been accompanied by an attitude of prudence and flexibility. This has prevented any upsurge of ill-feeling among the citizens of Catalonia.

The return of the President of the Generalitat, Josep Tarradellas, to Catalonia. A Royal Decree dated October 17, 1977, named the honourable Josep Tarradellas President of the Generalitat of Catalonia. On October 21, President Tarradellas arrived in Madrid from France to visit King Juan Carlos I and the President of the central Government, Mr. Adolfo Suárez, with whom he had been negotiating the restitution of the Generalitat and the institutions for the self-government of Catalonia since June. On October 23, a multitudinous concentration of Catalans in the Passeig de Maria Cristina, in Montjuïc, welcomed Tarradellas back amidst ovation and clamour. This put an end to more than forty years of forced submission for the Catalan nation. This step was made possible by the persistence and strong will of the citizens of Catalonia as well as by the recent democracy implemented in Spain.

Constitution of the Presiding Council of the Parliament of Catalonia in 1980. On April 10, 1980, the Parliament of Catalonia was constituted, for the first time after the fall of the IInd Republic. This was the result of popular will as manifested in the March elections. The Parliament was presided over by the Honourable Mr. Heribert Barrera, Esquerra Republicana de Catalunya. The Honourable Mr. Isidre Molas, Partit dels Socialistes de Catalunya, and the Honourable Ms. Concepció Ferrer, Convergència i Unió, were its vice-presidents.

Assembly Hall at the Parliament of Catalonia. The sessions of the Parliament of Catalonia take place in this hall. This image was taken in the constitutive session on April 10, 1980, after the autonomous parliament elections in March. The Parliament represents the people of Catalonia, since its members are chosen by the citizens in whose name they act. From its democratic origins the Parliament draws its greatest strength and creates the Generalitat as the key institution from which all the others emanate. The Catalan Parliament, unlike the Parliament of the State, which is organized in two chambers, has only one chamber. Like all democratic parliaments, it is independent from the executive and judicial powers, as well as from any other institution either of the State or any of the autonomous territories of Catalonia.

Investiture speech of Most Honourable Mr. Jordi Pujol before the Parliament of Catalonia. On June 21, 1988, after the victory of the coalition, Convergència i Unió in the elections held on May 29, the recurrent candidate to the Presidency of the Generalitat pronounced an investiture speech of remarkable political content. Mr. Jordi Pujol made an emphatical affirmation of Catalonia as a nation, and in so doing stated that in this context it was not possible to compromise or capitulate. "The time is over — he said — when a nation without a State saw no other goal but to have its own. But the time is not over in which nations, with or without a State, seek on the one hand supranational integration — the process of integration of Europe being the clearest example —, and on the other hand its own identity. They seek to deepen and reinforce what they are, and to project themselves as they are. At the same time they dismiss anything attempting to diminish them, to lessen them or to put them aside".

Tàpies recreates Catalonia's national history. The Tàpies Hall, in the Generalitat Government building, was inaugurated in 1990. It shows that the present situation is the result of a long historical process. Antoni Tàpies, a painter of international prestige, has intended to link, in this mural, the present situation of his country with the signs of a period which has long gone by, the period from 1208 to 1387. It was a time of Catalan splendour, as reflected in the *Quatre Grans Cròniques*. The vigorous strokes in the mural attract the viewer's attention to two letters: a J, which stands for James I, and a P, which stands for Peter III the Ceremonious.

The Palace of the Generalitat, headquarters of the Catalan Government. In the words of the President of the Generalitat, the Honourable Mr. Jordi Pujol, "the Palace of the Generalitat is the most outstanding piece of medieval civil architecture in the capital of Catalonia. In addition to its five hundred years of history, and its architectural and artistic value, the works of art accumulated over the course of the centuries and the political and social events that have taken place there in moments of glory as well as tragedy, this palace is also one of the few medieval buildings in Europe, which having been originally planned as quarters for a political institution, continues as such in our days".

The Queen of England in the Sant Jordi Hall. In October 1988, the President of the Generalitat, the Honourable Mr. Jordi Pujol, received the Queen of England, Elizabeth II, together with her husband the Duke of Edinburgh. The President of the Government of Catalonia showed the sovereigns of Britain the Sant Jordi Hall while explaining certain historical and present-day facts about the political life of the country. Queen Elizabeth II signed the Golden Book of the Generalitat and received from President Pujol — as can be seen in the photograph — a replica of the sculpture of Sant Jordi, patron saint of Catalonia and England. It is a reproduction of the original sculpted by Melcior Bravo de Sarabia in 1536.

Síndic de Greuges or Ombudsman's Office building. Only the late nineteenth century neoclassical façade remains of the old Marquis of Alfarràs' palace, which had been built in 1774. This fine building is now the seat of the Síndic de Greuges (Ombudsman), an institution which had been foreseen in the 1979 Statute of Autonomy, and which was brought into being by Catalan Law 14/1984. The historical precedent for this institution can be found in the figure of Sweden's Ombudsman. The Síndic de Greuges has been very active, and has drawn up two documents which aim to supply the Parliament, in an entirely impartial fashion, with a reflection — which is often critical — on the shortcomings of the public administration and the complaints made by the citizens of Catalonia.

Gothic-Renaissance quarters of the Consultative Council of the Generalitat. This image — obligatorily oblique — shows the recently restored Centelles Palace, a magnificent exponent of the gothic-renaissance style in Barcelona's gothic quarter. Today this building quarters the Consultative Council of the Generalitat of Catalonia. This body has the responsibility for ensuring compliance with the Spanish Constitution and the Catalan Statute of Autonomy. Its pronouncement is mandatory whenever the Generalitat or the Parliament of Catalonia wish to file a recourse with the Spanish Constitutional Court.

The Sant Pau Hospital, a Modern Style jewel. The Sant Pau Hospital in Barcelona is one of the most impressive architectural works of Catalan Modernist Style. It was designed in 1901 by the architect Lluís Domènech i Montaner, and it comprises various wards separated by gardens, some of which are the work of his son and successor Pere Domènech i Roura. The main entry features the façade seen here that corresponds to the Administration Pavilion. Its design obeys a strictly symmetrical design and shows withits original the artistic sensitivity of his author, with its original polychromous tiles. The Generalitat of Catalonia is responsible for the field of health and social assistance, and architectural, artistic and historical heritage.

The principal staircase of the Moja Palace, Baroque architecture of the 18th century. The Moja Palace, together with the Palau de la Llotja, the Palau de la Virreina and the Palau dels March de Reus, is one of the most outstanding pieces of baroque 18th century architecture in Barcelona. Apart from its original architectural solutions, it is remarkable for its paintings of "El Vigatà", an independent artist unconstrained by the academic of his time. Santiago Alcolea, professor at Barcelona University and a scholar of the Palace, writes that "He does not know of any organic group in the Iberian Peninsula that had the importance that this Barcelona collection did during the last quarter of the 18th century". This picture shows the principal staircase of the Palace, which leads to a noble floor, executed in white veined marble of splendid appearance.

The hall of Animal Life Systematics. The hall of Animal Life Systematics, with its warm reminiscence of the beginning of the century, has lately grown in importance. In 1987 it received a magnificent donation with more than 400 birds and 16,000 butterflies. To house this and all other collections of lepidoptera, the museum has installed a room equipped with "compactus" — a mobile cabinet system on rails, which will greatly help storage and access, as well as scientific work.

A unique combination at the Tàpies Foundation. A unique combination of periods and styles is to be found in this image, which shows us the current Tàpies Foundation building. On the one hand, the Modernist façade, work of the architect Domènech i Montaner, which was built between 1880 and 1885 by Montaner and Simon, a publishing company which was to last for one hundred years. And on the other hand, the sculpture with metal filament decoration which crowns the structure, a work which Antoni Tàpies — the artist who created the Foundation — has called *"núvol i cadira"* (cloud and chair).

The Zoological Museum of Barcelona, a modernist building. One of the buildings constructed for the World Exhibition of 1988, still standing and commonly known as Castell dels Tres Dragons (the Castle of the Three Dragons) is a modernist work by the architect Domènech i Montaner. It is today the quarters of the Zoological Museum of Barcelona. Over the last few years, this museum has been suitably restored in order to fulfil its cultural role in modern society while at the same time preserving the traditional role as zoological museum. "We hope", says Carme Prat, curator of the museum, "that it will become known as an example of equilibrium between respect for tradition and efficiency in carrying out its scientific and cultural role".

Miró Foundation: the promotion of contemporary art. The Miró Fundation building is in Montjuïc park. It is the work of the Catalan architect Josep-Lluís Sert. It was inaugurated in 1975. As was the wish of the great universal artist, Joan Miró, the foundation concentrates on the study and popularization of his work, as well as the promotion of avant-garde contemporary art. After the death of the artist, in 1983, a permanent collection of contemporary art is on display as a homage to the centre's founder. This foundation has received various prizes, among which the Council of Europe prize for the best museum in 1978 is particulary significant.

A relief by Picasso presides over the College of Architects. A drawing in relief on stone, by Picasso, featuring a popular Catalan festival, presides the frieze on the Official College of Architects of Catalonia and the Balearic Islands, near Barcelona cathedral. The College is a professional body which has played, and continues to play an important role in the field of architecture and the different plastic arts. Some years ago calculation, structure calculation and town planning information offices were installed. It also holds the Historical Town Planning, Architecture and Design Archives.

The Catalan language in commerce. The normalization of the use of the Catalan language in all the aspects of social life is one of the basic objectives of the present Government of Catalonia. The advertisements used in commerce are practical instruments for increasing the presence of Catalan in this domain. Lately, several campaigns have been promoted with an aim to encourage the Catalanization of commercial advertising, both inside and outside commercial centres.

Human development and entertainment for youth. The Catalan autonomous Government has full powers in the area of policy for youth. During the summer holidays a series of alternatives are offered to young people to allow them to broaden their horizons and to come into contact with other young people from all over Catalonia and Europe. The Catalan Institute for Services to Young People, offers various activities in the fields of architectural patrimony, archaeology, protection of nature, community work, agriculture, animal farming, environmental studies and tourism for the young, among others. Familiarization with the environment often involves excursions, camping, trekking and adventure on the mountain rivers.

Tourism in Catalonia, present at international conferences. Among the real powers granted by the Statute of Autonomy, there is one covering tourism. Ever since the formation of the first autonomous Government, the corresponding department undertook intense activity for the promotion of tourism in Catalonia — inland as well as on the coast — in all the world. A suitable policy regarding publications presenting available offers to tourists in Catalonia together with frequent participation in international symposia has resulted in an extraordinary increase in the number of visitors to our country. If in 1980 the number of visitors was about 11,830,000 people, in 1987 the number increased to 15,325,000, or 28.3 percent of all people visiting Spain.

A library incorporated into an old church. An old church in Ulldecona, no longer used for religious services, has recently been converted into an exhibition room, auditorium and library. In addition to a bibliographic collection which was already there, this library now holds more than 10,000 volumes. The rooms are distributed in two levels to make the most of the available space.

La Bisbal d'Empordà, Historical archives in a castle. This castle-cum-palace in La Bisbal d'Empordà, located in the middle of the town, was the ancient office of the episcopate back in the 12th century, as evidenced by the Romanic chapel inside. It was restored in the 14th, 16th and 17th centuries, and is today a magnificent piece of civil architecture with a coronet of many merlons. At present it houses the Historical Archives of the county, which include documents on the towns that form it, a fund of notary deeds since 1865, a photographic archive with more than 4,000 units and other patrimony and cartography relating to archives from the 19th century. It also has a library and a newspaper collection. It has a microfilm reader machine and photographic laboratory.

Folk historical theatre in Olesa de Montserrat. On May 1, 1987 the new Theatre of *La Passió* was inaugurated. Every year at Christmas and Easter a dramatic play representing the life and passion of Jesus Christ takes place there. This theatrical piece is the product of a long historical process and greatly attracts the interest of the public. As with other forms of popular drama, it can be related to sacred representations of a liturgical character that were performed inside the temples during the Middle Ages. The oldest documentation on *La Passió d'Olesa* (The Olesa Passion) is dated 1642, and we know today that during the 17th and 18th centuries this work was performed in warehouses and oil mills. Until the middle of the 20th century the text used in this play was that of Trinitarian Antoni de Sant Jeroni. In 1948, however, a poet from Olesa introduced a new composition, a narration of remarkable dramatic force.

The Amphitheatre of the Barcelona Royal Academy of Medicine. The prestige of the amphitheatre of the Royal Academy of Medicine of Barcelona has old origins. The title of Royal was granted to it in 1786. For many years it did not have its own quarters until it was finally established in the building of the Academy of Surgery, built during the period 1762-1764. In the last century it was given the faculty to teach in its Department of Applied Medicine. At present the academies with boards in Catalonia are governed by the Generalitat and are defined as public right corporations, their purpose being the execution of research in the fields of science and the arts.

Training the Catalan police in times of democracy. The autonomous police force of Catalonia, which bears the historical name of Mossos d'Esquadra, is a security force which in only ten years has received careful preparation both at a human and at a technical level. It is a police force that was put into service in the context of a democratic society. It must logically be versed with the use of arms for those cases in which they are called for. But its challenge is to achieve a thorough degree of professionalism: always using the resources and functional means that are not contradictory with the principal objective of protecting individual citizens, their property and rights.

Premises of the research division of the Generalitat. This is the equipment of the Electrical Laboratory, the first one installed on the site of the General Tests and Research Laboratory, an organism depending on the Industry and Energy Departament of the Generalitat. This General Laboratory also quarters laboratories for mechanical, construction, container and packing techniques, acoustics and vibration, and gas and electronic research. It also carries out activities in support of private laboratories in the textile, leather, automobile and die and casting fields. This General Laboratory has also subscribed cooperation agreements with the Catalan universities to facilitate the exchange of scientific ideas and information, and to identify possible inadequacies in meeting the demand for research.

Engineering and the beauty of nature at the Susqueda dam. In the gorgeous natural beauty of Les Guilleries, human engineering has left its technical mark. Here is the dam of Susqueda which, together with that of Sau, provides fresh water for the city of Barcelona. Among the powers granted in the Statute of Autonomy there is that of authority over rivers and hydraulic works. An Act of the Parliament of Catalonia, dated July 1987, regulated the exercise of this authority and created the necessary administrative bodies: the Water Board (Junta d'Aigües) and the Sanitation Board (Junta de Sanejament).

The most significant unions in Catalonia. Catalonia has historically pioneered the structuring of the union movement in true organizations. There was an initial Bakuninist influence that would later on result in the creation of the Unió General de Treballadors (UGT), of socialist tendency. Some years later, in 1911, the Confederació Nacional del Treball (CNT) was formed, under anarchist inspiration, and had a significant role during the second and third decade of this century in Catalonia. These organizations were both born in Barcelona. During the years of dictatorship, they survived police repression in clandestinity. With democracy, things have changed. A new union force, Comissions Obreres, formed during the last years of Franco, achieved a commanding role while the CNT suffered a set-back. With a clear nationalist orientation, the Confederació Sindicalista de Catalunya has emerged in recent years. We show here the emblems of the unions we have mentioned.

SECRETARIAT NACIONAL DE CATALUNYA

Confederació General del Treball (CNT)
Comitè Confederal • Catalunya • Secretariat Permanent

Confederació Sindical de Catalunya

Emblems of the various politic groups present in the Parliament of Catalonia. These are the different emblems belonging to the political parties represented in the Catalan Parliament. It is necessary to point out that some of these political groups already existed before the transition period from dictatorship to democracy started, helping to make that step possible. This is the case of Esquerra Republicana de Catalunya (ERC), Convergència i Unió, Partit Socialista Unificat de Catalunya (which now has the initials IC) and the sectors that were later to form the Partit Socialista de Catalunya (PSC). In the same way the political options would not be the same had the State not organized itself in autonomous regions with the capacity for self-government. Nonetheless, Catalonia — which is a nation — shows important differences relative to other autonomous regions. When examining the position of the different political parties, it is necessary to take into consideration the weight that they give to the assertion of the Catalan nation.

Main façade of the Parliament of Catalonia Palace. As Francesc Vicens wrote, "There is probably no other legislative assembly occupying a building constructed for a purpose so distinct from its current use". In effect, the Parliament of Catalonia occupies the same building that long ago was used as an arsenal of the Ciutadella , a fortification built by order of Philip V to have a repressive instrument against the city of Barcelona. Behind this close-up of the sculpture *Despair*, by Josep Llimona, the main façade of the Parliament exhibits the functional grace of the military architecture of the 18th century, reflecting balance and harmony, and achieved using local materials: stone from Montjuïc and red tile.

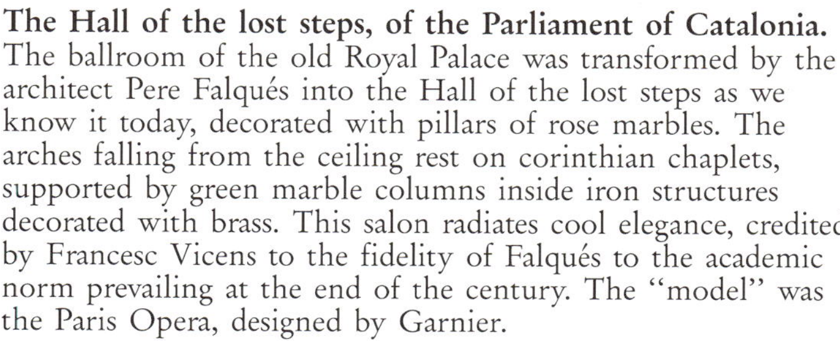

The Hall of the lost steps, of the Parliament of Catalonia. The ballroom of the old Royal Palace was transformed by the architect Pere Falqués into the Hall of the lost steps as we know it today, decorated with pillars of rose marbles. The arches falling from the ceiling rest on corinthian chaplets, supported by green marble columns inside iron structures decorated with brass. This salon radiates cool elegance, credited by Francesc Vicens to the fidelity of Falqués to the academic norm prevailing at the end of the century. The "model" was the Paris Opera, designed by Garnier.

Honour staircase of the Parliament of Catalonia. The building which today houses the Parliament of Catalonia has been the object of some changes historically. The alterations of this building — which had been the arsenal of the Parc de la Ciutadella Fortress Park —, to become a Royal Palace were directed since 1889 by Pere Falqués, municipal architect of Barcelona. This honour staircase which was built in marble, covered by an impressive dome cast in iron with decorated glasses, was designed by him.

Catalonia, a land of fine and varied wines. In the word of a well-known expert, Jaume Ciurana, "Catalonia has always been a land of good wine. The grapevine, as did civilization, came across the sea, with the Greeks and Romans. Our own history as a society has been, at all times, related to the grapevine and wine. See the cellars in the medieval monasteries, the adventure undertaken by our sailing vessels in the commercial routes of America, the 'Cathedrals of wine', huge cooperative wine cellars created by people and the drive of the Mancomunitat de Catalunya at the beginning of this century". Considering the geography, climatic conditions and the varieties of grapevine cultivated, Catalan wines are quite varied. There are official origin denominations such as Penedès, Alella, Tarragona, Priorat, Empordà, Costa Brava, Conca de Barberà, Terra Alta and Costers del Segre. Visual examination of the colour and transparency of a wine is a critical step in its production.

L'Espanya Industrial Park, avant-garde architecture. This expanse, once occupied by the large plant of La España Industrial, the most important cotton/textile company of Catalonia for over a hundred years, is today the location of the Espanya Industrial Park, one of the last works of modern avant-garde architecture realized by the Basque architect Luis Peña Ganchegui. The site has the aspect of a modern Roman thermal spring, with a navigable lake as its central element. It is surrounded by rows of seats dominated by ten cylindrical towers which are at the same time surveillance and illumination points. The decoration is made up of sculptures of various inspirations such as the dragon with a slide.

Panoramic view of Barcelona harbour. This view of Barcelona harbour, seen from the castle on the Montjuïc hill, suggests to us what Rufus Festus Avienus, Roman voyager and geographer of the 4th century, saw: that Barcelona was a city with a natural seaport. Less precise testimonies indicate that sailing ships already used this port in the 5th century BC. The natural harbour was used until Alfons V gave Barcelona the privilege of building an artificial seaport. The harbour has grown along the centuries to assume its actual configuration with nearly 400 ha of surface and major facilities and services available. It is used by 250 ocean lines and it ranks 28 among European seaports in volume of traffic.

Beach and mountainside camping sites. Tourism has played an essential role in the economic development of Catalonia in recent years. At present, it accounts for more than 15% of the GNP, and employs 12.5% of the working force. The varied geographic morphology has favored the development of this sector. Catalonia's camping sites and facilities have a capacity for 294,000 people. These sites are distributed between beach and mountain zones. These pictures show one of each.

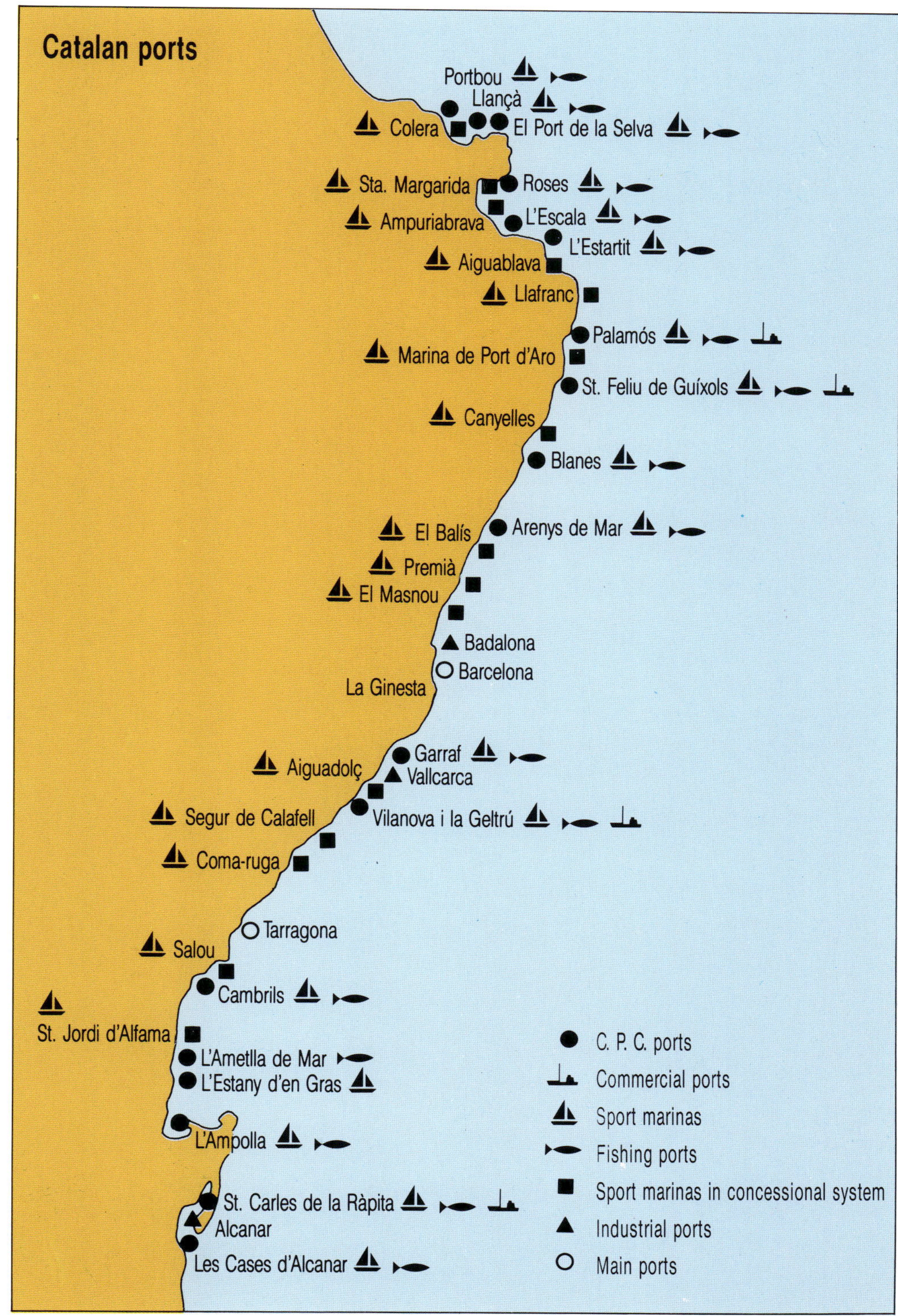

Map of Catalan ports. The Greek and Roman cultures, two of the most determinant ones that existed before the time of Christ, came to Catalonia across the sea, unfolding their sails towards our shores and leaving here many lasting marks. Ever since then coast has been the centre of many industrial and commercial activities. Today, however, tourism and leisure are an important aspect of the dialogue between Catalonia and the world, especially with the rest of Europe. The Catalan seashore offers magnificent views but also many sport centres. This map shows the marinas along the 580 km of our coast.

The Fair of Barcelona: 12 000 exhibitors per year. The vitality of Catalan society has made Barcelona a meeting point for international commercial and industrial meetings. More than a century ago, Barcelona organized the World Exhibition of 1888. More spectacular and monumental was the World Exhibition of 1929, some pavilions of which still form part of the area of the Barcelona Fair — seen here from an aerial camera. In this area of 250,000 m^2, more than 30 international events take place every year, attracting more than 12,000 exhibitors and 2 million visitors.

Barcelona, a European city by choice and geographical situation. Barcelona is the bi-millennial capital of a millennial nation. The original nucleus was a small Roman colony named Barcino. It was situated on the top of a hill, Mons Taber, surrounded by walls with its centre in the place occupied today by the Plaça de Sant Jaume. On this Roman city were constructed the main buildings of the medieval city. The urban development which transformed Barcelona into a large city took place in the second half of the 19th century, thanks to the vision of architect Ildefons Cerdà. Today Barcelona has become a cosmopolitan city and drives the Catalan economy, being representative of cultural and artistic trends and, in consequence, a nucleus of attraction for the citizens of a Europe without frontiers.

A replica of the first Catalan railroad. In 1948, to celebrate the first hundred years of railroads in Catalonia — and the Spanish State —, La Maquinista Terrestre i Marítima built railway cars and carriages and wagons which were a replica of those serving the line between Barcelona and Mataró in 1848.

Adjacent to Barcelona harbour, the "Zona Franca". These pictures show us a panoramic view of the "Zona Franca" adjacent to Barcelona's harbour, a place for the storage and transformation of foreign goods. This area is connected to one of the most important sectors of the city's industrial belt, the old county of Baix Llobregat, where various industries are located, the most important one being those associated with chemistry and metallurgy.

The Barcelona Stock Exchange: dealing in a gothic atmosphere. The sessions of the Barcelona stock Exchange took place until recently in a great gothic hall with three wings, named the Llotja, that was finished in 1392 and is today part of a neoclassical building. Commodity dealing, however, was already organized in the last third of the 13th century. Organized financial transacting was started in Barcelona in the year 1401 with the creation of the *taula de canvi*. During its long history, the Barcelona stock exchange adopted some peculiarities (the *dobla* and the *compte d'efectes bancaris*) that later on were to be used by other foreign financial centres. In the last few years, the Barcelona stock exchange, seen here in full activity, has made an effort to adapt to the present times. It ranks second among Spanish exchanges with 25% of total volume, and about 300 companies — Catalan, Spanish and foreign, are listed.

Catalonia, Spain's factory, a European region. Besides having served as the motto for the Barcelona's international Exhibition of 1985, as can be seen here, *Catalunya, la fabrica d'Espanya* (Catalonia, Spain's factory) these words were an irrefutable reality during the period 1833-1936. In fact, in 1833 Josep Bonaplata installed the first steam-powered industry. In 1900 the dominance of Catalan industry within Spain embraced all productive aspects except the food industry. To a great extent this role was fueled by the driving force of the capital of Catalonia, Barcelona, a city with an industrial driving force similar to the great industrial British cities. At present, with the growing industrialization of Spain, Catalonia works to become a modern and structured country projected towards Europe, a European region in equilibrium between Barcelona, Toulouse and Montpellier.

The complicated co-existence of two languages. In both the private and public sector — as can be seen in this picture —, the co-existence in Catalonia of the two official languages, Catalan and Castillian, is patent. This situation of even legal status for both, provided for in the Statute of Autonomy, is clearly not the best situation for Catalan, a language that suffered strong political repression which rendered it weak and defenceless. The Catalan Government is active in the defence of the Catalan language (Catalonia's own natural language) against harmful effects. In this way its full recovery as the national language of Catalonia is ensured. One activity is the placing of signs in the most visible public locations.

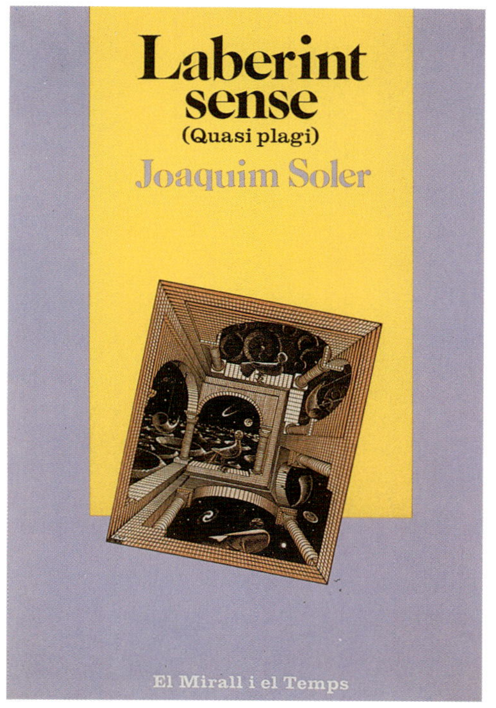

Some writers and books of the Generation of the '70. This collage of book covers illustrates the work of a group of Catalan writers called "Generation of '70", since it was during that decade that they became known to the public. All of them are in the peak of their literary production, and now that the situation is back to normal, the regime of dictatorship over and language barriers have disappeared, they have the opportunity to connect with a sector of readers much larger than fifteen years ago.

Projection abroad for today's Catalan literature. One of the most important traits of the eighties has been the substantial increase in literary translations. If at the beginning of the decade translations from other languages to Catalan proliferated, at present, at the century end, there are many books written in Catalan which are translated into foreign languages. Carme Riera, Quim Monzó and Sergi Pàmies are some examples. During the last ten years 58 Catalan books have been translated to other languages. We coincide with literary critic Isidor Cònsul who says: "Literary prestige is also measured by its international dynamism, by its capacity to conquer the external world".

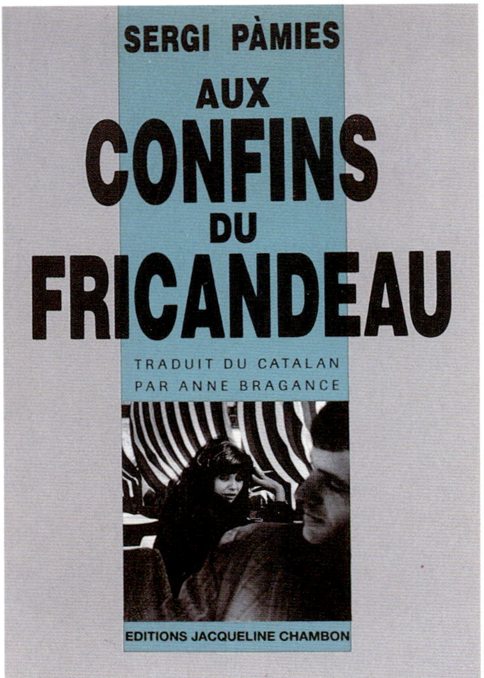

A network of more than two hundred Catalan periodicals embracing the entire territory. One of the basic objectives of Catalonia's linguistic normalization is to increase the offer of periodicals written in Catalan. Since the end of the dictatorial regime in 1975, new magazines and newspapers have emerged, some of national coverage and some — most of them — of more limited scope. The historical foundations of periodicals in Catalonia are notorious. Jaume Guillamet, a scholar of printed matter, says that "the wars at the end of the 18th and beginning of the 19th centuries gave rise to the publication of periodicals. At present there are about two hundred periodical publications in Catalan, not including newspapers."

PUNT
DIARI
INDEPENDENT, CATALÀ, COMARCAL I DEMOCRÀTIC
Moscoso defensa la creaci
servei de traducció al S
Nº 1
LOTERIA
SETMANARI DE L'ALT
EMPORDÀ
Vandalisme a la
EL 9 NOU
PERIÒDIC INDEPENDENT DE LES COMARQUES D'OSONA I DEL RIPOLL
ANY XII. Nº 913 Dilluns, 24 d'abril de 1989
Una banda de joves té
bona part dels
Avui comença una nova edició de la Lliga de bàsquet amb Barça
AVUI
Dimarts, 19 de setembre de 1989
Preu: 65 ptes.
Estudi sobre el saldo fiscal negatiu entre el que paga Catalunya i el que es rep de Madrid
L'Estat gestiona el 65 per cent
de la despesa pública catala
La Generalitat decideix sob
Barrionuevo promet una solució per a TV3 a València
Diari de Barcelona
Dimarts / 19 Setembre / 1989
Madrid controla la despesa
catalana
El tram olí
Litoral s'o
Torta caiguda del tèxtil i el calçat
El PCUS inicia avui el debat per trobar solucions a la qüestió nacional
"La Caixa" obre la temporada amb una mostra del seu fons d'obres d'art
XARXA
Els fenòmens "Poltergeist"
1939: aquell gener de fa cinquanta anys
Mites i realitats sobre la leucèmia
Posi una Preysler en la seva vida
Tintín fa seixanta anys
Segona època, nº
Gener 1989
275 pts. / 14 f.f.
Revista mensual d'actualitat
REVISTA D'HISTÒRIA
L'AVENÇ
FEBRER 1989 · 400 PTES.
NÚM. 348 / NOVEMBRE 1988 / 260 PTES.
Nous arguments i nous autors a la València de sempre per J.G. Mota
Itinerari poètic de Marià Manent per Ramon Oteo i Sans
Ens prendrem seriosament d'una vegada el teatre infantil? per Joaquim Vila
SERRA D'OR

La neu allí a l'hivern s'arremolina,
glaçant-se en l'escalada gegantina
d'aquell roquer *fantàstic* coliseu,
i avui al desglaçar-se sa ruïna,
l'absis apar de trossejada *Seu.*

Ploren de fil a fil *totes les roques*
i llança la gelera per cent boques
sinistres harmonies i espetecs;
dels penyalars, *com d'esberlades soques,*
se sent la cruixidera *i los gemecs.*

Allí amb ses fades Flordeneu plorosa
del seu amor lo fred cadavre *posa,*
per mausoleu *donant-li el Canigó;*
set braçades de neu tindrà per llosa,
la lluna cada nit per llantió.

Així que deixen el cadàver damunt la neu, dalt la collada apareix l'escuder que en veure Gentil mort i en poder de les fades fa esglaiat el senyal de la creu. Corre vers ell i aferrant-s'hi l'arrenca de les mans de Flordeneu. La goja llença un crit esgarrigós i fuig amb ses companyes, mentre l'escuder, carregat amb les estimades despulles del seu senyor, bosc a través davalla tot afligit a Sant Martí.

Quan hi arriba pel senderó de la serra, pel camí que puja de Castell acaba d'arribar-hi la comitiva dels dos comtes, i ell, en veure'ls, diposita als seus peus damunt la gespa de la prada el cos inanimat del *malaguanyat* Gentil.

Com un faig del Pirineu abatut per un llamp de la tempesta, el comte Tallaferro cau aplomat a terra; després, incorporant-se, agafa el cadàver del seu fill i l'estreny contra el seu pit llançant tristos sanglots.

70

De sobte es refà, s'aixeca encès per la ira, gira al seu voltant els ulls congestionats i crida amb veu de tro:

—Qui ha mort el meu fill?

Guifre confós i esgrogueït es retira vers l'ermita, però lleial contesta: —Jo!

Com un llampec Tallaferro treu l'espasa que creua voladora l'espai cap al cor del seu germà. Però el bisbe Oliba, *amatent*, dóna una empenta al culpable i el fa entrar dintre l'ermita, i, entrant-hi ell també, d'una revolada tanca la porta i passa el *forrellat*.

Ferit pel viu dolor del seu penediment, Guifre cau als peus del bisbe, son germà, i li confessa el seu crim espantós. No li fa res la mort, ja que des d'ara dóna la vida per ben perduda, però com a cristià vol salvar la seva ànima.

La capella ressona als cops de massa dels punys de Tallaferro que cauen damunt la vetusta porta i l'esquerden. Llavors repenja el seu cos en la part que més fort gemega i amb un esforç titànic aconsegueix *esbotzar-la* i obrir de bat a bat el temple.

71

sortida, que pareixia com si saltàs a cercar menjar, forçada per la necessitat; secs els braços; les mans com a sarments; de mig cos en avall semblava compàs o forqueta de dues pues; caminava amb pausa; i si res se li descomponia, li sonaven els ossos com els fustets de sant Llàtzer; la parla, hètica; la barba, llarga, que per no gastar no se la tallava i deia que les mans del barber per la seva cara li feien fàstic. Duia barret els dies de sol, ratat amb mil gateres i guarnicions de greix; la sotana era miraculosa, perquè no sabieu quin color tenia, que així, sense pèl, semblava cuiro de granot, i altres deien que era il·lusió; de prop semblava negra i blavenca d'enfora; no gastava coll ni punts i anava sense cenyidor; de manera que amb els cabells llargs i la sotana curta i miserable semblava un lacai de la mort. Cada sabata podia ser la tomba d'un filisteu. A la seva cambra, ni aranyes hi havia; conjurava els ratolins perquè no es menjassin els rosegons de pa que guardava; dormia a una màrfega en terra i sempre de costat per no gastar llençol. Era, en una paraula, arxipobre i protomisèria.

Aquí doncs vaig venir a parar. Com que no vaig veure gats, vaig demanar allò com era.

—Gats? —va dir un criat antic, tot entendrit i ploricós—. I qui us ha dit que els gats són amics de dejunis i penitències? Pel greix que traginau, ja es veu que sou nou a la casa.

Es va asseure el llicenciat Cabra, va beneir la taula, i vàrem fer una dinada eterna, això és, sense principi ni fi. Varen dur un

tancat. En arribar-hi vaig descobrir que el meu pare havia estat tan generós amb tothom que havia gastat totes les meves rendes, i va resultar que jo era tan pobre que amb prou feines tenia diners per pagar el pa que havia de menjar cada dia!

— —

Aleshores, mentre jo estava tancat a Montsó, els rics-homes aragonesos van dividir-se en bàndols que es barallaven entre ells, i sovint venien al castell perquè jo sortís i anés a favor dels uns o dels altres. I com que vaig veure que tota la terra es perdria si jo no imposava l'ordre i restablia la justícia, vaig prendre la determinació d'anar-me'n del castell.

Vaig cridar dos rics-homes de la meva confiança perquè m'ajudessin a marxar fos com fos i un bon dia, als nou anys, vaig abandonar Montsó a punta d'alba per anar amb la meva gent, que em va rebre amb gran alegria. Com que havien sentit a dir que al comte Don Sanxo no li havia agradat gens que jo me'n volgués anar de Montsó i que s'acostava per combatre'ns, un cavaller va deixar-me el seu gonió per protegir-me. I aquesta va ésser la primera vegada que vaig prendre les armes!

En arribar a Saragossa tothom estigué molt content de la meva vinguda.

— —

Com que jo era petit i no tenia ningú que m'ajudés i em donés bons consells, molts nobles van aixecar-se contra mi sense respectar la meva autoritat. Als onze anys vaig haver d'enfrontar-me amb Don Pero Ferrandes i vaig anar-lo a assetjar a la seva vila d'Albarrasí, i als quinze estava combatent contra En Guillem de Montcada, que era el noble més important de Catalunya; però el ricshomes sempre triomfaven perquè s'ajudaven entre ells i en canvi a mi el meu consell sempre em traïa i em feia capitular.

— —

22

música, art que conreaven havent dinat en cors a quatre o cinc veus, i de vegades sobre un tema improvisat. Aprengué a tocar la mandolina, l'*espineta*, l'arpa, la flauta germànica, la viola i el *sacabutx*.

Això durava una hora, l'hora de la digestió, que era seguida d'evacuacions naturals, i immediatament per nous estudis que solien durar tres hores o més: aleshores hom s'ocupava de repassos, escriptura i humanitats. En acabar sortien tots amb un jove gentilhome de la Turena, anomenat Gimnaste, el qual ensenyava a Gargantua l'art de cavalleria. Calia canviar de vestimenta i muntar un corser, al qual feia fer cent curses, fer tombarelles, saltar fossades i entrebancs, girar un petit cercle, adés a dreta, adés a esquerra. També trencava —no pas llances, que res no hi ha de més estrafolari que vantar-se d'haver trencat en torneig o en batalla tantes llances o més, perquè això també ho sabria fer qualsevol fuster: el que cal vantar és la llança que trenqui tants o tants enemics. Doncs, amb la seva llança acerada, verda i rígida, Gargantua trencava una tanca, esclafava un *arnès*, desarrelava un arbre, destrossava una sella d'armes, un casc o un guantellet. I ho aconseguia bo i armat de cap a peus.

Ningú com ell per ben plantar dalt de cavall, per saltar d'una sella a l'altra tot galopant, per muntar sense estrep i amb la llança al puny, per guiar sense brides. Aprengué a donar cops de destral, a brandar la pica, a esgrimir el mandoble, la bastarda, l'espasa castellana, la daga i el punyal; adés armat, adés desarmat, amb escut, a la capa. Caçava el cérvol i la daina, l'isard i l'ós, el senglar, la llebre, la perdiu, el faisà, l'avitarda. Lluitava, corria i saltava; però no a tres passes el salt, ni a peu coix, ni a la teutona, perquè, segons Gimnaste, aquests salts no serveixen de res a la guerra; sinó que saltava per travessar una fossa, o per salvar una tanca, o bé a sis passes per escalar una tàpia; i sabia enfilar-se a finestres posades a l'alçada d'una llança. Nedava en aigua profunda, del dret, al revés, de cantó, amb tot el cos, amb els peus només, amb una sola mà; travessava el Sena bo i portant, sense mullar-lo, un llibre a la mà. Remava i guiava les barques contracorrent, es mantenia a la *resclosa*, governava les veles. Sortia de l'aigua per

44

45

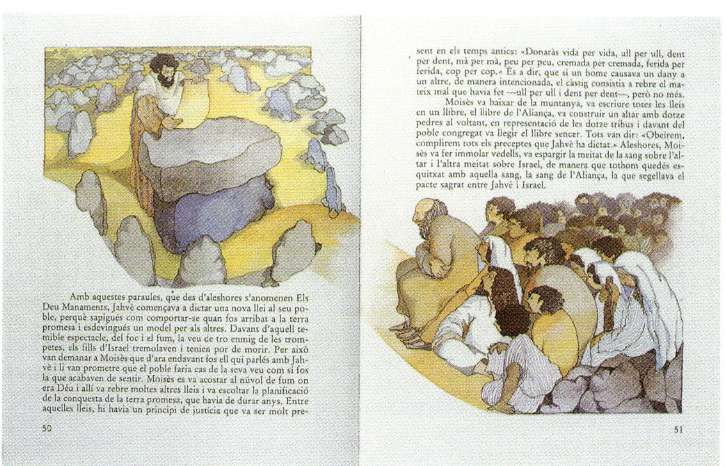

Amb aquestes paraules, que des d'aleshores s'anomenen Els Deu Manaments, Jahvè començava a dictar una nova llei al seu poble, perquè sapigués com comportar-se quan fos arribat a la terra promesa i esdevingués un model per als altres. Davant d'aquell temible espectacle, del foc i el fum, la veu de tro enmig de les trompetes, els fills d'Israel tremolaven i tenien por de morir. Per això van demanar a Moisès que d'ara endavant fos ell qui parlés amb Jahvè i li van prometre que el poble faria cas de la seva veu com si fos la que acabaven de sentir. Moisès es va acostar al núvol de fum on era Déu i allí va rebre moltes altres lleis i va escoltar la planificació de la conquesta de la terra promesa, que havia de durar anys. Entre aquelles lleis, hi havia un principi de justícia que va ser molt pre-

50

sent en els temps antics: «Donaràs vida per vida, ull per ull, dent per dent, mà per mà, peu per peu, cremada per cremada, ferida per ferida, cop per cop.» És a dir, que si un home causava un dany a un altre, de manera intencionada, el càstig consistia a rebre el mateix mal que havia fet —ull per ull i dent per dent—, però no més.

Moisès va baixar de la muntanya, va escriure totes les lleis en un llibre, el llibre de l'Aliança, va construir un altar amb dotze pedres al voltant, en representació de les dotze tribus i davant del poble congregat va llegir el llibre sencer. Tots van dir: «Obeirem, complirem tots els preceptes que Jahvè ha dictat.» Aleshores, Moisès va fer immolar vedells, va espargir la meitat de la sang sobre l'altar i l'altra meitat sobre Israel, de manera que tothom quedés esquitxat amb aquella sang, la sang de l'Aliança, la que segellava el pacte sagrat entre Jahvè i Israel.

51

A la fi va alçar-se, damunt la terra escocesa, el sol que havia d'aclarir la lluita decisiva. A punta de dia Macbeth havia rebut una nova que l'avisava de la proximitat del perill. Un exèrcit de deu mil homes —deien— s'acostava a marxes forçades i era a punt d'arribar. En saber que l'enemic arribava, Macbeth va sentir-se tot

72

d'una animat per la fúria dels combats propers. Les seves ordres, curtes, precises, van ésser trameses ràpidament al nucli més gros del seu exèrcit, acampat vora el puig, i les tropes triades del castell van estar tot seguit sobre les armes.

Macbeth havia dat, com a cabdill expert, totes les ordres

73

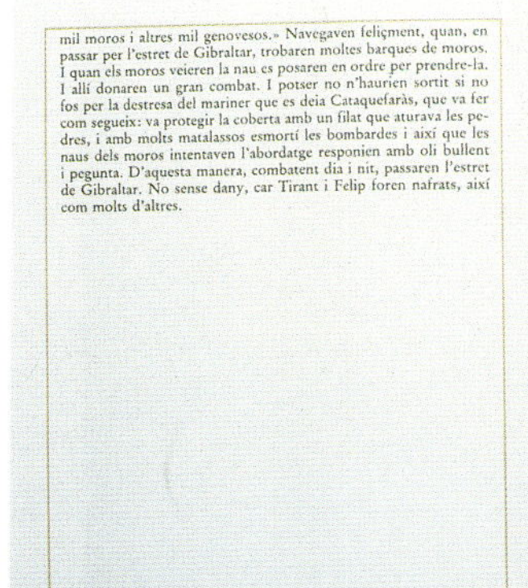

mil moros i altres mil genovesos.» Navegaven feliçment, quan, en passar per l'estret de Gibraltar, trobaren moltes barques de moros. I quan els moros veieren la nau es posaren en ordre per prendre-la. I allí donaren un gran combat. I potser no n'haurien sortit si no fos per la destresa del mariner que es deia Cataquefaràs, que va fer com segueix: va protegir la coberta amb un filat que aturava les pedres, i amb molts matalassos esmortí les bombardes i així que les naus dels moros intentaven l'abordatge responien amb oli bullent i pegunta. D'aquesta manera, combatent dia i nit, passaren l'estret de Gibraltar. No sense dany, car Tirant i Felip foren nafrats, així com molts d'altres.

34

TIRANT A SICÍLIA I A RODES

Quan el Rei de Sicília sabé que del Ponent venien a Palerm aquells que en l'estret de Gibraltar havien tingut grans combats amb els moros, acordà dar-los acollida amb gran honor. Féu fer un gran pont de fusta de la terra fins a la nau, tot cobert de draps de ras, per tal que poguessin arribar a terra amb tota felicitat. I els portà a la ciutat i els féu molt bé aposentar i servir molt bones viandes. I tota la cort els rebé a palau, i el Rei tingué paraules amables per a tots,

35

Literary masterpieces for young people. Over the last few years editorial supply in Catalonia has expanded with the publication of some of the best pieces of universal literature, appropriate as reading material for the young. An essential ingredient for these books is to have good illustrations. Shakespeare, Rabelais, Quevedo, biblical Moses or Catalan authors with worldwide projection — Joanot Martorell, Verdaguer —, have today the valuable graphic contribution of internationally known illustrators such as Maria Rius, Irene Bordoy, Carme Peris, Fina Rifà, Montserrat Ginesta and Manuel Boix.

I no és que talment fos com ara

I no és que talment fos com ara. Canvia,
més que la terra, un home. Però aquest aire, errant
entre un cel penetrat de sol i la maragda
fosa en una blanesa humida pels terrossos,
alè que arriba i diu sols un mot de miracle,
joia que no entenem i sembla que s'oblidi...
Quasi torna una hora antiga, tal vegada,
com una font que puja pels pisos de la terra,
i és pura i clara sota del cel d'avui, feliç.
Són aquests camps de sempre, llunyans de llum d'infància,
arbres com ales, ombres sonores d'alegria,
i un fons ample de sol estès, tot acceptat.
Espais oberts on busca ja una tendra mirada,
busca potser afirmar-se, o perdre's, o el plomatge
fugaç i la bellesa dels camps que descobreix,
del mar llunyà. El mar vist arran de pedra i sorra,
quan duia un crit proper de goig, de blau, d'escuma
—o s'eixamplava amb una inquieta tristesa
de força i solitud, on s'enfonsava l'ombra.

Marià Villangómez, Honour Prize of Catalan Letters 1989. This serigraphy displays a luminous and delicate poem of Marià Villangómez i Llobet, decorated by his niece Sonya. This poet, born in Eivissa (Ibiza), had his first poems published in 1932, and has lately pleased readers with translations of the work of Thomas Hardy, the English poet of the colloquial meditation on life, beauty, love and death. Between 1932 and 1989 he authored several very high quality books of literature and poetry. In the opinion of poet Isidor Marí, also born in Eivissa, Villangómez is the best writer from Eivissa, the one who has best presented the true personality of the islands (the Balearic Islands).

Prize and winner of the *Catalònia Prize*, international biennial. Catalonia's long tradition in the field of book illustration inspired the Generalitat to create an international prize, named Catalònia Illustration Prize awarded every two years since 1984. The goal of this prize is to contribute to the recognition and praise of a profession with an enormous didactic, aesthetic, and humanist value. An average of one hundred and fifty draftsmen, from forty countries, have taken part in the first three editions. We show here the winners of the first two editions and the award, a work of the sculptor Josep M. Subirachs.

TV3, a communication tool and an instrument to promote Catalan. With the recovery of democratic rights, the enactment of the Constitution and the Catalan Statute of Autonomy, the doors of the media previously closed to Catalan, were opened. The establishment of TV3 in 1983, a television station broadcasting exclusively in Catalan, has been a decisive step towards linguistic normalization. It can be said that TV3 has been a genuine adult school for all those people who, owing to their origin, family roots or work, are far removed from those areas where Catalan is most widely used. Needless to say, it has also played an important educational role for young people. TV3 has invested heavily in technical means, as its facilities and equipment demonstrate. The impact of television is reinforced by radio broadcasts in Catalan by Catalunya Ràdio and Radio Associació, stations managed by the Generalitat.

An international Comic Exhibition in Barcelona. The last International Comic Salon took place in the Barcelona Drassanes in May 1990, and gained the necessary public and institutional support needed to achieve the level of renown sought by Catalan Comic artists. Today, Barcelona is already a site of annual encounters for Comic artists and editors, together with Lucca, in Italy, and Angoulême, in France.

FC Barcelona's Camp Nou, a stadium for 120,000 people. FC Barcelona's stadium is one of the most spectacular examples of modern architecture in Barcelona. This work by architects Mitjans, Soteras and García Barbón, was inaugurated in 1957. At present it can accommodate 120,000 people. Surrounding the stadium there are several sports facilities, the most important one being the Palau Blau-grana and the Mini-estadi. Barcelona FC — a football team founded in 1899 by Joan Gamper, a Swiss —, is considered among the most magnificent in the world and since its inauguration has played an important role as representative of Catalan society.

The Cycle Track, the first Olympic building. Situated in one of the most elevated points of Barcelona, very near the Collserola hills in the borough of La Vall d'Hebron, the Cycle Track is the first completed Olympic building. A creation of the architects Esteve Bonell and Francesc Rius, it is encircled by gardens and contains one sculpture-poem by Joan Brossa. These gardens communicate with the Laberint d'Horta (Horta Labyrinth), an area of luxuriant vegetation, surrounding a neoclassical mansion.

The Cervantes Park, in Barcelona, with its 11,000 rosebushes. This is a panoramic view, from an elevated point, of the Cervantes Park, an oxygenated area which is situated in the Diagonal in uptown Barcelona. This park boasts geometrically-shaped gardens, some in circles and semi-circles, and rosebushes that cover 4 hectares, half its surface. Those walking in the park have the opportunity to enjoy 11,000 rosebushes of more than 245 varieties.

Outside a residence for severely disabled people. Sant Salvador, a residence for severely disabled people, is one of the most recent accomplishments of an architectural style which serves health care, under the surveillance of the Generalitat of Catalonia. It includes five different architectural structures related to each other by means of open spaces, streets, paths and greenery. It has many ornamental elements, and exercises the attraction of architecture of the senses, utilizing the best elements of post-modern research, specially from Charles Moore and Californian architects.

"The spaces of Abraxas", designed in France by Ricard Bofill. "The spaces of Abraxas", in Marne-la-Vallée (France), is one of the latest works by Ricard Bofill. It is an array of three buildings: a "Palau" (palace), a theatre and an arch. Different styles are mixed, relating to sudden changes in scale. Each architectonic element — prefabricated — is used to the limits of disproportion, and the relationship between the different elements is underlined by inverted spacial structures, producing an astounding sensation. Bofill conceived this group as a residential area, making it visually distinct from work environments.

The bridge-sculpture of Calatrava. In the field of urban architecture, it is worth mentioning a bridge-sculpture, which was built by architect and engineer Santiago Calatrava. The bridge serves to communicate two populated and old boroughs of the city: Sant Andreu and El Poblenou. The surrounding grounds, previously used as part of a train station, will be converted into a park, according to a plan for the promotion of park areas within this densely populated city.

La Creueta del Coll Park and its *In praise of water.* The park traditionally known as "La Creueta del Coll" is one of the spaces that has been set aside for the "new Barcelona". The hill, rocky on one side — an old stone quarry —, has been transformed into a public space. An artificial lake has been built where small boats can navigate in winter, is used as a swimming area during the summer. This lake was designed by the architects Martorell and Mackay and exhibits a monumental hanging sculpture — *In praise of water* — which reflects upon the lake surface. The municipality has been able to keep and promote this natural space, in the centre of Barcelona, an oxygenated area for a city with a population far too dense.

The Millennium Bridge, with a span of 180 m. The Millennium Bridge over the Ebre river at Tortosa, is one of the most important undertakings of the administration of the Generalitat of Catalonia. The construction of the bridge and related accesses cost about 1,900 million pesetas. The bridge received this name since its inauguration in 1988 coincided with the celebrations of the first millennium of Catalonia. The bridge spans over 180 metres, making it the first in this class of steel arch bridges. The designers are engineers Julio Martínez Calzón and José Antonio Fernández Ordóñez.

Inside a modern kindergarten. Social service architecture promoted by the Generalitat is visible around the country in singular buildings combining aesthetics and functionality. This is, for example, the case of the kindergarten La Pomera, at Sant Joan Despí. The emplacement of the building uses the gentle incline of the terrain to organize the inside around a system of ramps. Situated in a well illuminated zone, the ramps come to represent a spirit of merriment that is characteristic of kindergartens, with their basic objective: educational play.

A sculpture by Joan Miró presides over the Plaça de l'Escorxador. Joan Miró, with his monumental and polychromatic sculpture *Woman and bird*, brightened up the ample space of the Plaça de l'Escorxador. This is now an additional space available for the relaxation of adults and the amusement of young people who navigate their toy sailing boats on the pond. In this picture, the profusion of palm-trees in the area near the bullring Les Arenes, can be seen. In addition, the park offers playgrounds amid pergolas, pine and eucalyptus trees.

The Mediterranean character of Barcelona seen from the Moll de la Fusta. The Mediterranean character of Barcelona and its people is most evident when walking along the port on a fair spring or autumn day. Over the course of time the people of Barcelona have built areas — platforms, terraces, balconies, sidewalks —, to facilitate contact with the Mare Nostrum. Lately, the Moll de la Fusta, a privileged spot that meets the Mediterranean waters, has been transformed by means of a careful renovation into an elevated terrace, garnished with palm trees and lamp-posts, where Barcelona's inhabitants and tourists can contemplate commercial vessels and yachts anchored in the nearby Yacht Club.

Joan-Josep Tharrats, avant-garde and unconventional painter. This piece, called *Vivace*, is a meaningful example of the aesthetic preoccupations of the painter during the sixties. The artist has also cultivated mural painting, scenery, lithography, pavements and ceramics. Tharrats is not worried about conforming to the classic definition of the avant-garde artist and is not interested in the massive diffusion of his work. As the art critic Francesc Fontbona wrote, "He is skeptical, liberal and obstinate, a man who despairs because among the privileged few who consume art, there are so few ever attaining their own ideas on artistic taste and judgement".

Tàpies, aesthetic research and humanistic objectives. Etching and collage, based on the profuse use of materials, are frequently used in the work of Tàpies in the late sixties and the beginning of the seventies. Tàpies, a universally famous artist, is constantly undergoing a process of evolution as a result of his steady activity in the field of aesthetic research. Lately, the painter has said that if he did not consider his work as useful to society, he would cease to produce: "If I have devoted myself to the research of interesting things, it has been because of my belief that they could help broaden the cognitive capacity of man, and at the same time foster some kind of solidarity".

Hernández Pijuan, from "decorativism" to free style drawing. *Indoor plant number 3* is an oil painting on canvas of Joan Hernández Pijuan, a painter formed in the Llotja school of Barcelona. Initially he created a "decorativist" style which progressively changed into a calculated and geometric figurative style. Besides Barcelona and Madrid, his work has been exhibited in Zurich (1965), Milan (1968), Johannesburg (1968), Cologne (1971), Geneva (1974) and, later on, in New York, Paris and Osaka. Lately he has favoured free style drawing, softer intonations and has shown a preference for themes from the botanical world (flowers, plants and trees). He holds a Professorship in the Fine Arts Faculty of the University of Barcelona.

Montserrat Gudiol, a painter of human intimacy. Montserrat Gudiol was educated in the study of restoration of medieval painting her family possessed. Since 1950 she has been devoted to painting on board, paper and drafting. An outstanding trait of her work is an attention to formal quality, and sometimes, an extraordinary fidelity to anatomy. But even more impressive is the profuse interior life transpiring from her works, which depict human images — which never play a role other than being human —, immerse in an atmosphere of meditation, contemplation and praying. Her works have been exhibited in various Spanish cities, South Africa, the United States and Canada. Some of them are part of the collection of the Museum of Modern Art of Barcelona.

Ràfols Casamada, painter, art teacher, writer. *Between the leaves*, acrylic on canvas, is the work of one of the most relevant Catalan artists of the last few years. Painter, teacher of art and design and a writer who has published various books, Albert Ràfols Casamada has experienced an evolution which has taken him from his initial post-impressionism to a poetic abstraction, "amorphous in its configuration", says the art critic Daniel Giralt-Miracle, "free and intelligent, fruit of a long maturing process, concentrating on atmosphare, themes, objects and graphisms associated with day-to-day life". On the occasion of a retrospective exhibition of his work (1947-1987), recently celebrated in Barcelona, Joan Teixidor said that this artist "has been forging his life and work in silence, without a voice".

Josep Guinovart, an artist of many ways of expression. *The escape* is representative of the pictorial work of Guinovart, who here used a mixed technique. The works of this Catalan painter are varied: drafts, graphic work, illustrations, decorations for theatres, tapestries, canvas, etc "His art" in merchant Matheos's opinion, "cannot be classified, and is one of the most vivid in today's world".

Relief with real objects by Grau Garriga. We are before one of Grau Garriga's paintings — *The shirt, painting (La camisa, pintura).* When this artist names one of his works "painting" he means something different from tapestries, drafts, sculpture or environmental pieces. On the other hand the use he makes of "collage" to obtain relief, a technique he has used often since 1965, becomes evident. The presence of real objects in his works may be due to several reasons: a will to embrace symbolism, chromatic and plastic significations as well as an attempt to incite psychological jolts.

Maximum purity of form in the work of ceramist Llorens i Artigas. This oval pitcher, which is a characteristic example of the art of ceramist Josep Llorens i Artigas, defines his artistic personality: maximum purity of forms, subtle treatment of colours and originality of enamels. Llorens i Artigas has won many prizes, and has had his work shown in Paris, Brussels, London, New York, Barcelona and Madrid. He cooperated with Joan Miró in various artistic works such us the UNESCO mural in Paris, the Maeght Foundation and Barcelona airport.

Xavier Corberó: metal as the basis of aesthetic abstraction. Xavier Corberó, educated in his father's studio, was born in a family which for more than three generations has been devoted to metal artistry. His first public appearance was in 1952, when he presented twelve pieces in the Hispano-American biennial. They were executed using repoussé techniques. From 1955 to 1958 he lived in London, where he worked with metal and stone in The Central School of Arts and Crafts. Back in Barcelona he exposed his series of small brass pieces inspired in the symbol/space relationship. Here we show one of the pieces exhibited in New York in 1988 under the title *Bishop, Bishop.*

Marcel Martí, from painting to abstract sculpture. Marcel Martí worked exclusively on paintings until 1953, when he made his first attempts at sculpture — according to Alexandre Cirici —, following the example of the Italians Marini and Manz. Later on he became interested in high temperature ceramics tending towards abstraction and creating organic-like forms which are symmetrical with respect to an axis and show a certain predilection for rough materials. This sculpture, called *Atnel Girona*, was made with a material called "corten" and is 10 metres high.

Stone, wood, brass and glass in the hands of Josep Maria Subirachs. Josep Maria Subirachs, a sculptor who began working in the forties, represents the shift from the postulates of *noucentisme* to those of the Avant-garde. From 1951, as a consequence of living in Paris, he turned to expressionism and later on initiated a period that would lead him to the abstract. His works were the first sculptures to be situated in public places after the war. In the sixties, Subirachs experimented with a combination of various materials: stone, wood, brass and glass. At present the artist's principal activity is working on sculptures for the Sagrada Família temple in Barcelona.

"Disseny a Catalunya", an itinerant ambassador. The exhibition "Disseny a Catalunya" ("Design in Catalonia") organized by the Barcelona Design Centre (Barcelona Centre de Disseny, BCD) and sponsored by the Generalitat, is an itinerant sample aimed at the promotion of Catalan design in its different facets: graphic, industrial, furniture and jewelry. "Disseny a Catalunya" began its international itinerary in Milan — one of the most important design centres in Europe — as a challenge to compare its own achievements with those of countries pioneering design. The Italian press gave good reviews to the overall quality of this exhibition that had a chair as its emblem. After Milan, there have been exhibitions in Barcelona, Berlin, Stockholm, and Nagoya, and others are planned.

Public places and interior design that facilitate communication. The eighties in Barcelona and other cities of Catalonia have been a period for achievements in the interior design of public places. Take "Velvet", shown in this picture, as an example: a music bar which is reached through a tunnel facilitating the passage from reality to the artificial atmosphere of ephemeral fantasies found when one is enjoying oneself and time loses its habitual meaning. The disposition of space in this and other similar places (Universal, Otto Zutz and KGB) pursues the same objective: to facilitate people relating to each other.

Interior design: from a public to a private environment. Another step in the adventure of post-modern interiorism is "Network" a music bar where there is a preference for everything American, where you can have American-style dinner since there is a small TV set on each table. The premises consist of a main floor and two basements. However the restless creativity of interior design is not only concerned with the design of public places. Today many people choose to create their own private atmosphere, which is modified and changed according to the evolution of taste and materials. To some extent, nearly everyone becomes a little bit of a designer with respect to their immediate domestic surroundings.

Useful versatility of the music bars. The designer of Nick Havanna, another music bar in Barcelona, is a pioneer of avant-garde design. Its spaciousness, meant to facilitate communication, makes it specially suitable for public meetings. In fact it has hosted, among other events, book presentations and meetings associated with political campaigns.

Graphic creativity: individual identity and universal language. Two examples of Catalan graphic design are shown here. One is a poster by Enric Satué and the other consists of four book covers made by Ricard Badia. It is said that there is a certain process of convergence in graphic creativity. Modern techniques foster the unification of solutions to the detriment of individual traits. It is difficult to maintain the author's own idiosyncrasy, or that of a given school or country. Works produced in New York, Paris or Tokyo are becoming more alike. This situation causes the desire to create differences of image, that, being unique to a specific country, speak a universal language.

***Sol Solet*, a performance in a book.** The theatrical company Els Comediants is responsible for the text and illustrations of the book *Sol Solet*, produced under the technical and artistic direction of the designers Salvador Saura and Ramon Torrente. It is a singular book made to give a free, sensuous, cosmic and literary version of the show *Sol Solet*, also created by Els Comediants. The covers, metal-like and shiny, invite the reader to travel through seven surprising books in search of the sun: mirrors, cut-out pictures, eyeglasses, perfumed envelopes and three-dimensional eyeglasses. This book, which has won international prizes, is edited by Edicions de l'Eixample and Institut del Teatre.

Posters, a genre dignified by designers. Posters have become a common variety of graphic production in Catalonia, as a consequence of an increased demand for communication in a society of masses. Although the poster is an element of only one use, professional graphic designers had dignified and converted it in an item for collection. As example take this poster titled *El català llengua mil·lenària*, designed by Ramon Robert, where the main text forms a circular column focusing the attention while the four pages of an ancient codex create an emblem.

The Foment de les Arts Decoratives operates since 1903. The concern with different aspects of design and decorative arts is nothing new in our country. Proof of this can be found in the Foment de les Arts Decoratives (FAD), founded in Barcelona in 1903. It is the main promoter in this field. Since then FAD has carried out many initiatives which project industrial and graphic design to the whole of Spain. The professional organizations that form part of FAD yearly call the Delta Prize for industrial design, the Laus prizes for graphic design and the FAD prizes for architecture and interior design, in different categories. On this double page we have reproduced the "Lampelunas lamp" (1986, Gold Delta), the "Coqueta chair" (1988 Gold Delta) and the 1986 interior design prize, awarded to the Badalona IV BUP Institute, as well as the competition poster for the Laus prizes and the Gold Delta which is awarded to the winners of the industrial design prize.

The miser, by Molière, under the direction of Flotats. _The miser_, one of Molière masterpieces, in the Catalan version of writer Xavier Bru de Sala, was represented in the Poliorama theatre in Barcelona under the direction of Josep Maria Flotats and was performed by his own theatre company. As it is known, the author presents, under a dramatic structure, an ideal of human wisdom and moral behaviour which, in spite of the fact that it is placed in the 17th century, is still relevant. The return of Josep Maria Flotats to Catalonia, from the Comédie Française were he worked, has been vital in the promotion of theatre in Catalonia. In a few years his company has performed _Cyrano de Bergerac_, by Rostand, and _Lorenzaccio_, by Musset among others.

The silent performance of Albert Vidal. Albert Vidal is not usually perceived as a theatre actor or mime artist. He is more definable as a one-man show, acting alone — generally in the open air — and his performances invite one to meditate on the human condition and its present circumstance. He has worked with Dario Fo's company and in the Piccolo Teatro di Milano in Italy. He has also performed in many countries. In Catalonia, in particular he has represented together with Carlos Santos, _El bufó_ (The clown) (1977) and _L'aperitiu_ (The aperitif) (1979). This image corresponds to his recent creation _L'home urbà_ (The urban man).

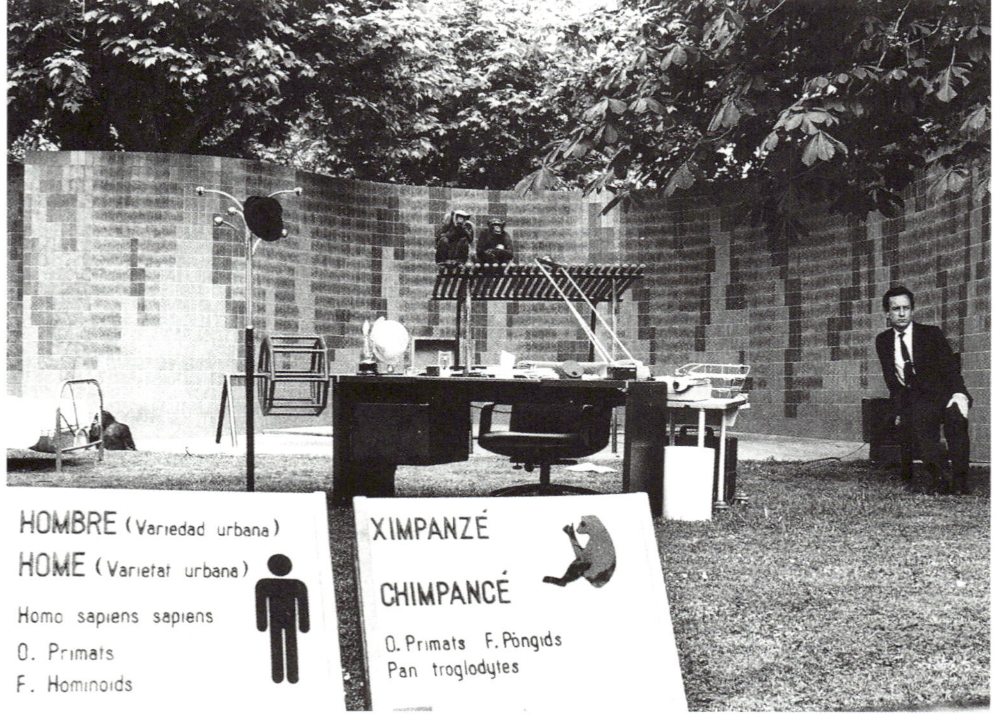

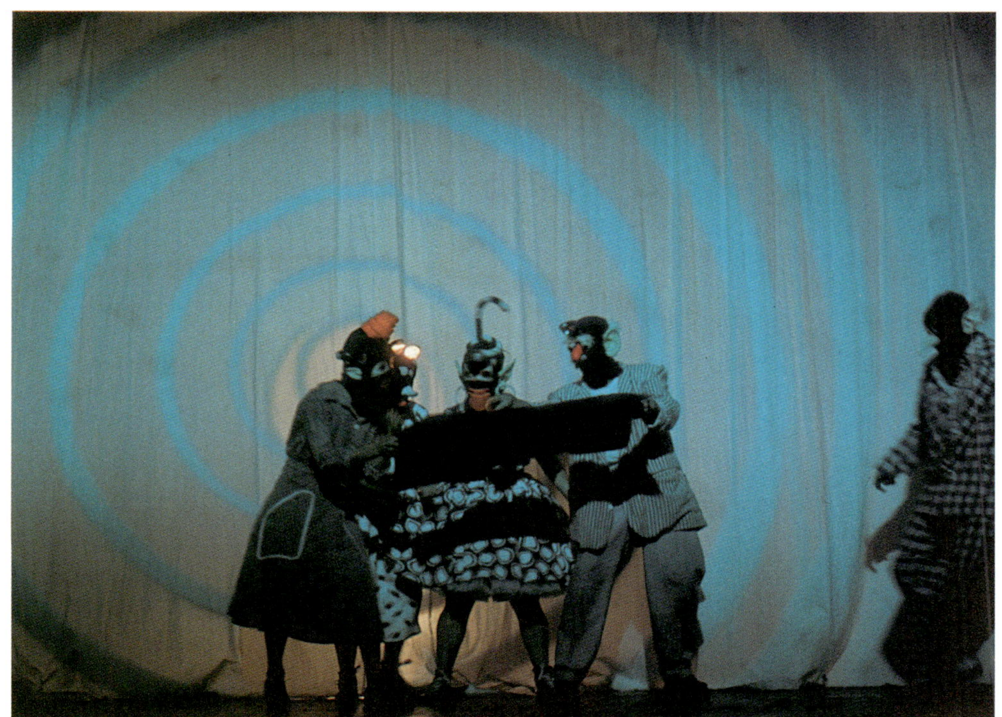

Els Comediants, a theatre company recreating the past. This scene corresponds to *La nit* (The night), a recent production of the theatre company Els Comediants. This Catalan company, founded in Canet de Mar, has specialized in street theatre, night shows and performances where public participation plays a relevant role. Their work, which includes a significant amount of study and research, is based in the iconography of folklore and country traditions and has contributed to the recovery of the cultural heritage of the past. Since 1971 it has produced dozens of plays and television programmes. It has also performed in many European countries including Germany, Denmark, France, Iceland and Italy.

Dagoll-Dagom, a new style for the Catalan musical. The *Mikado*, by Gilbert and Sullivan, in the Catalan version translated by Xavier Bru de Sala, is, according to Joan Anton Benach, "The most finely elaborated performance of Dagoll-Dagom", a theatre company whose objective is to produce plays for all Catalan audiences. "If among the different audiences we were given the choice — they say — we would undoubtedly choose the young, those nearly of an adolescent age, people who fill music locals and who have forgotten — or perhaps simply have never been told —, that theatre can also be exciting and entertaining, full of emotion and life". This is the inspiring objective of Dagoll Dagom, a group coming together in 1973, having represented dozens of theatrical pieces and which has specialized in musicals such as *La nit de Sant Joan* (St. John's Eve), *Glups!!*, *Antaviana* and *Mar i cel* (Sea and sky), to mention but a few.

El Molino, an old and emblematic variety theatre. This rudimentary wind mill, presenting a white-and-red nocturnal façade, is the most visible trait of one of Barcelona's best known night clubs. At the end of the 19th century it was specialized in variety performances, in which cheeky humor and feathered "vedettes" had a great following. At the beginning its name was "Petit Palais" and later on "Petit Moulin Rouge", a name which lent it a pretentious Parisian air. In 1939 it took on its present name. Over the years El Molino has become a joyful and spontaneous symbol of Barcelona's nightlife attracting locals and foreigners alike.

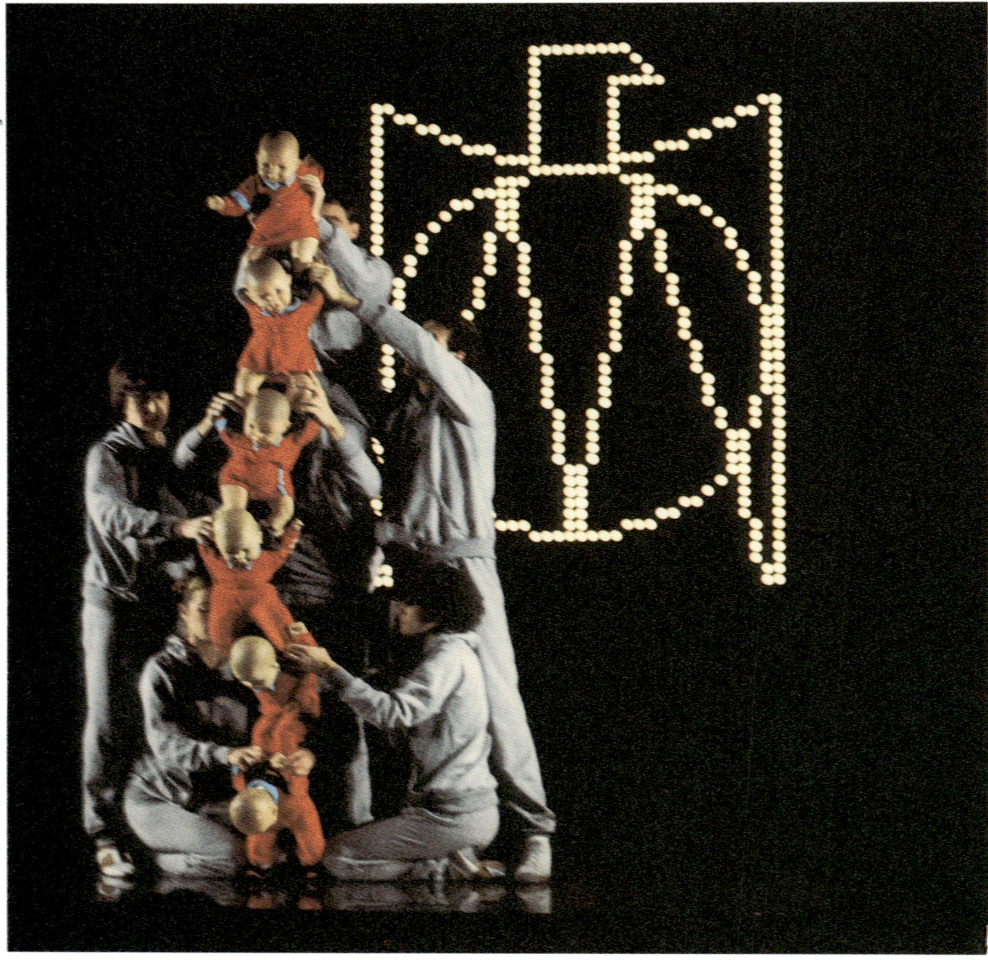

Els Joglars: more than twenty five years with the public. Els Joglars, founded in 1963 as a mime group — influenced by Marcel Marceau and Italo Riccardi —, has consolidated its status over the course of more than twenty-five years becoming a theatre company which creates its own plays. Over the past few years they have staged *M-7 Catalònia* (1978), *L'Odissea* (The Odyssey) (1979), *Laetius* (1980), *Olympic Man Movement* (1981) — two scenes of which are shown here. Their latest show was called *Columbi Lapsus*. The group has also made programmes for foreign television, has acted frequently outside Catalonia and has participated at international theatre festivals.

La Fura dels Baus, entertainment or provocation? In 1979, Catalan theatre saw the birth of a company which has recently consolidated its artistic progress: La Fura dels Baus. They started off as a street theatre group, later taking to the stage, performing not only in Catalonia and other European countries, but also in Japan and Australia, where they have staged "provocative" works. In a series of works such as *Accions* (1983), *Suz-o-Suz* (1986) and *Tier Mon* (1988), these players often shock their audiences and cause them to reflect about the contemporary human condition and the characteristics of preparation and physical discipline associated with circus artistes. They base their work on the spectacular, concentrating on those elements which make a strong impact.

El Tricicle, creators of "dumb" drama. Almost all Catalan theatre companies have gradually come round to writing their own material. They are authentic stage and dramatic text creators. In the case of the El Tricicle, they are creators of silence, be it comic or dramatic. This is because their three components (Gràcia, Mir, and Sans) perform a kind of drama without words which often brings the techniques and resources of Old American comic cinema to mind (Harold Lloyd, Buster Keaton or the great Charlie Chaplin himself). In the last few years, the following of their works must be mentioned: *Manicòmic* (1982), *Exit* (1984), *Slàstic* (1986), works with which they toured several European countries. They also work in several television series.

The Teatre Lliure, quality and variety of theatrical pieces. The Teatre Lliure started up its theatrical activities in December 1976, and has ever since functioned as a cooperative company. The Lliure has distinguished itself for the quality and variety of its adaptations, mainly based on texts by world-class authors: Shakespeare, Brecht, Ibsen, Marlowe, Büchner, etc. This image corresponds to *One of the last evenings of the Carnival* (Un dels últims vespres de Carnaval), by Goldoni, directed by Lluís Pasqual who has distinguished himself as an extraordinary director.

Ramon Muntaner, an expert composer of music. Over and above his talent as a singer, Ramon Muntaner stands out as an expert composer of music. His work often involves setting music to the texts of contemporary Catalan poets, which he sings with the accompaniment of a fine musical ensemble. One of his best works was the music for *La plaça del Diamant*, a novel by Mercè Rodoreda which was made into a film, a play and a television series. He has also taken part in many other works for the audio-visual media.

Joan Manuel Serrat, a world famous singer. Joan Manuel Serrat is one of the best known singer-composers of the prolific literary musical movement which took place in Catalonia at the end of the fifties and was known as the "Setze Jutges" (Sixteen judges). Serrat was able to gain the esteem and respect of his public. In few years he became a true professional singer. Taking advantage of his fluency in the two languages spoken within his family (Catalan and Castilian) he has written splendid songs of his own and has made excellent musical recordings both of Catalan — Salvat-Papasseit — and Spanish — Antonio Machado and Miguel Hernández — poets. After twenty-five years in his professional career he is now a singer of worldwide fame.

Raimon, the singer of force, conviction and persuasion. Raimon (Ramon Pelegero Sanchis) is another important Catalan singer. Born in Xàtiva, in València, Raimon first sang in Catalonia at the age of 22, with devastating and electrifying energy. He was the cry of moving masses, becoming the key figure in the process of making young people aware of social and political affais in the sixties, in the period marked by the Franco regime repression. In addition to creating his own songs, he has put music to the work of contemporary poets such as Salvador Espriu, or historical ones such as Ausiàs Marc, Jordi de Sant Jordi and Roís de Corella. He had tremendous success in the Olympia, in Paris, and has performed and recorded his songs in the United States, France, Sweden, Germany, Mexico, Argentina and Canada, among other countries.

Marina Rossell, a poetic and powerful voice. Marina Rossell's voice is dramatic, poetic and powerful. She is one of the best equipped feminine singers to sway audiences into emotion. She entered the world of songs with the aid of Teresa Rebull, and eventually began to interpret difficult songs, pieces by Mikis Theodorakis and Rafael Subirachs, for example. She has been awarded prizes and has made successful records including *Si volíeu escoltar, Penyora, Bruixes i maduixes.*

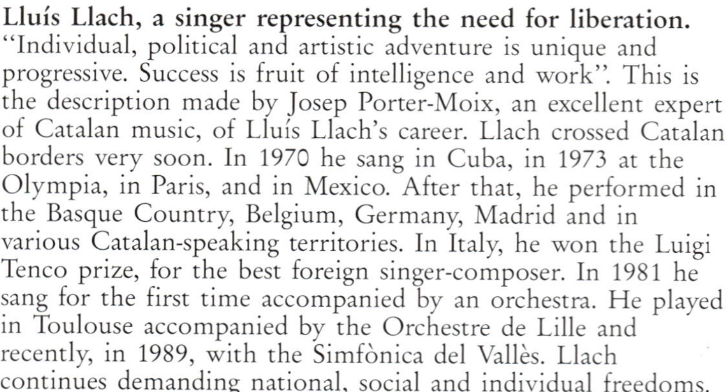

Lluís Llach, a singer representing the need for liberation. "Individual, political and artistic adventure is unique and progressive. Success is fruit of intelligence and work". This is the description made by Josep Porter-Moix, an excellent expert of Catalan music, of Lluís Llach's career. Llach crossed Catalan borders very soon. In 1970 he sang in Cuba, in 1973 at the Olympia, in Paris, and in Mexico. After that, he performed in the Basque Country, Belgium, Germany, Madrid and in various Catalan-speaking territories. In Italy, he won the Luigi Tenco prize, for the best foreign singer-composer. In 1981 he sang for the first time accompanied by an orchestra. He played in Toulouse accompanied by the Orchestre de Lille and recently, in 1989, with the Simfònica del Vallès. Llach continues demanding national, social and individual freedoms.

Maria del Mar Bonet, the musical charm of a Majorcan girl. The smile emanating from the face enshrouded in Maria del Mar Bonet's black hair is always accompanied by a charming voice gifted for the interpretation of songs. Since 1963, this Majorcan girl has delighted the Catalan Countries and the entire world with the power of her evocative voice. She has also performed, always in Catalan, in Denmark, England and France. In Paris she performed jointly with Moustaki. Later on she went to Venezuela, Poland, Yugoslavia and Italy. She has performed with Ovidi Montllor and with Pi de la Serra, and has put music to the lyrics of Joan Vergés, Josep Palau i Fabre and Bartomeu Rosselló-Pòrcel.

Tete Montoliu, a world famous piano player. This picture shows Tete Montoliu in a recital given in 1979 in the Palau de la Música in Barcelona, which was recorded live. Montoliu is considered to be one of the greatest jazz piano players in the world. His first international appearance was in 1961 when he played in the Berlin jazz festival. Since then, he has played in the most important jazz scenarios around the world. In 1977 he performed for the first time in the "Jazz Cathedral", Ronnie Scott's Club in London, with Georges Coleman. He has recorded more than fifty records mostly in Denmark, Holland, the United States, Germany, Italy and Spain. One of them was recorded with the participation of Chick Corea, a most celebrated jazz player.

Núria Feliu: a secure voice, a woman full of convictions. This is an image of Núria Feliu, an authentic and versatile singer, with a secure and penetrating voice. She is a woman of character and convictions and a cherished interpreter of both national and foreign pieces. Núria Feliu has sung all kinds of songs: Catalan, Brazilian and French authors, movie songs and cabaret themes. She has interpreted poems by Apel·les Mestres and Guillem d'Efak, lyrics by Albert Mallofré and Joan Manuel Serrat. She has also performed in theatres, on the screen, and in radio and television. She has been awarded national and international prizes. From her original home in Sants, she has taken her charming and melodious voice to the US, Switzerland, Venezuela, Montecarlo.

The *sardana*, a dance and an emotional motive. The *sardana*, which takes the shape of a ring made up of couples of dancers, is a dance of friendship. It requires precision, discipline, and rhythm in order to move to and fro, while keeping in time with the music and swinging in symmetry. It is also a motive of inspiration tending to become a symbol and an ideal. The poet Joan Maragall wrote "It is the sincere dance of a nation which loves and progresses through holding hands". It is a legitimate ideal, which stimulated the imagination of poets such as Max Jacob or Jules Romains, and moved the brilliant brush of Pablo Picasso, who depicted the *sardana* as an exploding circle of dancers adoring the peace pigeon.

Sardanes in Besalú. These dance groups, which we see decked out in the country's traditional dress, can be found in the main plaça of any Catalan city or town. They are testimony to the vitality of the *sardana*, an unmistakably Mediterranean dance which seems to descend from those of ancient Greece. The sardana is a joyful but restrained dance, even in its most exalted passages.

A *cobla* playing *sardanes* makes for a jolly atmosphere. Any pedestrian, whether local or foreign, can enjoy the lively air coming from the musical instruments of *cobles*, who play in many *places* in our towns and cities. The *cobla* is a specific form of musical ensemble that plays *sardanes*. Many scholars have tried to determine its origin without being able to specify with any degree of accuracy. We know, however, that the first written references to the *sardana* are dated in the second half of the 16th century, and that from the second third of the 19th century, the progression of the *sardana* can be traced up till the present day. Its popularity and vigour may be due to the fact that, as the composer Enric Morera says, the *sardana* "is a dance, a hymn and a song".

The interior of the Gran Teatre del Liceu, Barcelona's Opera House. With its ample orchestra section, five upper levels and seating for 3,500 people, the Liceu is the artistic setting that has given Barcelona universal renown. It was inaugurated in 1847, and was refurbished and redecorated in 1861, after suffering a fire, by a team directed by Josep Mirabent. At that time, it discontinued the representation of short comedies and Castilian drama and concentrated on opera, ballet and concerts. In its more than one hundred and forty years of existence, the Liceu has introduced many of the top voices of all times: Gayarre and Masini (1880-1890), Caruso (1902), Renata Tebaldi (1953), Maria Callas (1959), Plácido Domingo (1966), and Catalan opera singers such as Victòria dels Àngels (1944), Montserrat Caballé (1962), Jaume Aragall (1961) and Josep Carreras (1969). Ballerinas such as Anna Pavlova (1930), Margot Fonteyn (1966) and ballet dancers such as Rudolf Nurejev (1969) have also performed here, as well as conductors such as Richard Strauss (1901) and Igor Stravinsky (1924).

Victòria dels Àngels, a world famous soprano. Victòria dels Àngels, who is without doubt a universally known soprano, started her career in the Barcelona Liceu Theatre in 1945, with *Le nozze di Figaro*, and acted regularly there until 1950 and also in the 1955, 1956, 1958, 1961 and 1967 opera seasons. In 1949 she sang for the first time in Paris with Gounod's *Faust*; in Covent Garden in London with *La bohème*, by Puccini; and in the Teatro alla Scala in Milan. She made her debut in 1951 in the New York Opera House. An artist of delicate quality and a modest woman with great personality, Victòria dels Àngels was elected Member of Honour of the Saint George Royal Academy of Fine Arts (Reial Acadèmia de Belles Arts de Sant Jordi) in 1981.

Montserrat Caballé and Josep Carreras, opera singers world famous. Montserrat Caballé, soprano, and Josep Carreras, tenor, have brilliant careers and have gained the favour of the public in the most demanding theatres and auditoriums around the world. Montserrat Caballé was educated in Barcelona and started performing in Italy. She has been contracted many times by the Metropolitan Opera House in New York, and has a vast opera repertory. Montserrat Caballé discovered the quality and potential of Josep Carreras, who in the sixties was acclaimed in London, Milan, Paris and New York, performing operas by Verdi, Puccini, Giordano and Donizetti. After suffering a serious illness, Josep Carreras has returned to the scenarios and is now at the peak of his professional career.

L'Orfeó Català, the country's leading choir. L'Orfeó Català, possibly the most famous choir in Catalonia. It has performed for nearly a century in the marvellous scenario of the Palau de la Música Catalana, in Barcelona, which is surrounded by lusch Modern Style decoration. It was founded by Lluís Millet and Amadeu Vives, who led the choral society movement in Catalonia. It also had an international projection. In 1962 it made the European debut of *El Pessebre*, an oratorio by Pau Cassals, in Florence. In 1969 it presented, for the first time in Catalonia, the full version of J. S. Bach's *Christmas Oratorio.*

Discipline, precision and quality: the motto of the St. George Choir (Coral Sant Jordi). The St. George Choir is another choral association which has won domestic and international acknowledgement for its discipline, precision and quality. This group was founded by Oriol Martorell in 1951. It has cooperated in the mise-en-scène of theatrical and choral symphonic pieces. Its ample repertory includes Catalan and foreign folk songs, medieval and contemporay polyphonic music. This ensemble is a founding member of the Fédération Européenne de Jeunes Chorales.

Cantiga Choir (Coral Cantiga): international recognition. Since Josep Anselm Clavé created the first choral society, "L'Aurora", in 1845, Catalonia has been a dynamic and sensitive country with regard to music and choral interpretation. Today, a century and a half later, several groups stand out for their quality and for the international recognition they have attained. Among them is the Cantiga Chorale, founded in 1961 within Els Lluïsos de Gràcia cultural association. Its repertoire is very wide and includes diverse styles. It frequently participates in symphonic choral performances for radio and television.

Càrmina Chorale (Coral Càrmina) a singular repertoire. Of more recent creation than the Cantiga Chorale but on a similar level of performance, the Càrmina Chorale was founded in Barcelona in 1972. Its repertoire is wide, and distinguishes itself from other groups in its inclusion of unusual genres and pieces. It performs frequently in symphonic choral concerts, and has made various recordings. The Càrmina Chorale has been successful in numerous European cities.

Fashion shows: "Gaudí" Men's Show and "Gaudí" Women's Show. Backed by a long standing tradition which since the sixties has been led by pioneers such as Pertegaz, Balenciaga, Pedro Rodríguez and Assumpció Bastida, Barcelona is today one of the European fashion centres. The dynamism of original fashion design has led to the organization of two annual symposia dedicated to this activity: "Gaudí" Men's Show and "Gaudí" Women's Show. The images we see here correspond to models presented in the 1989 edition.

Andrés Andreu, an international fashion designer. The city of Barcelona has always been the centre of inspiration for fashion in Catalonia. Sometimes this has led to presentations of local creations, and at other times it has been a reflection of tendencies which have originated in Paris, London or Milan. Fashion designs produced in Barcelona by Pertegaz, Balenciaga, Pedro Rodríguez and Assumpció Bastida have been successfully exported. Today, at the beginning of the nineties, there are pioneers such as Andrés Andreu, whom we see in this picture.

Toni Miró: an invitation to the endless conquest of creativity. In the same line of fashion creativity we find Toni Miró, an ambitious professional who represents the present dynamics of fashion design in our country: "Barcelona is engaged in the conquest of fashion: the efforts multiply, demand increases, there is a tendency towards equilibrium between offer and demand. There are improved schools forming new designers, and institutional promotion has improved substantially". Miró speaks from a European perspective, where competition is present in the field of fashion design and there are no barriers protecting conservative or mediocre attitudes.

Dictionaries, international testimony of the language. The decade of the eighties has been characterized, among other things, by the intensification of the projection of Catalan culture beyond its borders. The Catalan Government has cooperated in this task through its presence in many international arenas, as well as through the promotion of translations of national literary works into other languages. Alongside this, however, has been the initiative of society at large. This is the case of publishing companies which have provided the Catalan language with the opportunity, by way of dictionaries of coming into the sphere of the world's major languages.

LLEI 7/1983, de 18 D'ABRIL, DE NORMALITZACIÓ LINGÜÍSTICA A CATALUNYA

EL PRESIDENT DE LA GENERALITAT DE CATALUNYA

Sia notori a tots els ciutadans que el Parlament de Catalunya ha aprovat i jo, en nom del Rei i d'acord amb el que estableix l'article 33.2 de l'Estatut d'Autonomia, promulgo la següent

LLEI

El català, llengua pròpia de Catalunya. La llengua catalana, element fonamental de la formació de Catalunya, n'ha estat sempre la llengua pròpia, com a eina natural de comunicació i com a expressió i símbol d'una unitat cultural amb profundes arrels històriques. A més, ha estat el testimoni de la fidelitat del poble català envers la seva terra i la seva cultura específica. Finalment, ha servit molt sovint d'instrument integrador, facilitant la més absoluta participació dels ciutadans de Catalunya en la nostra convivència pacífica, amb total independència de llur origen geogràfic.

Situació precària actual. Forjada en el seu territori i compartida després amb altres terres, amb les quals forma una comunitat lingüística que ha aportat al llarg dels segles una valuosa contribució a la cultura, la llengua catalana es troba des de fa anys en una situació precària, caracteritzada principalment per l'escassa presència que té en els àmbits d'ús oficial, de l'ensenyament i dels mitjans de comunicació social.

Causes de la precarietat. Entre les causes i els condicionants d'aquesta situació, hom en pot enumerar uns quants de decisius. En primer lloc, hi ha la pèrdua de l'oficialitat del català fa dos segles i mig, arran dels decrets de Nova Planta, els quals imposaren el castellà com a únic idioma oficial, mesura que fou reforçada en ple segle XX amb les prohibicions i les persecucions contra la llengua i la cultura catalanes desfermades a partir del 1939. En segon lloc, la implantació, a mitjan segle XIX, de l'ensenyament obligatori comportà que el català fos bandejat de les escoles de Catalunya, en les quals, fins al 1978 i llevat d'alguns curts períodes, només s'ensenyà preceptivament el castellà i en castellà. En tercer lloc, l'establiment a Catalunya d'un gran nombre de persones majoritàriament castellanoparlants s'ha produït durant molts anys sense que Catalunya pogués oferir-los estructures sòcio-econòmiques, urbanístiques, escolars i d'altra mena que els haurien permès una incorporació i una aportació plenes a la societat catalana, des de les seves

3

A language undergoing a process of normalization. There are two elements of the current Law of Linguistic Normalization which first attract the reader's attention. The first one is that the Catalan is "Catalonia's own language and the natural tool for communication" among Catalan people, although they also have to learn Spanish. The second is the acknowledgement of the poor situation the Catalan language is in, due to its scant presence in the public administration, public education and the media. Seven years have elapsed since the enactment of this law, and the situation has improved, but we are far away from reaching the final goal.

Catalan enters the commercial world. The process of normalization in the use of Catalan cannot be barred. Knowledge of Catalan by all the population is ensured through its generalized teaching in schools. In practice, the use of Catalan grows in spite of a gloomy initial outlook, thanks to the prestige of its institutional use and the role of Catalan television. However, Catalan has not made similar progress in the areas of commercial and industrial activities. In this respect, we must acknowledge that the city of Barcelona lags behind the rest of Catalan cities. Walking the streets of Manresa, Berga, Girona or the *plaça* in Vic depicted here, we will see that most commercial advertising is written in Catalan.

Linguistic immersion: a method of learning Catalan. Catalan inhabitants who were born elsewhere want their children to be completely integrated in Catalonia. They would like them not only to learn Catalan in school, but to study all subjects in Catalan. It is because of this that there has been an institutional promotion of "linguistic immersion". This is a pedagogical system for learning languages other than one's own, which consists in introducing the student in an atmosphere where all things are done using the language to be learned. In Catalonia, by using this method, we have applied a system made popular in Quebec (an autonomous territory in Canada where French is spoken), by the psychologist and pedagogue Lambert. It was surprisingly successful in Quebec. In Catalonia, in spite of some difficulties, it is also achieving good results.

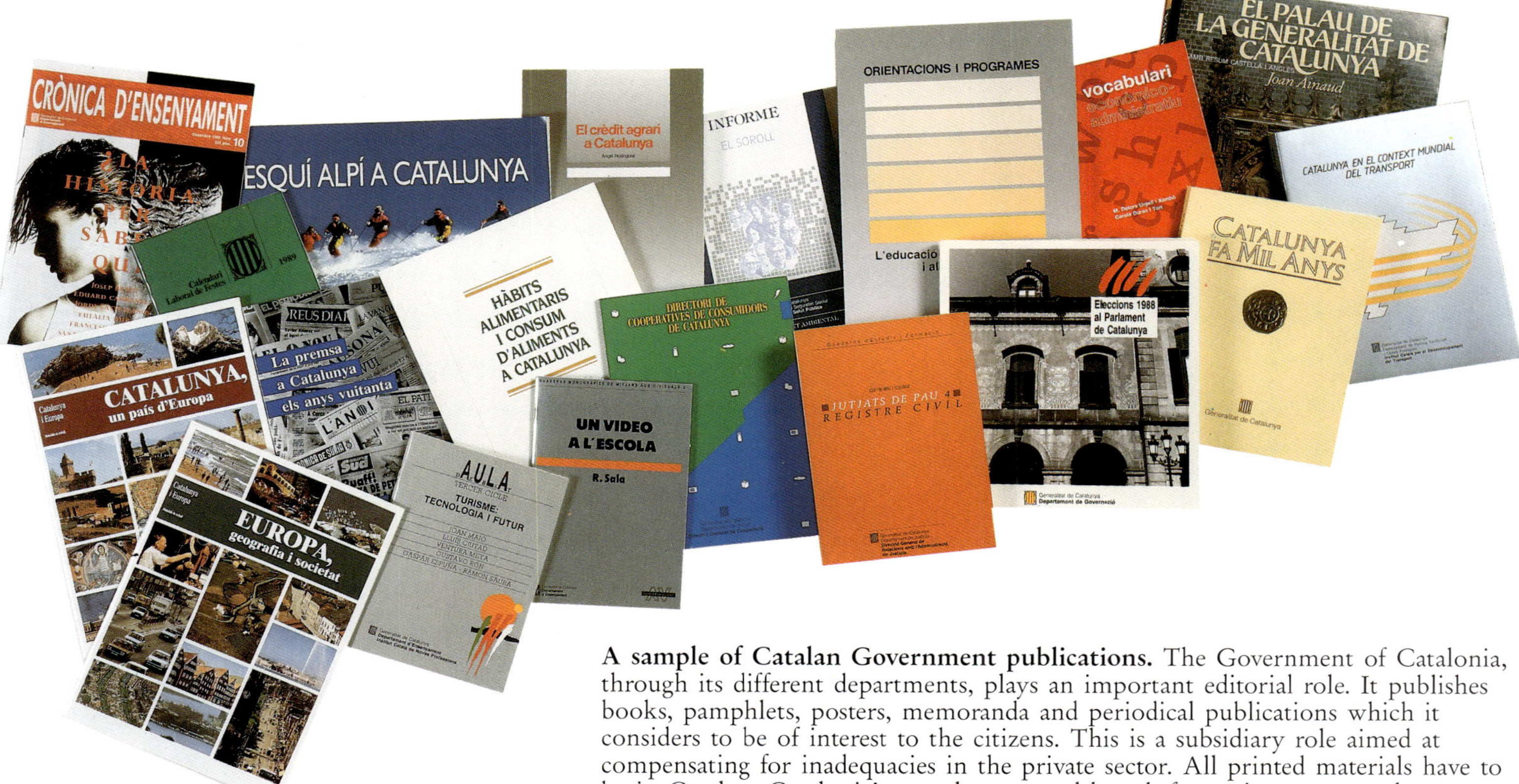

A sample of Catalan Government publications. The Government of Catalonia, through its different departments, plays an important editorial role. It publishes books, pamphlets, posters, memoranda and periodical publications which it considers to be of interest to the citizens. This is a subsidiary role aimed at compensating for inadequacies in the private sector. All printed materials have to be in Catalan, Catalonia's own language, although for various reasons there are translations into Spanish, English, German, French, Italian and other languages.

The importance of Catalan in restaurants and bars. The aim of linguistic normalization campaigns undertaken in restaurants and bars is to increase the use — oral and written — of Catalan in menus, price lists, advertisements, recommendations and all other types of communication. The Government of Catalonia makes available to businesses the necessary technical means to accomplish this, but equally important is the participation of professional associations, hotel management schools, and salesmen.

CHAPTER III

A COUNTRY WHICH IS PROGRESSING

This book is a brief account of the past and present of Catalonia, as well as a look at what she hopes to become in the future. It is published when the country has already celebrated her first Millennium anniversary. We have followed the History of Catalonia on a long trek which has led us up to the present day.

The world has changed a lot since the Catalan nation began its adventure. The world is now becoming a place where events are increasingly taking on a world-wide significance; a place which is criss-crossed with a dense network of communications, converting all countries into witnesses of the complex and dynamic vitality of the planet.

It is no less true to say, however, that no one wilfully gives up his or her identity, and daily experience shows us that each country strives to conserve its own characteristics. Catalonia is no exception. The country has begun its second millennium with two vital assignments ahead of her. The first is to ensure her survival as a nation, after emerging from the long tunnel of oppression. The second is to assert herself and make her contribution to the world at large.

The current President of the Catalan Government, the Most Honourable Mr. Jordi Pujol, is very explicit on the subject of the role Catalonia is to play in the context of the nations of the world. "Do not be surprised" he declared "if I speak of our future with optimism; not only with faith and hope, as I have done for years, and with confidence in ourselves, but with manifest optimism. Now that the situation has changed and now that the effort we made resisting has borne fruit, it is time to discover a new horizon for Catalonia".

TAKING UP POSITIONS IN THE EUROPEAN CONTEXT

Throughout her history, Catalonia has considered and felt herself to be a European country. In her more dynamic moments, Catalan culture has had an open, outgoing spirit and has sought to link up with what was going on beyond her frontiers. One need only remember the intensive and long-standing Catalan presence in the Mediterranean countries at the time of the zenith of the Catalan-Aragonese Crown in the 13th and 14th centuries. It is logical that cultural symbiosis should have caused the assimilation, both in the Principality and in the other two Catalan-speaking countries (the contemporary kingdoms of Valencia and Majorca), of the Humanist spirit which at that period existed in élite circles in Sicily, Naples and Sardinia, territories which had been conquered over the course of several reigns, from Peter II (1276-1285) to Alphonse IV the Magnanimous (1416-1458).

It would serve little purpose to try and proclaim the European nature of Catalonia over the last two centuries. However, it would be unjust to make no mention of the fact that the intellectual movement associated with the birth of the *Renaixença* was closely related to the romantic movement which at the time was very Present in European culture.

It must therefore be clear that it is not gratuitous to say Catalonia has a strong European vocation. This is true not only in the passive sense of Catalonia being a beneficiary of ideological fashions or artistic styles from Europe, because, at times, Catalonia has come out with her very own propositions for the whole continent. Someone has even said, that the Modernists had aimed to make Catalan culture the national culture of Europe.

What must be appreciated about this lofty ambition is the desire to make Catalan culture universal.

Nevertheless, Europe must not merely be seen as a

conglomeration of cultures that are open to exchange and mutual inspiration. It is also just as much an economic community about to unify its domestic market. In terms of economy, Catalonia is primarily a country which is open to international trade. Once the liberalization of the Spanish economy began in the sixties, the Principality progressively recovered her traditional verve for exporting and importing.

Spain joined the EEC on the 1st of January 1986. This event gave rise to a series of challenges for the Catalan economy. From that moment onwards, Catalan society began to adapt to the new European context. This process aims to enable our country to become accomodated to the full EEC transformation process which begins on the 1st January 1993. A huge effort will no doubt have to be made because Catalonia has a lower degree of development than the EEC average, as well as important infrastructural shortcomings.

Until now, the leading role in the configuration and development of Community Europe has been played by the States. Lately, however, and increasingly so, the regions of Europe are making their presence felt and aspire to carry out a significant role parallel to that of the States. European regionalism advances along two paths: the first of these is theoretical, and involves the acknowledgement, in certain cases, of national political entities with their own economic potential or distinct cultural identity. The second path is practical and organizational, and aims to achieve maximum operativity and real impact on the already existing institutions: the AER (Assembly of European Regions) and the Council of Cities and Regions of Europe.

The fact that the President of the Government of Catalonia has been elected president of the AER and that the mayor of Barcelona has also been appointed President of the Council of the Cities and Regions of Europe is a powerful support for Catalonia in Community Europe. Indeed Catalonia holds regular contacts with three economically developed regions of Europe and is considered to be one of the "four motors of Europe". There is no doubt, therefore, that a new period is beginning during which the objectives of self-government for the European regions with entity and capacity will receive a remarkable boost.

STRATEGY AND POLICIES

The Catalan Government has already drawn up policies for different areas such as economy, society, agriculture, industry, technology, education, professions, ecology, culture. These policies, considered as a whole, offer an overall strategy guaranteed to cope with all the problems raised by full incorporation into Europe in the forthcoming turn of the century. The different departments of the Generalitat Government are very much involved in this activity, as is the Catalan Pro Europa Board (Patronat Català Pro Europa), a body which was specially set up by the Government for this purpose.

Economy and finance

Despite the fact that Catalonia has a higher degree of development than the Spanish average, the country — as we mentioned before — is still below the EEC average. She must therefore take full advantage of available time to bring in necessary changes in her economic structure in a gradual and non-traumatic fashion. These changes must above all promote professional training, measures against unemployment, the development of rural areas and the modernization of agriculture, and encourage the building of new public infrastructure works such as the modernization of the railways and the construction of new major roads. The request for investment funds needed to carry out these projects, which are also of interest to the EEC, has been received with favour — and in certain aspects, possibilities of backing — by the EEC institutions.

In the context of finance, the key role played by the savings banks is also significant. The Caixa d'Estalvis i Pensions de Barcelona is the first financial institution in the Spanish State and one of the first in Europe. The Caixa de Catalunya and other Catalan financial entities also have a remarkable presence in the world of finance and banking. On the other hand, banking in Catalonia is almost entirely dominated by Spanish and foreign institutions. The Barcelona stock exchange is the second most important exchange in the State, accounting for 25% of the overall activity in this field. The shares of about 300 companies are quoted there.

Agriculture

In the first two years of EEC membership, Catalan agriculture suffered from the lack of coordination between the central and autonomous administrations. This was basically due to the incorrect interpretation of the powers Catalonia possesses in the area of agriculture. Despite these political difficulties and others f a financial kind, agricultural policies have been carried out with the adaptation of the sector to the new EEC structure as a constant reference point.

Furthermore, long-term policies have also been established. These policies aim to attain the following objectives: to encourage cooperation between the central and autonomous administrations; to ensure the participation of Catalonia in the general State agricultural policy; to improve the quality of products and commercialization processes; and to bring agricultural organizations into line with those of other countries in the EEC.

Industry

The establishment of the single European market as from 1993 gives rise to the birth of the largest consumer block in the world: 323 million inhabitants. With this impressive prospect as a point of reference, the Catalan industrial sector must take steps in the right direction. It must seek optimum financial backing and must operate — both when purchasing and selling — with the forthcoming constitution of a single-based economic unit in mind. Catalan industry has good prospects for participation in the EEC single market. But this calls for the following measures: a concerted effort for the promotion of technological research and development; the improvement of product quality, safety and design; the improvement of the commercial distribution network; the modernization of enterprises to adapt them to the characteristics of the European industrial set-up; and the close observation of new legislation brought out by the EEC.

Technology

Priority treatment is obviously needed for the advance of technological innovation and research if the country is to be brought up to required EEC standards. It must be borne in mind that Catalonia is still a long way below the European average in this field. Only 0.3% of the country's Gross Domestic Product is set aside for technological research, while the equivalent figure rises to 1.9% in the EEC, 2.5% in Japan, and 2.7% in the United States. The Generalitat Government, through the Catalan Pro Europa Board and the Enterprise Information and Development Centre (Centre d'Informació i Desenvolupament Empresarial, CIDEM), gives out information on the principal innovation and research programmes (BRITE, RACE, ESPRIT, etc.), and makes them available to Catalan enterprises.

Education

One of the fields calling for swift and decisive action to stop the country falling far behind European standards, is the professional training and preparation of young people. After the publication of the report called *The Europe of the Citizens* in June 1985, major projects associated with education have been appearing.

Examples of these are the COMETT and ERASMUS programmes, aimed at encouraging a European approach to the joint cooperation between universities and enterprises. Several proposals have also been made for the teaching of languages and the introduction of new technologies into the world of education. With EEC projects and the situation of our country in mind, the Catalan Government set up the Catalan New Professions Institute

(Institut Català de Noves Professions), which, amongst other activities, pinpoints future professional and educational needs, and focusses reconversion programmes on these areas.

Services. Tourism

The size of the services sector in Catalonia is similar to the average in EEC countries in terms of proportional share of the Gross Domestic Product. Within the structure of the sector, however, tourism is a highly developed subsector.

It must be noted that Catalonia is today the most important tourist area in Europe and that the expectations for the forthcoming years are highly encouraging. The Single Market implies an increase in local EEC tourism, as well as a more competitive context. This will call for the modernization of the tourist product and an improvement of the offer.

The commercial services subsector is already adapting to a new situation characterized by a major increase in the availability of consumer products and the establishment of large commercial centres in urban districts.

Professional activity

Not only are merchandise, products and services that circulate freely since the begining of 1993. Individuals from EEC countries are also free to move around Europe in their professional capacities. EEC professionals are thus able to come and work in Catalonia, and the Catalans have the option of working in any EEC member State. At present,
the standards of our professionals are at the same level as in the rest of EEC countries. However, the incorporation of new technologies into work systems and the modification of the legal framework of specific activities are factors that should not be overlooked.

Environment

With the introduction of the Single European Act, environmental protection takes on even greater importance. The Generalitat of

Catalonia, which has legislative powers in the area of the environment (within the general framework of Spanish State legislation), as well as executive competence over the question of industrial waste and sewage disposal in State waters on the Catalan coast, has already adapted its regulations to EEC requirements. Recently the Generalitat has created a Department which is to be exclusively involved in this area.

Cultural policy

One last very important point is the question of cultural policy. Europe has always been a leader in the quest for new achievements and new ground for the development of cultural expression. Appropriate conclusions have been drawn regarding this question, as history bears out. Nowadays, however, we are immersed in a world dominated by industrialized cultural agents, with greater facilities for exchange amongst cultures — and even among civilizations — and with an increase in the number of people benefiting from cultural products. This situation calls for serious reflexion on what has correctly been termed "European culture". EEC countries have elaborated a basic programme covering five fields: the creation of a European cultural area; the promotion of the European audio-visual industry; access to cultural resources; cultural training; and interchange with the rest of the world's cultures.

Catalonia, a country with her own specific brand of culture, which is different from that of Spain, is at present seeking to make its presence felt and to find its place in the varied and polyvalent context of European culture. We will once more refer to this subject at a later stage.

DYNAMICS AND CAPACITY FOR DEVELOPMENT

Catalonia before the challenge of Europe

Action within the territory

The challenge represented by full integration into Europe obliges Catalonia, and particularly the public sector, to resort to her full range of drive and capacity for development. It is vital to modernize and extend service networks. In this context, the projects drawn up may be placed into three groups: road network, railways and water supply.

As regards the Road Plan, part of the planning and execution work has been initiated on the optimum network plan for the following twenty-five years. Apart from the Barcelona byways, which relieve traffic problems in the city centre and enable the city to be crossed without entering it, various sections of motorway are to be built, and the one joining two important industrial cities — Terrassa and Manresa — has been completed, extending the Barcelona-Terrassa motorway as far as the E-09 section of the European Emerald Network. Another project of special importance, for the effect it will have on the whole country, is the Transverse Axis Road. It will take advantage of already existing roads, crossing Catalonia in an East-West direction, joining Lleida with the Mediterranean coast, by way of Cervera, Manresa, Vic and Gerona.

As regards railway network projects, Catalonia is shortly to start building a new line between Barcelona and the French border. It will have an international gauge, enabling the connection with the European High Speed Train network. Furthermore, the connection with important Spanish cities — Zaragoza, Madrid and Sevilla — and the establishment of an efficient railway communication with

Europe will improve both the passenger service and goods transport.

Another of the basic services to ensure development and future prospects is the water network. Without water it is impossible for a human settlement to survive. If the supply of water is not guaranteed, the progress of a country is uncertain. There is enough water in Catalonia, but a system for its rational use has not yet been established. At this moment, the autonomous Government of Catalonia has the powers and responsabilities it needs to guarantee the fulfilment of a coherent and efficient policy of water exploitation. Generalitat of Catalonia activity is aimed at improving the usage of water resources by way of the introduction of modern technologies. Catalonia can now boast of works already in service or projects under way, apart from projects which are to be carried out in the future. Let's see the realizations: the diversion of water from the Ter to the Maresme, Vallès and Barcelona areas; the Abrera plant for Barcelona and Baix Llobregat area consumption, and, a little later on, for the Penedès and Garraf areas too; the recovery of Ebre delta canal excess water for industrial purposes as well as for Camp de Tarragona and Baix Penedès borough use; the Rialp reservoir to improve the regulation of the river Segre and to introduce new irrigation works into the Garrigues and Segarra counties; and the Llosa de Cavall reservoir, to make full use of the river Llobregat.

Looking ahead, the Government of Catalonia Administration pays special attention to all those elements that affect the complete water cycle, so that water returns to the environment after proper treatment, respecting the balance of nature and the environment, and enabling it to be reused or returned to the sea without risk of pollution.

New technological centres for industry

The Automobile Applied Investigation Institute has finished the construction of a trial track complex and an automobile laboratory, which fulfil all the requirements of similar centres at an international level. The Institute contributes, in this way, to technological improvement, and to the increase in the quality and progress of the automobile in the social, industrial and academic contexts.

In the field of technology, the Catalan Autonomuos Administration has constructed the General Tests and Research Laboratory, which basically aims to cooperate with industry by way of tests and research on specific technical problems raised by private companies, by individuals or by the public administration. In order to face up to the challenge of the European single market, the Generalitat's Department of Industry and Energy has put several laboratories into service: the mechanical structure laboratory, the termotechnical laboratory, the illumination and photometry laboratory, the fire detection laboratory, the robot technology laboratory, the laser application centre and the advanced chemistry pilot plant.

Part of the infrastructure of this complex has been co-funded by the European Regional Development Fund (ERDF).

The promotion of agriculture, and protection of the environment

In the agricultural field, the Generalitat Government's major concern is to take action in the more depressed zones of the country. There are five main projects aimed at strengthening irrigational infrastructures, and correspond to the canals of Algerri-Balaguer (la Noguera), Segarra — Les Garrigues and Les Garrigues Baixes (Segarra, Les Garrigues, Urgell and Segrià), the canal of Low Ter (Baix Empordà) and of L'Aldea-Camarles (Baix Ebre) and of Xerta-river Sénia (Baix Ebre and Montsià). Another project is the so-called "*Regs del riu Montsant*", which will benefit the Priorat, the county with the lowest individual income rate in Catalonia. This project foresees the transformation of 1,450 hectares of dry agricultural lands into irrigated cropland, as well as the construction of three reservoirs.

The Department of Agriculture, Livestock and Fisheries carries out intensive research work at the Agricultural Food Stuffs Research and Technology Institute (Institut de Recerca i Tecnologia Agroalimentària, IRTA). A new IRTA centre has been built at Cabrils. It is representative of the high technological level achieved in the agricultural research field.

In the field of research, the Catalan Government also pays special attention to agricultural professional training of a double nature — combining theory and practice — for a more efficient and satisfactory incorporation of young people into activities in this sector. Two achievements stand out in this direction: the Solsonès Agricultural Training School and the Santa Coloma de Farners Forestry School.

In the line of faithfulness to demands for protection of ecological reserves, the Catalan Parliament enacted (in December 1990) a Law for the Conservation of Flora and Fauna in the Medes islands sea-floor area, on the Costa Brava, near L'Estartit port. There are further norms for the protection of several areas of great ecological land and sea wealth.

To govern, protect and communicate the country

Besides those physical actions carried out within the territory — actions which we have already mentioned — the Government must also see to the moral action concerning the country's inhabitants, the organization of society, the protection of people and their patrimony, the prevention of special situations which may affect the whole community of the country.

Within the wider framework of the set of laws that affect territorial organization, Catalonia has brought back a territorial unit with historical roots and a geographical and commercial justification, the *comarca* or county. As time passes, so the *comarques* (counties) behave more and more as authentic local bodies, with their own juridical character, with specific powers and responsibilities and autonomy for the fulfilment of their own objectives. The validity of the recovery of the *comarca* as a territorial unit capable of running the country depends, to a large extent, on the county councils, institutions which are to be the basis of local administration activity. The standard of living of the inhabitants of Catalonia and the guarantee for the equality of opportunities for citizens throughout the territory depend on the organizational capacity and efficiency of these councils.

The growing concern over the protection of individuals and their belongings is worthy of mention. The Emergency Coordination Centre was created in 1990 to this effect. It has been conceived and designed as a back-up instrument for all those organizations and authorities with responsibilities in cases of emergency, public disaster or widescale catastrophe.

Within the narrow margin offered by the autonomous competences in this area, the Police School of Catalonia has taken on a more solid structure, and now has the means with which to form an élite security force, the Mossos d'Esquadra, with specialists in various aspects of this profession.

The need to coordinate communications services in an organized and coherent fashion, and the lack of radioelectric channels with which to do so, has led the Generalitat to create an integrated telecommunications network. There are basically three kinds of radio communication and data transmission systems. Communications between radio units (Autonomous Police, Fire Brigades, Town Halls, Hospitals, etc.). Communications between mobile and portable unit users in local areas of a limited range. And communications between regular stations at local or branch headquarters, from points integrated in the microwave network.

The system basically comprises 82 posts which act as base stations in a trunking system and as repeater stations of the microwave digital multichannel links. These stations are situated in regional rings which are united by an inter-regional or national ring.

Health, social welfare and administration of justice

If we are to consider the question of the standard of living every citizen of a developed country may aspire to, we must examine the future projects associated with health and social security. Catalonia, through the Generalitat's Department of Health and and Social Security Catalan Health Service currently benefits from a decentralized health service, which is structured in a balanced division of the territory into health regions, with a remarkable level of autonomy. The establishment of the new system will logically lead to a new hospital policy based on the promotion of county hospitals, on the exploitation to the full of those already existing resources and on the progressive application of advanced technology. One of the novelties which must be pointed to in the period 1990-95 is the *"Vida als anys"* ("Life to years") Programme, of social and sanitary care for elderly people with chronic illness. In this field of health, the existence of the Nuclear Magnetic Sounding Centre at La Vall d'Hebron Hospital, and the creation of the High Technology Hospital Diagnosis Ward for the improvement of a good many pathologies, must also be mentioned.

As important a field as that of health is individual welfare within society. The Government of Catalonia, by way of its Department of Social Welfare, is active in the most depressed areas of towns and cities. Among the overall actions one must mention the Interdepartmental Minimum Income Insertion Plan (PIRI), which offers aid and training for people with low incomes. Apart from this the number of old people's homes and resource centres for the training of adults has increased. One of the objectives motivating the activity of this Department of the Government is to bring the Administration's services closer to the citizens and enable them to obtain a quick and suitable response to their needs. Finally, there is also another area which calls for permanent attention: that of the homes for people with profound psychic disabilities, which are also being created as the need for them appears.

The Government of Catalonia's Department of Justice is working with a view to the future, and aims to contribute to the improvement of the overall efficiency of the judicial system. Intensive action is carried out in those fields it holds powers and responsabilities in. Worthy of special mention are, for example, the construction of centres related either with the penitentiary or the Justice for Minors fields: a Preventive Penitentiary centre at Sant Esteve Sesrovires; a penitentiary hospital at Terrassa or the Minors Observation and Treatment Centres at Lleida and Girona, a Girls Treatment Centre at Girona, and the Penitentiary Centre at Quatre Camins at la Roca del Vallès. With the future incorporation of powers and responsibilities in the Justice

Administration field, the Generalitat Government has begun a series of rationalization activities and the automatization of the judicial offices, the improvement of judicial buildings and the construction of new offices.

Commercial structure and tourist offer

Catalonia has traditionally been a country with a special flare for commerce. In the 13th and 14th centuries, as well as being a military power, the country had been responsible for commercial enterprise throughout the Mediterranean sea. At the end of the 20th century, and as part of the growing tendency towards a tertiary economy and a greater stress on the quality of products and services, it is necessary to adapt commercial structures and activities to the new situation. The lines of reform advocated by the Department of Commerce, Consumer Affairs and Tourism are: the promotion of the modernization process for small and medium-sized commercial enterprises; the improvement of collective commercial infrastructure; and special attention and technical assistance for the salesperson.

Catalonia has for centuries been a country with a special attraction for tourists and foreigners. Having both sea and mountains, its natural beauties and plentiful samples of historical and current artistic interest contribute to this continous flow of tourists. In this context, the Generalitat Government's line of activity will be aimed at: creating new accomodation centres and modernizing ones that already exist; promoting nautical and sports centres and encouraging winter sport tourism (eg. and cross-country skiing).

Aims in education and culture

At the beginning of the nineties, Catalonia faces the challenge of having to incorporate a new educational system that is to be adopted throughout the Spanish State — a system which will substantially modify the current structure, because it makes education compulsory from three to sixteen years and redefines the educational levels. To make the application of the new system

as correct and efficient as possible, it was necessary to have a precise and through description of the educational reality of the country. This is the task the Generalitat Government's Department of Education has set about fulfilling with the preparation of the School Map of Catalonia. It lays down schooling plans for the next ten years. The School Map establishes the way to ensure the right of junior citizens to a better education, and to make their eventual incorporation in society more harmonious and satisfactory. The Catalan University Map undergoes substantial changes. Since 1990, the Pompeu Fabra and the Ramon Llull Universities have been added to the three already existing. The university centres at Girona, Lleida, Vic and Tarragona-Reus are also to be modernized for the year 2000.

As regards the future of culture, it is obvious that Catalonia is working harder than ever on two fronts, now that it has the competences with which to do so. The first front involves the conservation of the spiritual heritage accumulated over the course of the centuries by the Catalan people, and which is the country's foremost treasure. The second front involves the promotion of the creative stimulus which is to ensure the survival of the Catalan community insofar as it is unique and contributes to the wealth of the huge and varied collage of the world's cultures.

In the field of infrastructure, the obligation of seeing to new needs and new aspirations has crystrallized in several projects which are to be carried out in the first years of the nineties. We are referring here to the Barcelona Music Auditorium which has two concert halls: one for symphonic concerts, with a capacity for 2,600 people, and another for chamber music concerts, with a capacity for about 700. One characteristic about this Auditorium is that it houses the Music Museum, an Advanced Music Studies Centre and a Sound and Score Library.

Catalonia, a country which has played an important role in the evolution of contemporary art — at an international level — has a contemporary Art Museum as from 1992. The aim of this museum is to have an art collection which is representative of the major artistic tendencies to have sprung up since the fifties, both at a national and a international level, and also to act as an arts promotion centre, organizing exhibitions and documentation and research facilities.

The National Theatre of Catalonia has been conceived in two separate buildings. The first one has a monumental nature and will have two halls: one with a capacity for 1,000 people, designed in a traditional fashion for performances of the classical repertoire; and another for experimental or avant-garde theatre with capacity for 400 viewers. The second building will have a workshop for the production of stage sets, and facilities for the training of new actors and theatre technicians.

Outside Barcelona, two important projects have been completed. The National Archives, at Sant Cugat del Vallès, conceived of to store and conserve historical documentation associated with Catalonia and documents produced by Generalitat Government bodies. The second realization is the Science and Technology Museum at Terrassa. It is situated in a fine Modernist building, and has collected about 5,000 articles related to the world of science, technology and industry.

Towards a more technical approach to sports pedagogy

As a result of a long sports tradition, Catalonia now has a remarkable amount of sportsmen in every speciality. This was the reason for the creation of the High Sports Performance Centre at Sant Cugat del Vallès. However, this sector, which in the field of competition and its pedagogy requires an increasingly specialized form of technical training, calls for change in the way its trainers are prepared. It is for this reason that those responsible for sport and education in the Catalan autonomous administration, have organized a programme for the modernization of sports education. This programme involves the unification of trainer preparation criteria, this enabling the homologation of Catalan studies and titles to those existing in EEC countries.

The incorporation — both academic and administrative — of European system requirements enables Catalonia to become involved in the ERASMUS project and to benefit from the exchange of technicians throughout the EEC.

Apart from seeing to the pedagogical aspects of sport, the Generalitat's General Secretary's Office for Sport pays special attention to the country's sports organizations. A computer plan

has already been put into service. It responds to the Administrative needs of federations, clubs, organizations, sportsmen and citizens, providing all kinds of information and communication associated with sport.

The task of society

In the miscellanious section we have presented on Catalan social life, in which the dynamics and the will for development must be fully taken into account, especially with regard to the future, we have only made reference to the task carried out by the public sector as such. However, it must be remembered that Catalonia has always based its progress on the vitality of the private sector. It is probably due to the fact that periods of self-government have been short-lived over the course of the country's history and that progress has come by way of private initiative and the cooperation initiatives between the private and the public sectors which are producing excellent results. As an example of this we must mention the Catalan Research Foundation which has created the Supercomputer Centre of Catalonia, which is linked up to international networks.

THE BARCELONA OLYMPIC GAMES

In 1992, Catalonia was faced with an exceptional challenge which put all the country's capacity as an organizer and as a host to test: the celebration of the Olympic Games. On the 17th October 1986, Barcelona (a Mediterranean city resulting from two thousand years of a history marked by the passage of Greeks, Romans, Visigoths, Arabs, Franks, as well as people from other more recent nations), was chosen as host city of the 25th Summer Olympic Games. Dreams had come true, and Barcelona, an open and hospitable city, the capital of the Catalan nation, celebrated the great event.

It would not have been possible to justify Barcelona's candidature as host city of the Olympic Games, if, apart from her historical background, she had not had a solid economic and commercial infrastructure behind her. Nor would the Games had been a success without the enthusiasm of Pasqual Maragall, mayor of Barcelona, and the good management of the Barcelona Olympic Committee.

There is yet another factor favouring nomination of Barcelona as the Olympic city: the passion for sport. This fact was recognized by the father of the modern Olympic movement, Baron Pierre de Coubertin, who in 1926 declared: "Before coming to Barcelona, I thought I knew what a sporting city was...". Half a century later, Mr. Avery Brundage, president of the International Olympic Committee, corroborated this opinion about this outstanding feature of the city. "I have discovered", he said, "a new aspect about the feeling for sport: here in Barcelona, sports centres are primarily for those who practise them...". This praise must not lead to senseless complacency. Nevertheless, it has contributed towards strenghthening morale in the face of a challenge of such importance as the 1992 Olympic Games.

Three dates for renovation: 1888, 1929, 1992

Barcelona, apart from being the capital of Catalonia is one of the great cities of the Mediterranean. A city is a live being which needs to continually modernize itself and stimulate its own vitality with new projects. For this reason, Barcelona has undertaken major expansion and modernization projects twice during its recent history: with the 1888 Universal Exhibition, and with the International Exhibition in 1929. Both exhibitions gave the city a different look, enriching its urban texture and strengthening its metropolitan character. They also acted as platforms for the promotion of its European image and universal projection. The year 1992 is the third transcendental moment in the evolution of a city that the Ibers founded over twenty-six centuries ago.

The objectives Barcelona set itself for the year 1992 — objectives which must nonetheless be seen in the context of the horizon of the year 2000 — may be grouped in three fields of activity.

The road network

The first of these fields involves the road network. Barcelona is an excessively densely populated city, and needed a ring road to facilitate a quick bypass system around the city. This was made possible by way of the construction of two sizeable projects: the coastal bypass ("Ronda Litoral") and the bypass which passes through the higher part of the city ("Ronda de Dalt").

This ring road, which completely surrounds the city without a break, forms a large 36 km circle which acts as a traffic distributor for the different areas of the capital and also links up all Catalan motorways.

The bypass — great throughway within the city's structure — has carried out an essential link-up role between the four Olympic areas we will refer to later on. The extension of the peripheral road network facilitates the clearance of excess traffic from the city centre. It is thought that about 900,000 vehicles are able to enter and leave the city daily without any difficulty.

The importance of these projects has called for cooperation between the local, autonomous and State administrations.

The second activity area is centred on two new throughways: the Western Axis, situated in the vicinity of Tarragona street, and which crosses the city from north to south; and the Eastern Axis, which involves the reconversion of a large space which extends from Plaça de les Glòries to the old Nord Station. This part of the city is set aside for cultural and leisure activities. In the setting of a vast square, which is called Plaça de les Arts (Arts Square), three important cultural buildings have been built: the Barcelona Music Auditorium, the National Theatre of Catalonia and the Aragon Crown Archives, which have already been mentioned as new cultural centres.

The four Olympic areas

The first two objectives, the bypasses, were a key aspect to the Barcelona of the year 2000, where as the third was more closely associated with the 1992 Olympic Games. It involves the construction of four Olympic areas called: La Vall d'Hebron, Diagonal, Vila Olímpica (Olympic Village) and Montjuïc.

The La Vall d'Hebron area is situated in the north of the city, and covers 87 hectares. The promotion of this area, where a very modern cycle track already existed, involved the construction of more sports areas and new urban parks. The area that is to be more closely associated with the Olympic Games has been equipped with the following installations: a sports complex with indoor *frontons* (Basque "pelota" courts), tennis courts and archery competition ranges and practice areas.

The Diagonal area is in the north-western part of the city, and has for many years been the area with most sports facilities: FC Barcelona's Camp Nou football stadium, the Pslau Blau-grana, the Miniestadi (small football stadium), the Royal Polo Club, the El Turó Tennis Club and the Barcelona University sports facilities. With the year 2000 in view, urban development of the area is to be completed with the construction of a new sports complex, the preparation of can Rigal park and the construction of a new road to link Barcelona with the adjoining town L'Hospitalet de Llobregat, which is also the second largest city in Catalonia.

A new urban area: Vila Olímpica (Olympic Village)

Among all those operations which have been undertaken in Barcelona in the period leading up to the turn of the century, the Olympic village is the most important in terms of urban regeneration. Apart from the recovery of four kilometres of beaches, it means the creation of a new coastal district, fully incorporated into the city, which modifies and modernizes the whole seafront. The Olympic Village is in one of the places in which industrial development concentrated most factories at the turn of the century. This new urban area has its own beaches and parks where citizens may relax and take their leisure. It has been called "Icària", because the first working class settlements in last century's El Poblenou had taken on this name in honour of the settlement which Étienne Cabet, a Utopian socialist, founded at that time in the USA. In this part of the Olympic village there is a new marina, where both sailing and motor boats may moor. The New Congress Hall (Palau de Congressos), a commercial centre and a coastal services complex are completed with the construction of maritime parks, involving new beaches and green belt areas for leisure.

Finally, Montjuïc is to be the area concentrating the great sports installations which make up the so-called "Anella Olímpica" or Olympic Ring. The development of the Montjuïc area, an isolated mountain 173 metres above sea level, was carried out for the Barcelona International Exhibition in 1929. Some of the current Barcelona Fair and Municipal Stadium buildings date from that period. The Stadium has been modernized and has been the major setting for the 1992 Olympic Games, having considerably increased its capacity to 70,000 spectators. Besides modernizinng all the interior part of the building, the external façade has been done up conserving the style of its first period, symbolizing in this way the historical wish of Barcelona to host the most important of all sporting events — the Olympic Games.

The Palau Sant Jordi (St. George Palace) is truly remarkable. It consists of the principal sports pavillion and another multi-use construction. The original conception of its design is the work of Arata Isozaki who envisaged a large surface covered in metal space mail 45 m high, presenting a visual image that blends with the sinuous forms of Montjuïc mountain.

Another of the components of the Olympic Ring is the National Physical Education Institute of Catalonia, which has been conceived of as a University Sports Faculty, with a capacity for 1,000 students and 100 teachers.

In order to blend this whole sports complex with the surrounding countryside, the Migdia park, which is to occupy 52 hectares, has been planned. This park includes a new botanical garden and an open-air auditorium with a capacity for 100,000 people. Montjuïc mountain has always been this city's green belt area, but from now on it will also be a key spot for sports, cultural and leisure activities.

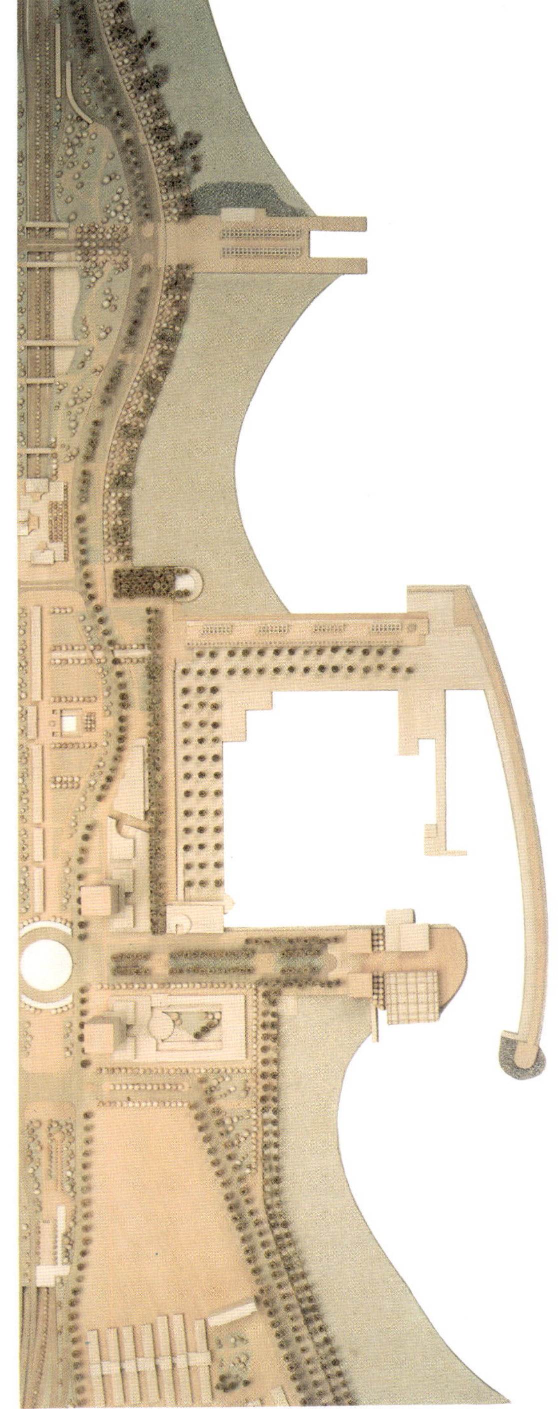

A unique challenge in the history of Catalonia

Barcelona, in keeping with the city's traditions as a seat of culture, undertook an ambitious programme called *Olimpíada Cultural* (Cultural Olympiad). In this way the original Hellenic concept of Olympiad (a four-year period) was recovered, having the Summer Games as its culmination. Festivals and exhibitions were the basis of the Cultural Olympiad. The festivals will cover different fields — theatre, dancing, classical music and jazz — and the exhibitions will feature monographic themes each year.

The economic impact of the Games has been of remarkable dimensions. To cover infrastructure works, equipment and sports installations, direct investment amounting to 900,000 million pesetas was required. The overall effect of the Olympic Games on the economy of the Spanish State is almost 2.8 billion pesetas. It has also involved the dedication of over 75,000 people a year, during the 1989-1992 four-year period.

The challenge of the Olympic Games has been, therefore, extraordinary — an occasion without precedents in the history of Barcelona and Catalonia. It is not only the city of Barcelona that has been put to test by this grand occasion, but the whole nation. It is the whole of Catalonia that has responded before the world for the technical capacity, the quality of its citizenship, the solidity of its social make-up and, when all is said and done, its national consistency.

THE IDENTITY OF A SMALL NATION

When looking into the future, a country such as Catalonia — a nation without a state of its own — must analyse its real chances of survival, and preserve its identity through the periods of change any country is exposed to on its passage through history.

It has been said many times that Catalonia is a "small" country. From a geographical and demographic point of view, this statement is undoubtedly true. However, from a moral point of view, there is no such thing as "important" countries or "less important" countries. This is especially true if these so-called "small" countries continually show a will to exist, overcoming the obstacles they find in their path.

If we consider the great ages of the history of mankind, countries, nations and states are born, develop, undergo change and die, giving way to new human groups which will mark a new age of mankind. If we take a closer look at shorter periods — centuries or millennia — during which a specific group holds together, retaining its group memory and accumulated experiences in what may be termed its "national or group spirit", then we have come face to face with a case of a stubborn will to survive. All countries with a basic quota of internal coherence and sense of identity have a will to survive through time and a certain determination to "perpetuate" themselves. This is exactly Catalonia's case at a time when the country is embarking upon its second millennium.

However, the historical circumstances we are faced with are not altogether favourable. It would seem that this situation, which is characterized by an ever-developing and continually expanding technology, does not respect the cultural identity of each country. In our own natural European context, we detect the presence of an ever-perfecting and inexorable form of technoculture. Today's

Europe is characterized, among other features, by the loss of individual identity, by the empire of computer-programming, by control of public opinion, by the standardization of education, by market strategies, by the generalization of mental trends, and by the invasion of social habits of all descriptions. Needless to say, this situation is not limited to Europe, and is the same the world over.

It would be absurd and unjust to qualify all these phenomena as "bad" or undesirable. But there is no doubt that the sum of all these elements — especially when there is no control — tends to weaken the cultural identity of different countries. The general feeling is that one sole universal culture (of a prefabricated, superficial and alienating kind) is beginning to prevail over us, more or less perceptibly, dictated by the most powerful economic groups and obedient to the interests of the countries with the greatest stock of natural resources.

Certain present-day thinkers propose we pay special attention to the creation of art and the promotion of literature as an antidote to the progressive deterioration of the various cultures. The limitless expressions art is capable of producing, especially in the case of the literature of different languages, must compensate for the worrying threat facing the identities which define the nations concerned. We must bear in mind that there is only one Earth, but not just one man, and, as the Portuguese thinker José Saramago says, "each culture is a universe: the space which separates them is the same as the space linking them together, just as the sea, here on Earth, both separates and joins together the continents".

If we see Europe and the world as puzzles made up of different cultures — each one endowed with its own particular identity — each piece making its vital contribution to the overall harmony, it is understandable that the Catalan culture should strive to survive and surpass itself. It is therefore logical that at this stage in the integration of the countries of Europe, Catalonia should reassert her identity. It is not in the least strange that Catalan culture should not be resigning itself to deterioration and disappearance, or to hibernation as a marginal or residual culture.

We may conclude that Catalonia must attain three objectives in order to ensure her survival in future years. The first is to consolidate her identity, a subject we have studied in depth in this book. The other two objectives are to ensure her cultural permeability and the projection of her image abroad.

By permeability we mean the internal will of every human group to be receptive and to incorporate what other contemporary cultures are coming up with in their own continuous process of creation.

By projection abroad we mean permanent readiness and effort to make other cultures participate in the wealth of output generated by the spirit and genius of the country, in every possible area of creativity. It is not really possible to speak of a "unique culture" unless a highly developed identity is achieved. Neither would it be proper, however, to highlight this "uniqueness" if the cultural context of a country were not given the scope it needed to rise up above itself, for the benefit of neighbouring cultures, alongside which she is to mark a specific era of mankind.

On the threshold of a second Millennium, and confiding fully in the capacity and determination of the citizens of his country, the current President of the Catalan Government made the following observations: "There is one future which is in the hands of God. It is not for me, nor for anyone else, to meddle in this area. We can only have faith in its outcome. But there is another brand of future which is within our reach, and though I do not know if it ensures us another thousand years of life or not, I know that it does indeed ensure — if we so wish — a particular way of passing through the world, a way of living, creating and contributing towards making Catalonia a worthy nation".

The Catalan Pro Europa Board — a connection nexus. At the beginning of November 1986 a branch of the Catalan Pro Europa Board (Patronat Català Pro Europa) was inaugurated in Brussels in front of the European Community headquarters. The picture shows this event, which President Pujol attended. The Generalitat of Catalonia does not have a say in the integration process. It is interested, however, in following up and analyzing the possible consequences that it will have for Catalonia. This is the objective of the Catalan Pro Europa Board, which is entrusted with promotion, coordination, and cooperation with other private entities, and is also involved information and documentation activities related with the Community and its interaction with our country.

Community financial aid for road construction. During the first two years of Spain's membership in the European Community, Catalonia has been granted financial aid by most of the different Community funds. More specifically, it has received aid from the European Fund for Regional Development (EFRD) for projects jointly undertaken with the Generalitat of Catalonia. In 1988, the Generalitat submitted 20 projects (11 for railroad transportation, 6 for roads and hydraulic works, 1 for road transportation and 1 for industry). This picture shows one of the roads for which financing was granted; it stretches from Manresa to Puigcerdà.

Meeting to draw up the Single European Act. This picture was taken at the meeting convened by the representatives of the different member States in order to elaborate the European Act, which was completed in Luxembourg on February 17th, 1986. The introduction to this treaty, which substitutes previous ones and lays down the basis for the Community, expresses the conviction that the idea of a united Europe and the results already achieved in the political and economical fields, both correspond to the will of a democratic community which considers the European Parliament, elected by universal suffrage, to be an indispensable means of expression. The article affirms that "the objective of the European Community is to jointly cooperate to achieve a united Europe".

Catalonia, the European Community, and 1992. This is a picture of the official presentation of the book *Catalunya a la Comunitat Europea* (Catalonia in the European Community) at the Sant Jordi Hall in the Palace of the Generalitat of Catalonia. This book includes a sectorial study on the impact that full European Community membership will have on Spain in 1992, when the European Market is created. This book is an essential instrument for those wanting to understand the evolution of the Catalan economy within Europe during the first two years of integration, and also for those interested in the formulation of plans to further adapt to the consequences of the implementation of the European Act.

The Parc Tecnològic del Vallès (El Vallès Technological Industrial Estate), focus of industrial activity. In Catalonia there is a high degree of industrial concentration around the city of Barcelona. Eighty percent of the work force and 78 percent of the total production in Catalonia is concentrated in its industrial belt. Over the last few years the Vallès county has experienced continued expansion due to industrial promotion under the name "Parc Tecnològic del Vallès". Several reasons made this area the obvious choice for this project: the availability of a qualified work force, the proximity to Barcelona's harbour and airport, and the existence of a transport and communication network. As a consequence, many national and multinational companies have set up in this area.

Segments of the motorway between Barcelona and Terrassa. The motorway network in Catalonia has grown constantly over the past twenty years. In 1970 there were 130 km of motorway in use. In 1987 this figure was already up to 599 km. The rest of the road network is made up of 10,571 km of primary and secondary roads. The main axis is the highway traversing Catalonia from north to south. It branches near Tarragona towards Lleida and continues until Saragossa. There are also shorter segments with high traffic volume connecting the most dynamic industrial nuclei: Barcelona-Mataró and Barcelona-Manresa crossing Terrassa and Sabadell, as shown in this picture.

The systematic control of motor vehicles: A means of avoiding accidents. The experience gathered by the Industry and Energy Department in the field of technical control of motor vehicles *Inspecció Tècnica de Vehicles* has resulted in an increase in the number of sites this Department disposes of throughout the counties of Catalonia. One of them, located in the Bages, can be seen in this picture. Among the most important irregularities detected are deficiencies in the suspension, brake systems, and axles. Without doubt the control of these deficiencies has contributed to a decrease in the number of road accidents.

Refrigeration techniques applied to wine. The Catalan Wine and Vineyard Institute (Institut Català de la Vinya i del Vi, INCAVI) has taken steps in support of the modernization of this important agricultural and industrial sector. Among other actions a yearly programme to train technicians in the most recent advances in wine elaboration and control has been drawn up. It also divulges the use of refrigeration techniques as applied to wine and related activities. Another important part of its technological support consists of providing wine companies with refrigeration equipment, similar to that seen in this picture.

Systematic actions against water pollution. The main objective of the Sanitation Board (Junta de Sanejament) is to combat water pollution through the financing of projects (water treatment plants, collectors for sewage, water purifiers, etc.). The Sanitation Board is an autonomous body of the Generalitat responsible for the coordination of planning with the various administrations. In 1985 it installed a water purifier station, on the river Anoia, in Igualada, as can be seen in this picture. In later years it has carried out works on the rivers Ter, Llobregat, Besòs and Segre.

Room for "in vitro" culturing in the IRTA. This is a room for "in vitro" culturing in the Vegetable Genetics department of the Agricultural Food Stuffs Research and Technology Institute (Institut de Recerca i Tecnologia Agroalimentària, IRTA) of the Generalitat in Cabrils. The objectives entrusted to IRTA by the Agriculture, Livestock and Fisheries Department of the Government of Catalonia are the following: to foster research and technological development in the agro-industrial field; to facilitate the adaptation of scientific advances into practical uses; to foster its own research as a means for technological transference; and to coordinate these activities with other government agencies and private companies so as to optimize the use of available resources.

Geothermal station of Samalús. Cooperation between the European Community and the Generalitat in the field of energy has crystallized in the form of finance for a series of specific projects: territorial and time distribution of the demand for energy, electrification of isolated country houses and geothermal exploitation. The geothermal station at Samalús, depicted here, constitutes a good example of the latter. This station is used as a source of heating for greenhouses and to harvest algae for protein and domestic heating.

The treatment of industrial waste. The Sewage Board (Junta de Residus), an agency associated with the Territorial Policy and Public Works Department, has promoted the construction of several treatment plants. This has made it possible for Catalonia to eliminate most of the industrial waste generated here. This picture shows a scale model of an industrial waste treatment plant. According to a plan previously established by the Generalitat, there were twelve authorized companies for industrial waste treatment at the end of 1989. The Sewage Board also exercises technical examination and inspection functions to ensure that legal norms are complied with.

University library in Lleida. Over the last few years, college education, which is heavily concentrated in Barcelona, has experienced a process of decentralization which has been beneficial in facilitating the access of Catalan society to higher education. There are now college faculties in Lleida, Girona and Tarragona, most of which are associated with one of Barcelona's colleges. In Lleida, there are Law, Philosophy and Literature faculties. The latter faculties share this library, which is located in a space of modern inspiration, which is luminous, functional and austere.

A permanent centre for the exhibition of products of craftsmanship. The Generalitat Permanent Arts and Craft Centre was inaugurated in 1986 in the Passeig de Gràcia in Barcelona. It occupies 1,300 m^2, and is an excellent showplace for the exhibition of Catalan craftsmanship. Craftsmanship in Catalonia is backed by a long standing tradition, but lacks sufficient means to advertise itself. In the country there are many zones of interest, such as Olot (religious imagery), La Bisbal d'Empordà and Verdú (ceramics), Sant Hilari Sacalm (fire-elaborated wood), Breda and Miravet (pottery) and Vall del Riu Ges, in Osona (carpentry).

The Santa Mònica Art Centre; a space for contemporary art. Contemporary art centres have proliferated in Europe during the eighties and have become an alternative to conventional museums. They do not attempt to collect, store and preserve art pieces — as museums do. Contemporary art centres fix their sight on the present and future, are attentive to the present-day situation and try to encourage creativity. The Santa Mònica Art Centre inaugurated in 1988 by the Culture Department of the Generalitat, is a great place for the exhibition of contemporary art. Artists from the Basque country, València, *chicanos* from Los Angeles (USA) or Germans from Cologne, have lately exposed in this new institutional space devoted to contemporary art.

Educational effort to breach the gap between Catalonia and Europe. Several actions in the educational field are being undertaken to place Catalonia at the level required by integration into Europe. One of the most relevant ones is the introduction of computing technology in the classrooms. The goal is not only to provide hardware, but to furnish educational material and, more above all, to teach how to use it. This is the aim of an educational programme known as "Educational Computer-Programming Programme" ("Programa d'Informàtica Educativa", PIE) of the Education Department of the Generalitat, which operates with the support of the European Social Fund. There are people who are already qualified to create computer-supported teaching materials, which are more and more necessary in a society that evolves at the same pace as computing sciences.

Incorporation to the European arts. Our country has always been open to artistic initiatives from Europe. As a result of this, our incorporation to the task of building a common European artistic space — one of the aims of the European Community programme — has not been difficult. Over the last few years artists from other European countries have exhibited their work in Catalonia. As an example we can say that in 1985 the Culture Department of the Generalitat sponsored an exhibition of Holland's contemporary artists, with the title *Original d'Amsterdam*. Alphons Freijmuth was one of the selected artists. Shown here is one of his works called *Brandende Balk* (Burning balk). He is a disconcerting painter due to the use he makes of colour and shape that provokes certain dramatic tension.

El Masnou marina: one of thirty-six. El Masnou, constructed in 1975, offers a complete array of possibilities for water sports as well as facilities to moor all types of boats and vessels. Over the last few years, Catalan sea ports have either adapted or built new facilities in order to keep pace with the growing demand for sport vessels. There are thirty-six nautical facilities along the 580 km of Catalan coast with over 10,381 mooring points. The Generalitat, which controls 95 percent of them, manages the facilities and promotes the number as well as overall quality of sea-sports facilities.

Ski lifts in Vaquèira-Beret. Vaquèira-Beret is one of the better equipped ski stations in Catalonia. It is situated at the eastern end of the Aran valley, close to the source of the river Garona which flows towards France. It is surrounded by high mountains and its steep inclines are appropriate for skiing. In clear contrast, Pla de Beret is the most suitable place for cross-country skiing, making for a varied winter sports offer. The ski resorts is equipped with many facilities, and in its surroundings many hotels can be found, as well as apartment buildings, shops and entertainments. It all ensures a comfortable and pleasant stay. At present there are twelve ski stations in Catalonia, making it a privileged spot for the practice of winter sports.

The TGV, a necessity for communicating with Europe. Good communications are a must for a country forming part of the Europe of the nineties. Catalonia today stands a good chance of competing internationally because it has managed to build a suitable highway network connected to Europe and the rest of Spain, thanks to effort and planning coming mainly from the private sector. Now is the time to work in the same way on the railroads. Because of this, the Government of Catalonia has proposed to the Spanish Central Government that the width of Spanish railroads be adapted to the European standard. It also advocates for the construction of a high speed train (TGV) like the one seen in this picture, covering the route Paris-Le Mans.

A sports marina for all kinds of competitions. On the occasion of the Olympic Games, the city of Barcelona will enjoy a new sports marina which we can see in this photograph of its construction. It will serve for sailing competitions as well as for pleasure craft. It has an extension of 7 hectars of harbour and 6 of pier, and has been designed to form a harmonizing element within the coastal façade of Barcelona. This new port is a symbol of the perpetuation of the links between the city and the Mediterranean, which extend back to prehistoric times.

The Vallvidrera tunnel, an access into Barcelona. The Vallvidrera tunnel is, according to landscape experts, the most complex operation to have been carried out in the Barcelona metropolis and its surrounding area. In the political context, its construction has required the support of all political organizations involved. This major work exemplifies the will to improve the connection between the capital and the Vallès area, an industrial county in full growth, overcoming the obstacle of the Collserola range. Those responsible for this new fast means of communication have been aware that they were operating in the heart of an area rich in vegetation — an age-old green belt area for Barcelona — and have managed to combine the transformation process with respect for the natural environment.

A giant in the Barcelona landscape. Barcelona's geographical environment has changed since technology has managed to place a "giant's" foot of cement and iron on one of the highest spots in the Collserola range. The "giant" is the work of North American architect Norman Foster, and is 268 m high. It is a construction which function as a telecommunications tower and which starts to function for the Olympic Games. The central core, made of thirteen metal floors, was raised from the ground in an operation without precedent in the world. The series of cables that raised the body of the "giant" is the same one to sustain the construction in the air. A spectacular lift climbs up as far as the panoramic view-floor 115 m above ground level, over 600 m above sea level.

To assist the lives of the less fortunate. In Sant Joan Despí, near the city of Barcelona, the Generalitat of Catalonia has created this residence for the severely mentally handicapped. A civilization concerned with the economic progress and well-being of its healthy members cannot be called humane unless it also makes the effort to care for its less fortunate members.

Caring for the elderly, a responsibility of the just. As important as one's health is one's social well-being at every age. Caring for the elderly, for those who have contributed their efforts to the progress of their country and, for that matter, to all of humanity, is the responsibility of a just society and a demonstration of its concern for the dignity of the individual. This terrace is part of the Residence for the Elderly, recently established by the Department of Social Welfare of the Generalitat of Catalonia. Next to the residence is a Resource Centre for Adult Education.

Museum of Science and Technology. These pleasing views are from the interior and exterior of the Museum of Science and Technology of Terrassa, established in the old Aymerich i Amat modernist style textile factory. The objective of this museum is to gather a complete model of the evolution of science and technology, as related to the country's industrial development. The museum is now in the final phase of remodeling and preparation, but it already disposes of an important base: more than 5,000 pieces in all.

Inside, an exhibition of old cars. Among other exponents of the technical world, the Terrassa Museum brings together a collection of old cars which have been made in Catalonia. This is the case of those made at the beginning of this century by the company Hispano Suiza de Automóviles — a factory created by a soldier called Emilio La Cuadra and a Swiss technician called Marc Birkigt in 1899. The society which founded the car factory underwent various changes and, in the twenties, began to make aeroplane engines. After the Civil War, in 1946, it was absorbed by the National Industry Institute (INI) and gave rise to the company Empresa Nacional de Autocamiones (ENASA). Hispano Suiza cars were always considered to be luxury vehicles.

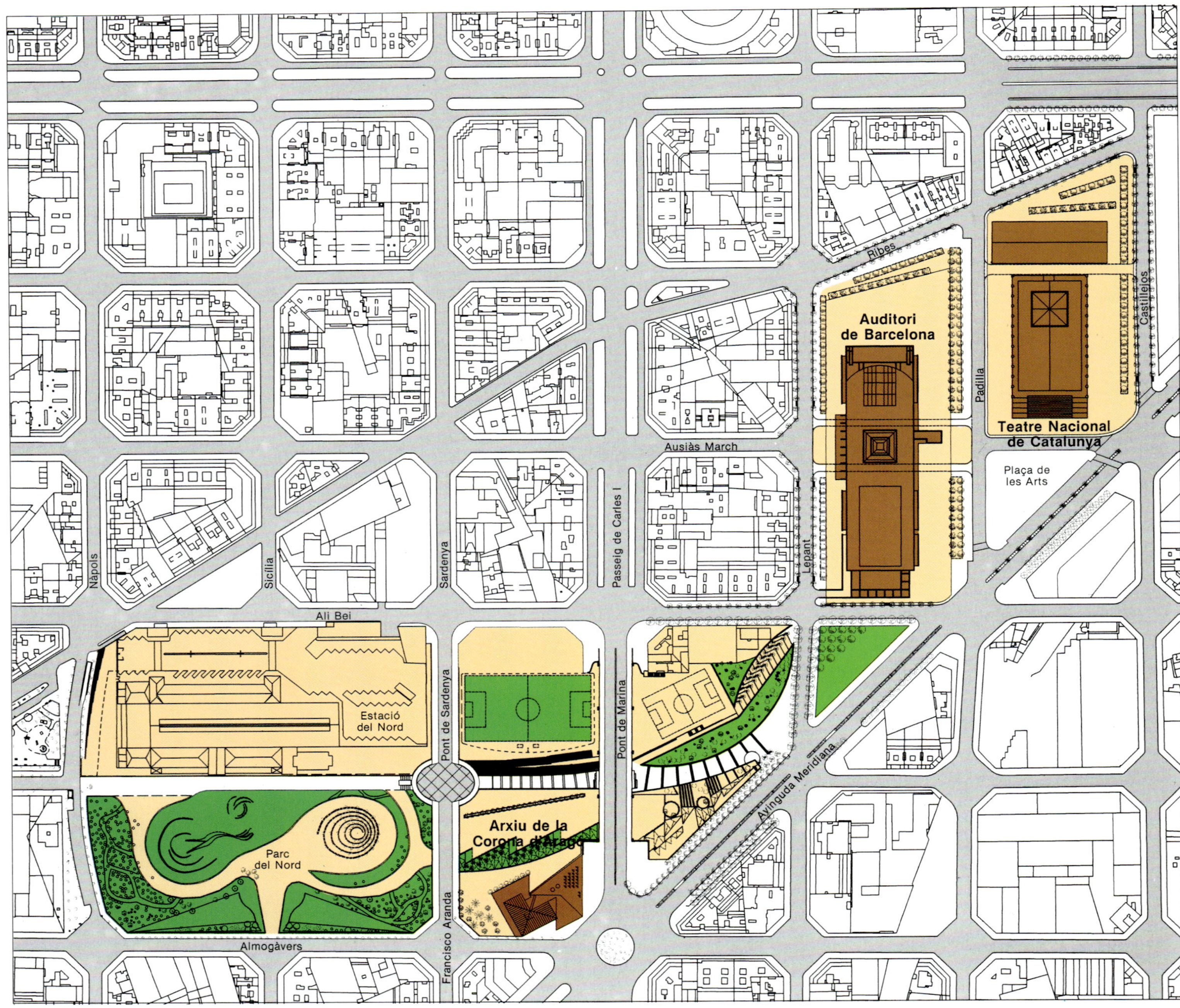

New and ample spaces for culture. The National Theatre of Catalonia, the Barcelona Auditorium and the Crown of Aragon Archives are concentrated on a huge 90,000 square metre area, which had formerly been occupied by the old Estació del Nord, the terminal station for all passenger trains until 1972. The plan shows areas set aside for the practice of sports and those reserved for park and garden areas. These latter areas are benefitting from the presence of the sculptures "Cel caigut" (Fallen Heaven) and "Espiral arbrada" (Tree-clad Spiral), the work of the North American artist Beverly Pepper. The building of the old train station has been rehabilitated and adapted for sports and leisure activities.

The new Music Auditorium of Barcelona. In this final stretch of the twentieth century, Catalonia is working towards creating the infrastructures demanded by the fruits of its modern-day culture. Barcelona, which already had two important musical centres — the Liceu Theatre, built in the 19th century, and the Palau de la Música, from the turn of the century — will soon boast another, with the new Music Auditorium which can be seen in this model. It will consist of two concert halls: one for symphonic music and the other for chamber music. A singular characteristic of this auditorium is that it will include the Museum of Music, a centre for Advanced Musical Studies, and a library for books, recordings, and musical scores.

The National Archives of Catalonia. One of the most important projects in the cultural infrastructure of Catalonia is the National Archives. The project is based at Sant Cugat del Vallès, near Barcelona, an area which has a rapid an efficient communication with the city. This archive — a model of which can be seen here — has as its primary function the gathering and conservation of historical documentation related to Catalonia, as well as that produced by the bodies of the Government of the Generalitat.

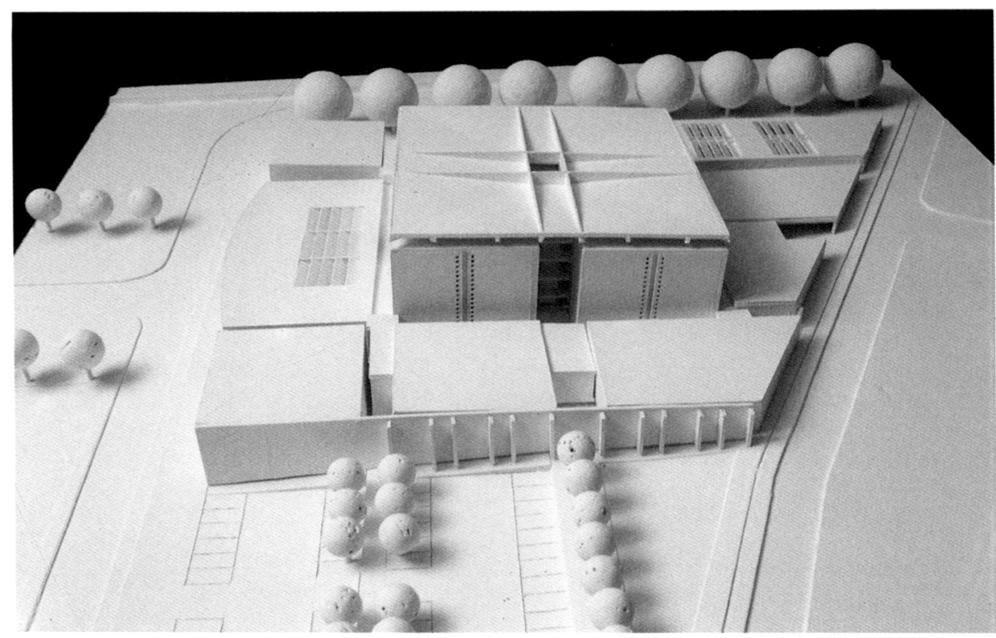

The Museum of Contemporary Art. The city of Barcelona, and Catalonia in general, have played a singificant role in the evolution of contemporary art, on a worldwide scale. One need only recall the names of Picasso or Miró, Dalí or Tàpies. It is for this reason that the city needed a Contemporary Art Museum. The objective of this museum is to exhibit a representative collection of the most important artistic tendencies to have taken root since the fifties, on a national and international level. At the same time, it will be a centre for the promotion of the arts, a platform for exhibitions, and a resource centre for documentation and research.

The National Theatre of Catalonia. Model of the National Theatre of Catalonia, made up of two independent buildings. Situated at the intersection of the city's major arteries (Gran Via, Meridiana and Diagonal), it will constitute, along with the Music Auditorium, the most important cultural centre in Barcelona. The theatre is divided into three zones: the Hall, the *Sala*, and the *Casa*. The Hall resembles an interior patio and will serve as a meeting point. The *Sala*, the heart of the building, has a circular form and an inclined orchestra pit, which directs the spectator's attention to the stage. The Hall and the façade of the *Sala* are enshrouded in a big glass superstructure.

A new building for the General Aragonese Crown Archives. This building will house the archives that have until now been kept at the Palau del Lloctinent, a 16th century building in the heart of the Gothic Quarter. The importance of these archives lies in the fact that they possess the document fund of the old Royal Catalonia-Aragon Chancellery, to which other document funds such as the Royal Diplomatic Charters (13th-18th centuries) a series which includes 50,000 items, must be added. The new building, designed by Roser Amadó and Lluís Domènech, has a large capacity. The storage area has 15 Kilometres of shelves.

An authentic motor-racing stadium at Montmeló. This illustration can really be said to be an historical document. It dates to the opening day of the Circuit of Catalonia, situated in Montmeló, on September 29th 1991, on the occasion of the Spanish Formula 1 Grand Prix. Since 1975, Catalonia, a country with a great following of motor-racing events, had not had suitable facilities to be a centre of World Championship qualifying events. Now it has: 4,747 metres of track, with a spectacular winding course, which holds a capacity audience of more than 60,000 spectators. The highest tribute it has received at this initial stage is from the President of the International Motor-racing Federation: "This circuit, an authentic motor-racing stadium, is the best in the world".

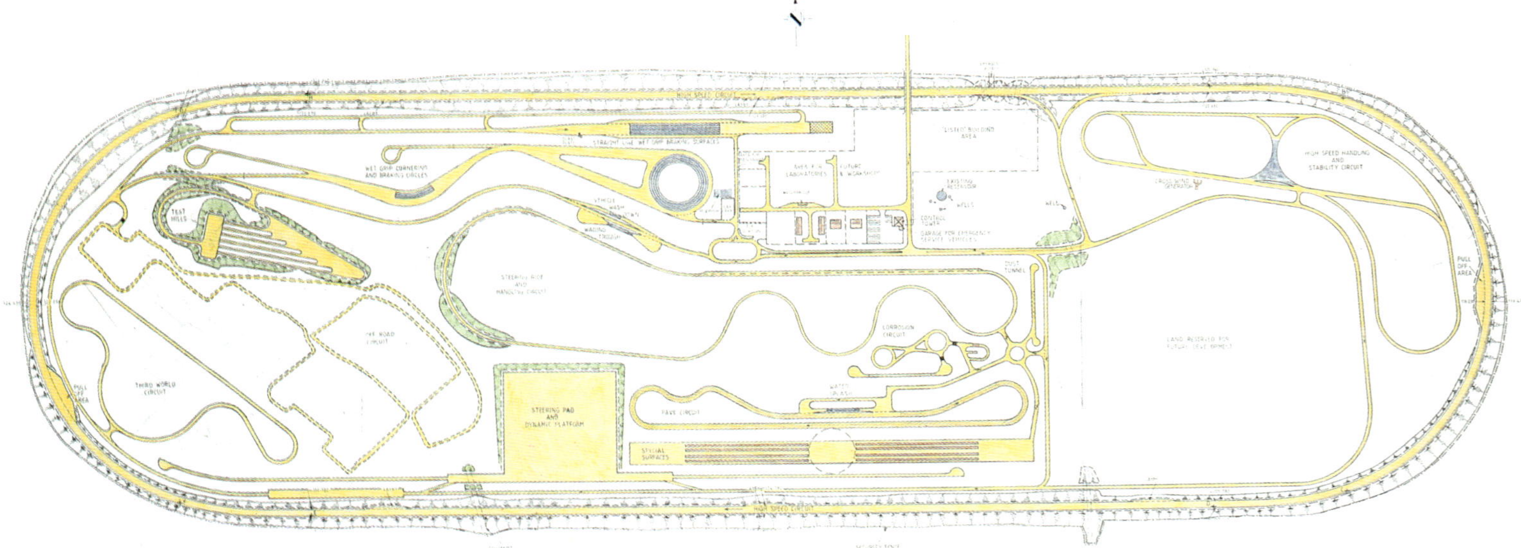

Plan for the automobile test circuit. With the above map, we may get a glimpse of the test circuit which the Generalitat of Catalonia Institute for Applied Research on the Automobile will put into operation very soon. Apart from this complex of tracks, the above-mentioned Institute has announced plans for a laboratory for the automobile. Both projects will, without doubt, contribute to the improvement of technology and to the role of the automobile in various areas: social, industrial, and academic.

Water for 2,500,000 people. This model, proof that aesthetics need not be incompatible with large-scale hydraulic projects, describes in miniature the future Llosa de Cavall dam. This new reservoir, located in the flow of the Cardener River, guarantees a reliable water supply for 2,500,000 inhabitants of the city of Barcelona and its surrounding areas. Llosa de Cavall, proposed by the Generalitat to the central Spanish Government as an alternative to the Jorba reservoir project, has clear economic and social advantages.

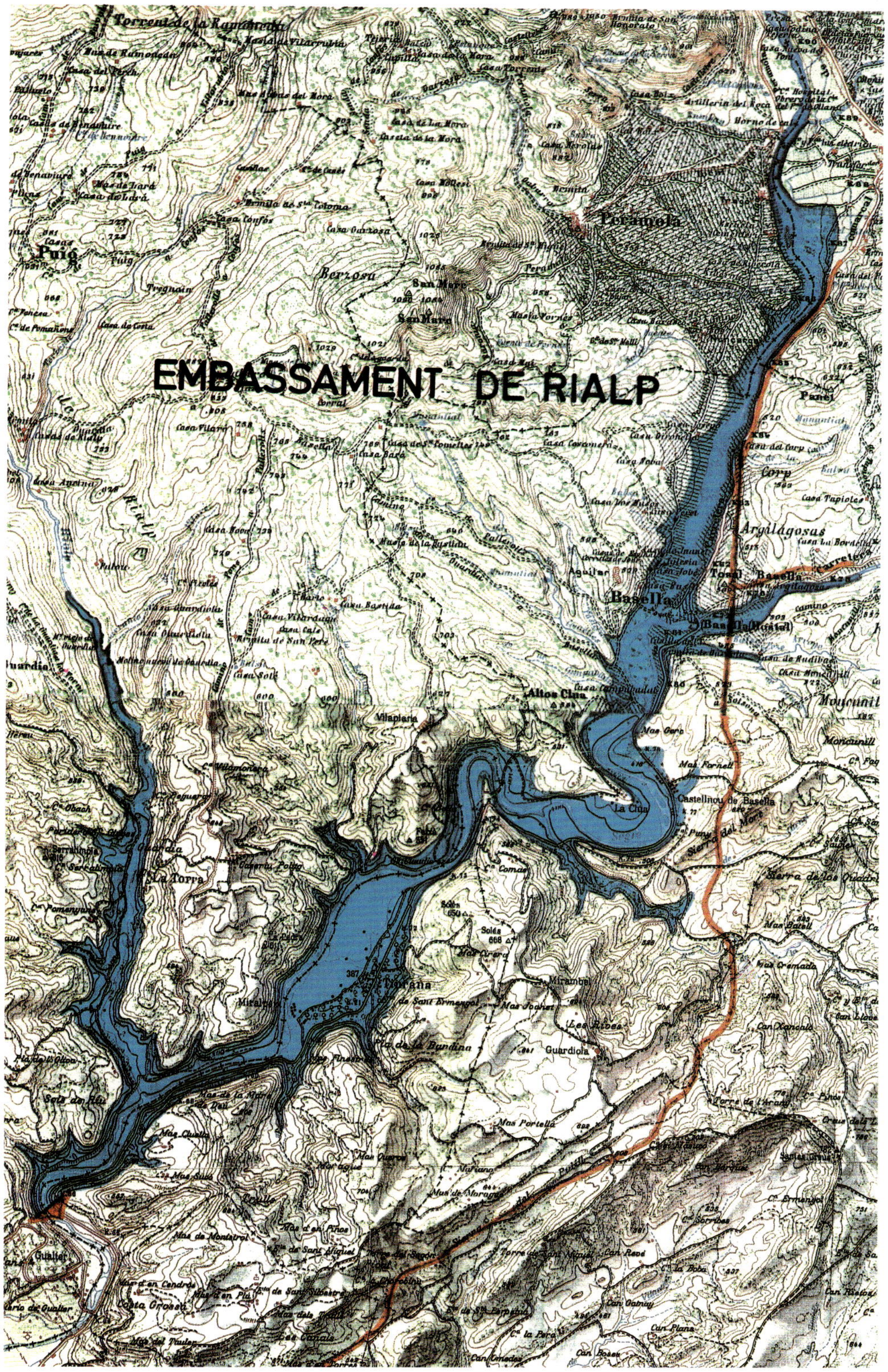

Rialp, a reservoir to take advantage of the Segre. One of the most important water resource projects which have been carried out is the resevoir of Rialp, which makes more efficient use of the Segre River basin. The water collected at Rialp allows 50,000 hectares in the regions of Garrigues and Segarra to be converted into irrigated farm land. The Catalan Statute of Autonomy guarantees Catalonia the right to develop its own policies for the supply, regulation and maintenance of water, and the construction of Rialp puts that directy into practice.

Experiments and research for industry. The autonomous administration of Catalonia has begun the construction of the General Tests and Research Laboratory. The purpose of this multi-disciplinary entity is to collaborate with industry through the carrying out of tests and research projects addressing specific technical problems proposed by private industry, by individuals, or by the administration itself. This laboratory is still in the development phase. Nevertheless, it already possesses 16 technological areas, including: electricity and physical experimentation, mechanics, electronics, chemistry, rubber and plastics, construction, accoustics and vibrations, computer sciences, and laser applications.

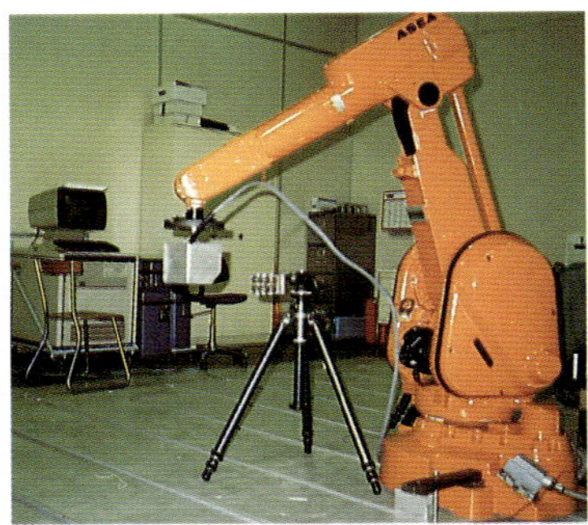

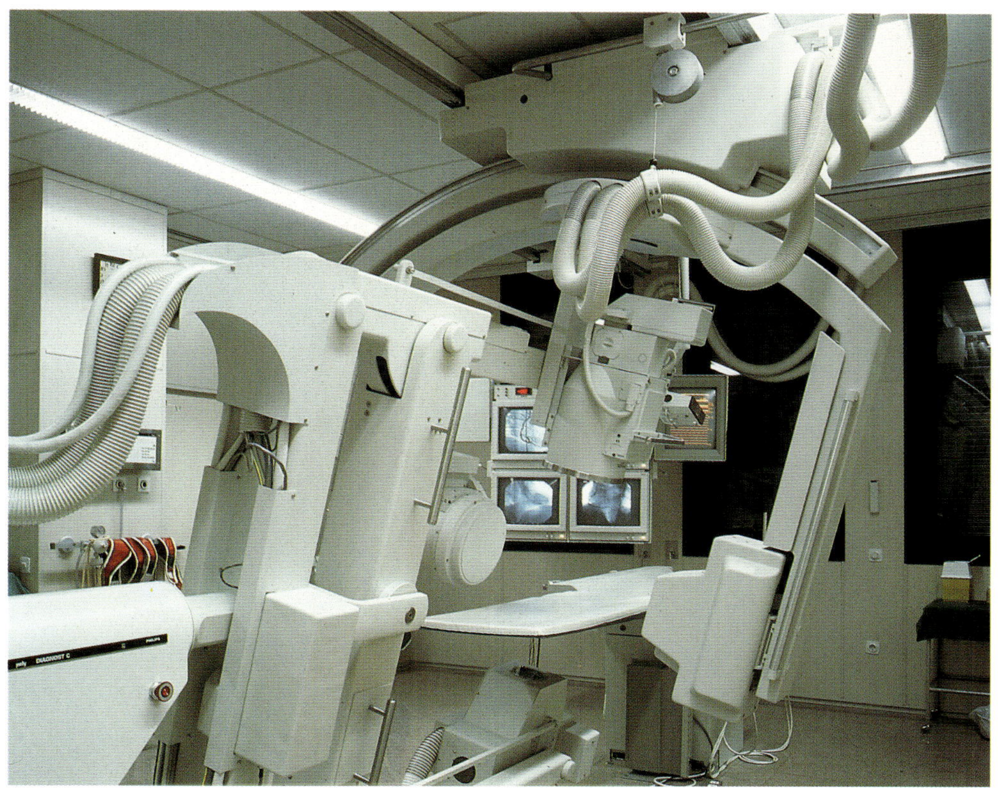

New technology to see inside the heart. The technique of cardiac catheterism is based on a combination of powerful x-ray emissions and on the most advanced system of image transmission. The catheters, made out of fiber optics, make it possible to see the inside of the heart and even of the blood vessels. Coronary angioplasties, the elimination of atheroma which obstruct the artery walls, and the re-establishment of the blood flow: all of these procedures are made possible by this apparatus, without the need for surgery.

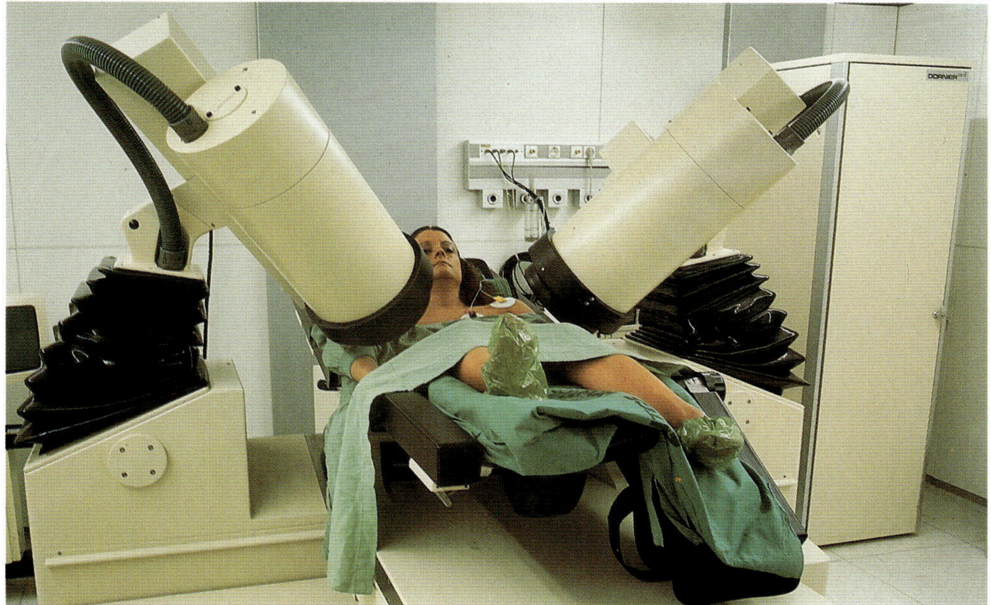

Elimination of calculi without surgery. The medical application of high technology is producing some quite revolutionary results. One example is extracorporal renal lithotrity through shock waves, a new therapeutic technique to fragment the calculus lodged in any part of the urinary system. After the fragmentation, the calculi are eliminated naturally. The advantages of renal lithotrity are evident: there is no surgical intervention, the treatment is ambulatory and does not require hospitalization, and no convalescent period is required.

The ecological riches of the Medes islands. The well-being and quality of life on the planet depend on man's respect for nature. The human community of any territory must respect the land. One of the great ecological riches of Catalonia is the marine life of the Medes Islands, small isles off the Costa Brava. The government has recently intensified the protection of the flora and fauna that thrives beneath the blueness.

Agricultural technical training. Apart from its research role, the Department of Agriculture, Livestock and Fisheries of the Government of Catalonia directs special attention at professional development in these areas of the labour market. The preparation of students always has a double orientation — the combination of theory and practice — which facilitates a more efficient and satisfactory incorporation of the student into his future profession. The Agricultural Training School of the Pyrenees, in Bellestar, pictured here, is one project that must bear such fruit.

A new building for the Police School of Catalonia. The spacious Police School of Catalonia, which is the centre where the country's autonomous and local police forces receive instruction, is in the Vallès Oriental county, near Mollet. Modern installations, sports grounds, well-selected staff with the contributions of specialized pedagogues from countries with great traditions in this field, and, above all, a conception of future agents as officials offering services to the citizens, are the keys to the prestige this school is gaining. Among the installations, one must single out those for practice with firearms, which were used for the 1992 Olympic Games shooting events.

More human and dignified internment of prisoners. The construction of this spacious Penitentiary and Preventive Centre, located at Can Duran de Brians at Sant Esteve Sesrovires, is one of the results of self-government in the area of prison administration. The modern and functional conception of an establishment such as this, in a natural setting, without doubt contributes to the completion of several objectives: the reduction of overcrowding among those completing a sentence; improved prison services and greater possibilities for social reinsertion; increased jobs, and greater security for all of the nation's citizens.

To avoid isolation in emergency times. The need for citizens throughout Catalonia to be able to contact their government in times of crisis (floods, fires, snowstorms, etc.) has led the Generalitat to develop a plan for an integrated telecommunications network. In the case of an interruption in traffic or in the telephone service, this network will establish a radio link between the municipal governments and the various branches of the Generalitat government: the Autonomous Police, the Fire Department, Civil Protection, Public Health, etc. This project will begin in two phases, which must be completed in 1992 and 1995.

Barcelona setting for the anti-fascist Olympics. *Olimpíada Popular* (Popular Olympiad) was the name given to the athletic games to be celebrated in the Montjuïc stadium in Barcelona from the 19 to the 26 of July, 1936. These games were intended to be a replica of the Berlin Olympics, in the same year Hitler used them in favour of Fascism. The *Olimpíada Popular* was jointly financed by the Generalitat of Catalonia, the Republican Spanish Government and the French Government. 5,000 athletes from different countries were inscribed to participate. When these games had to be cancelled due to Franco's coup, 200 of these athletes enrolled in the Republican Army. They were the first members of the International Brigades.

The Baron de Coubertin: re-creator of the Olympic Games. Pierre de Fredy, Baron de Coubertin, was responsible for the recuperation of the tradition of the Olympic Games, a national event in Greece — both sporting and cultural — that were celebrated every four years in Olympia as from the year 776 BC. The restoration of the Olympic Games took place in May 1894. It came as a consequence of a pedagogical and social movement that recognized the beneficial influence that sports have in the integral development of young people, the development of a consciousness considering mankind as a universal collective and promoting a better understanding among men.

Samaranch, president of the International Olympic Committee. Catalan-born Juan Antonio Samaranch is the current president of the International Olympic Committee (IOC), a post he has held since 1980. It was Mr. Samaranch who announced the selection of Barcelona as the host city to the 25th Summer Olympic Games at the Palais de Beaulieu (Lausanne, Switzerland), in the presence of Pasqual Maragall, Barcelona's mayor. A little after this photograph was taken (it features the session at which the members of the IOC debated and voted the candidature), enthusiasm broke out and Barcelona's victory was celebrated by all, all the more since Barcelona had failed to get the nomination in the years 1924, 1936 and 1972. The work and prestige of Mr. Samaranch was vital for the selection of Barcelona as host city to the Olympic Games. The capacity of those institutions involved in the organization of the Games, especially Barcelona City Hall, is a full guarantee for success.

The Olympic Village, an important urban improvement for Barcelona.
The Olympic Village — an 165-acre complex — with a marvellous projection towards the sea in the form of a marina (as can be seen in the photograph) housed athletes participating in the 1992 Olympic Games. It is the most important urban development operation undertaken in the city in the last few years. This urban complex modified and redefined the sea-front of the historical Poblenou district, one of the principal industrial centres in the first half of this century. The two original skyscrapers presiding over the Olympic Village account for 28,000 m^2 of offices, which housed the administrative and organizational services of the Barcelona Olympic Committee during the Games.

The Olympic Ring (Anella Olímpica), with the Mediterranean in the background. The Montjuïc area concentrates the set of sports installations that make up the so-called "Olympic Ring": the Stadium, the Sant Jordi Hall, the Picornell swimming-pools, the National Physical Education Institute of Catalonia — headquarters of the future Sports University Faculty — the 130 metre high Calatrava telephone Communications Tower, and other competition areas. Its situation is priviliged because it is set in a mountainside 170 metres above sea level. In this photograph it can be seen in the background. It is surrounded by the kind of vegetation which nature and the wise criteria of garden designers have conserved over the course of time.

The Montjuïc Olympic Stadium: 1929-1992. Conserving its exterior historical façade, the one built on the original 1929 building, a team of Catalan architects (Margarit, Buxadé, Correa and Milà), along with the Italian Gregotti, drew up a new project for the Montjuïc Olympic Stadium, the interior of which may be seen in the photograph below. The beauty of the surrounding gardens, its privileged situation on the side of the mountain and its nearness to the sea, make the Stadium particularly attractive. It has a capacity for 70,000 spectators. Despite the dificulties involved in the adaptation of the former building, athletes have ratified the ideal conditions of the Stadium for competitions.

The Palau Sant Jordi, architecturally unique. The Palau Sant Jordi is unique and includes the principal sports area, with a capacity for 17,000 spectators and a contiguous multiple use construction. The originality of the architectural conception may be put down to the Japanese architect Arata Isozaki, who designed a large covered surface of spatial metal mesh. The accompanying visual image fits in with the sinuous forms of the natural site it occupies, Montjuïc hillside. In this Palace, the gymnastics, handball and volleyball events were held in the Barcelona 1992 Olympic Games.

A multi-use indoor area. The interior characteristics of this indoor area, the roof of which permits pleasant natural lighting, make it the ideal place for all kinds of non-sporting activities. This dynamic city and its surrounding area, accounting for three and a half million people, will doubtless benefit from this extraordinary hall to celebrate artistic and cultural events of many different kinds.

A sports faculty which respects "Noucentista" architecture. This building of exquisite symmetry, bearing the name of National Physical Education Institute of Catalonia, is situated in the Montjuïc mountain Olympic Ring area. It is the location of the Catalan Sports University. During the Olympic Games it hosted the wrestling events. The creators of this project — Peter Hodgkinson and Ricard Bofill — have stated that their intention was to achieve a pure form of approximation to the "Noucentista" style reflected in the 1929 Montjuïc constructions, by making use of advanced technology. Despite the large volume of the building — they state — it has been designed in such a way as to blend into the general environment of the mountain and its gardens.

The Bernat Picornell Swimming-pools. They were originally built in 1968 with a view to hosting the European Swimming Championships, which were held in Barcelona in 1970. They have been completely modernized for the 1992 Olympic Games. In the Olympic Games, they were used for swimming events, synchronized swimming, waterpolo finals and swimming events in the modern pentathlon. The Bernat Picornell complex is made up of an open-air competition pool; a pool for diving, also open-air, and a covered pool for warming up sessions of participants in the different competitions.

An area with excellent sports infrastructure. The north-eastern sector of the city has for years been the best equipped for the practice of sport: one may list Barcelona Football Club installations (stadium, "Blau-grana" Palace, "Miniestadi" and Ice Hall), the Royal Barcelona Polo Club, RCD Español's Sarrià stadium and Barcelona University's sports area, among others. They all go up to make the Diagonal Olympic Area, setting of several competitions: football, riding, roller-skate hockey, judo etc. Barcelona Football Club's stadium, "Camp Nou", can be seen in the foreground of this photograph.

Camp Nou, the largest stadium in Europe. Among the sports installations located in the Olympic area of Diagonal, is the stadium of Futbol Club Barcelona, or Camp Nou. Inaugurated in 1957, it has been expanded several times and is currently the largest in Europe, with a capacity for 120,000 spectators. The combination of fields that form part of the club made it very useful for many of the Olympic sports: hockey, baseball, handball, volleyball, and ice hockey, among others.

The Palau Blau-grana, scene of international competitions. The Palau Blau-grana, the site of many victories of Barcelona's basketball team and setting for important international play-offs, was also one of the attractions during the Olympic Games of 1992. Opened in 1971, it is a sports centre which is particularly well-equipped for basketball, handball and volleyball.

The High Standard Sports Centre is preparing athletes for 1992. The Generalitat of Catalonia recently created the High Standard Sports Centre, located in Sant Cugat del Vallès, near Barcelona, with the basic aim of facilitating the preparation of athletes and sportsmen and women for top ranking sports competitions, with its high-technology installations. At present, 168 sportsmen and women from different federations, specialists in 14 Olympic disciplines, are in training.

Aptitude check-ups for top level competition. In the sphere of research into preparation for top-class sporting events, the Generalitat of Catalonia is carrying out aptitude and performance check-ups in various Sports Medicine Centres which are spread across Catalan Territory. A task of medical and psychological control and biological performance of top class sportsmen and women is also being carried out by way of the High Standard Sports Study Centre.

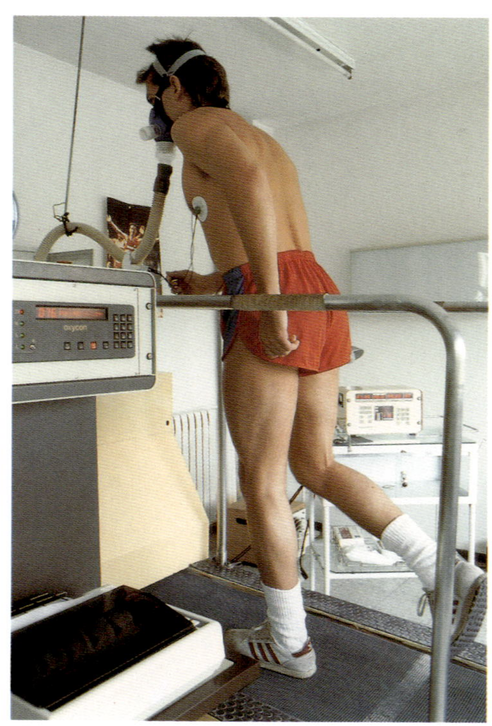

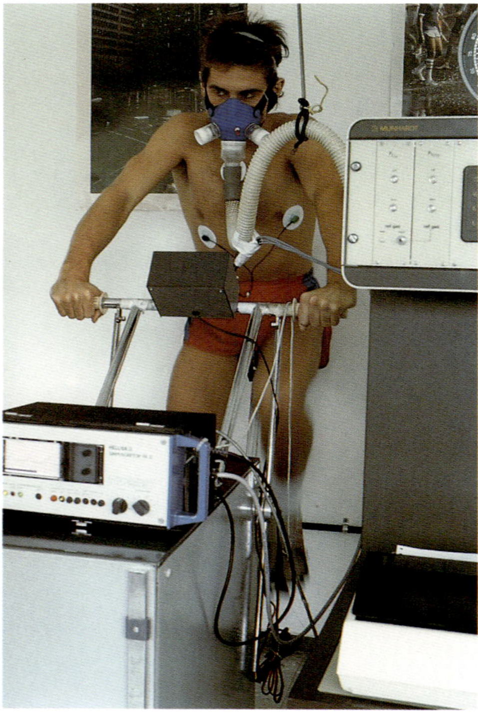

The Cycle Track, centre of an Olympic area. The Vall d'Hebron is one of the four sites where Olympic activity took place in 1992. The existence of a very modern cycle track with pleasing architectural features will also make it the site of future sporting activity among the city's residents. The zone was complemented with a sports centre with a complex interior of courts for tennis and "fronton", and areas for training and archery competitions, apart from the cycle track pictured here.

ANNEXES

UNIVERSAL FIGURES OF CATALAN CULTURE

Many cultures in the world have had an influence in specific ways on universal culture and the progress of humanity. This is clear from the work of great figures who have taken their place in history for their special contributions which now form part of universal culture.

Catalonia and the Catalan Countries (Catalan-speaking countries which until the 18th century formed part of a confederated State) are linked as the heirs to a long and common cultural tradition. Thus, in this brief selection of figures, we have taken as point of reference the cultural boundaries of the Catalan Countries, which exceed the strictly administrative borders of today. The great men and women who have disseminated and advanced the values of the spirit, knowledge, arts and sciences, take their places within a common culture, and not necessarily within the borders resulting from circumstantial and conventional factors.

These biographical sketches have been prepared by Josep M. Cadena in cooperation with Josep-M. Puigjaner.

PERE NOLASC
(?, 1180 - Barcelona, 1249)

Founder of the Order of Mercy, a congregation which was active in the redemption of captives. Pere Nolasc was born near Barcelona, in a house called Les Puelles. The son of merchants, and a merchant himself, he learned personally of the Christians who

lived as captives of the Saracens. When he was only twenty years old, he sold all of his goods to rescue the captives. Afterwards, he began to ask for alms. When he had enough money collected, he set off for the lands dominated by the Arabs (València, Andalusia, North Africa), and returned with liberated men and women. Within a period of a few months, some of his friends, wealthy merchants of Barcelona, and members of the nobility, learned of his work and gave him money and land to help him to go on with his difficult task.

According to legend, the Virgin Mary appeared to him one night and told him to create an order devoted to liberating Christian slaves. Pere Nolasc told Ramon de Penyafort, a distinguished jurist, about his dream and Ramon de Penyafort answered that he too had had the same dream, and that the king himself had the same idea. As a result, the Order of Mercy was born in August 1218, first with a civil character, until 1235, when Pope Gregory IX authorized its transformation into a religious order under the rule of Saint Augustine. Its members added a fourth vow to the three existing ones; it was the vow to redeem captives, and they promised to temporarily substitute those captives in danger of losing their Christian faith.

The Mercedaries had great importance in the Mediterranean and wherever there was slavery and pirates.

The feminine branch was founded in 1261 by Maria de Cervelló. In 1860, the Institute of Mercedaries was founded by the Mercedary Pere Nolasc de Trenas.

Pere Nolasc was canonized in 1688, as was Maria de Cervelló in 1692.

RAMON LLULL
(Palma de Mallorca ?, *c.* 1232/33 - Palma de Mallorca, after 1315)

Without doubt, Llull is the greatest gift the Catalan countries gave to Medieval European culture, in the sciences, letters, and music. His father took part in the conquest of Majorca. Ramon Llull (Raymond Lully) was born on that island under the rule of James I of Catalonia and Aragon (called the Conqueror), and was the tutor and later the chief assistant to James II when he inherited the thrown. Deeply religious and a connoisseur of the Christian and Arabic cultures which then dominated that part of the world, he set out to convert the infidels to Christianity. His life was full of risks, and the zeal of a missionary. He formulated an *Art abreujada de trobar la veritat* (Brief Art for Finding the Truth), which he considered essential to the conversion of Arabs to Christianity, but his best known works were Blanquerna and the *Llibre d'Amic e Amat*. He preached in Tunis and debated with Islamic theologians. According to legend, he was martyred at Bugia, but he probably died in Majorca.

The works of Ramon Llull — 250 titles in all — have given way to a philosophical systematization known as Lullism, which takes its place in the realm of Christian platonism, influenced both by Latin authors of the twelfth century and oriental thought. Llull wrote in Catalan, Latin, and Arabic. The majority of Llull scholars are located in Germany. The Raimundus Lullius Institute of the University of Freiburg im

Breisgau continues to publish Llull's unedited Latin works. In the eighteenth century, Professor Salzinger sent the most important collection of works in Latin by Llull to Mainz. Nevertheless, there have been and continue to be specialists in this exceptional Majorcan's work all over the world.

JOANOT MARTORELL
(Gandia, Safor, *c.* 1413/1415 - 1468)

Knight and writer. As a knight, Martorell was known as a keen observer of the need to right wounded honour, an avenger, a fighter, a protector of juridical and military canons, and a tireless traveller. It is known that in 1438 he went to England to advise King Henry VI to accept the judgment of a fight to the death that he wanted to wage against the knight Joan de Montpalau for not having kept his word to marry his sister, Damiata. It was there he had the time to read books, to get to know the sumptuous English Royal Court, and to form the idea for what would be the most famous chivalrous novel of the era, *Tirant lo Blanc*.

After returning to the Kingdom of Valencia, he continued his knightly duties. He later went to Portugal, and probably England again. What is known for certain is that on January 2, 1460, he began to write the novel, which would not be seen until November 20, 1490, when his editor, Nicolau Spindeler, published it after the author's death. It has been written, and probably with good reason, that *Tirant lo Blanc* is the best European novel of the fifteenth century, as well as the first modern novel. Miguel de Cervantes wrote: "I will tell you the truth, my friend, that for its style this is the best book in the world" The renowned critic Martí de Riquer, specialist in Medieval literature, said the following: "*Tirant* is a militarily serious novel, empassioned, amusing in many marginal episodes, and above all, joyful. Joanot Martorell writes with intricate detail of the singular battles between knights, or fights to the death, the precise fencing movements of the contenders, and the function of the offensive and defensive weapons". This will not surprise anyone who knows of the battles he fought during his life.

Tirant lo Blanc, successful in the latter half of the fifteenth century, re-edited by Marià Aguiló in the last quarter of the nineteenth century, and again during the twentieth, it is once again a world-wide best seller, perhaps because of the revival of medieval literature set off by Umberto Eco and his novel *The Name of the Rose*. Since 1984, it has been translated into English, Spanish, Finnish, Italian, Dutch, Romanian, and is currently being translated into German, French and Chinese.

JOSEP DE CALASSANÇ
(Peralta de la Sal, la Llitera, 1557 - Rome, 1648)

Theologian. Having followed the directives of the recently held Council of Trent, he acquired a solid philosophical and theological preparation. He occupied various posts of responsibility. First, as a secretary to the bishop of Lleida, Gaspar de la Figuera. Later, as the right hand man to the bishop of La Seu d'Urgell, Andreu Capella. He served during an era in which the spririt of the Council was being encouraged among the priests and secular members of the Diocese. He carried out several duties as priest of the parishes of Claverol and Ortoneda, and as an archpriest of Tremp. In recognition of his talent,

Dr. Calassanç was sent to Rome to attend to certain ecclesiastic affairs of his bishopric.

In Rome, at the sacresty of the church of Santa Dorotea, Josep de Calassanç began to devote himself to his most cherished vocation: the education of poor children. In fact, without knowing it, he established the first public Christian school of modern times; no one was asked if they could pay or who their family was. Genís Samper, the biographer of Josep de Calassanç, said that the mothers who took their little children to the school said: "This teacher is either a fool or a saint".

The Reapers' War (1640) — the Catalan revolt against Philip IV, the King of Spain — delayed by some years the foundation of schools based on his model. Several years would pass and, after the death of the so-called "saint of the children", the first Piarist School in Catalonia and indeed in Spain opened in Moià in 1683. The Piarist Order currently has some 2,000 members, spread out in some two hundred centres throughout the world.

In 1829, the first school was opened in Figueres, the Religious Institute of the Daughters of Mary, founded in Arenys de Mar by Paula Montalt, who followed the Piarist approach to the education of young girls. There are more than 1,000 missionaries in more than 80 centres in various countries in Latin America, Asia, Africa and Europe. Josep de Calassanç was canonized by Pope Clement XIII in 1765.

PERE CLAVER I SOBOCANO
(Verdú, Urgell, 1580 - Cartagena, Nueva Granada, 1654)

A Jesuit missionary who achieved sainthood for his work with the sick, the incarcerated, and especially, the black slaves of Nueva Granada, present-day Colombia. After studying in Barcelona, Girona, and Palma de Mallorca, the Jesuit order sent him to finish his education in Bogota. There he developed, against the will of the wealthy class, an important evangelistic influence which he directed at cultural improvements and protecting the dignity of every human being.

According to one story, he knew many languages spoken by the slaves, making use of some of the interpreters he had trained earlier, and he helped himself with some illustrated plates that reinforced the explanations. After baptising them, Pere Claver accompanied them whenever possible on the road to faith. Records from the period said that he baptised nearly 300,000 slaves. His biographer, Enric Puig, added that "he still found time for the lepers and the prisoners. The world of pain was his world, and the outcasts were his people".

The Council of Tarragona of 1727 proclaimed him an apostle of the West Indies, and Pope Leo XIII canonized him in the year 1888. That Pope, in one of his writings, stated, "After the life of Christ, no one has moved my soul as profoundly as the great apostle Saint Pere Claver". His house in Verdú is a museum, and his following is one of the most extensive in the Latin-American nations.

ANTONI MARIA CLARET I CLARÀ

(Sallent de Llobregat, Bages, 1807 - Fontfroide, Languedoc, 1870)

Theologian. The son of weavers, he was very interested in the machinery used in textile manufacture. He abandoned the idea of devoting himself to industrial technology and in 1829, entered the Seminary of Vic, where he was a disciple of Jaume Balmes. His religious vocation caused him to be first parish priest of his village, Sallent, and later at Viladrau. At the same time, the strong desire to preach moved him to travel for seven years throughout Catalonia, with the title of "apostolic missionary"; in this role he achieved anextraordinary popular following. He complemented his oratory activity with writing. He published books, pamphlets, stamps, and flyers, aimed always at his particular audience. He founded a publishing house in order to multiply propagandistic and communicative activity. In oral, as in written communications, he insisted on the use of Catalan, the language of those he was trying to reach. Dr. Carles Cardó wrote of him: "One can say that Father Claret made all Catalans of his time read Catalan".

In order to increase the efficency of preaching, he promoted the creation of a group of priests who would devote themselves primarily to that task, under the bishop's direction. This was the seed of the missionary congregation known as the Children of the Immaculate Heart of Mary, founded in 1848. Less than one month later, he received the appointment as archbishop of Santiago, Cuba. Pere Codina, his most recent biographer, asserts that in this period his principal concern was the community, and the recognition of the necessity to reform certain social and economic structures. Bishop Claret devoted himself to the dissemination of books on agricultural techniques; he also founded the first savings banks in all of Latin America, defended the black slaves, and called for the establishment of arts and vocational training in prisons.

The works carried out under his rule as bishop were so significant that the historian Hugh Thomas calls him the only "enlightened bishop" of the period in Latin America. Those very social actions, though, were also the cause of an attempt on his life in 1856 in the village of Holguín.

In March 1857, he received a royal order calling him to Madrid. Upon arriving at the Court, he was informed that he had been named confessor to Queen Isabella II, a position which he occupied under certain conditions, the first of them being that he would never be called upon to intervene directly in political life. In that era, the clergy's primary objective was to promote spiritual and scientific balance. The revolution of 1868 dethroned Isabella II. Antoni Maria Claret went into exile in Paris, where he lived for several months. In April 1869, he went to Rome to participate in the First Vatican Council. He died in the Cistercian monastery of Fontfroide, near Narbonne (Languedoc) in October 1870.

He was canonized in the year 1950, and, along with the above-mentioned men's congregation, the women's Immaculate Mary Apostolic Institute of Education, has branches the world over.

NARCÍS MONTURIOL I ESTARRIOL

(Figueres, Alt Empordà, 1819 - Sant Martí de Provençals, Barcelona, 1885)

Although the American Robert Fulton constructed a submarine vessel for Napoleon in the year 1800, it is believed that Narcís Monturiol invented the first submarine. The *Diario de Barcelona* described to its readers the first public display of that singular vessel in the port of Barcelona on September 23, 1859. "The first motion of the *Ictíneo* was a vertical descent, ten meters down, a position which it maintained for twelve minutes. Later, during the second half of that period, it ascended and descended three consecutive times without creating more than a ripple. Just afterwards, changing course to south-west, it navigated between two waters and different depths, some two hundred metres in the space of six minutes, climbing and lowering several times and, turning in a circle, changing course again to the north, in a straight line for some six hundred metres". This journalistic description, undisputed by anyone in attendance that day, is evidence that the object in question was a true submarine, that is, a vessel capable of navigating under water. That vessel, from auspicious beginnings, was designed for underwater exploration and coral extraction. General O'Donnell, the Spanish De-

fence Minister, who attended the demonstration, was enthused with the vessel because he saw in it a new weapon for war at sea. The government of Isabella II, however, was not interested. The second *Ictíneo*, which was equipped with a covered canon, was completed on October 2th, 1864. Monturiol tried out the vessel as an instrument of war, but it needed to be perfected. This model was equipped with a steam engine. On October 22th, 1867, the self-propelling *Ictíneo* navegated on the surface of the water, but the necessary financing for further perfection was not secured. The company founded by the inventor and his friends went out of business. The vessel was seized and sold as scrap to pay off the company's debts. Isaac Peral, who years later invented another submarine which was successful and changed the strategies of war at sea, always recognized that Monturiol had preceded him.

Narcís Monturiol invented various machines such as, for example, one that made exercise books and another for making cigarettes, but neither of these machines were successful, and he died in poverty and oblivion.

He also had an interest in politics, and was inspired by the Icarian ideals of Étienne Cabet.

ANTONI GAUDÍ I CORNET

(Reus, Baix Camp, 1852 - Barcelona, 1926)

Architect and creator of monumental buildings constructed in accordance with an original form which was often inspired in nature and which incorporated many elements of popular culture. Arabic art and the Gothic and Baroque styles combined to give way to truly creative architectural forms. Barcelona is the site of the greatest number of Gaudí's constructions, including Milà House — popularly known as "la Pedrera" (the stone quarry); the Batlló House (1904-1906), the Güell Palace (1886-1891), Güell Park (1900-1914) and the Sagrada Família temple, his project as from 1883 on.

In 1918 on he began to devote himself heart and soul to the Sagrada Família temple, which he described to Prat de la Riba as the cathedral of Catalonia. Gaudí devoted the last part of his life to the search for a figurative-structural synthesis in the form of a personal and inimitable geometrical form. Profoundly religious, it has been said of him by Salvador Tarragó that "we must interpret this attitude as a historic form of a will to absolute perfection and as a form of transcendental justification for his work". Aside from his devoutness, he also displayed a deep sense of civic pride, a great love for the language of his land and a sensitivity for its social problems. The temple, which he left unfinished and which has been continued by popular demand and as a collective work, for its religious significance, represents the culmination of the spiritual symbology of its creator. The Sagrada Família is a monument of great international renown and an obligatory stop for anyone visiting Barcelona. Gaudí is the most important Catalan architect of all times and one of the most interesting figures in nineteenth century.

ISAAC ALBÉNIZ I PASCUAL

(Camprodon, Ripollès, May 29, 1860 - Cambo, Lapurdi, Basque Country, May 18, 1909)

At the age of four he gave a piano recital at the Romea Theatre in Barcelona. At six, he was already studying in Paris with Marmontel, and later at the Conservatory of the same city and at the Conservatory in Madrid. He developed his career as a concert pianist performing Scarlatti, Bach, Mozart, Beethoven, Schumann and Chopin.

In 1874, he studied with Judasson and Reinecke at Leipzig, and later at the Conservatory in Brussels where he underwent an intense period of study and obtained first prize in piano (1879). From there, he began his career as a composer, an activity he would never abandon.

In 1883, Albéniz moved to Barcelona where he met Felip Pedrell, a defender of Wagnerism, cultivator of musicology, rejuvenator of Iberian polyphony of the Golden Age, and mentor of Albéniz, Granados and Falla.

From 1883 to 1885, he introduced himself into the cultural life of Catalonia, attending the meetings of the Quatre Gats cabaret, with Picasso, Romeu, Rusiñol, Casas, etc. In 1883, he played at the Gran Teatre del Liceu, and the following year at the Teatre Líric. It was decisive that Albéniz heard Pau Casals at the Café Tort in the Carrer Gran de Gràcia; he wrote a letter of recommendation to the Count of Morphy, secretary to the Queen Regent, presenting the young Casals.

D'Indy, Dukas, Ravel, Fauré and in a special way Debussy, all valued the creative world of Albéniz and his capacity for innovation. His friendship with Franz Lizst helped him discover a stronger sense of creativity. These influences helped bring him to a level of maturity, from which would spring his ever-important pianistic work. One must mention as well certain influences on his various pianistic languages and styles, such as Chopin, Schumann, and the afore-mentioned Lizst. The Iberian Peninsula and its people and landscapes were his source of inspiration.

Between the years 1900 and 1905 in Tiana, shortly after the invention of the phonograph by Edison, he recorded at the home of Mr. Regordosa some improvised works, his only known recordings. They were later edited by an American company.

His *Suite Ibèria* is one of the crowning works of modernism, and of all European art of his time. It opened new perspectives in pianistic technology and had an influence on the movements of the French vanguard. Of *El Albaicín*, which forms part of the *Suite*, Debussy told him: "There are few works with its value". *Ibèria* clearly influenced the later works of both Debussy and Ravel.

Isaac Albéniz died on May 18, 1909 at Cambo. His remains arrived on June 6 at the central train terminal, where they were solemnly received, in a land proud to have been the birthplace of one of Catalonia's most universal figures of the time.

PAU CASALS I DEFILLÓ

(El Vendrell, Baix Penedès, 1876 - San Juan de Puerto Rico, 1973)

Cellist, orchestra conductor and composer. Casals turned the cello into a solo instrument and revolutionized performance and pedagogical techniques. An internationally praised concertist since 1899, when he first

played in Paris, he achieved a singular interpretative perfection.

He founded the famous Cortot-Thibaud-Casals trio, which Isaye calls "a three-headed god". He founded the Pau Casals Orchestra in Barcelona in 1920, and in 1926, the Workers' Association of Concerts, which until 1939 played a great musical and pedagogical role. That same year, at the end of the Spanish Civil War, he took up voluntary exile in Prada (Roussillon-French Catalonia). In 1950 he created the Pau Casals festivals of Prada and Puerto Rico. He composed, among other works, the *Hymn of the United Nations*, which was first played in 1971 at the headquarters of the United Nations in New York; he also composed *El Pessebre*, with words by Joan Alavedra. This second piece was intended as a message of peace and humanity, and he played it all over the world. He was awarded an honorary doctorate from New York University, and earned the admiration of the greatest figures of his day (from the Tzar of Russia, who called him to Saint Petersburg, to the most simple of folk), not only for his art, but also for his ethical attitude in favour of the national rights of his country (Catalonia), world peace, and the victims of the wars. He refused to perform not only in Franco's Spain, but also in Hitler's Germany (and so had to emigrate from France during the Nazi occupation), and in Mussolini's Italy. Perhaps that is why Albert Einstein said: "Pau Casals has understood perfectly that the world is in greater danger from those who tolerate or encourage evil than from those who do evil".

In 1972, one year before his death at the age of 97, the United Nations awarded him their peace prize. On that occasion, U Thant, Secretary General of the UN, pronounced the following words: "Pau Casals has glorified his life with truth, beauty and peace. As a man and as an artistic genius, you personify the ideals symbolized by this Medal of Peace which the United Nations offers you with profound respect and admiration".

ENRIC GRANADOS I CAMPIÑA

(Lleida, 1876 - the sea, near Dieppe, 1916)

Composer and pianist, he was able to project refined harmonies of a romantic nature through prodigious technique at the piano. His artistic tendencies coincided with those eager to renovate the arts during the "Modernist" movement. He founded the Society of Classical Concerts and cooperated with the majority of the great musicians of his time (Pau Casals, Jacques Thibaud, Camille Saint-Saëns). In 1914, he triumphed with his work *Goyescas* at the Pleyel Hall in Paris.

Among his most famous compositions are *Doce danzas españolas, Siete valses poéticos*

and *Capricho español*, among other works, all for the piano; he wrote also *María del Carmen* for the *zarzuela* theatre and many other lyrical works, such as *Picarol*, *Follet* and *Liliana*. Among his symphonic works mention must be made of *Tres danzas españolas* and the poem *The Divine Comedy*. He also composed chamber music, the most famous work of which was *Quintet for Piano*. He travelled to New York, along with his wife, to attend the debut of the stage version of *Goyescas* and, upon returning to Europe, the ship was sunk by a submarine. His tragic death, at the height of his career, moved music lovers the world over.

IGNASI BARRAQUER I BARRAQUER

(Barcelona, 1884 - 1965)

Ophthalmologist. The son of Professor Josep-Antoni Barraquer i Roviralta — who was himself one of the pioneers of the Catalan study of ophthalmology — he continued his father's work and found new sur-

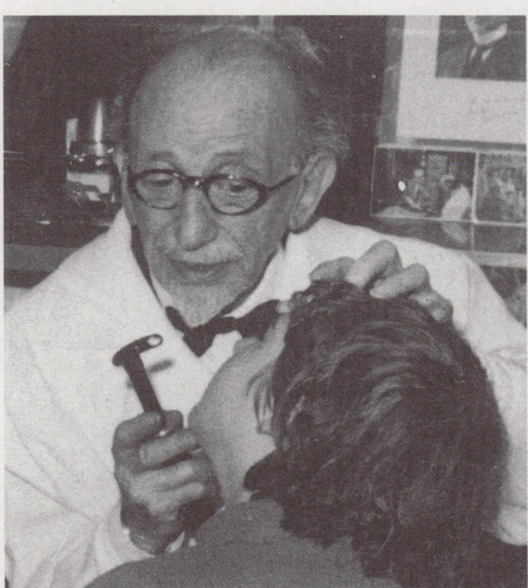

gical methods which gained acceptance all over the world. Especially relevant was his technique in extracting crystalline with the use of a suction cup, the vacuum of which could be regulated. This procedure facilitated the safe extraction of the cataract. With slight technological improvements, this is the system used today. He performed thousands of such operations.

In 1947, he founded the Barraquer Institute of Ophthalmology in Barcelona, a prestigious centre of medicine and research, drawing patients from all over the world. He also created the Eye Museum, a collection of perfectly preserved anatomical pieces. He founded when deceased, the Eye Bank, through which people could leave their eyes, when deceased, for others who could need them. His sons Josep-Ignasi and Joaquim have followed in their father's footsteps: the older, founder of the Barraquer Institute of Bogota, developed a new clinical technique to modify the curvature of the cornea; and the younger, director of the Barraquer Institute of Barcelona, is the innovator of an original technique for extracting crystalline in cataract surgery, called "enzymatic zonulolysis", as well as the inventor of various microsurgical instruments.

JOAN MIRÓ I FERRÀ

(Barcelona, 1893 - Palma de Mallorca, 1983)

An internationally acclaimed artist, the creator of a new visual language which combined the sensations that came to him from his native land — the family farmhouse at Mont-roig — with the dreams produced from the contemplation of the Mediterranean sky from the island of Majorca. Although he experimented with cubism, fauvism and surrealism, he discovered an intensely personal language, with symbols for woman, bird, moon, sky and kite, describing a world of complex beauty through great formal simplicity. The blues, greens and reds of Miró are unique. His work, which includes painting, sculpture, engravings and tapestry, can be found in the most important museums in the world. In

Barcelona he created, with a generous donation, the Centre for Studies in Contemporary Art — Joan Miró Foundation —, and in Majorca there is another foundation bearing his name.

Miró's international fame took off in 1928. That year, the Museum of Modern Art in New York acquired two paintings that had been recently exhibited in Paris. In 1944, he began to work closely with the great Catalan ceramist Llorens i Artigas. The results of their work were excellent, and were exhibited in Paris and New York in 1956. A series of his murals are on permanent display at the UNESCO headquarters in Paris, at Harvard University in the United States, at Barcelona airport, and at the Palace of Congresses in Madrid.

"CHARLIE RIVEL"

(Cubelles, Garraf, 1896 - Sant Pere de Ribes, Garraf, 1983)

The son of a poor family, Josep Andreu i Laserre (his real name) dedicated his life to the circus, continuing the family tradition. His first successes were achieved in Paris

between 1925 and 1930. It was there he delighted the spectators of the Medrano Circus, performing with his brothers Polo and René in a comical act and in another on a low trapeze. As from 1935, he began a new period and performed alone. From his repertoire two numbers especially stand out: the one with a fat and ridiculous opera singer and the Charlie Chaplin "Charlot" act. Chaplin himself, after seeing a performance in which Rivel imitated him, said, "Either you're imitating me, or it's me who's imitating you". Truly, praise such as this is the most sublime recognition of the artistic quality of Josep Andreu.

Rivel was an international clown and a clown for all audiences. He was understood everywhere. Everyone liked him, from little children to old people. This universal understanding was due to the fact that Josep Andreu respected the fundamental laws of the traditional circus clown: movement and mime. A gesture was enough, along with facial expressions, a natural and spontaneous cordiality, and the ability to discover or reveal the sentiments and the lives of the people watching him; it was in this way he communicated an inner world, an interpretation of the world, that he wanted to share with those around him.

Except for his later years, Charlie Rivel performed little in Catalonia. Fame obliged him to make continual tours of Europe, especially Germany, Switzerland, and Scandinavia. No one doubts in comparing him with the best clowns of all times: Lou Jacobs, Groch, the Fratellini Brothers, Oleg Popov, Pompoff and Teddy, etc. He received innumerable honours.

He spent his last years in his home town, at his house in Cubelles, surrounded by the objects — nearly a museum — that he had collected during his long artistic career. A book entitled *Poor Clown* contains his memoirs. We would here like to recall a sentence that belies his intelligence and concern for humanity: "Wars would end if the governments, instead of sending diplomats to the UN, sent instead their best clown".

JOSEP TRUETA I RASPALL

(Barcelona, 1897-1977)

Surgeon. As the chief physician of the Caixa de Provisió de Socors (House of the Provision of Assistance) of Barcelona, he began in 1929 to experiment with a new procedure for the treatment of open fractures, to avoid the onset of gangrene. In those times there were no antibiotics with which to treat infections, and his method proved very effective during the Civil War in field hospitals. Exiled to England in 1939 and a professor of Oxford University, his medical technique was accepted by the allied armies of World War II and met with magnificent results. It saved millions of lives and spared thousands of soldiers from undergoing amputations. His method of treatment was applied to more than 300,000 injured in the terrible Battle of Dunkirk. After the war, in 1948, he was named Chief Professor of Surgery and Orthopaedics at Oxford University.

With the economic help of Lord Nuffield, he created the "Nuffield Orthopaedic Centre" at Oxford University, a large orthopaedic hospital with great research capacity. In 1960, he presided over the Congress of the International Society of Orthopaedics and

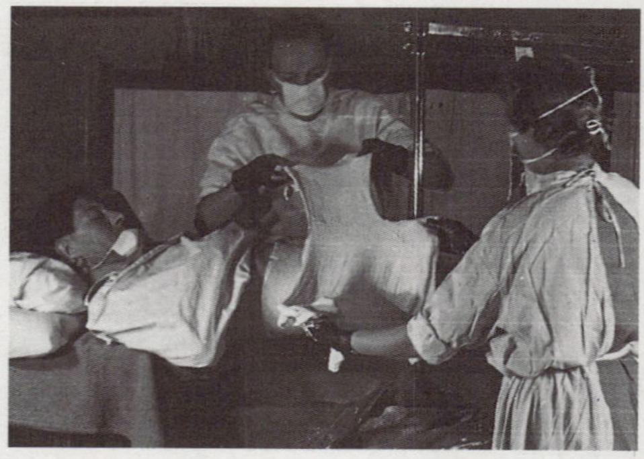

Traumatology in New York. He published many notable scientific works, which are still consulted by specialists.

In the area of medicine, Dr. Trueta was responsible for two other important contributions on the treatment of war wounds. The first was a study of renal circulation, the kidney's functions and its illnesses. The second was his research into the formation and growth of bones. A member of various academies and an honorary Ph. D. of many universities, Trueta is considered a universal scientist with deep Catalan roots. He was a member of the Catalan Council of London and was personally responsible, over a period of ten years, for the Catalan broadcasts on the BBC. One of his better known works, apart from those published in relation with his surgical speciality, is *The Spirit of Catalonia*, which makes the Catalan situation known to the Anglo-Saxon world.

FRANCESC DURAN I REYNALS

(Barcelona, 1899 - New Haven, USA, 1958)

Medical researcher who achieved world-wide fame for his work on the viral etiology of cancer, a disease from which he himself died. Disciple of August Pi i Sunyer in Barcelona, he worked in the Pasteur Institute of Paris where, in 1925, he discovered an important factor of infectious diffusion which, within specialized circles of medicine, carries his name. He also carried out important research at the Rockefeller Institute of New York (from 1926 to 1938) and at Yale University (New Haven, Connecticut), where he was a brilliant professor and director of research.

This universal Catalan was the recipient of several honours including an honorary doctorate from the Hahnemann Medical College of Philadelphia; the Prize of the American Anti-Cancer Association; the Prize for Research Medicine awarded by the Ann Fuller Memorial Foundation, and membership in the Institut d'Estudis Catalans as from 1947.

His most important works on cancer were collected in the book *Virus y Cáncer*, published in Barcelona in 1971 in homage to his work and on the occasion of the Fifth International Congress on Biochemistry. His wife, Maria Lluïsa Ayala i Bayón, doctor in sciences at the Sorbonne and associate professor of pathology at the Albert Einstein College, where she worked under the auspices of the National (American) Cancer Institute, continued the work of her husband. The Duran i Reynals family has given the country a number of illustrious professionals. His brothers were the lawyer and politician Estanislau Duran i Reynals (Barcelona, 1894-1950), the *noucentista* writer Eudald Duran i Reynals (Barcelona, 1891-Paris, 1917), and the *noucentista* and rationalist architect, Raimon Duran i Reynals (Barcelona, 1895-1966).

JOSEP LLUÍS SERT I LÓPEZ

(Barcelona, 1902 - 1983)

Architect and urban planner. The nephew of the painter Josep M. Sert, who painted the council room of the League of Nations in Geneva, the hall of the Rockefeller Centre in New York, the cathedral of Vic and other important buildings. Josep Lluís Sert, with a decorative style rooted in the Baroque, was the first to epitomize the rationalist movement in Catalonia. He occupied a position in the European avant-garde, gathering within the architectonic language of rationality the beginnings of the Mediterranean spirit. A member of the Catalan Architects and Technicians for the Progress of Contemporary Architecture (Grup d'Arquitectes i Tècnics Catalans per al Progrés de l'Arquitectura Contemporània, GATCPAC), he contributed to the Macià Plan — a project for expanding Barcelona, along with Le Corbusier —, and the project for the City of Rest and Relaxation in the coastal zone south of Barcelona. Other early joint works of his, include the Casa Bloc, a housing site in Sant Andreu de Palomar (Barcelona), and the Central Antituberculosis Dispensary. In cooperation with Lacasa, he constructed the Spanish pavillion for the International Exhibition in Paris, and, in exile because of the Spanish Civil War, he worked in urban centres in Brazil, Peru and Colombia. He directed the College of Architecture at Harvard, succeeding Gropius, and he completed important architectural works throughout the US and Canada.

Sert felt strongly in touch with his identity as a Catalan and the Mediterranean spirit. "In my architecture", he said, "the presence of the Mediterranean element is fundamental, a nostalgia for climate and light, of all those visual contacts received in the years of youth in the country where I was born". For that reason, he often came from the US to work in a Mediterranean atmosphere. Between the years 1955 and 1956, he built the beautiful studio of the painter Joan Miró in Palma de Mallorca. Later, due to his friendship for the painter, he designed the building which houses the Joan Miró Foundation in Montjuïc Park, which opened to the public in 1975. One of the architectural objectives of Sert in this work was to take maximum advantage of sunlight. The use of white in the interior establishes an ample and peaceful atmosphere that facilitates the communication

between the artistic object and the person contemplating it. Sert introduced a new concept of museum, removed from the static and rigid atmospheres of certain older ones. Because, he said, "The way I see it, a museum is a centre of artistic activity, and not only an exhibition site. It is a place where the arts should be seen in the light of the participation of the public".

SALVADOR DALÍ I DOMÈNECH
(Figueres, Alt Empordà, 1904 - 1989)

A painter of rare perfection and prodigious imagination, decorator and writer. He took shrewd advantage of the mass media to achieve status as a world-wide figure. He enjoyed a close relation with the poets and artists of the "Generation of 1927", formed in the "Students' Residence of Madrid". In the late twenties, he took up residence in Paris, where he was the most brilliant of the surrealists. At the advice of his future wife Gala H. Diakonova, he moved to the United States in 1939, where his calculated eccentricities met with great success and his painting became well-known and appreciated. He took his place divorced from orthodox surrealism, a group from which he was expelled by André Breton, who accused him of being a Fascist. Set designer, figurine sculptor, decorator, illustrator, designer and poster artist, he took part in many activities, both artistic and commercial.

His painting was rooted in *noucentisme* and passed through a cubist phase before arriving at what he himself called a "paranoic-critical" stage, with a predominance of dream-like scenes rendered in great technical detail. Perhaps the high point of his artistic production can be found in works like *Blood is Sweeter than Honey* (1927), *Persistence of Memory*, (1931), and *Premonition of the Civil War* (1936).

During the Spanish Civil War (1936-1939), he took up residence in Italy, where he occupied himself with religous, historical and

allegorical themes. Perhaps the most famous painting of that era is *The Christ of St. John and the Cross*. He held numerous exhibitions the world over, some of them retrospectives (London, Paris, Madrid, Ferrara). He played an active part in the diffusion of Catalan modernism. He also collaborated in some of the films directed by Alfred Hitchcock and his friend Luis Buñuel.

In 1974, he inaugurated a museum dedicated to his work in Figueres, the most visited by foreigners in Catalonia. He created the Gala-Dalí Foundation, entrusted with administering his heritage. His controversial will and testament and the economic interests surrounding his work have created a still-unresolved flurry among the institutions who stand to gain an important part of his work.

ANTONI TÀPIES I PUIG
(Barcelona, 1923)

Antoni Tàpies is one of the most universally famous painters of our time. During the 1940s, influenced by Joan Miró and Paul Klee, he developed surrealist figurativism. He later ventured alone into new terrain, with works ranging from portraiture to dream-like abstraction. In the mid 1950s, he began to move towards informalism, and to work with a variety of materials (sand, clothing, straw) in a "collage" format. In the seventies, his work took on clear political overtones, opposing in a militant fashion the dictatorship of General Franco and in support of the recovery of the rights and the freedom of his country, Catalonia. It was also in that decade that his work began to take the form of sculpture, a medium which he further developed in the eighties with the use of terra cotta. Tàpies has illustrated literary texts and has made a notable contribution to bibliographic production in general and to the libraries of the rare book collector in particular.

Later, after the Peking exhibition of 1989, the influence of oriental art became apparent in his painting. In fact, however, his interest in the aesthetics of the Far East can be traced back to the 1940s, and is visible in a series of works: *Collage of rice and ropes*, *Figure of newspaper and thread*, etc.

Tàpies himself offered the key to interpreting his work with the following statement: "I have been able to make my paintings objects whose power resides in the paintings themselves, without them having to describe the world we see". Despite the lack of artistic sensitivity he has identified in the art world today, his work attempts to touch society's collective conscience. The artist has gone so far as to say that if he did not believe that his painting had a role to play in society, then he would no longer paint. Antoni Tàpies has written various books reflecting on the nature of art, including *The Practice of Art* (1970), *Art Against Aesthetics* (1974), and *Towards a Modern and Progressive Art* (1985).

Since 1976 and up to the present, several retrospective exhibitions of his work have been held throughout the world: (Tokyo, 1976; New York, 1977; Rome, 1980; Amsterdam, 1980; Madrid, 1980; Venice, 1982; Milan, 1985; Vienna, 1986; Brussels, 1986, etc.) He has been honoured with an impressive collection of prizes in recent years, including the Prize of the City of Barcelona (1979), the Wolf Prize (1982), the Rembrandt Prize (1983), the Gold Medal of the Generalitat of Catalonia (1983), and the Grand Prize for Painting of France (1984). He is a member of the fine arts academies of Berlin, Vienna and Stockholm, and holds a doctorate from the Royal College of Art in London.

A famous modernist-style building in Barcelona, now crowned with one of the artist's metallic sculptural structures, currently houses the Tàpies Foundation, at the centre of which is a library rich in important resource material on modern art and its evolution, created with the objective of stimulating an understanding of art as well as oriental spirituality.

VICTÒRIA DELS ÀNGELS LÓPEZ I GARCÍA
(Barcelona, 1923)

Known around the world by this name, Victòria dels Àngels studied at the Conservatory of the Gran Teatre del Liceu, in Barcelona, between 1939 and 1942. She made her official debut at the Palau de la Música Catalana in 1944 while still a student. During the 1944-1945 season, she sang for the first time at the Liceu in Barcelona with *Le nozze di Figaro* (by Mozart) and later performed *Clorinda* (by Monteverdi), *La serva padrona* (by Pergolesi) and *Susanna* (by Wolf-Ferrari). She continued to perform at the Liceu during the years 1946, 1947, 1948, 1949, 1950, 1956, 1957, 1959, 1961 and 1966.

She embarked upon her international singing career in the 1949-1950 season, travelling through Europe and America. She made her debut at the Paris Opera with *Faust* (by Gounod), and later was received enthusiastically at Covent Garden of London, where she performed *La bohème* (by Puccini). During that same season, she visited the city of the "bel canto", the "Teatro alla Scala" of Milan, with a recital. Months later, Victòria dels Àngels triumphed in Milan with *Ariadne auf Naxos* (by R. Strauss) and *Don Giovanni* (by Mozart). She sang at Carnegie Hall in New York that same year, and in 1951 performed *Faust* at the Metropolitan Opera House. Between 1951 and 1971, she sang at the Edinburgh Festival. In 1961, she opened the Festival of Bayreuth, where no other Catalan singer had ever performed.

She is recognized as one of the greatest concert performers, and specialises in ancient Spanish music, pre-Baroque and Baroque repertoire, German *lied*, French songs and the music of our composers — whom Victòria dels Àngels has managed to make known to all the major concert halls of the world — and her repertoire includes more than 1,200 works, comprising 60 different programmes.

The prizes awarded to Victòria dels Àngels are numerous. They include: the Gold Medal of the Liceu of Barcelona (1955), the Gold Medal of the City of Barcelona (1958), the Oscar for Recordings in the United States for her recording of *Madame Butterfly*, and the Edison Prize (1963) for the quality of her performances. In Spain, she has been honoured with the National Music Award of the Ministry of Culture (1978). In 1981, she was named Honorary Fellow by the Saint George Royal Academy of Fine Arts (Reial Acadèmia de Belles Arts de Sant Jordi). And in 1987, she received an honorary doctorate from the University of Barcelona.

Artur Llopis has said that the exceptional art of Victòria dels Angels "is not especially impressive for its volume or for its impetuousness, but it is particularly fascinating for its magical delicacy, for its clear translucence, for its variety and ineffable expressivity in its sweetness and in its pathos." The Norwegian soprano Kirsten Flagstad, after hearing Victòria dels Àngels, wrote her the following: "I heard you yesterday afternoon as Margarida in *Faust* and was enthused. It is very rare to find a mature voice that is so perfectly directed. What a pleasure to know a role word by word".

Apart from her exceptional quality, achieved through rigorous dedication and study, the openness and complete sincerity of her performances are the keys to Victòria dels Àngels' success, an eminent opera singer who recognizes the importance of communicating with her audience. She has said, in that respect, that "the public is fifty percent of what we are."

MONTSERRAT CABALLÉ I FOLC

(Barcelona, 1933)

Soprano. She studied singing and piano at the Liceu Conservatory in Barcelona, and began in the lied modality with Conxita Badia, a soprano as well as a singing professor. In 1957, she obtained a three years grant to complete her studies in Basel and to sing there as a beginner. In 1960, she moved to Germany (Bremen), where she performed for three more years, and later moved on to Austria. She had still not accomplished what she dreamt of: to sing in Barcelona. That happened in 1962, when she took the stage at the Gran Teatre del Liceu for the first time. From there, she began to perform in various Latin American countries: Mexico, Peru, Brazil, Puerto Rico, and Argentina. In 1965, she made her major debut at the Metropolitan Opera House in New York. Thus began a brilliant international career. In 1967 she took the most prestigious stage in the world: La Scala in Milan.

Montserrat Caballé possesses an incredible repertoire of 102 operas, in addition to *lieder*, *zarzuelas*, and popular Catalan songs. As a singer, of course, she has her favorites. It has been said that the operas she performs with greatest satisfaction are *Salomé* and *Madame Butterfly*. Apart from her prodigious talent, Montserrat Caballé bases her continued success on the perpetual and profound study of the works she performs and on her familiarity with the styles of various composers. She herself has declared: "I insist on the need for great musical training, which has been my lifelong obsession".

JOSEP CARRERAS I COLL

(Barcelona, 1946)

Tenor. At the age of eleven, he took the stage at the Liceu Theatre in Barcelona for the first time, and performed the role of the child in *El Retablo de Maese Pedro*, by Manuel de Falla. His authentic debut as a professional, also at the Liceu, took place in 1970, when he played opposite Montserrat Caballé — his artistic mentor — in the opera *Norma* by Bellini. From then on he successfully performed on the most important stages in the world: the Metropolitan Opera House in New York (1974), Covent Garden in London (1974), Teatro alla Scala in Milan (1975), and Salzburg (1976). When he

seemed to be on the brink of world-wide fame, a grave illness forced him to stop performing. Medical science and his strong will, however, contributed to his recovery. He has recovered his success, and has demonstrated his humanity by sponsoring several concerts for charity.

His lyric voice, full of feeling, permits him to be the greatest performer of the operas of Verdi, Puccini and Donizetti. He is considered world-wide as the greatest tenor of the eighties. His repertoire also includes popular Catalan songs. In 1984, he was given the Gold Medal of the Generalitat of Catalonia.

CATALONIA AS SEEN BY NON-CATALANS

All nations are defined by characteristics or traits that can be accurately applied in a general way, despite the stereotypes that are passed down through the ages. A nation's geography, economy, political life and historical circumstances explain its nature and the environment it creates. It is natural that a nation situated between the Iberian Peninsula and the continent should be visited over the centuries by travellers who have recorded their impressions and opinions of it.

It seems an interesting idea to include in the supplementary pages of a book which attempts to portray a nation in all of its aspects, a few brush strokes by authors the world over who have set out to paint full or partial portraits of the ancient and modern Catalan and of the world around him.

The reader will observe that their order of appearance is strictly chronological.

"Each one of those gentlemen of Catalonia are the devil incarnate, as no other being of the land or the sea is. It would please God that they were reconciled with the Church! — for these are people who could lay conquest to the entire world and smite all infidels."

Words of **POPE HONORIUS IV,**
according to the historian Ramon Muntaner
(1265-1336)

"Barcelona is set on the edge of the sea, a very suitable situation for commerce. Even so, trade is not as strong as in the past, and so the city is not as rich as it was before, and even less so with the presence of the Court in Castile. It is a very beautiful city, large and populous. One does not see particularly notable or fine buildings, but in general the houses are very pretty throughout the city, and so, as they say with such precision, it is a city through and through, something which, in my opinion, is most admirable; in this, it is better even than Florence.

"Even so, if I am not mistaken, it cannot truly be compared to Florence, which surpasses it in the splendour of its public and private buildings and which has prettier and cleaner streets, although Barcelona boasts of sharing this last characteristic. The surrounding countryside is fertile for miles around. But if one travels three or four leagues from the city, he will find himself in savage territory, in which there are a few sparse villages, far apart and of little importance.

"Catalonia is called a Principality and not a Kingdom, and it has its own privileges and laws, without which the King cannot rule them. I still have not come to understand what it obtains from this."

FRANCESCO GUICCIARDINI
Ambassador of Florence
(1483-1540)

"The Catalan language is the language of the courtiers and was spoken by those Princes.

"Because the Catalan nation, which until then had contended for the sea with Pisians, Venetians and Genoese, was very feared, and had gained great honour with foreigners, with whom they had great wars in older times, of much repute and honour in that city.

"The King (Peter IV) left Pina one day, and went to sleep in Candasnos, and then to Fraga, and when he saw that town, he told Sir Bernardo de Cabrera to rejoice, that this was Catalonia, and he began to praise it and say fine things of it, of the loyalty of the Catalans, and cursing the land of Aragon: and such was the general sentiment of the Kings, because since they succeeded the Count of Barcelona, they always had Catalonia as their natural and ancient country, and conformed completely to their laws and customs, and the language they used was Catalan, and it was spoken by all the most important courtiers of those times."

JERÓNIMO ZURITA
Aragonese historian
(1512-1580)

"Barcelona, that beautiful city, head of that nation that surpassed all those of Europe in nobility, beauty and decor."

FATHER JUAN DE MARIANA
Castilian Jesuit, historian
(1536-1624)

"I came to Barcelona, archive of courtesy, shelter of foreigners, hospital of the poor, home of the valiant, vengeance of the offended and pleasing site of firm friendships, and in its setting and beauty, unique. And although my experiences there have not been pleasant, but rather sorrowful, I leave unburdened by sorrow for having seen this city."

"...The courteous Catalans are temperamental, frightening; pacific, mild; people who easily give up their lives for honour, and fight for the chance to defend one another, which is the way to surpass all other nations in the world."

MIGUEL DE CERVANTES
Castilian writer
(1547-1616)

"The Catalans are a monstrous abortion of politics. Free with a master; for this reason the Count of Barcelona is not dignity, but rather verbage and naked voice. They have a prince the way the body had a soul to live, and as this prince wrongfully speaks out against their desires and vices, they wrongfully speak out against his privileges and exemptions. They say that they have a Count, as one says he has a certain number of years, being the former who possesses the latter."

FRANCISCO DE QUEVEDO
Castilian writer
(1580-1645)

"Barcelona, capital of the wise, model of honesty, touchstone of Kings."

"...The Catalans know how to be friends to their friends; they are also bad with their enemies; it is clear that they think much be fore beginning a friendship, but once it has begun, it is eternal..."

BALTASAR GRACIÁN
Aragonese writer and ecclesiastic
(1601-1658)

"The Catalans, for the most part, are of a hard nature; their words are few and seem to form a language of its own, with very brief clauses and diction; they respond greatly to any offense, and so are inclined to vengeance; they value highly their honour and their word, and no less their privileges, for among the other nations of Spain, it is they who love their liberty.

"Those different voices are still conserved in Catalonia, although they are impressively united around the cause of their defense, something well worth noting, for although among them there is a great range of opinion and sentiment, they have joined strongly around a purpose, and thus diversity and age-old disputes never give rise to a division; a good example to show or confound the pride and disparity of other nations whose success in certain areas depends on a union of spirits."

FRANCISCO MANUEL DE MELO
Portuguese historian and military man
(1608-1666)

"The abundance and the delights of Catalonia have not softened its inhabitants; on the contrary, they have always been warriors and those from the mountains have been especially ferocious; but despite their bravery and their extreme love of liberty, they have been subjugated throughout history: the Romans, the Visigoths, the Vandals, the Saracens: all have dominated them."

VOLTAIRE
(FRANÇOIS-MARIE AROUET)
French writer and thinker
(1694-1778)

"Catalonia is almost throughout extremely mountainous. The nature of the country appears to have great influence on that of the inhabitants, who are a hardy, active, industrious race, of a middle size, brown complexion, and strong features; their limbs well knit together, and by education and practice inured to the greatest fatigues (...) The loss of all their immunities, and an enormous load of taxes, have not been able to stifle their independent spirit."

HENRY SWINBURNE
English writer and traveller
(London, 18th century)

"Although Catalonia has not received Nature's favours, it is the best and richest part of the Peninsula, the most well-mannered, and that which best helps the traveller... And in what does their felicity consist? In their flexibility and in their refusal to partake of vain feuds or overindulgence. If in Spain everyone were Catalan in their actions, we would all benefit from riches and a more powerful State. Catalonia is a tiny England within Spain. No one doubts this, but everyone refuses to imitate it."

FRANCISCO MARIANO NIFO
Spanish journalist
(1719-1803)

"I would like to point out some special characteristics of this Principality, which should be appreciated for the industriousness of its inhabitants, for its tireless search within and without for the means to improve its fortune. It is not in the Catalan's nature to rest on his laurels; on the contrary, he actively finds solutions and opens up new paths, always at the exclusion of indulgence and lassitude.

"Catalonia is known as one of the most populous provinces of Europe, and the Catalans are known to be as hard-working as those of the most hard-working province. It is not that I believe that the population could not acquire greater wealth, or that the work of the arts and professions could not reach greater perfection. The erudite Rev. Jayme Caresmar, known for his literature and his diligent research of history through the Archives of this province, is of the opinion and has demonstrated that Catalonia was, up until the fifteenth century, richer, more populous, more cultivated and more fertile than it has been since then, and furthermore, that a quarter of the Principality's villages have since disappeared, leaving only their names."

ANTONIO PONZ PIQUER
Spanish historian and erudite
(1741-1782)

"The Catalans are the most industrious people of Spain. Their manufacturing, fishing, navigation, commerce and law are unknown to the rest of peninsula. They are not only useful in times of peace, but even more so during war. The manufacture of cannons, weapons, uniforms and saddles for the army, the transport of artillery, munitions and foodstuffs, the formation of excellent light troops: all of this comes from Catalonia. The fields are cultivated, the population grows, riches increase, and to be sure, this nation seems a thousand leagues away from Galicia, Andalusia and Castile. But their temperament is difficult, dedicated only to their own profit and gain. Some call them the Dutch of Spain. My friend Nuño says that this province will flourish as long as it is not infiltrated with personal luxury and the mania for ennobling the artesans: two vices that would occupy the genius that has until now made them wealthy (...)

"I have just arrived in Barcelona. The little that I have seen assured me that what Nuño told me about the genius of the Catalans and the usefulness of this Principality is the truth. For a pair of provinces such as this, the king of the Christians could trade his two Americas. More riches could the crown gather from the industriousness of these people than from the poverty of millions of Indians. If I were the leader of all of Spain, and I had to chose from among its people to select my servants, I would make the Catalans my butlers."

JOSÉ CADALSO
Spanish military man and writer
(1741-1782)

"Today I would like to take you, my friend Goethe, to a land which can only be compared with two others in Europe. A land where the landscape and its inhabitants have formed a reciprocal and marvellous union, and where even the foreigner who has for an instant distanced himself from the world and from man, contemplates, with singular sentiments, the hamlets and cities that stretch out before him and go on for as long as the eye can see. I want to take you, my friend, to the refuge of Montserrat, near Barcelona.

"I have spent two unforgettably beautiful days there, during which I have not tired of remembering you. Your *Secrets* form a living part of my memory. I have always loved that beautiful poem which I find seeped in a marvellously human and yet elevated sentiment, but I had never associated it with my own experience until I discovered this land. It is not that this experience has made it more precious, but rather it has made it more intimately mine."

"...The two provinces through which one enters and leaves Spain, Biscay and Catalonia, have remarkably similar landscapes: mountains, an abundance of trees, and beauty. The vegetation is also similar, for example, the oaks. But Catalonia is larger and prettier: the mountains and the valleys have more personality and the vegetation, like the orange trees, aloes and palm trees, although scarce, is milder and more meridional. The greatest difference is between the inhabitants. The Basques, especially the men, surpass the Catalans in confidence, cleverness and the expression of their courage, but the Catalans, especially the women, have a softer and more tender bearing. The Basques are mountain people and are closer to the state of nature. The Catalans are active and industrious, but are also reflective and calculating in business. The Catalans are also strong, brave and quick, but they do not possess the delicacy of the Basques".

KARL WILHELM VON HUMBOLDT
German diplomat and philologist
(1767-1835)

"To speak to you of the Principality of Catalonia I would need the art with which Rousseau paints what he imagines. In Valencia I saw nature laugh. In Catalonia I saw man fight against nature, impose laws upon it, make it obey, and surprise his fellow man. I have not travelled to Holland nor to Venice. Without having seen them I know what was achieved through a love of liberty accompanied by moderation and virtue. All of that seems little in comparison to what I am describing to you. Mountains as high as ours, too steep for the ox to climb, or for the plough to master; sandy and rocky land cut continuously without achieving a level surface; extreme dryness in places that cannot be irrigated; these are great inheritances, rich gardens, well-distributed stretches of grapevines, fields sowed with wheat and corn; forests of olive and cork. Every mountain is the object of admiration for the curious traveller. The poplar trees run along the mountain ridges, and the green leaves hurt by the morning sun and, beaten by the wind, refresh the view and make one reflect that this is where the virtuous labourer offers to the Supreme Being the fruit of his work."

MANUEL LORENZO DE VIDAURRE
Peruvian writer and jurist
(1772-1841)

"For a long time, Catalonia has governed itself. Since the middle of the eleventh century it had its own particular laws and local customs, with which Count Raymond Berenguer, in the year 1068, set down in place of the Gothic laws, which had fallen into disuse. It had its own particular states, composed of three orders: the clergy, the nobility, and the municipalities, which shared the legislative power with the sovereign. No law could be passed without the simultaneous agreement of both of these powers, and the king, on taking the throne, was obliged to swear to maintain these customs. Apart from this independent form, the Catalans had particular and quite extensive privileges, among which we point out the following: first, that the voluntary donations given to the kings could never be considered taxes; second, to never be judged, in civil or criminal cases, by any law other than the law of Catalonia; third, that the judges be chosen from among their compatriots; and finally, that one's property could not be confiscated for any crime, except for crimes committed against the king.

"The Catalans are reproached for their dryness of character and their rudeness of expression. This portrait may have some foundation, but if one searches for its origin and at the same time considers his excellent qualities, no one would take pleasure in speaking ill of them. The Catalans, accustomed under the kings of Aragon to sharing legislative power with the sovereign, to not recognizing his prince except as the Count of Barcelona, to paying taxes only when they wish, to forming only the troops they want to, to considering themselves as participants in the sovereign authority, have, as a result, a notion of independence that has been perpetuated over the years. From this they derive a pride that is unique to this province and an imperative tone, of which there still remain some traces. These minor defects have perhaps contributed to the success of their great enterprises. It is often necessary to be proud of not being defeated in order to attain victory; and when one is endowed, as are the Catalans, with a tireless activity and a patience that endures all tests, one must succeed, as they have done, in the riskiest adventures. Commerce seems to have a special attraction for them: it is the base of their riches, and its influence extends through their arts and in their studies."

ALEXANDRE DE LABORDE
French nobleman, scholar, and traveller
(1773-1842)

"The province of Catalonia is the richest and most active in Spain. Their many factories of wool, linen, paper, iron, cotton, leather, sockets, etc., give the pleasant spectacle of a hard-working people who owe their prosperity to the tireless application of their individuals and carry out a very lucrative commerce in the other provinces and abroad. Although the Catalans inhabit a rocky and mountainous terrain, their industrious hands have cultivated even the most inhospitable spots."

ISIDORO DE ANTILLÓN
Spanish geographer and politician
(1778-1814)

"It seems to me that the Catalans find themselves in the same case as the metallurgic industrialists of France. These gentlemen want just laws, with the exception of the law of customs, which they like to tailor to their taste. The Catalans demand that every Spaniard who wears cotton should pay four francs a year so that Catalonia may exist in the world.

"The Spaniard from Granada, from Malaga or from Coruña cannot buy English cloth, which is excellent and costs one franc a rod, for example, and must buy Catalan cloth, of far inferior quality and at three francs the rod.

"These people are republican and secretly admire Jean-Jacques Rousseau and *The Social Contract*; they pretend to value what is *useful for everyone* and to detest the injustices from which the minority profits; that is, they detest the privileges of the nobleman *which they do not share*, and they want to continue enjoying the privileges of commerce, which in other times have driven them to absolute monarchies. The Catalans are liberals in the same way that the poet Alfieri was, a count who hated the kings, but who considered the privileges of the counts sacred."

STENDHAL (HENRI BEYLE)
French writer
(1783-1842)

"In crossing through the formidable and immense fortifications of Barcelona, with a munitions port, drawbridges, poterns and bastions, everything decries a city in arms. But after the triple siege of cannons, and the isolation from the rest of Spain through banditry and civil war, the sparkling youth strolls under the sun along the Rambla, a long avenue lined with trees and buildings, like our boulevards. The women, beautiful, charming and coquettish, are worried about the crease of their shawls and the play in their fans; and the men, with their cigars, laughing, chatting, looking sideways at the women, talking about Italian operas and giving the sensation that they are not too concerned with what happens outside their walls. But when night arrives, the opera ends, the guitars have disappeared and the city becomes the domain of peaceful strollers, the only sound one can hear, alongside the monotonous rumour of the sea, are the sinister shouts of the guards and the shots, even more sinister, which are occasionally fired, quick and rapid, now far, now near, and always at the first light of dawn. Then everything is silent again for an hour or two, and the bourgeois seem to sleep peacefully while the port awakes and the sailors begin their daily bustle."

GEORGE SAND (AURORE DUPIN)
French writer
(1804-1876)

"The Catalans are the most industrious, business-like, enterprising people in Spain; they are the Scotch of this country, as the Andalusians are the Irish, and the Asturians the Welsh. They are sober, laborious, honest, enthusiastic for progress, proud of their own, looking up to France for example and competition, and down on the surrounding provinces with contempt and pity.

"Wherever there are trade, fabrics, enterprise, there you are sure to find Catalans; in England, in America, in the East, they have everywhere, and in all ages and times, carried their insatiable love of enterprise and activity. They are vehement, austere, revengeful, and generally not capable of great feeling or lasting friendship, and egotism seems to be a pivot around which all their actions turn. They are besides destitute of stability in their own political principles, and have sold themselves always to the highest bidder; but it must not be forgotten that in their hearts and souls they are neither Spaniards nor French, they are Catalans; and in their eyes, there is only one Cataluña, and Barcelona is its prophet. Their religion reaches superstition; their activity degenerates into feverish craving; their love of liberty has led them to bloodshed, excesses, and rapine. They hold the commerce of Spain in their hands, and have been justly defined, as a province, the Spanish Lancashire. Cataluña has been always the centre of rebellion, the focus of republicanism and democracy; it is the feeder of Spain, its stomach, which is the centre and cause of all disease in the great body. They are patient and daring soldiers, excellent sailors, and model smugglers and mountain guerrillas."

HENRY O'SHEA
English writer and Spanish diplomat
(1838-1905)

"The sea came up to here," a merchant told me in his odd and pintoresque store (there everything is small commerce) where I had taken refuge to see how, across the little plaza, the octogonal towers of the façade of Santa Maria del Mar and the colored rose-window that illuminated it like the glow of brilliant gems. From this church the *condottieri* of the sea left, to direct the great fleets armed by the rich and lofty Catalan businessmen and which fell like flocks of birds of prey over the rocks of the Mediterranean, where they constructed, as they passed, their nests of glory and blood. The Balearic Islands, Sicily, Greece, Asia Minor, were the heroic periods of an uninterrupted exploit renovated over the course of three centuries, and within a step of these galleys, kingdoms and principalities were born. Today the adventure has ended, but the positive spirit, audacious and reminiscent of a time which every Catalan carries within him, suddenly obliges him to march in dense and formidable columns, serious, obstinate, coldly furious through the streets of Barcelona, breaking and destroying. To conquer what? A new world of wealth and well-being, Paradise. And where is it? Up ahead, he knows, where this red flag with black letters reading "Long live the social revolution."

JUSTO SIERRA
Mexican historian, politician and pedagogue
(1848-1912)

"I have travelled much in my life, pushed by the itch of curiosity, and I have come across people of all possible nationalities and positions, but I have never come across a group of people as sincere and pure of heart as in Catalonia, the poetic land of the troubadors.

"Let us speak of the social life of Catalonia, its customs, industries, arts and literature. We find ourselves before the interesting and original surprise which makes this picturesque corner, bathed by the Mediterranean, a different nation from anything we have seen in Spain before.

"The Catalan writer would have enough time to die of starvation twenty times before receiving some profit from his work. Coroleu, despite the quantity of marvellous writing that would have made him rich if it were in French, must live off the sale of the oil and wine from his modest farm near Barcelona.

"This is one of the characteristics of all Catalan writers, without exception: none of them can live off literature as an artisan would, and none wants to. Literature is like his lover; he loves it passionately, but can only see her secretly, when he has fulfilled his obligations. Probably for this reason, his love for her is so strong and so honest. When I present these people to you by their names, you shall be convinced.

"In the first place, they have as their milestone the glory of the country, the development of its wealth, education, science, arts and industry. With constance and obstinacy of that goal in mind, changing little by little our sentiments and sincerely loving his country, the Catalans praise it (...)

"The Catalans have fame in Spain as egoists and unpleasant people, but under close observation I have become convinced that this is the result of a historical and impassioned enmity. The Catalan, as a person, devotes himself fully and tirelessly to work, knows how to administrate money in his everyday affairs; at the same time, in the case of some social problem or collective need, or simply a question of public utility, there is no one more general and more human and with greater spirit. I was in Barcelona when the telegraph arrived with news of the disaster in Andalusia. Without cries, or noise, or grandiloquent words, committees for the collection of donations were formed immediately.

"One cannot say that the Catalan does not have a sociable character, but as the serious person that he is, he choses his acquaintances and friendships carefully, and does not form them with the first person he meets. If a Catalan tells you that you are his friend, you may put your faith in his words; they will not disappear in the wind. The Catalan will always help you, he will rescue you from any mishap, and will be disinterestedly and completely at your service. I can only compare Catalan hospitality with our own, the Russian. The foreigner who arrives in Barcelona with good recommendations feels at home from the first moment."

ISAAC PAVLOVSKI
Russian writer
(1852-1924)

"There is no hate in Catalonia, nor in Barcelona, nor is there envy either. The Spaniards from the other regions have been constantly pondering and exalting the industrious spirit of the Catalan — it is the other Spaniards who invented the phrase: "the Catalans get bread out of rocks" — and with this they have revived and excited that native vanity that is so strongly rooted and grows beneath the Mediterranean sun. And this vanity, this petulant pride and arrogant petulance that fills the air of Barcelona, makes the other simple and modest folk — the Castilian, for his other defects, is simple and modest even in his arrogance —, upon finding himself in that atmosphere of aggressive petulance, feel hurt and bothered.

"This boastfulness, no doubt fed by the interested adulation of foreigners, is accompanied by a pernicious selfishness and is the source of all kinds of unjust judgements. The native of Barcelona, and the Catalan in general, complains that the rest of Spain does not know him and so judges them harshly out of their ignorance, which is true; but it is no less true, and rather more true, that they know the rest of Spain even less than the rest of Spain knows them, and that out of their ignorance they judge it much more injustly than the rest of Spain judges them."

MIGUEL DE UNAMUNO
Spanish philosopher, novelist and essayist
(1864-1936)

"I discard, my dear friend Américo Castro, a long speech or judgement and classification of the Hispanic dialects which for years could have been familiar to me, and I do not dispute the importance or grandeur in the political domain of the more important Hispanic provinces. I will limit myself to Catalonia and mentally reconstruct its linguistic literary history since the Middle Ages up until our time. Can one deny the richness and originality, the vast dominion of Catalan, which echoed strongly, audaciously, brilliantly, in Greece itself, which blossomed and was invigorated aside its sister language, Provençal, and was the expression of a great people; giving life to ideas, to commerce, and for centuries (until the Renaissance), producing its own remarkable art, the prose of brilliant chroniclers, the poetry of the most select and strongest spirits absorbed in grave and mystic meditations such as Ausiàs Marc? Was it not through Catalan that the elegant poetry of Dante was introduced into Castile and later to the entire peninsula? Did not the doctrines, phantasies and knightly tales of Ramon Llull echo the world over?

"The fact that the central province has come to dominate and rule the destiny of hispanic literature, called national literature, does not diminish the value of this exuberant manifestation of Catalan spiritual life with the language of the Catalans. Neither the lethargy of coming centuries nor the absorption carried out by the throne of the most powerful nation, can erase the indestructible riches of Catalan culture."

ARTURO FARINELLI
Italian erudite, writer in various languages
(1867-1948)

"As, for example, the Institut d'Estudis Catalans. I have the most pleasant and long-lasting impression of this cultural centre. I admire in it first the copious Cervantian collection, the first in the world, rich in original editions, of rare and unique copies, of the finest printing and binding, a bibliophile's delight.

"Barcelona is a *façade*, Unamuno has said. My passing observation does not confirm the accuracy of this judgement, for what it negatively implies about the solidity and intensity of its culture. It is true that these people take care of the façade, and in that I see nothing wrong; but behind the façade, I see, in the home of the Catalans, the inside: I see an artistic hall, a copious library, a comfortable dining room, abundant and well-cultivated gardens. In general, I see that status which is the root of all grandeur and the secret of all triumph: energy. And this energy is the same when it takes the form of the will as when it takes the form of the imagination. Along with a visibly positive character, calculating, utilitarian (let us not forget that it is here in Barcelona where D. Quijote is vanquished); along with a powerful drive for work which sends smoke from the factories of Sants, Sabadell and Terrassa to the sky, one also sees the persistence of artistic instinct which made this people, in its day, the propagators of an ideal of refined and knightly poetry.

"And there is another character to the force, another manifestation of the energy, which you may observe as much in the lofty tendencies of the culture as in the arrangement of a garden or the design of a street lamp: the longing to be original, the aspiration to produce something of their own.

"All of this sum of energies which we can see in the atmosphere is concentrated and resolved in one idea, in an inspiring sentiment: the idea that Catalonia is the country, the true and glorious country, and the pride in belonging to it. *Civis romanus sum!* And this, the most intimate depth, transcends and rises to the surface with a fervour of a hot spring. There is no one who with any facility for observation, could come into contact with these people and not perceive, at first glance, the interior impulse that lifts and stimulates them; of a common personality that with every passing day acquires a greater awareness of itself, and a firmer and loftier notion of its capacities and destinies. Whatever the final result of this spiritual restlessness, no one can fail to recognize that a collective sentiment of such intensity is a force, and a force that is not likely to end in nothing."

JOSÉ ENRIQUE RODÓ
Uruguayan intellectual, writer and politician
(1872-1917)

CATALAN LAND
How close I am to you... without
[knowing how,
oh Catalan land!
Land of the coasts of green coves,
of the people of white houses,
of the hills of fresh pines,
of the open plains of rich land,
land which has known how to make
[a bucolic rumour
of the fertile rumblings of the factories,
of the solemn and gentle men
who know how to belong to yesterday
[and to tomorrow.
How close I am to you..., without
[knowing how,
oh Catalan land!

GREGORIO MARAÑÓN
Spanish physician, historian and writer
(1887-1960)

"Of the *Catalan nationality* there is no doubt that one can speak of the fact that there exists a common language and historico-cultural conscience, strongly perceived as such. The problem that I pose is precisely the play between this underlying fact of *stable community* and the existence of a political demand for sovereignty, at times realized, at times frustrated; at times forgotten, other times resurgent. The historical dialectic between *nationality*, a long-term fact, *nationalism*, a restless awareness, and *nation*, a politically organized group: this is what I am interested in studying."

PIERRE VILAR
French historian
Text published in 1962

"Beyond compromise and conditions, there exists a Catalan way of life in which I see three essential characteristics. First, a love for the concrete reality of the material world and the consequent appreciation of beauty, and the fruition of this material world as a thing valuable in and of itself. Secondly, the attribution of an intrinsic value — with reference to his earthly end — to the life of man in the world. And, in third place, the adaptation, at the same time labourious and ironic, of man to his own limits and to the limits with which, in his concrete reality, things are presented to him."

PEDRO LAÍN ENTRALGO
Spanish philosopher and writer
Text published in 1971

"I also think it necessary that the Catalans depart from that purely defensive attitude and adopt the conviction that they possess a language with as much creative capacity as Castilian or any other, and that it is up to them to give this Catalan language the full Iberian resonance that it should have. And naturally, we shall do everything in our power to make known the creative reality of Catalonia, of course. But it is especially the Catalans to whom this task falls, and we cannot by any means play a paternalistic role, even in a subtle way, because we do not have the right to.

"And the Catalans must understand that they must fight for themselves and they must fight for their lands; of course, in the area of politics, but also in the area of work well done — we have mentioned Eugeni D'Ors above — so that it will be seen by people like the Castilians who, in any case, are more disposed, and better endowed, to understand Catalonia than they were fifty years ago."

JOSÉ LUIS ARANGUREN
Spanish professor of philosophy and writer
Text published in 1983

"The Catalan, in his region, feels intensely 'at home'; when he is away, his nostalgia is so strong, he so misses certain forms of immediate familiarity, that he feels in some way like a 'foreigner', and this overrides in him an awareness of belonging to a larger house. Many Spaniards are scandalized — perhaps this is the best word — when they learn that most Catalans feel 'more Catalan than Spanish'. The phenomenon is clear and unequivocal; but I don't think that if it is interpreted correctly, it should be the cause of any scandal.

"Most Spaniards think that Spain is 'more important' than their region; one must put it 'first', 'above' — and other spacial images. They feel 'Spanish of such-and-such a regional variety'. In some regions, in general — but not exactly — those regions in which other languages besides Spanish are spoken, the case is not quite so clear.

"The Catalans cannot conceive of being anything but Catalans. For other Spaniards, there is a certain margin of 'fate' in their regional condition: they are Castilians, or Extremadurans, or Asturians, but they could have perhaps been something else. The Andalusians, if they ever reflected on the question, would probably think 'what else would they be if not Andalusians?' but they are such with spontaneity, I would say vegetively and as something obvious. The Catalans feel radically a part of the world of Catalonia, they need to enjoy it, feel sure of it, never question it."

JULIÁN MARÍAS
Spanish professor of philosophy and writer
Text published in 1966

"I see the landscape of Catalan culture in a completely mature and modern situation. It seems to me that Catalonia — naturally, as a function of the cultural circulation characteristic of our time — has recovered its role as transit point, as modernizing filter between Europe and the Peninsula. Whether we look at poetry, the novel, literary criticism, or whether we examine the arts, and even the so-called lesser arts, as light music is now considered, Catalonia seems to receive all of the influences of our time and to add to them. Furthermore, this variety and multiplication, this curiosity and creation, are not the mere result of a simple cultural loan: one arrives there upon penetrating the indigenous forms and currents of foreign thought (...). Altogether it is the index of the existential vitality of the Catalan culture, actively inserted in the framework of modern manifestations, something that promises a truly bright future."

GIUSEPPE E. SANSONE
Italian professor of Romance Languages

"In search of the essence of Catalonia the keen eye and the attentive ear will find many clues in popular culture and legend. Kings and heroes, demons and dragons and comic characters all sway along in the festival processions or figure in mime and song. None of them represents any single incontrovertible truth about the Catalans. But it is a sign of maturity that the grave *sardana*, an expression of *seny*, and the licentious *Patum de Berga* with its strong dose of *rauxa*, can both flourish at one and the same time: it is a wise nation that devises an appropriate outlet for all its impulses."

ALISTAIR BOYD (LORD KILMARNOCK)
English writer and politician
Text published in 1988

"And so it can be understood that the role of Barcelona, city and port, is essentially Catalan. Nevertheless, there are also, thanks to the same considerations of nature, an Iberian role of the first order and the most important condition of its development is the increase in the Spanish market. In effect, Spain can become for Europe a source of agricultural products and of raw materials and an interesting market for the important industrial products from abroad or transformed in Catalonia. It is understandable why the Catalans have protested about the backwardness of Spain, which limited its own development as intermediaries, and why they have sought in Spain a leading role. Its port must follow this tendency in the interior as a means of continuing in its role as the only great Spanish outlet to the Mediterranean."

JACQUELINE ORVAL
French journalist
Text published in 1936

"As it is known, man, like the animals, has a particular hormone, adrenaline, which increases its presence in the blood and muscles in moments of fear, to put us in a state of special alert. Those who live as Catalans need another special hormone which I would call 'CUM'. All Catalan speakers who defend the right to that language's normalized existence should have great reserves of 'CUM'. Especially in moments of exhaustion, a good dose of 'CUM' is needed. And to change established habit, a strong first dose of 'CUM' is called for. 'CUM' means *'consciència'n un més'* or *'convenç-ne un més'* (convince one more) or *'crea un multiplicador (més)!'* (create one more multiplier).

"Catalonia, I mean the Catalonia formed by the Principality (with the North and Andorra) the Valencian Country and the Balearic Islands, is the most populous nation and the most culturally and economically productive in modern-day Europe that has not achieved one of those independencies (relative in the area of economics among others) of which other European nations — some of them even smaller — enjoy. This seems to me a clear sign of a lack of 'CUM' in the past. In German we would say: *'Katalonien hat den richtigen Moment verschlafen'*: Catalonia, sleeping, has let its moment pass. The nations of the Portuguese and the Dutch, and later the Polish, the Hungarians, the Romanians, the Czechs and the Slovaks, the Albanians, the Norwegians, the Icelandic, etc., have taken advantage of the propitious historical moments to do that which gave a sure guarantee of the future: to fight until their neighbours let them exist with political independence. The grave 'defect' of the Catalans is, then, as seen from outside, to not have been as alert as in the hymn *Els Segadors* and to have wanted to reach a pact, and to co-exist when those pacts were more dangerous than a firm position demanding the right to live without their neighbour's interference. I repeat that this pacific position of the Catalans is also very pleasant and comfortable for their neighbours, but for the Catalans...

"The Germans have taken a heavy burden on their shoulders: the Second World War, begun by Hitler, which has cost the lives of 60 million people. It is fair, then, that territorial reclamations not be made from Germany. But the Catalans have not committed any such upheaval and have the logical legitimacy to demand their territory, objectively contained within the limits of the Catalan language. It is, then, an injustice that another people with another language continue wanting to rule in Catalan territory."

TIL STEGMANN
German professor of Romance Studies
at Frankfurt
Text published in 1988

"The idea of beginning again, of starting to walk, which characterizes the Catalan nationalist movement of the nineteenth century, can be clearly recognized in the terminology it created. *Renaixença*: this is the motto of the period and concepts such as *regeneració* and *renovació* are frequent. The self-image of the Catalan national movement is that of a renaissance that gradually makes its way into all areas of life. Maragall goes back to the theological essence of thought during the Renaissance and applies to Catalonia the concept of palingenesis, which means that after a long night of death — the centuries of Catalan decadence — a new life is awakened. It is no coincidence that it is a vocabulary similar to that with which the writers of the sixteenth century (let us recall Calvin's commentary on the Gospel according to St. John) tried to show the process of return.

"*Renaixença*, in a general sense, means the recuperation and the new creation of that which can be considered a national identity for Catalonia. At the same time, *Renaixença* does not at any time mean the return to that which had already existed; it was never a *restoration* (although the conservative-restorative thought had as its focus the Catalan movement of the nineteenth century). In the long run it was seen that the *Renaixença* had another objective: the creation of a modern Catalan culture comparable to the industrial nations of Europe."

HORST HINA
German professor of the Depart.
of Modern Languages at the University
of Freiburg im Breisgau
Text published in 1978

"These quick lines on Bishop Mariano Martí necessarily remind me of other Catalans resident in Venezuela who, like other brave folk from diverse latitudes, opened then and continue opening today powerful furrows in the areas of culture, industry, commerce and crafts. Many of them have turned out to be excellent emulators of the incomparable *don* Mariano. I shall only be able to mention a few among the many whom I recall in a rapid reflection.

"The first, without doubt, for his scope and his international merits, is that eminent physiologist, the late Augusto Pi Suñer, whose tireless mastery and brilliance contributed so much to the modernization of our medicine from 1937 onwards. An eminent professor, he created such a following that his name has seemed to revitalize itself and survive thirty years later, when in the halls of the Alma Mater one of his students, now with grey hair like his mentor before him, shares the knowledge imparted by the great man, whom I had the chance to meet when his shoulders were already weighed down with years. His brother, *don* Carlos, is also owed a debt by the Venezuelans for his detailed, prolonged, and fertile research which has allowed our historians to gain great knowledge from the English archives, in the foreign papers referring to Miranda and to Bello."

MAURO PÁEZ
Venezuelan researcher
Text published in 1970

CATALAN PRESENCE IN THE WORLD

This annex consists of information dealing with the Catalan presence in the world. It includes several kinds of information: Catalan social clubs and meeting places for Catalans and followers of our country; universities and non-university centres throughout the world where the Catalan language is taught; entities whose objective is the study or promotion of issues related to Catalan cultural or scientific life. And, finally, those public and private organizations representing the Catalan Government or other institutions.

The information collected herein has been provided by Josep Nubiola, Head of the Service of Institutional Affairs of the Generalitat of Catalonia Presidency Departament, or extracted from *Presència catalana al món*, an essay by Xavier Tudela.

CATALAN SOCIAL CLUBS AND ASSOCIATIONS AROUND THE WORLD

AFRICA

EQUATORIAL GUINEA

Grup de Catalans
Address:
c.o. Sr. Pere P. Simarro
Apartado de Correos 560
Bata

NORTH AMERICA

CANADA

Casal Català
Centre Paul-Sauvé
4000, Rue Beaubien est 300
Montréal, Québec H1X 1H6
Telephone: 1.514.729 12 94

Centre Català el Gresol
Address:
c.o. Sr. Josep Sabater
510 Innes Street
Nelson B.C. V1L 5E9

Casal Cultural Muntaner
Address:
2775, Rue Sasseville
Ste. Foy, Québec G1W 1A1

Casal dels Països Catalans
Address:
P.O. Box 6660 Postal Station A
Toronto, Ontario M5W 1X5

Esbart Català de Colúmbia Britànica
Address:
30746-3640 East Hastings Street
Vancouver, B.C. V5K 2A6

MEXICO

Centre Català
Address:
Apartado Postal 1-1121
Guadalajara, Jalisco 44100

Orfeó Català, A.C.
Marsella, 45
Colonia Juárez
Deleg. Cuauhtemoc 06600 México D.F.
Telephone: 52.5.525 09 25

Casal Català
Address:
Local, 55 Plaza Dorada
Puebla, Pue.

USA

Casal dels Catalans de Califòrnia
Address:
P.O. Box 91142
Los Angeles, Ca 90009

Casal Català
The Florida Catalan Society
University of Miami
Coral Gables, F1 33124
Telephone: 1.305.284 43 03

American Institute for Catalan Studies
Address:
c.o. Sr. David Cardús
14314 Cindywood
Houston, Texas 77079

Associació de Catalans de l'Àrea de Washington
Address:
P.O. Box 9481
Washington D.C. 20016-9481

CENTRAL AMERICA

COSTA RICA

Casal Català
Address:
Apartado 3861
San José 1000

CUBA

Societat de Beneficència de Naturals de Catalunya
Consulado 68 (entre Genios y Refugios)
Centro Habana, 2
La Habana

GUATEMALA

Casal Català
Address:
17 Ave. 11-73, Zona 15,
VH III Guatemala

PUERTO RICO

Casal Català
Address:
c.o. Sr. Josep M. Bernada
Box 1406 Carolina
Puerto Rico 00628

DOMINICAN REPUBLIC

Casal Català
Address:
Apartado Postal 437
Santo Domingo D.N.

SOUTH AMERICA

ARGENTINA

Casal de Catalunya
Chacabuco, 863
1069 Buenos Aires
Telephone: 54.1.23 41 41

Obra Cultural Catalana
Address:
Casilla de Correos, 77
Sucursal 6
1406 Buenos Aires

Les Quatre Barres
Machado, 1560
1712 Castelar, Buenos Aires
Telephone: 54.1.629 73 09

Casal Català
Urquiza, 1612
Córdoba

Casal Català
Address:
Bolívar 3283/85
7600 Mar del Plata

Centre Català
San Juan, 1436
5500 Mendoza
Telephone: 54.61.23 38 75

Agrupació Catalana
Address:
Ruta 8, km 225
2700 Pergamino

Centre Català
Entre Ríos, 761
2000 Rosario
Telephone: 54.41.25 52 98

BRAZIL

Casal Català
Address:
Rua Buenos Aires, 466 (Batel)
08230 Curitiba PR

Associació Cultural Joan Miró
Address:
Av. Cidade Jardim, 280, 5º
CEP 01454 São Paulo

Grup de Catalans
Address:
c.o. Sr. Jacint Vila
Caixa Postal 9963
CEP 01051 São Paulo

CHILE

Centre Català
Av. Suecia, 414-428
Santiago de Chile
Address:
Casilla de Correos 2278

Centre Cultural Català
Address:
Casilla 161
Viña del Mar

COLOMBIA

Comunitat Catalana
Address:
c.o. Sr. Pere Jané
Apartado Nacional 1481
Bogotá D.E.

ECUADOR

Casal Català
Address:
Casilla de Correos núm. 1321
Guayaquil

Casal Català
Address:
Vàncouver, 333 e Italia
Quito

PARAGUAY

Centre Català
Cerro Corá, 276
Asunción

URUGUAY

Casal Català
Francisco Araucho, 1186
Montevideo
Telephone: 598.2.79 90 22

VENEZUELA

Centre Català
Final Tercera Avenida
Los Palos Grandes (entre 10 y 11)
Caracas
Telephone: 58.2.283 75 35

Associació Països Catalans
Address:
c.o. Sr. Jaume Alberdi
Apartado 4084
Puerto de la Cruz

ASIA

PEOPLE'S REPUBLIC OF CHINA

Casal Català
Address:
c.o. Sr. Ramon Santaulària
Agència Efe
Jianguomenwai 2-2-132
Beijing

UNITED ARAB EMIRATES

Grup de Catalans
Address:
c.o. Sr. Joan Dedeu
P.O. Box 3242
Sharjah

EUROPE

AUSTRIA

Casal Català
Address:
Zentag, 1228
1050 Wien

BELGIUM

Casal Català
Address:
Desguinlei 194
2018 Antwerpen

Centre Josep Carner
Address:
c.o. Sra. Mercè Roca
Rue Van Artevelde, 161, Bte. 30
1000 Bruxelles

FRANCE

Casal Català
Address:
Boîte Postale 469
16001 Angoulême-Cedex

Cercle Català
89, Rue Jean de Bernardy
13001 Marseille
Telephone: 33.91.62 16 32

Casal de Catalunya
41, Rue Berzélius
75017 Paris
Telephone: 33.1.42 63 06 81
Address:
c.o. Sr. Jaume Mir
SQ. Roger-Martin-Du-Gard C4
Villeneuve-La-Garenne

Centre Cultural Català
2, Rue Saint Mathieu
66000 Perpignan
Telephone: 33.68.35 38 91

Casal Català de Tolosa de Llenguadoc
7, Rue Novarts
31300 Toulouse

GERMANY

AKL
Grup de Treball Països Catalans
Address:
c.o. Sr. Francesc Sala-Duch
Maria-Hall-Str. 44
6072 Dreieich

Associació Catalana
Address:
c.o. Sr. Jordi Lloveras
Postfach 10 23 02
43 Essen 1

Casa Nostra
Address:
Affentorplatz, Affentorhaus, 2
6000 Frankfurt-Main 70

Casal Català, E.V.
Address:
Am Graswege, 32
3 Hannover 1

Casa Nostra
Address:
Postfach 1122
7141 Möglingen

Associació de Gent de Parla Catalana
Address:
Brüder Grimm Strasse, 28
3501 Niestetal 2, Kassel

Amics de Pau Casals
Address:
c.o. Sra. Matilde Romagosa
Lange Herzogstraβe, 46
3340 Wolfenbüttel

ITALY

Catalans a Roma
Address:
Via Eugenio II, 18
00167 Roma

LUXEMBOURG

Centre Català
Address:
24, Avenue Victor Hugo
1750 Luxembourg

NETHERLANDS

Centre Català
Address:
c.o. Sra. Roser Misiego
Anthoni Spatzierhof, 29
10 65 SJ Amsterdam

Casal Català
Address:
c.o. Sra. Montserrat Pérez Bastar
Nightingalestr. 60
2131 EC Hoofddorp
Amsterdam

NORWAY

Club Català de Noruega
Address:
Olaf Schousvei, 1
0572 Oslo

SPAIN

Centre Català
Gral. Primo de Rivera, 12, entl.
03002 Alacant

Centre Català de Biscaia
Address:
Alameda San Mamés, 38, 6° C
48010 Bilbo/Bilbao

Casa Catalana
Av. Comte de Sallent, 16
07003 Ciutat de Mallorca
Telephone: (971) 25 13 59

Centre Català
Poeta Juan Ramón Jiménez, 2
14012 Córdoba
Telephone: (957) 27 42 21

Llar Catalana
Address:
Apartado de Correos 2117
A Coruña

Cercle Català
Plaza de España, 6 (Ed. Catalunya)
28013 Madrid
Telephone: (91) 241 60 90

Casal Català de Menorca
Address:
Concepció, 6, 1r
Maó, Menorca

Casa Catalana
Murga, 44
35003 Las Palmas de Gran Canaria
Telephone: (928) 37 33 01

Cercle Català de Navarra
Aralar, 46, 1a dcha.
31004 Iruñea/Pamplona
Telephone: (948) 23 98 63

Casal de Catalunya a Guipúscoa
Café Guria
P° de la República Argentina, s/n
2004 Donostia/San Sebastián
Telephone: (943) 41 11 70

Casa Catalana
Fernando el Católico, 23
50006 Zaragoza
Telephone: (976) 45 78 24

SWEDEN

Les Quatre Barres
Address:
Humlegarddsgatan, 17, 2tr OG
11446 Stockholm

SWITZERLAND

Casa Nostra
Address:
Postfach 213
5430 Wettingen 1
Baden-Wettingen

Casa Nostra
Address:
c.o. Sra. Concepció Kühner
Friedhofstrasse, 2
4127 Birsfelden
Basel

Casa Nostra
Address:
Postfach 2
3144 Gasel
Bern

Casa Nostra
Address:
Case Postale 60
1211 Genève 16

Centre Català de Lausana
Av. des Acacias, 8
1008 Prilly
Telephone: 41.21.51 30 02
Address:
c.o. Sr. Gabriel Montoliu
Av. Général Guisan, 50
1800 Vevey

Casa Nostra
Address:
Weiherhof, 23
8604 Volkestwil
Winterthur-Schaffhausen

Casa Nostra
Address:
Postfach 17
8060 Zürich

Casa Nostra de Suïssa
Address:
Postfach 17
8060 Zürich

OCEANIA

AUSTRALIA

Associació Cultural Catalana
Address:
P.O. Box 263
Annerley 4103
Queensland (Australia)
Brisbane

Casal Català de Sidney
Address:
N. 2 Firts Ave.
Canley Vale 2166
New South Wales (Australia)

Spanish Society of North-Queensland
(Grup Català)
Address:
c.o. Sr. Benet Droguet
42, Alice Parkside
Ayr 4807
Queensland (Australia)
Townsville

Casal Català de Victòria
Address:
P.O. Box 17
Highett 3190
Victoria (Australia)
Melbourne

UNIVERSITIES AND CENTRES OF CATALAN STUDIES

NORTH AMERICA

CANADA

University of Alberta
Faculty of Arts. Department of Romance Languages
103 Arts Building
Edmonton, Alberta
Canada, T6G 2E6

University of British Columbia
Department of Hispanic Studies

2075 Westbrook Mall
Vancouver, British Columbia
Canada, V6T 1W5

University of Saskatchewan
Department of Hispanic Studies
Saskatoon, Saskatchewan
Canada, S7N OWO

University of Toronto
Department of Hispanic and Portuguese Studies
Toronto, Ontario
Canada, M5S 1A1

MEXICO

Universidad Nacional Autónoma de México
Ciudad Universitaria
04510 México DF

PUERTO RICO

Universidad de Puerto Rico
Facultad de Humanidades, Departamento de Estudios Hispánicos
Recinto de Río Piedras
00931 Puerto Rico

USA

Arizona State University
Department of Foreign Languages
Tempe, AZ 85281

Boston University
College of Liberal Arts, Department of Modern Foreign Languages
718, Commonwealth Ave
Boston, MA 02215

Brown University
Department of Hispanic and Italian Studies
Providence, RI 02912

Bryn Mawr College
Department of Philosophy
Bryn Mawr, PA 19010

Calasanctius School
167, Windsor Ave
Buffalo, NY. 14209

California State University
Department of Modern Languages
Chico, CA 95929

Columbia University
Department of History
New York, NY 10027

Eastern College
Department of Languages
Saint Davids, PA 19087

Georgetown University
School of Languages and Lings
Washington D.C. 20057

Illinois State University
Dept. of Foreign Languages
Bloomington, IL 61761

Indiana University
Department of Spanish and Portuguese
Bloomington, IN 47405

Kent State University
Department of Spanish
Kent, OH 44242

Marquette University
Department of Spanish
Milwaukee, WI 53233

Marshall University
Department of Modern Languages
Huntington, WV 25701

Michigan State University
Department of Romance Languages
E. Lansing, MA 48824 1027

New York University
Department of Spanish and Portuguese
19, University Place
New York, NY 10003

North Carolina State University
Department of Foreign Languages
Raleigh, NC 27650

Northwestern University
Department of Spanish and Portuguese
Evanston, IL 60201

Ohio State University
Department of Spanish
190, North Oval Drive Columbus, OH 43210

Princeton University
Department of Art and Archaeology
104, McCormick Hall
Princeton, NJ 08544

Rutgers
The State University of New Jersey
Faculty of Arts and Sciences
Department of Spanish and Portuguese
New Brunswick, NJ 08903

State University of New York
Department of Romance Languages and Literatures
Binghamton, NY 13901

Syracuse University
Department of Foreign Languages and Literatures Spanish and Portuguese
206 H.B. Crouse
Syracuse, New York 13244. 1160

Tennessee Technological University
Department of Foreign Languages
Cookville, TN 38505

The Catholic University of America
Department of Spanish
Washington D.C. 20017

The University of Pennsylvania
Department of Spanish
Philadelphia, PE 19014

UCLA
Department of Spanish and Portuguese
Los Angeles, CA 90024

University of Buffalo
Department of Modern Languages and Literatures
Faculty of Arts and Letters
910 Clemens Hall
Buffalo, NY 14260

University of Arizona
Department of Spanish
Tucson, AZ 95721

University of California
Department of Spanish and Portuguese
Santa Barbara, CA 93106

University of California/Centre d'Estudis Catalans
Department of Spanish and Portuguese
Berkeley, CA 94720

University of Colorado
Department of Spanish and Portuguese
Boulder CO 80309

University of Connecticut
Department of Spanish Studies
CT 06268

University of Florida
Department of Spanish
Gainesville, FL 32601

University of Georgia
Department of Modern Languages
Moore College Athens
GA 30602

University of Illinois
Department of Spanish, Italian and Portuguese
Urbana, IL 61801

University of Massachusetts
Department of Spanish and Portuguese
Amherst, MA 01003

University of Miami
Department of Foreign Languages
Coral Gables, FL 33124

University of Michigan
Department of Spanish
Ann Arbor, MI 48104

University of New Hampshire
Department of Spanish and Classics
Durham, NH 03824

University of North Carolina
Department of Spanish
Chapel Hill, NC 27514

University of Rhode Island
Department of Languages
Kingston, RI 02881

University of South Florida
Department of Foreign Languages
Tampa, FL 33620

University of Texas
Department of Spanish and Portuguese
Austin, TX 78712

University of Texas
College of Fine and Applied Arts
Division of Arts and Design
San Antonio, TX 78285

University of the South
Department of Spanish
Swanee, TN 37375

University of Washington
Department of Romance Langs.
Seattle, WA 98195

University of Winconsin-Madison
Department of Spanish
590, Lincoln Drive
Madison, WI 53706

Vanderbilt University
Department of Spanish and Portuguese
Nashville, TN 37235

West Virginia University
Department of Foreign Languages
Chitwood Hall
Morgantown, WV 26506

Western Maryland College
Department of Foreign Languages
Westminster, MA 21157

Yale University
Department of Spanish and Portuguese
P.O. Box 10. A Yale Station
New Haven, CT 06520

SOUTH AMERICA

BRAZIL

Universidade Santa Úrsula
Rua Fernando Ferrari, 75
22260 Rio de Janeiro

NON-UNIVERSITY STUDY

Casa de Rui Barbosa (linked to the Culture Ministry)
Rua São Clemente, 134
22260 Rio de Janeiro

ASIA

JAPAN

Waseda University
Language Teaching Institute
1-6-1, Nishi-Waseda Shinjuku-ku
Tokyo 161

EUROPE

AUSTRIA

Universität Salzburg
Institut für Romanische Philologien der Universität Salzburg
Akademiestr. 24
5020 Salzburg

Universität Wien/Vienna
Institut für Romanistik der Universität Wien.
Schlickgasse 4/2. Stock
1090 Wien

BELGIUM

Université Libre de Bruxelles
Vrije Universiteit Brussel
Instituut Voor Taalon-berwijs
Pleinlaan, 2. 1050 Brussel

BULGARIA

University of Sofia
«Kliment Ohridski»
Faculty of Classical and Modern Literature
Chair of Ibero-Romance Philology
15 Ruski Bd
1000 Sofija

CZECHOSLOVAKIA

Universita Karlová
Ovocný trh. 5
Praha 1

DENMARK

Aarhus Universitet
Romansk Institut
Nordre Ringgade 1
8000 Aarhus C

Københavns/Copenhaguen Universitet
Romansk Institut
Njalsgade 78-80
2300 Kobenhavn S

Odense Universitet
Romansk Institut
Campusvej 55
5230 Odense M

FINLAND

University of Helsinki
Helsingin Yliopisto
Ibero-Romaanisten Kielten Oppituoli
Hallituskatu 11-13
SF-00100 Helsinki 10

FRANCE

Université de Bordeaux III
Institut de Langues Romanes
Esplanade Michel de Montaigne
Domaine Universitaire
33045 Talence Cedex

Université des Langúes et Lettres de Grenoble III
Institut de Langues Romanes
Domaine Universitaire
Saint Martin d'Hères 25
38040 Grenoble Cedex

Université de Limoges
Institut de Langues Romanes
Allé André Maurois
F-87065 Limoges Cedex

Université de Lyon II
Institut de Langues Romanes
86, rue Pasteur
69365 Lyon Cedex 2

Université Paul Valéry Montpelhièr III
Institut de Langues Romanes
Route de Mende, BP 5043
34032 Montpellier. Cedex

Université de la Sorbonne-Nouvelle-Paris III
Institut Ibérique Gay-Lussac
17, place de la Sorbonne
75230 Paris Cedex 05

Université de Paris-Sorbonne-Paris IV.
Centre d'Études Catalanes de l'Université de Paris IV
9, rue Sainte Croix de la Bretonnerie
75004 Paris

Université de Poitiers
Institut de Langues Romanes
15, rue de Blossac
86034 Poitiers Cedex

Université de Provence
Institut de Langues Romanes
29, Ave. Schuman
13621 Aix-en-Provence

Université de Haute-Bretagne Rennes II
Institut de Langues Romanes
6, avenue Gaston Berger
35043 Rennes Cedex

Université de Sciences Humaines-Strasbourg II
Institut de Langues Romanes
22, rue Descartes
67084 Strasbourg Cedex

Université de Toulouse-le-Mirail Toulouse II
Institut d'Études Hispaniques et Hispano-Américaines
Département de Catalan
109 bis, carrièra Vauquelin
31058 Toulouse Cedex

GERMANY

Karl-Marx-Universität
Sektion Theoretische und angewandte Sprachwissenschaft

Augustus-Platz 9
7010 Leipzig

Universität Augsburg
Lehrstuhl für angewandte
Sprachwissenschaft (Romanistik) der Universität Augsburg
Alter Postweg 120
8900 Augsburg

Universität Bamberg
Romanische Sprach- und Literaturwissenschaft
Postfach 1549
8600 Bamberg

Freie Universität Berlin
Fachbereich Neuere Fremdsprachliche Philologien
Institut für Romanische Philologie
Habelschwerdter Allee 45
1000 Berlin 33

Universität Bielefeld
Sprachenzentrum 1
Fakultät Für Geschichte
Postfach 8640
4800 Bielefeld 1

Freie Universität Berlin
Sprachenzentrum 1
Fakultät Für Geschichte
Postfach 8640
4800 Bielefeld 1

Universität Bochum
Romanisches Seminar
Postfach 10 21 48
4630 Bochum 1

Universität Bonn
Romanisches Seminar
der Universität Bonn
Am Hof. 1
5300 Bonn

Universität Bremen
Romanisches Seminar
der Universität Bremen
Postfach 33 04 40
2800 Bremen 33

Universität Erlangen-Nürnberg
Institut für Romanistik
Bismarckstr. I
8520 Erlangen

Universität Frankfurt
Institut für Romanische Sprachen und Literaturen der J.W. Goethe Universität
Gräfstraße 76
Postfach 11 19 32
6000 Frankfurt am Main 11

Universität Freiburg im Breisgau
Romanisches Seminar der Albert-Ludwigs-Universität
Werthmannplatz 3
7800 Freiburg im Breisgau

Johannes-Gutenberg-Universität
Fachbereich 23 (FAS)
An der Hochschule 2
6728 Germersheim

Universität Göttingen
Seminar für Romanische
Philologien der Universität
Göttingen. Nikolausbergerweg 25
3400 Göttingen

Universität Hamburg
Ibero-amerikanisches Forschungsinstitut
Romanisches Seminar der Universität Hamburg
Von-Melle-Park 6
2000 Hamburg

Universität Heidelberg
Romanisches Seminar der Universität Heidelberg
Seminarstraße 3
6900 Heidelberg

Universität Kiel
Romanisches Seminar der Universität Kiel
Leibnizstr. 10
2300 Kiel

Universität Köln/Cologne
Romanisches Seminar der Universität Köln
Albertus-Magnus-Platz
5000 Köln 41

Universität Konstanz/Constance
Fakultäten für Literaturwissenschaft und für Sprachwissenschaft
Postfach 5560
7750 Konstanz

Universität Mainz
Romanisches Seminar
Postfach 3980
6500 Mainz 1

Universität München/Munich
Romanisches Seminar der Universität München Ludwigstraße 24
8000 München 22

Universität Münster
Romanisches Seminar der Universität Münster
Spanisch-portugiesisch-lateinamerikanische Abteilung
Bispinghof 3
4400 Münster

Universität Paderborn
Romanistisches Seminar
Postfach 1621
4790 Paderborn

Universität Regensburg
Institut für Romanistik
Gebäu. de PT. Universitätsstraße 31
Postfach 397
8400 Regensburg

Universität Trier
Frachbereich II (Romanistik)
Postfach 3825
5500 Trier

Universität Tübingen
Romanisches Seminar der Universität Tübingen
Wilhelmstraße 50
7400 Tübingen

Universität Würzburg
Romanisches Seminar der Julius-Maximilians-Universität
Sanderring 2
8700 Würzburg

CATALAN CULTURE COURSES FOR ADULTS

Bildungszentrum der Stadt Nürnberg
(Vokshochschule) Rollnerstr. 15
8500 Nürnberg

Kreisvolkshochschule Wolfenbüttel
Stöberstr. 11-15
3340 Wolfenbüttel

HUNGARY

Eötvös Loránd Tudomànyegyetem
Spanyol Tanszék
1364 Budapest, Pf. 107

IRELAND

University College
Department of Spanish
Cork/Corcaigh

ITALY

Università degli Studi di Bari
Istituto di lingua e letteratura spagnola e portoghese
Via Garruba, 6/b
70122 Bari

Università Magisterio di Firenze
Istituto Ispanico
Via di Parione, 7
50123 Firenze

Università degli Studi di Cagliari
Dipartimento di Filologie e Letterature Moderne
Facoltà di Lettere e Filosofia e di Magisterio. Sa Duchessa
09100 Cagliari

Università Cattolica del Sacro Cuore
Istituto di Letterature Medioevali e Moderne.
Facoltà di Lettere
Largo A., Gemelli,
20123 Milano

Istituto Universitario Orientale
Seminario di Studi dell'Occidente Medievale e Moderno
Cattedra di Lingua e Letteratura Catalana

Piazza S. Giovanni Maggiore, 30
80134 Napoli

Università degli Studi di Napoli
Dipartimento di Filologia Moderna
Via Porta di Massa, 1
80133 Napoli

Università degli Studi di Perugia
Istituto di lingue e letterature straniere
Via del Verzaro, 4ª
06100 Perugia

Università degli Studi di Roma «La Sapienza»
Facoltà di Lettere e Filosofia
Dipartimento di Studi Romanzi
Piazzale Aldo Moro, 5
Città Universitaria
00185 Roma

Università degli Studi di Roma «La Sapienza»
Facoltà di Magisterio
Piazzale Aldo Moro, 5
Città Universitaria
00185 Roma

Università degli Studi di Torino
Dipartimento di Scienze Letterarie e Filologiche
Via S. Ottavio, 20
10124 Torino

Università degli Studi di Venezia
Facoltà di Lingue e Letterature Straniere
Seminario di Letterature Iberiche e Iberoamericane
Ca'Garzoni-Moro
San Marco 3417
30124 Venezia

NETHERLANDS

Universitat Estatal d'Amsterdam
Gemeentelijke Universiteit van Amsterdam
Spui 21
Postbus 19268
1000 GG Amsterdam

Universitat Estatal d'Utrecht
Rijksuniversiteit Utrecht Spaans, portugees en ibero-amerikaans instituut
Drift 29. 3512 Utrecht

NORWAY

Universitetet Oslo
Romansk Institut Avd. B. Blindernveian, Blindern Oslo, 3

POLAND

Jaguiellon University of Cracow
Institute of Romance Philology
Krakòw

RUMANIA

Universitatea din Bucuresti
Linguistics Institute
Spiru Haret, 12
3515 Bucuresti

SPAIN

Universidad Complutense de Madrid
Facultad de Filología
Departamento de Hispánicas
Ciudad Universitaria
28003 Madrid

Universidad de Salamanca
Facultat de Filosofía y Letras
Departamento de Lingüística Románica
Plaza Anaya, 2/n
37001 Salamanca

NON-UNIVERTSITY STUDY

Escuela Oficial de Idiomas de Madrid
Jesús Maestro, s/n
28003 Madrid

SWEDEN

Göteborgs Universitet
Institutionen för romanska sprak
Lundgrensgatan 7
412 56 Göteborg

Stockholms Universitet
Romanska institutionen
106 91 Stockholm

Uppsalas Universitet
Romanska institutionen
Box 513
751 20 Uppsala

SWITZERLAND

Universität Basel
Romanisches Seminar der Universität Basel
Stapfelberg, 7
4051 Basel

Université de Fribourg
Séminaire de Langues et Littératures Ibériques
1700 Fribourg

Universität Zürich
Romanisches Seminar der Universität Zürich
Plattenstrasse, 32
8028 Zürich

UNITED KINGDOM

University of Aberdeen
Department of Spanish
King's College
Aberdeen, Scotland-2UB

University of Bath
School of Modern Languages
Claverton Down
Bath BA 2 7 AY

The Queen's University of Belfast
Department of Spanish
Belfast, Northern Ireland BT7 INN

University of Birmingham
Department of Hispanic Studies
P.O. Box 363
Birmingham B15 2TT

University of Bradford
Modern Languages Centre
Bradford, West Yorkshire BD7 1 DP

University of Bristol
Department of Hispanic and Latin-American Studies
15, Woodland Road
Bristol BS 8 1TE

University College of Wales
Department of Hispanic Studies
P.O. Box 78
Cardiff/Caerdydd-CF1 1XI

University College of Wales
Department of Romance Studies
Singleton Park
Swansea. Wales SA2 8PP

University of Cambridge
Fitzwilliam College
Department of Spanish
2, Sidgwick avenue
Cambridge CB3 9DA

University of Durham
Department of Spanish
Elvet Riverside, New Elvet
Durham DH1 3JT

University of Essex
Department of Literature
Wivenhoe Park
Colchester, Essex CO4 3SQ

University of Leeds
Department of Spanish and Portuguese
Leeds LS2 9JT

University of Liverpool
Department of Hispanic Studies
PO. Box 147
Liverpool L69 3BX

University of London
Westfield College
Department of Spanish
Finchley Road
London NE3 7ST

University of Nottingham
Department of Hispanic Studies
University Park
Nottingham NG7 2RD

University of Oxford
Faculty of Medieval and Modern Languages
Taylor Institution St. Giles
Oxford 0X1 3NA

University of Sheffield
Department of Hispanic Studies
Sheffield S10 2TN

University of Southampton
Department of Spanish
Southampton S09 5NH

University of St. Andrews
Department of Spanish
Castle Cliff, The Scores
St. Andrews, Scotland KY15 9AL

NON-UNIVERSITY STUDIES

Catalan Culture Courses for Adults
Sra. Marta Cardona
416 Wakefield Road. 68
Huddersfield HDS 9XJ

Marylebone
Paddington Institute Quintin Kynaston Branch
Marlborough Hill
London NW8

USSR

Leningradski Universitet
Fakultet Filologii
Otdelenie romanskai linguistiki
Universitetskaja nabereznaja, 11
Sankt Petersburg 1

Moskovskij Universitet
Fakultet filologii Otdelenie Ispanskogo
Portugalskogo jasikov
Leninskie Gory
Moskva

YUGOSLAVIA

Republiski Komité za Kulturo
Comkarjeva, 5
61000 Ljubljana

OCEANIA

AUSTRALIA

La Traobe University
Department of Spanish, Portuguese and Catalan
Bundoora, Victoria. 3083

CENTRES FOR THE STUDY OF CATALAN CULTURE

NORTH AMERICA

USA

American Institute for Catalan Studies
14314 Cindywood
Houston, Texas 77079

North American Catalan Society
Dept. of Romance Langs.
State Univ. of New York
Binghamton, NY 13901

ASIA

JAPAN

The Japan-Catalonia Friendship Association
Saló de Catalunya
Toda Build, 4F, Ginza 7-14-7,
Chuo-ku Tokyo

EUROPE

GERMANY

Deutsch-Katalanische Gesellschaft/ Associació Germano-Catalana
See Oficina Catalana.

Oficina Catalana
Katalanisches Kulturbüro
Jordanstr. 10
6000 Frankfurt am Main 9
Tel.: (49-69) 70 73 44
Fax: 707 37 45

Biblioteca Catalana de Frankfurt
Institut für Romanische Sprachen und Literaturen der J.W. Goethe-Universität
Postfach 11 19 32
6000 Frankfurt am Main 11

ITALY

Associazione Italiana di Studi Catalani
c.o. Giuseppe Grilli
Via Canalone All'Olivella 21
08135 Napoli

Associazione Italiana di Studi Catalani
c.o. Giuseppe Tavani
Via G.B. Morgagni, 35
00161 Roma

UNITED KINGDOM

Anglo-Catalan Society
c.o. David George. Dept. of Romance Studies University College of Wales
Singleton Park
Swansea SA28PP

PUBLIC AND PRIVATE ORGANISMS OF REPRESENTATION ABROAD

CIDEM

Av. Diagonal, 403, 1r
08037 Barcelona
Tel. (93) 217 20 53

CIDEM OFFICES OUTSIDE CATALONIA

San Francisco
50 California Street
CA 94111 San Francisco

New York
747 Third Avenue, 20th. floor
NY 10017 New York

Tokyo
Shuwa Kioocho TBR Building 1214
5-7, Kojimachi, Chiyoda-Ku
102 Tokyo-Japó

Brussels
Rue Archimède, 5, 4ème
1040 Bruxelles

COPCA (Consortium for Commercial Promotion)

Av. Diagonal, 550, pral. 1a
08021 Barcelona
Tel. (93) 209 05 66

CATALAN PRO EUROPA BOARD

Bruc, 50, 2n
08010 Barcelona
Tel. (93) 318 26 26

LOCAL BRANCHES

Brussels
Rue Archimède, 5-9ème
B-1040 Bruxelles
Tel. 07.322.23 03 30

Girona
Gran Via de Jaume I, 46, 5è
17001 Girona
Tel. (972) 22 20 92

Lleida
Anselm Clavé, 2, 6è
25007 Lleida
Tel. (973) 23 92 84

GENERALITAT GOVERNMENT DELEGATION

Official Chamber of Commerce, Industry and Shipping

Madrid
Montalbán, 9, 1° dcha.
28014 Madrid
Tel. (91) 532 33 23

Av. Diagonal, 452
08006 Barcelona
Tel. (93) 219 13 00

CATALAN LITERATURE TRANSLATED INTO OTHER LANGUAGES

A complete list of contemporary Catalan literary works translated into other languages is being gathered at present by the Catalan Literature Institution, an organ of the Catalan Government. The annex herein presented, then, is only a partial approximation to the presence of Catalan literature in other languages. It is an attempt to guide the reader, pending the publication of the complete list which is expected in the near future.

AMADES, Joan (Barcelona, 1890-1959)
L'origen de les bèsties.
L'origine des bêtes: petite cosmogonie catalanae. French version and presentation by Marlène Albert-Llorca. Carcassonne: Garae/Hésiode, 1988.

BARTRA, Agustí (Barcelona, 1908 - Terrassa 1982)
Ecce homo. Foreword by Francesc Vallverdú. 3th ed. Barcelona: Edicions 62, 1982.
Last poems 1977-1982. English version by D. Sam Abrams. Barcelona: North American Studies Institute, 1984. Bilingual edition.

BENGUEREL, Xavier (Barcelona, 1905)
El testament. 7th ed. Barcelona: Club Editor, 1984.
Testament. Polish version by Jadwiga Karbowska. Warszawa: Instytut Wydawniczy Pax, 1982.

CABRÉ, Jaume (Barcelona, 1947)
La teranyina: un estiu maleït. Barcelona: Edicions Proa, 1988.
La toile d'araignée. French version by Patrick Gifreu. Perpignan: Chiendent, 1984.

CARNER, Josep (Barcelona, 1884 - Brussels, 1970)
Auques i ventalls. Prologue and edition by Joan Ferraté. 3th ed. Barcelona: Edicions 62, 1989.
Poems. English version by Pearse Hutchinson. Oxford: Dolphin Book, 1962. Bilingual edition.

CATALÀ, Víctor (L'Escala, 1873-1966) (Pseud. of Caterina Albert i Paradís).
Solitud. 6th ed. Barcelona: Edicions 62, 1988.
Samota. Czech version and preface by Jan Schejbal. Praha: Odeon, 1987.

CUCURULL, Fèlix (Arenys de Mar, 1919)
Poemas escolhidos. Portuguese version of poems by: *El temps que se'ns escapa* and *Ara no us puc dir.* Selection and translation by Stella Leonardos. São Paulo: Monfort Editor, 1968.
Pustinya. Bulgarian version by Svetoslav Kolev. Sofia: Prodzdat, 1968.
O último combate. Portuguese version by Manuel de Seabra. Lisboa: Clube Bibliográfico Editex, 1957.
A miragem. Portuguese version by Manuel de Seabra. Lisboa: Clube Bibliográfico Editex, 1959.
Antologia do conto moderno. Portuguese version and preface by Manuel de Seabra. Coimbra: Editorial Atlántida, 1950.
O silencio e o medo. Portuguese version by Manuel de Seabra. Lisboa: Livros de Brasil, 1961.
Quase uma fabula. Portuguese version by Fernando Mendes. Madeira Tomar: Nova Realidade, 1969.
Dois Povos Ibéricos. Portuguese version by Carlos Loures. Lisboa: Assino and Alvim, 1975.

ESPINÀS, Josep M. (Barcelona, 1927)
El teu nom és Olga. 14th ed. Barcelona: Edicions La Campana, 1989.
Dein Name ist Olga: Briefe an meine mongoloide Tochter. German version by Hans Leopold Davi. Zürich: Pendo, 1988.
Tu nombre es Olga: cartas a mi hija mongólica. Spanish version. Prologue by J. M. Gironella. 7th ed. Barcelona: Edicions La Campana, 1987.
Your name is Olga: you call her mongol, we call her by her name, her friends call her by the name. English version by Pamela Waley; prologue by Claire Rayner. London: Unwin Hyman, 1989.

ESPRIU, Salvador (Santa Coloma de Farners, Selva 1913-Barcelona 1985)
Cementiri de Sinera; Les Hores. Prologue by Francesc Vallverdú. 4th ed. Barcelona: Edicions 62, 1986.
Kimitíri tis Sinéra. Greek version by Kosta E. Tscrópulos. Athina: Astrólabos/Euthíni, 1983.
Sinera cemetery. English version by James Eddy. Barcelona: American Studies Institute, 1988. Bilingual edition.
Llibre de Sinera. 2th ed. Barcelona: Edicions 62, 1985.
Livre de Sinère. French version by Fanchita González Batlle. Paris: François Maspero, 1975. Bilingual edition.
La pell de brau. 6th ed. Barcelona: Edicions 62, 1985.
Die Stierhaut. German version by Fritz Vogelgsang. Frankfurt am Main: Vervuert, 1985.
La pell de brau. English version by Burton Raffel; Marlboro: Marlboro, 1987.
La piel de toro. Spanish version by José Agustín Goytisolo; Barcelona: Lumen, 1983. Bilingual edition.
Primera història d'Esther; Antígona. 9th ed. Barcelona: Edicions 62, 1988.
The story of Esther. English version by Philip Polack. Sheffield: The Anglo-Catalan Society, 1989.
Cristallo di parole. Anthology in Italian in charge of Giulia Lanciani. L'Aquila; Roma: Japadre, 1989.
Lord of the shadow: poems. Anthology in English in charge of Kenneth Lyons. Oxford: Dolphin Book, 1975. Bilingual edition.
Salvador Espriu: izbrannoje perevod s katalonskogo. Anthology in Russian by Je. Babun i N. Mat'aš. Moskva: Raduga, 1987.

FOIX, J. V. (Barcelona, 1893 - 1987)
Gertrudis. Edited by J. Vallcorba. Barcelona: Edicions dels Quaderns Crema, 1983.
Gertrudis; suivi de, KRTU. French version by Anna Domènech and Philippe Laoue-Labarthe. Paris: Christian Bourgois Editeur, 1987.
KRTU. Edited by J. Vallcorba Plana. Barcelona: Edicions dels Quaderns Crema, 1983.

KRTU: *und andere Prosadichtungen.* German version by Eberhard Geisler. Frankfurt am Main: Vervuert, 1988.
Poésie, prose. French version by Montserrat Prudon and Pierre Lartigue. Cognac: Le Temps qu'il fait, 1986.
When I sleep, then I see clearly. Anthology of poems, English version by David H. Rosenthal. New York: Persea Books, cop. 1988. Bilingual edition.
GARCÉS, Tomàs (Barcelona, 1901)
Vers i prosa. Illustrations by Carme Garcés. Barcelona: Editorial Joventut, 1981.
The span of compassion: selected poems 1931-1985. English version by D. Sam Abrams. Barcelona: North American Studies Institute, 1985.
GIMFERRER, Pere (Barcelona, 1945)
Fortuny. Dutch version by Annemieke van de Pas. Amsterdam: Uitgeverij De Arbeiderspers, cop. 1988.
LLOR, Miquel (Barcelona, 1894 - 1966)
Laura a la ciutat dels sants. (6 th ed. Barcelona: Edicions 62, 1988.
Laura. French version by Pascale Bardoulaud. Nîmes: Éditions Jacqueline Chambon, 1988.
Laura en la ciudad de los santos. Spanish version. Barcelona: Ediciones Destino, 1987.
LLULL, Ramon (Palma de Mallorca?, 1232/33 - 1315-16)
Ramon Llull: vida, pensament i obra literària. Anthony Bonner and Lola Badia. Barcelona: Empúries, 1988
Arbre dels exemples o Arbre Exemplifical.
Arbre des exemples: fables et proverbes philosophiques. French version by Armand Llinarès. Paris: Librairie Honoré Champion, 1986.
Llibre d'Amic e Amat (Included in the Libre d'Evast i Blanquerna). Prologue by Lola Badia. Barcelona: Edicions 62 i La Caixa, 1982.
Le livre de l'ami et de l'aimé. French version by Max Jacob. Montpellier: Fata Morgana, 1987.
Livro do amigo e do amado. Portuguese version by Esteve Jaulent. São Paulo: Ediçoes Loyola: Leopoldianum, cop. 1989.
Llibre de les bèsties. (Included in the Llibre de meravelles. Prologue of Joaquim Molas. Barcelona: Edicions 62 i La Caixa, 1980).
Il libro delle bestie. Italian version by Loretta Frattale. Palermo: Novecento, 1987.
Le livre des bêtes. French version by Patrick Gifreu. Vinça: Chiendent, 1985.
MANENT, Marià (Barcelona, 1898 - 1989)
La collita de la boira. Barcelona: Edicions 62, 1987.
The shade of mist: selected poems. Anthology translated into English by D. Sam Abrams. Barcelona: North American Studies Institute, 1984.

MARTORELL, Joanot (Gandia, 1413/1415 - 1468)
Tirant lo Blanc. Adapted by Maria Aurèlia Capmany; illustrations by Manuel Boix. Barcelona: Edicions Proa, 1989. Adapted version for children.
Tirant lo Blanc. English version by David H. Rosenthal. New York: Schoken Books, 1988.
Tirant lo Blanc. Dutch version by Bob de Nijs. Amsterdam: Uitgeverij Bert Bakker, 1988.
Tirant Valkoinen. Finnish version by Paavo Lehtonen. Jyväskylä; Helsinki: Gummerus, 1987.
Tirante il Bianco. Italian version by A. M. Annicchiarico anf others. Roma: La Tipografica, 1984.
MOIX, Terenci (Barcelona, 1945)
El dia que va morir Marilyn. 8th ed. Barcelona: Edicions 62, 1985.
El día que murió Marilyn. Spanish version by José Manuel Velloso. Barcelona: Plaza & Janés, 1984.
Le jour où est morte Marilyn. French version by Gabriel et Vicky Saad. Paris: Le Chemin Vert, 1987.
O dia em que Marilyn morreu. Brazilian versions by Eduardo Brandão. Rio de Janeiro: Globo publishers, 1987.
MONZÓ, Quim (Barcelona, 1952)
...Olivetti, Moulinex, Chaffoteaux et Maury. Barcelona: Edicions dels Quaderns Crema, 1980.
O'Clock. English version by Mary Ann Newman. New York: Ballantine Books, 1986.
...Olivetti, Moulinex, Chaffoteaux et Maury. French version by Patrick Gifreu. Marcevol: Chiendent; Villelonge d'Aude: Atelier du Gué; Lyon: Fédrop, 1983.
MORA, Víctor (Barcelona, 1931)
Els plàtans de Barcelona. 6th ed. Barcelona: Laia, 1984.
Barcelonai platánok. Hungarian version by Konrád Júlia. Budapest: Kozmozs Könyvek, 1977.
MUNTANER, Ramon (Peralada, 1265-Ibiza, 1336)
Crònica. Edited by Marina Gustà. Barcelona: Edicions 62.
Cronache catalane del secolo XIII e XIV. Italian version by Filippo Moisé; introduction by Leonardo Sciascia. Palermo.
OLIVER, Maria Antònia (Manacor 1946)
Estudi en lila. 4th ed. Barcelona: Edicions La Magrana, 1989.
Study in lilac. English version by Kathleen McNerney. London; Sidney; Welligton: Pandora, 1989.
OLLER, Narcís (Valls, 1846-Barcelona, 1930)
La papallona. 5th ed. Barcelona: Selecta-Catalònia, 1988.

La papallona. French version. Preface by Émile Zola. Bilingual edition.
PÀMIES, Sergi (Paris, 1960)
T'hauria de caure la cara de vergonya. Barcelona: Edicions dels Quaderns Crema, 1986.
Aux confins du fricandeau. French version by Anne Bragance. Nîmes: Jacqueline Chambon, 1988.
PÀMIES, Teresa (Balaguer, 1919)
Testament a Praga. Barcelona: Destino, 1971.
Oporoka v Pragi. Slovakian version. Zalozba «Komunist». Drzavna zalozba slovenije, 1983.
Testamento en Praga. Barcelona: Ediciones Destino, 1972.
Dona de pres. Barcelona: Editorial Proa, 1975.
Mujer de preso. Barcelona: Editorial Aymà, 1977.
Vacances aragoneses. Barcelona: Edicions Destino, 1980.
Vacaciones aragonesas. Zaragoza: Heraldo de Aragón, 1981.
Memòria dels morts. Barcelona: Editorial Planeta, 1981.
Memoria de los muertos. Barcelona: Editorial Planeta, 1981.
PEDROLO, Manuel de (L'Aranyó, 1918-Barcelona, 1990)
Mecanoscrit del segon origen. 30th ed. Barcelona: Edicions 62, 1988.
Bigarren Jatorriko Makinizkribua. Basque version by Jokin Lasa. Donostia: Elkar, cop 1989.
Mecanoscript: verslag van een nieuw begin. Dutch version. Rotterdam: Lemniscaat, 198?.
PERUCHO, Joan (Barcelona, 1920)
Les històries naturals. 7th ed. Barcelona: Edicions 62, 1989.
Le hibou: histoires-presque-naturelles. French version by Montserrat Prudon. Paris: Julliard, 1988.
Las historias naturales. Spanish version. Prologue by Antoni Comas. Barcelona: EDHASA, 1978.
Natural history. English version by David H. Rosenthal. New York: Alfred A. Knopf, 1988.
Natuurtlijke historiën. Dutch version by Bob de Nijs. Amsterdam: Uitgeverij Bert Bakker, 1989.
Le storie naturali. Italian version by Angelo Morino, Sonia Piloto di Castri. Milano: Rizzoli, 1989.
Der Nachtkauz. German version by Sabine Ehrhart. Munich/Vienna: Carl Hanser Verlag, 1990.
Natural history. English version by David H. Rosenthal. London: Martin Secker and warbury, 1989.
As histórias naturais. Portuguese version by Artur Guerra. Lisboa: Editorial Teorema, 1990.

RACIONERO, Lluís
La Mediterrània i els bàrbars del Nord. 4th edition, Barcelona: Laia, 1986.
Die Barbaren des Nordens. German version by Roberto de Holanda. Düsseldorf/Wien: Econ Verlag, 1986.

RIBA, Carles (Barcelona, 1893-1959)
Estances. 2th ed. Barcelona: Edicions 62, 1984.
Poems. Anthology. English version by J. L. Gili. 2th ed. rev. Oxford: Dolphin Book, 1970.

RIERA, Carme (Palma de Mallorca, 1948)
Te deix, amor, la mar com a penyora. Prologue by Guillem Frontera. 27th ed. Barcelona: Laia, 1988.
Balkons met triestre dromen. Dutch version by Marga Demmers. Amsterdam: Sara/Ven Gennep, 1988

RODOREDA, Mercè (Barcelona, 1909-Girona, 1983)
La plaça del Diamant. 29th ed. Barcelona. Club Editor, 1987.
Auf der Plaça del Diamant. German version by Hans Weiss; prologue by Gabriel García Márquez. Frankfurt am Main: Suhrkamp, 1984.
Colometa. Dutch version by Elly de Vries Bovée; prologue by Gabriel García Márquez. Amsterdam: Uitgeverij de Bezige Bij, 1987.
A Diamant tér. Hungarian version by Tomcsányi Judit. Budapest: Európa Könyvkiadó, 1978.
Diamanttorget. Swedish version by Jens Nordenhök; Stockholm: Författarförlaget Fisher & Rye, 1989.
A Plaça do Diamante. Portuguese version by Mercedes Balsemão. Lisboa: Publicações Dom Quixote, 1988.
La Place du Diamant. French version by Bernard Lesfargues with the collaboration of Pere Verdaguer. Paris: Gallimard, 1986.
I Platía ton diamantion. Greek version by Dína Sidéri. Athina: Dórikos, 1987.
La Plaza del Diamante. Spanish version by Enrique Sordo. Barcelona: EDHASA, 1984.
Ploscad diamant. Bulgarian version by Maja Genova, Corbadzijska. Sofia: Izdatelstvo Narodna Kultura, 1986.
The time of the doves. English version by David H. Rosenthal. London: Arena Book, 1986.
Ipuin Hautatuak (short stories). Basque version by Maite González. Donostia: Elkar, 1984.

SALVAT-PAPASSEIT, Joan (Barcelona, 1894-1924)
Poesies completes. Edited by Joaquim Molas. 6th ed. Barcelona: Ariel, 1988.
Selected poems. Anthology. Versions and introduction by Dominic Keown and Tom Owen. Sheffield: Anglo-Catalan Society, 1982.

SEABRA, Manuel de (Lisbon, 1932)
Els exèrcits de Paluzie. Barcelona: La Magrana, 1982.
Bumaznyje soldatiki. Introduction and version in charge of M. Kij i A. Sadikova; Moskva: Raduga, 1985.

VERDAGUER, Jacint (Folgueroles, 1845-Vallvidrera, 1902)
Canigó. 4th ed. Barcelona: Edicions 62, 1988.
Canigó. French version. Toulouse: Privat, 1986.

VILLALONGA, Llorenç (Palma de Mallorca, 1897-1980)
Bearn o La sala de les nines. 13th ed. Barcelona: Club Editor, 1983.
Bearn o La sala de las muñecas. Spanish version. Madrid: Alianza, cop. 1987.
Béarn ou Le cabinet des poupées de cire. French version by Denis Fernández-Recatalà. París: Acropole, 1986.
The Doll's room. English version by Deborah Bonner. London: André Deutsch, 1988.
Mallorcai udvarház vagy a babaszoba. Hungarian version by Tomcsányi Zsuzsanna. Budapest: Európa Könyvkiadó, 1982.
Bearn of de Poppenkammer. Dutch version by Bob de Nijs. Amsterdam: Vitgeverij Wereldbibliotheek, 1991.
La sala delle bambole. Italian version by Ettore Finazzi Agrò. Roma: Editori Riuniti, 1976.
Un estiu a Mallorca. 3rd edition. Barcelona: Club Editori, 1983.
Un été à Majorque. French version by Raphaël Carrasco and Jorge Serra. La frasse: Éditions Verdier, 1988.

INTERNATIONAL BIBLIOGRAPHY ON CATALONIA

This bibliography gathers information on books published in recent years in German, English, Spanish, French and Italian concerning Catalonia and the various facets of Catalan culture. In the selection of its contents, special attention has been paid to the accessibility of the material, and journal articles have been included only when their topic has not been treated in book form.

The bibliography is structured in eight large groups of materials — general, social sciences, science and technology, art, Catalan language, Catalan literature, geography, and history — and is further divided into subgroups. Within each section, the works are listed by the author's last name and, in the case of books and articles with more than three authors, by the first word in the title.

Following the multilingual bibliography, a body of fundamental reference works published in Catalan is also classified in order to facilitate access to useful and current information while giving evidence to the levels of publishing and intellectual activity in Catalonia at the present time.

This bibliography has been prepared by Jordi Llobet i Domènech, Amadeu Pons i Serra, Montserrat Prat i Serra, and Jordi Roqué i Figuls, with the collaboration of Joana Crespi i Gonzàlez (music), Montserrat Galera i Monegal (geography), and Concepció Isern i Ferrando (art).

MULTILINGUAL CATALAN BIBLIOGRAPHY

GENERAL WORKS

CATALAN CULTURE

«Barcelone: de Raymond Lulle à Manuel Vázquez Montalbán». In *Magazine littéraire* / dir. Jean-Claude Fasquelle. Paris: Magazine littéraire. No 277 (mai 1990). Pages 16-63.

Barcelone baroque et moderne: l'exubérance catalane / dir. Oscar Caballero, Brigitte Ouvry-Vial. Paris: Autrement, 1986. 288 pages. (Villes et créateurs).

Boyd, Alastair. *The essence of Catalonia: a traveller's guide to Barcelona and its region.* Barcelona: Muchnik, 1988. xi, 324 pages.

Briesemeister, Dietrich. «Katalonien und Deutschland: ein Überblick über die kulturgeschichtlichen Wechselbeziehungen». In *Zeitschrift für Katalanistik.* Vol. 1 (1988). Pages 11-35.

Català, llengua europea; foreword by Antoni M. Badia Margarit. Barcelona: Cercles de Normalització i La Crida, 1988. 64 pages.: illus. Text in French, English, German, Spanish.

Catalan review: international journal of Catalan culture / ed. Manuel Duran, Josep Roca Pons. Vol. 1, nº 1 (June 1986). Barcelona: Quaderns Crema, 1986. Half-yearly.

Catalonia culture / dir. Fèlix Martí. 1 (1986). Barcelona: Centre Unesco de Catalunya, 1986. Half-yearly. Editions in English, French, Spanish.

Cien años de cultura catalana: 1880-1980. Palacio de Velázquez. Parque del Retiro. Junio-Octubre, 1980. Madrid: Ministerio de Cultura. Dirección General del Patrimonio Artístico, Archivos y Museos, 1980. 278 pages.

Europäische Kulturtage Karlsruhe 1983: Kunst und Kultur Kataloniens: Setmanes Catalanes Karlsruhe 19.09.—10.11.83. Karlsruhe: Stadt Karlsruhe Kulturreferat, 1983. 120 pages.

Ferrater Mora, José. *Las formas de la vida catalana.* Madrid: Alianza, 1987. 128 pages. (Biblioteca de Cultura Catalana; 13).

Granell, Francesc. *La Catalogne.* Paris: Presses Universitaires de France, 1988. 127 pages. (Que sais-je; 2426).

Hina, Horst. *Castilla y Cataluña en el debate cultural 1714-1939.* Translated from German by Ricard Wilshusen Callicó. Barcelona: Península, 1986. 459 pages. (Historia, ciencia, sociedad; 195).

Hina, Horst. *Kastilien und Katalonien in der Kulturdiskussion 1714-1939.* Tübingen: Max Niemeyer, 1978. xiv, 382 pages. (Forschungsprobleme der Vergleichenden Literaturgeschichte; 7).

Lüdtke, Jens; Pous, Antoni. *Informationen über Katalonien: Geschichte, Sprache, Literatur.* Tübingen: Romanisches Seminar, 1970. 79 pages.

«Paesi Catalani, I». In *Minoranze.* Milano: CIEMEN. Anno 4, no 14-15 (2-3 trimestre 1979). 74 pages. Monographic issue.

Parés i Maicas, Manuel; et al. *Approach to Catalonia.* Bellaterra: Universitat Autònoma de Barcelona, 1985. 140 pages.

Press in Catalonia in the eighties, The. Barcelona: Generalitat de Catalunya. Departament de Cultura, 1988. 94 pages.

Puigjaner, Josep-Maria. *Arte y Cultura de Cataluña.* Barcelona: Grup Promotor-Santillana, 1980. 88 pages.

Puigjaner, Josep-Maria. *La Catalogne: un pays millénaire.* Barcelona: Generalitat de Catalunya. Entitat Autònoma del Diari Oficial i de Publicacions, 1989. 88 pages.

Puigjaner, Josep-Maria. *Catalonia: a millennial country.* Barcelona: Generalitat de Catalunya. Entitat Autònoma del Diari Oficial i de Publicacions, 1989. 88 pages.

Puigjaner, Josep-Maria. *Catalogna: un paese millenario.* Barcelona: Generalitat de Catalunya. Entitat Autònoma del Diari Oficial i de Publicacions, 1989. 88 pages.

Puigjaner, Josep-Maria. *Katalonien: ein tausendjähriges Land.* Barcelona: Generalitat de Catalunya. Entitat Autònoma del Diari Oficial i de Publicacions, 1989. 88 pages.

Puigjaner, Josep-Maria; López i Garrido, Adriana. *Ser catalán, ¿qué es eso?* Barcelona: Hogar del Libro, 1984. 126 pages. (Navidad; 76).

Québec-Catalogne: deux nations, deux modèles culturels / sous la direction de Gaëtan Tremblay et Manuel Parés Maicas. Québec: Ministère des Relations Internationales du Québec. Université du Québec, 1987. 258 pages.

Read, Jan. *The Catalans.* New York: Faber & Faber, 1979. 223 pages.

Relaciones de las culturas castellana y catalana: encuentro de intelectuales. Sitges, 20-22 diciembre 1981. Barcelona: Generalitat de Catalunya. Departament de la Presidència, 1983. 196 pages.

Riquer, Martí de; et al. *Catalonia.* Barcelona: Luna Wennberg, 1983. 260 pages., 1 sheet of folding map.

RIQUER, Martí de; et al. *Catalonia.* Barcelona: Luna Wennberg, 1984. 251 pages., 1 sheet of folding map.

RIQUER, Martí de; et al. *Catalonia.* Barcelona: Luna Wennberg, 1988. 253 p., 1 sheet of folding map.

RIQUER, Martí de; et al. *Catalonia.* Barcelona: Luna Wennberg, 1988. 241 pages., 1 sheet of folding map.

SAGNES, J. *Le pays catalan.* Pau: Société de nouvelles éditions régionales, 1984. 875 pages.

SALVI, Sergio. «Catalunya». In *Le nazione proibite: guida a dieci colonie «interne» dell' Europa occidentale.* Firenze: Vallecchi. 1973. Pages 143-207.

STEGMANN, Tilbert. «Katalonien: keine Region, sondern eine Nation». In *Europas unruhige Regionen* / ed. Rainer S. Elkar. Stuttgart: Ernst Klett, 1981. Pages 179-194.

STEPHENS, Meic. «The Catalans». In *Linguistic minorities in Western Europe.* Llandysul, Wales: Gomer Press, 1976. Pages 605-632.

TRUETA I RASPALL, Josep. *The spirit of Catalonia.* Barcelona: Institut d'Estudis Catalans, 1985. 198 pages.

VELA, Leonor. «Bibliografía catalana: panorama general». In *Nuevo hispanismo: revista crítica de literatura y sociedad.* Madrid: Universidad Internacional Menéndez Pelayo. Nº 2 (primavera 1982). Pages 207-232.

ZURLETTI, Michelangelo. *Catalani.* Torino: EDT, 1982. 256 pages.

PSYCHOLOGY

FIGUEROLA I MUSSONS, Glòria; MUSE, Mark-Dana; PÉREZ I SALANOVA, Mercè; «The State of Psychology in Catalonia». In *International Journal of Psychology.* Vol. 23, nº 4 (1988). Pages 513-524.

SIGUAN, Miquel; et al. «Miquel Siguán». In *Anthropos: revista de información y documentación.* Barcelona: Anthropos. Nº 48 (abril 1985). Monographic issue.

SPORTS

Guía del turismo náutico en Cataluña: la costa y los puertos deportivos / dir. Olga Castells i Schener, Gerard Gelonch i Monné. Barcelona: Generalitat de Catalunya. Departament de Política Territorial i Obres Públiques, 1985. 189 pages.

Guide to sailing in Catalonia. The catalan coast: anchorages, ports and mooring facilities / dir. Olga Castells i Schener, Gerard Gelonch i Monné. Barcelona: Generalitat de Catalunya. Departament de Política Territorial i Obres Públiques, 1986. 189 pages.

Passió i mite de l'esport: un viatge artístic i literari per la Catalunya contemporània / selecció: Joaquim Molas; foreword: Antoni Dalmau i Ribalta. Barcelona: Diputació de Barcelona, 1986. 134 sheets. Illust. Text in Catalan, Spanish, English and French.

PRIESTLEY, Gerda K. «The role of golf as a tourist attraction: the case of Catalonia, Spain». In PRIESTLEY, Gerda K. *The development of tourism in the area surrounding important tourist zones.* Sousse, Tunisie: International Geographical Union, 1988. Pages 385-394.

Snow in Catalonia. Barcelona: Generalitat de Catalunya. Departament de Comerç, Consum i Turisme, 1984. 47 pages.

SOCIAL SCIENCES

SOCIOLOGY

CANDEL TORTAJADA, Francisco. *Los otros catalanes.* 4ª ed. Barcelona: Península, 1972. 324 pages. (Ediciones de bolsillo; 184).

CORBELLA, Josep Maria. *Social communication in Catalonia.* Barcelona: Generalitat de Catalunya. Centre d'Investigació de la Comunicació, 1988. 68 pages.

GINER, Salvador. *The social structure of Catalonia.* London: The Anglo-Catalan Society, 1980. VIII, 78 pages. (The Anglo-Catalan Society occasional publications).

MALUQUER SOSTRES, Joaquim. *L'assimilation des immigrés en Catalogne.* Genève: Droz, 1963. 156 pages. (Travaux de droit, d'économie et de sociologie; 10).

PI-SUNYER, Oriol. «Elites and noncorporate groups in the European Mediterranean: a reconsideration of the Catalan case». In *Comparative studies in society and history.* Cambridge. N. 16, 1 (1974). Pages 117-151.

PI-SUNYER, Oriol; PI-SUNYER, M.J. «Occupational images and ethnicity: some observations on the attitudes of middle class Catalans». In *Human organization.* Washington. N. 34, 3 (1975). Pages 229-300.

NATIONALISM AND POLITICS

CASALS, P.; et al. *Libro blanco de Cataluña.* Buenos Aires: Ediciones de la Revista de Catalunya, 1956. 489 pages. Text in Spanish, English and French.

Cataluña: esa desconocida para España: a propósito de 200 artículos de prensa / Club Arnau de Vilanova; prólogo de José Luis L. Aranguren. Barcelona: Península, 1983. 120 pages. (Col. Temas de historia y política contemporánea; 17).

DESSENS, André. *L'Espagne et ses populations.* Bruxelles: Complexe, 1977. 412 pages. (Pays et populations; 4).

GARCÍA VENERO, M. *Cataluña: Síntesis de una región.* Madrid: Editora nacional, 1954. 372 pages, 1 sheet. (Las Tierras de España; 3).

HANSEN, Edward C.; SCHNEIDER, J.; SCHNEIDER, P. «From autonomous development to dependent modernization: the Catalan case revisited: a reply to Pi-Sunyer». In *Comparative studies in society and history.* Cambridge. N. 17 (1975). Pages 236-241.

HÉRAUD, Guy. *Peuples et langues d'Europe.* Paris: Denoël, 1966. 270 pages.

MARÍAS AGUILERA, Julián. *Consideración de Cataluña.* 2ª ed. Barcelona: Aymà. 1974. 184 pages.

MERCADÉ I DURÓ, Francesc. *Cataluña, intelectuales, políticos y cuestión nacional: análisis sociológico de las ideologías políticas en la Cataluña democrática.* Barcelona: Península, 1982. 219 pages. (Temas de historia y política contemporáneas).

MERCADÉ I DURÓ, Francesc; HERNÁNDEZ, Francesc; OLTRA, Benjamín. *Once tesis sobre la cuestión nacional en España.* Barcelona: Anthropos, 1983. 154 pages. (Conciencia y Libertad; 2).

MODERNE, Frank; BON, Pierre. *Les autonomies régionales dans la constitution espagnole.* [S.l.]: Economica, 1981. 168 pages. (Études juridiques).

OLTRA, Benjamín; et al. *La ideología nacional catalana.* Barcelona: Anagrama, 1981. 208 pages. (Ibérica).

PETRELLA, Riccardo. *La Renaissance des cultures régionales en Europe* / préface de Carlo Scarascia Mugnozza. Paris: Entente, 1978. 317 pages. (Minorités).

PI-SUNYER, Oriol. «Catalan nationalism: some theoretical and historical considerations». In TIRIYAKIAN, Edward A.; ROGOWSKI, Ronald. *New nationalisms of the developed West.* Boston, MA: Allen & Unwin, 1985.

PI-SUNYER, Oriol. «Dimensions of Catalan nationalism». In *Nations without state* / Charles R. Foster, ed. New York, NY: Praeger, 1980. Pages 101-115.

PI-SUNYER, Oriol. *Nationalism and societal integration: a focus on Catalonia.* Amherst, MA.: University of Massachusetts, 1983.

PRAT DE LA RIBA, Enric. *La nacionalidad catalana* / introd. de Carlos Seco Serrano. Madrid: Alianza, 1987. 112 pages. (Biblioteca de Cultura Catalana; 10).

PUIGJANER, Josep-Maria. «Annäherung an die politische und kulturelle Identität Kataloniens». In Ibero Americana Lateinamerika, Frankfurt: Klaus Dieter Vervuert. (1985), nº 1. Pages 3-11.

ROSSINYOL, Jaume. *Le problème national catalan* / préface de Guy Héraud. Paris; La Haye: Mouton, 1974. VIII, 710 pages.

SERRAHIMA, Maurici. *Realidad de Cataluña: respuesta a Julián Marías.* 2ª ed. Barcelona: Aymà, 1974. 155 pages. (Ensayo).

SOBREQUÉS, Jaume: VICENS, Francesc; PITARCH, Ismael E. *The Parliament of Catalonia.* Barcelona: Parlament de Catalunya, 1981. 118 pages.

VERGÉS, Oriol; CRUAÑAS, Josep. *La Generalitat et l'histoire de la Catalogne* / version française par Alain Verjat Massman. Barcelona: Generalitat de Catalunya. Departament de Cultura, 1986. 106 pages.

VERGÉS, Oriol; CRUAÑAS, Josep. *The Generalitat in the history of Catalonia* / translated by Richard Rees. Barcelona: Generalitat de Catalunya. Departament de Cultura, 1986. 106 pages.

VERGÉS, Oriol; CRUAÑAS, Josep. *La Generalitat nella storia di Catalogna* / versione italiana di Raffaele Pinto. Barcelona: Generalitat de Catalunya. Departament de Cultura, 1986. 106 pages.

VERGÉS, Oriol; CRUAÑAS, Josep. *Die Generalitat in Kataloniens Geschichte* / deutsche Version Guillem Raebel i Gumà. Barcelona: Generalitat de Catalunya. Departament de Cultura, 1986. 106 pages.

VERGÉS, Oriol; CRUAÑAS, Josep. *La Generalidad en la historia de Cataluña* / versión castellana de Santiago Alcoba Rueda. Barcelona: Generalitat de Catalunya. Departament de Cultura, 1986. 106 pages. ISBN 84-393-0465-X.

VINYES, Ricard; PLANA, Manuel. «Marxismo e questione nazionale nel socialismo catalano». In *Annali dell'Istituto Giangiacomo Feltrinelli.* 1983-1984. Pages 823-855.

ECONOMY

BALCELLS, Albert; RALLE, Michel. «Mouvement ouvrier et question nationale catalane de 1907 à 1936». In *Mouvement social.* N. 128 (1984). Pages 59-82.

Basic data on the economy of Catalonia. Barcelona: COCIN, 1977. 23 pages.

Catalogna: un paese per viverci, un paese per investirci. Barcelona: Generalitat de Catalunya. Departament de la Presidència, 1988. 96 pages.

Catalonia: a land to invest in, a land to live in. Barcelona: Generalitat de Catalunya. Departament de la Presidència, Direcció General d'Afers Interdepartamentals, 1988. 96 pages.

Catalonia: the country and its economy. Barcelona: Generalitat de Catalunya. Departament d'Economia i Finances, 1982. 90 pages.

Catalonia: the industrial apex of Europe and the Mediterranean. 2nd ed. Barcelona: Generalitat de Catalunya. Departament de la Presidència, 1986. 48 pages.

Économie de la Catalogne, L'. Barcelona: COCIN, 1981. 14 pages.

GARCIA, M.C. *Midi-Pyrénées et Catalogne dans l'Europe des banques: chiffres-clés, stratégies.* Toulouse: Banque de France, 1989. 27 pages.

GASÒLIBA, Carles A. *La Catalogne, un an après l'adhésion de l'Espagne à la CEE.* Paris: Éditions Hispaniques, [1987?]. 14 pages. (Études ibériques et Latino-Américaines Appliquées; 8).

GRANELL, Francesc. *Cataluña, sus relaciones económicas transnacionales y la CEE.* Barcelona: Vicens Vives, 1986. 151 pages.

LA FORCE, J.C. *The development of the Spanish textile industry, 1750-1850.* Berkeley, CA, University of California Press, 1965. XV, 210 pages. (Publications of the Bureau of Business and Economic Research, University of California, Los Angeles).

LAMBERET, Renée. *Mouvements ouvriers et socialistes: (chronologie et bibliographie): l'Espagne (1750-1936).* Paris: Les Éditions Ouvrières, 1953. 204 pages.

MUNS, Joaquim. *Bilan et perspectives de l'économie catalane.* Paris: Éditions Hispaniques, 1987. 16 pages. (Études ibériques et latino-américaines).

PI-SUNYER, Oriol. «The politics of tourism in Catalonia». In *Mediterranean studies.* (Malta) 1, 2 (1979). Pages 47-69.

Las Regiones de la Comunidad ampliada: tercer informe periódico sobre la situación y la evolución socioeconómica de las regiones de la Comunidad / Comisión de las Comunidades Europeas. Madrid: OPOCE, 1987. 182 pages. [Editions in French, English, Italian and German].

Setting up business in Catalonia. 3rd ed. Barcelona: Generalitat de Catalunya. Departament d'Indústria i Energia, 1989. 74 pages.

TRIAS I FARGAS, Ramon. *Introducción a la economía de Cataluña: un análisis regional.* Madrid: Alianza, 1973. 151 pages. (El libro de bolsillo; 491).

LAW

Autonomiestatut von Katalonien. [3. Auf.]. Barcelona: Generalitat de Catalunya. Entitat Autònoma del Diari Oficial i de Publicacions, 1987. 60 pages.

CAMILLERI, Gerard; GALIAY, Claude. «Le Statut d'autonomie de la Catalogne». In *Revue française de Sciences Politiques.* Vol. 30, nº 5 (1980). Pages 1012-1047.

Catalan Statute of Autonomy, The. 3rd. ed. Barcelona: Generalitat de Catalunya. Entitat Autònoma del Diari Oficial i de Publicacions, 1987. 56 pages.

Compilación del derecho civil de Cataluña. Barcelona: Generalitat de Catalunya. Departament de Justícia, 1985. 144 pages.

PUIG FERRIOL, Luis; ROCA TRIAS, Encarna. *Instituciones del derecho civil de Cataluña.* Barcelona: Bosch, 1987. 746 pages.

Statut d'Autonomie de la Catalogne. 3e éd. Barcelona: Generalitat de Catalunya. Entitat Autònoma del Diari Oficial i de Publicacions, 1987. 58 pages.

Statuto d'Autonomia della Catalogna. Barcelona: Generalitat de Catalunya. Entitat Autònoma del Diari Oficial i de Publicacions, 1987. 48 pages.

EDUCATION

ARNAU, Joaquim; BOADA, Humbert. «Languages and school in Catalonia». In *Journal of multilingual and multicultural development.* Clevedon, Avon. Vol. 7, N.º 2-3 (1986). Pages 107-122.

Education in Catalonia. Barcelona: Generalitat de Catalunya. Departament d'Ensenyament, 1987. 20 pages.

Enseignement en Catalogne, L'. Barcelona: Generalitat de Catalunya. Departament d'Ensenyament, 1987. 20 pages.

SIGUAN, Miquel. «Education and bilingualism in Catalonia». In *Journal of multilingual and multicultural development.* Clevedon: Bristol. Vol. 1, N.º 3 (1980). Pages 231-232.

SIGUAN, Miquel. «Language and education in Catalonia». In *Prospects.* Vol. 14, N.º 1 (1984). Pages 107-119.

ETHNOLOGY

AMADES, Joan. *L'origine des bêtes: petite cosmogonie catalane* / trad. et présentation de Marlène Albert-Llorca. Carcassonne: Garae / Hesiode, 1988. 380 pages.

BLANC, Dominique; ALBERT-LLORCA, Marlène. *L'imagerie catalane: lectures et rituels.* Carcassonne: Garae / Hésiode, 1988. 107 pages.: illus.

Conflict in Catalonia: images of an urban society / Gary W. McDonogh, ed. Gainesville, FL: University of Florida Press, 1986.

ESTEVA I FABREGAT, Claudi. «Acculturation and urbanization of immigrants in Barcelona: a question of ethnicity or a question of class». In *Acculturation and urbanization of immigrants* / Aschenbrenner, Collins (eds.). The Hague: Mouton, 1978. Pages 159-194.

ESTEVA I FABREGAT, Claudi. «Ethnicity, social class and acculturation of immigrants in Barcelona». In *Etnologia Europea.* (Goettingen). VIII, 1 (1975). Pages 23-43.

HALL, Jacqueline. *The Congress of Catalan Traditional and Popular Culture (1981-1982) /* summary and explanatory texts prepared by Jacqueline Hall. Barcelona: Fundació Serveis de Cultura Popular, 1986. 136 pages., 2 pict.

HANSEN, Edward C. *Rural Catalonia under the Franco regime: the fate of regional culture since the Spanish Civil War.* Cambridge: Cambridge University Press, 1977. X, 182 pages.

VERJAT MASSMANN, Alain. «Catalan Christmas». In *Catalan review.* Vol. 3, N.º 2 (dec. 1989). [20] pages.

SCIENCE AND TECHNOLOGY

ANDREWS, Colan. *Catalan cuisine: Europe's great culinary secret.* London: Headline, 1989.

Catalogne: vins et gastronomie. Barcelona: Generalitat de Catalunya. Institut Català de la Vinya i el Vi, 1988. 20 pages.

Catalonia: wines and gastronomy. Barcelona: Generalitat de Catalunya. Institut Català de la Vinya i el Vi, 1988. 20 pages.

The excellent wines of Catalonia. Barcelona: Generalitat de Catalunya. Institut Català de la Vinya i el Vi, 1988. 28 pages.

GARRABOU, Ramon; SERRA, Eva. «L'agricoltura catalana nei secoli XVI-XX». In *Studi storici.* V.; 21, nº 2 (1980). Pages 339-362.

Die Gastronomie in Katalonien / coord.: Marta Ribalta. Barcelona: Generalitat de Catalunya. Department de Comerç, Consum i Turisme, 1989. 32 pages.

Gastronomy in Catalonia / coord.: Marta Ribalta. Barcelona: Generalitat de Catalunya. Department de Comerç, Consum i Turisme, 1989. 32 pages.

HOYO, Josep del; et al. *Where to watch birds in Catalonia.* Barcelona: Lynx, 1989. 308 pages.

MAJORAL, Roser. «Catalonian agriculture». In *Treballs de la Societat Catalana de Geografia.* Barcelona: Societat Catalana de Geografia. Vol. 2, núm. especial (1986). Pages 87-104.

ART

PLASTIC ARTS

AGUILERA CERNI, Vicente. *Julio González.* (Madrid: Publ. del Ministerio de Educación y Ciencia, 1971). 57 pages: illus.

AINAUD DE LASARTE, Joan. *La peinture catalane: la fascination de l'art roman.* Genève: Skira, 1990. 158 pages: illus.

ARS Hispaniae: Historia Universal del Arte Hispánico. Madrid: Ed. Plus Ultra, 1947-1975. 20 vol.

Barcelona: spaces and sculptures: 1982-1986. Barcelona: L'Ajuntament, 1987. 167 pages.

Barcelona en joc.=Barcelona en juego.=Barcelona where the games are no game / dir. Josep A. Dols. Barcelona: Col·legi d'Aparelladors i Arquitectes Tècnics de Barcelona, 1986. 158 pages.

BASSEGODA NONELL, Joan. *El gran Gaudí.* Sabadell: Ausa, 1990. 610 pages. Text in Spanish.

BASSEGODA NONELL, Joan. *A guide to Gaudí.* Barcelona: Nou Art Thor, 1989. 64 pages.

BASSEGODA NONELL, Joan; et al. *Modernismo en Cataluña.* Barcelona: Nou Art Thor, 1976. 282 pages.

BOHIGAS, Oriol. *Reseña y catálogo de la arquitectura modernista.* Barcelona: Lumen, 1983. 2 vol. (Palabra en el tiempo; 49, 50).

CAROL, Màrius. *Cien años de diseño industrial en Cataluña.* Barcelona: Gustavo Gili: BCD, 1990. 149 pages.

Catalan designs for export 1989 / dir. David Fulton. Barcelona: Fundació BCD, 1989. 195 pages. (Publicaciones BCD).

Cataluña. Madrid: Fundación Juan March; Barcelona: Noguer, 1974, 2 vol. (Tierras de España) I: Introducción geográfica J. Vilá Valentí. Introducción histórica: Juan Reglà. Arte: José Gudiol. II: Introducción literaria: Martí de Riquer, Guillem Díaz-Plaja. Arte: Joan Ainaud de Lasarte, Enric Jardí, Alexandre Cirici, Francesc Fontbona, Daniel Giralt-Miracle.

CIRICI I PELLICER, Alexandre. *El arte catalán.* Madrid: Alianza, 1988. 408 pages. (Biblioteca de Cultura Catalana; 16).

CIRICI I PELLICER, Alexandre. *Barcelona paso a paso.* 3ª ed. Barcelona: Teide, 1988. 392 pages.

CIRICI I PELLICER, Alexandre. *Barcelona step by step /* translation: Bert Strauss, Frances Strauss. Barcelona: Teide, 1974. 165 pages.

CIRICI I PELLICER, Alexandre. *Miró and his world /* translation: Kenneth Lyons. Barcelona: Polígrafa, 1985. 245 pages: illus.

CIRICI I PELLICER, Alexandre. *Miró et son temps /* traduction française de Robert Marrast. 2ᵉ éd. Barcelona: Polígrafa, 1985. 245 pages: illus.

CIRICI I PELLICER, Alexandre. *Museos de arte catalanes.* Barcelona: Destino, 1982. 303 pages.

COGNIAT, Raymond. *Apel·les Fenosa.* (Texto en castellano, inglés, francés y alemán). (Barcelona): Polígrafa, s.a. 307 pages: illus. (Biblioteca de Arte Hispánico).

COLLINS, George Roseborough. *Antonio Gaudí von... unter Verwendung vieler vom Autor selbst gewählter deutschsprachiger Formulierungen und Ergänzungen übersetzt von Andreas Pollitz.* Ravensburg: Otto Maier, [1962]. 132 pages: illus. (Grosse Meister der Architektur; 4).

COLLINS, George Roseborough; BASSEGODA NONELL, Juan. *The designs and drawings of Antonio Gaudí.* Princeton, NJ.: Princeton University Press, cop. 1983. XX, 83 pages, 70 pict. sheets: illus.

CORREDOR-MATHEOS, José. *Jaume Mercadé.* (Madrid: Serv. de Publ. del Minist. de Educación y Ciencia, 1975). 93 pages: illus. 3 sheet. (Artistas Españoles Contemporáneos; 124).

CORREDOR-MATHEOS, José. *Miró posters* /catalogue of the posters by Gloria Picazo. Barcelona: Polígrafa, 1987. 269 pages: illus. col.

COSTA CLAVELL, Xavier. *Picasso: Picasso Museum, Barcelona: photographic report, complemented by a biography of the painter /* photograph by the Technical Department of Editorial Escudo de Oro. 3rd. ed. Barcelona: Escudo de Oro, 1987. 95 pages: illus. col. (Art in Spain; 14).

COURTHION, Pierre. *Pablo Gargallo* (suivi de) Catalogue raisonné par Pierrette Anguera-Gargallo. (Paris): '73 Société Internationale d'art du XX siècle, 1973. 185 pages: illus. (L'œuvre complet).

DEFFONTAINES, Pierre; DURLIAT, Marcel. *Espagne du Levant: Catalogne, Baléares, Valence* . [Paris]. Arthaud, [1975]. 298 pages: illus.

DEFFONTAINES, Pierre. «Le problème de la grande *Masia* de la Catalogne humide de l'Est». In *Cuadernos de Arqueología e Historia de la Ciudad.* Núm. 10 (1967). Pages 267-277.

DESCHARNES, Robert; NÉRET, Gilles. *Salvador Dalí: 1904-1989.* Köln: Benedikt Taschen, 1989. 224 pages. Text in German.

Design in Catalonia / Barcelona Design Centre. Barcelona: CIDEM, 1988. 143 pages.

Diccionario de artistas de Catalunya, Valencia y Baleares / dirigido por J. M. Ráfols. Barcelona [etc.]: Edicions Catalanes [etc.], 1980. 5 vols.

DURLIAT, Marcel. *Art Catalan.* Paris; Grenoble: Arthaud, D.L. 1963. 417 pages: illus., pict.

ERBEN, Walter. *Joan Miró: 1893-1983: the man and his work.* Cologne: Benedikt Taschen, 1988. 248 pages.

FERRAS, Robert. *Barcelona: croissance d'une métropole.* Paris: Anthropos, 1977. 616 pages.

FLORES, Carlos. *Gaudí, Jujol y el modernismo catalán* / Prólogo de George R. Collins. Madrid: Aguilar, 1982. 2 vol. (Imagen de España).

FONTBONA I DE VALLESCAR, Francesc; MIRALLES, Francesc. *Anglada-Camarasa.* Barcelona: Polígrafa, 1981. 338 pages: illus.

FONTBONA DE VALLESCAR, Francesc. «L'art catalan moderne». In *50 ans d'art espagnol: 1880-1930.* Bordeaux: Galerie de Beaux Arts, 1984.

GAYA NUÑO, Juan Antonio. *Jaime Mercadé.* Madrid: Ibérico Europeo de Ediciones, 1972. 24 sheets. (Panorama de la pintura contemporánea; 3).

GIMFERRER, Pere. *Antoni Tàpies und der Geist Kataloniens* / Übersetz. T.D. Stegmann. Frankfurt; Berlin: Propyläen, 1976. 382 pages.

GIMFERRER, Pere. *Tàpies and the Catalan spirit* / translated by Kenneth Lyons. Barcelona: Polígrafa, 1986. 382 pages: illus.

GÓMEZ DE LIAÑO, Ignacio. *Dalí* / [translation by Kenneth Lyons]. London: Academy, 1987. 33 pages. [94] pict. pages: illus.

GÓMEZ DE LIAÑO, Ignacio. *Dalí* / [traduction française: Joëlle Guyot et Robert Marrast]. París: Albin Michel, 1989. 92 pages, [46] pict. pages: illus. (Les Grands maîtres de l'art contemporain).

GÓMEZ DE LIAÑO, Ignacio. *Dalí* / [tradução: Aurelia Maria Pinheiro de Carvalho]. Rio de Janeiro: Ao Livro Técnico, 1988. 92 pages, [46] pict. pages: illus.

Homage to Barcelona: the city and its art (1888-1936) / introd. by Marylin McCully. New York, NY: Thames and Hudson, 1987. 328 pages.

JARDÍ CASANY, Enric; MANENT, Ramón. *El cartelismo en Cataluña;* trad. X.B. Barcelona: Destino, 1983. 160 pages. (Col. Libros de Arte).

JARDÍ CASANY, Enric. *J. Mir.* (Barcelona): Polígrafa, (1975). 264 pages; illus. (Biblioteca de Arte Hispánico).

JARDÍ CASANY, Enrique. *Jaume Mercadé.* Barcelona: Polígrafa, 1978. 272 pages; 26 cm.

JARDÍ CASANY, Enric. *Nonell.* (Text en English, French i German). (Barcelona): Polígrafa, (s.d.). 343 pages. (Biblioteca del Arte Hispánico).

JARDÍ CASANY, Enric. *Torres García.* (Translated into English by Kenneth Lyons). (Barcelona): Polígrafa, (Barcelona): Polígrafa, (1974). 287 pages: illus. (Spanish Art Library).

Joaquín Torres-García: época catalana (1908-1929): Museo Nacional de Artes Visuales, Montevideo, Uruguay, agosto-setiembre 1988: (catálogo de la exposición); texto y asesoramiento Enric Jardí. Barcelona: Generalitat de Catalunya. Comissió Catalana del Cinquè Centenari del Descobriment d'Amèrica, 1988. 84 pages: illus. Spanish-Catalan bilingual edition.

JUNYENT I SUBIRÀ, Eduard. *Catalogne romane* / photographies inédites de Jean Dieuzaide. La Pierre-qui-Vire: Abbaye Sainte Marie, 1960-1961. 2 vol. (La nuit des temps; 12-13).

Katalanische Kunst des 20. Jahrhunderts: art i modernitat als Països Catalans / edited by T.D.S... [et al.]. Berlin: Staatliche Kunsthalle, 1978. 343 pages. Bilingual edition.

MACKAY, David. *Modern architecture in Barcelona: 1854-1939.* London: The Anglo-Catalan Society, 1985. 80 pages: illus. (The Anglo-Catalan Society occasional publications; 3).

MALET, Rosa Maria. *Joan Miró* / [traduction française: Joëlle Guyot et Robert Marrast]. Paris: Albin Michel, 1983. 128 pages: illus. in colour. (Les Grands maîtres de l'art contemporain).

MALET, Rosa Maria. *Joan Miró* / [tradução: Francisco de Castro Azevedo]. Rio de Janeiro: Ao Livro Técnico, 1983. 128 pages: illus. in colour.

MARTINELL BRUNET, César. *Gaudí: his life, his theories, his work* / translated from the Spanish by Judith Rohrer; edited by George R. Collins. Cambridge, Mass.: The MIT Press, [1975]. 486 pages: illus.

MENDOZA, Cristina; MENDOZA, Eduardo. *Barcelona modernista.* Barcelona: Planeta, 1989. 176 pages. (Ciudades en la historia).

MIRÓ, Joan. *Joan Miró: selected writings and interviews* / edited by Margit Rowell; translations from the French by Paul Auster, translations from the Spanish and Catalan by Patricia Mathews. Boston: G.K. Hall, 1986. xiv, 326 pages, 24 pict. pages. (The Documents of Twentieth century art).

PALAU I FABRE, Josep. *Picasso.* Barcelona: Polígrafa, 1981. 21 pages, 53 pict. sheets. Edition in Spanish.

PALAU I FABRE, Josep. *Picasso;* translated by Kenneth Lyons. New Jersey: Chartwell Books, 1981. 22 pages; 53 pict. sheets.

PALAU I FABRE, Josep. *Picasso en Cataluña.* (Texto en castellano, inglés, francés y alemán). (Barcelona): Edic. Polígrafa, (1966). 257 pages: illus. (Biblioteca de Arte Hispánico)

PANE, Roberto. *Antoni Gaudí.* Milano: Edizioni di Comunità, 1964. 273 pages: illus. (Studi e documenti di Storia dell'Arte; 5).

PERUCHO, Joan. *Joan Miró and Catalonia* / translation by Kenneth Lyons. London: Alpine Fine Arts Collection, 1988. 214 pages: illus. in colour.

PLADEVALL I FONT, Antoni. *Así es Cataluña: guía del patrimonio arquitectónico.* 2ª ed. Barcelona: Generalitat de Catalunya. Departament de Cultura; Esplugues de Llobregat: Plaza y Janés, 1989. 515 pages, 32 map pages.

PLADEVALL I FONT, Antoni. *This is Catalonia: a guide to its architectonic heritage.* Barcelona: Generalitat de Catalunya. Departament de Cultura; Esplugues de Llobregat: Plaza y Janés, 1987. 516 pages: illus.

PLADEVALL I FONT, Antoni. *Voici la Catalogne: guide du patrimoine architectural.* Barcelona: Generalitat de Catalunya. Departament de Cultura; Esplugues de Llobregat: Plaza y Janés, 1988. 516 pages: illus.

ROHRER, Judith; et al. *Catalan spirit: Gaudí and his contemporaries.* New York, NY: Cooper-Hewitt Museum, 1987. 128 pages.

Sert: Mediterranean architecture / edited by M.L. Borràs. Boston, MA: New York Graphic Society, [1975]. 25 pages, 226 pict. pages: illus.

SOLÀ-MORALES, Ignasi de. *Gaudí.* Barcelona: Polígrafa, 1983. 127 pages. Text in English.

SUREDA, Joan. *La pintura románica en Cataluña.* Madrid: Alianza, 1981. 411 pages. (Alianza forma; 17).

TRENC-BALLESTER, Eliseu; YATES, Alan. *Alexandre de Riquer (1856-1920): the British connection in Catalan Modernisme.* Sheffield: The Anglo-Catalan Society, 1988. 139 pages: illus. (The Anglo-Catalan Society occasional publications; 5).

ZERBST, Ramer. *Gaudí: 1852-1926. Antoni Gaudí i Cornet, a life devoted to architecture.* Cologne: Benedikt Taschen, 1988. 239 pages.

MUSIC

BLUM, David. *Casals et l'art de l'interprétation.* Paris. Buchet: Chastel, 1980.

CASALS, Pau. *Ma vie racontée à Albert E. Khan.* Paris: Stock, 1970.

CHRISTEN, Ernest. *Pablo Casals.* Genève: Labor et Fides, 1956.

COLOMER, Claude. *Montserrat Caballé ou l'anti diva.* Béziers: Société de Musicologie de Languedoc, 1988.

CORREDOR, Josep M. *Conversations avec Pablo Casals.* Paris: Albin Michel, 1955.

Diguem no. Sagen wir nein!: Lieder aus Katalonien / ed. by Tilbert D. Stegmann. Berlin: Rotbuch, 1979. 159 pages. Text in German and Catalan.

DUEZ, Ann. *La Nova Cançó: réaffirmation d'une catalanité*. Bordeaux, 1986. 483 pages.

GAVOTY, Bernhard. *Victoria de los Ángeles*. Genève: René Kister, 1956.

KIRK, H.L. *Pablo Casals*. New York [etc.]: Holt, Rinehart and Winston, 1974.

New Grove dictionary of music and musicians, The / edited by Stanley Sadie. 7th repr. with minor corrections. London, [etc.]: Macmillan, 1989. 20 vol.: illus. Bibliographic references.

ROBERTS, Peter. *Victoria de los Ángeles*. London: Weidenfeld & Nicolson, 1982.

TREND, J.B. «Early Catalan music». In TREND, J.B. *The music of Spanish history*. Oxford, 1926. Chapter VI.

CATALAN LANGUAGE

ANGLO-CATALAN SOCIETIES

Anglo-Catalan Society: 1954-1979, The. Sheffield: University of Sheffield, 1979. 10 pages. It contains works published between 1955 and 1978.

Associació Internacional de Llengua i Literatura Catalanes, L'. Barcelona: Associació Internacional de Llengua i Literatura Catalanes. Publicacions de l'Abadia de Montserrat, 1983. 79 pages.

Associació Internacional de Llengua i Literatura Catalanes 1968-1986, L'. Barcelona: Associació Internacional de Llengua i Literatura Catalanes. Publicacions de l'Abadia de Montserrat, 1986. 134 pages.

Associació Internacional de Llengua i Literatura Catalanes 1986-1989, L'. Barcelona: Associació Internacional de Llengua i Literatura Catalanes. Publicacions de l'Abadia de Montserrat, 1989. 122 pages.

BARRAL I ALTET, Xavier. *L'ensenyament del català a Europa i Amèrica del Nord*. Barcelona: Arts Gràfiques Rafael Salvà, 1971. 202 pages.

Bibliografia catalana: libri 1978-1988: indici e copertine / Associazione Italiana di Studi Catalani. Napoli: Istituto Universitario Orientale, 1988. 202 pages: illus.

BOVER I FONT, August. «La catalanística y su difusión internacional en la actualidad». In *Hispanica Poznaniensia*. Poznań: Universitata Adam Mickiewicz. In print. Soon to be in print in Barcelona.

BRIESEMEISTER, Dietrich. «Bibliographie Katalanischer Veröffentlichungen in Deutschland seit 1945». In *Iberoromania: Zeitschrift für die iberoromanischen Sprachen und Literaturen in Europa und Amerika = Revista dedicada a las lenguas y literaturas iberorrománicas de Europa y América*. Tübingen: Max Niemeyer. Neue Folge, Nr. 9 (1979). Pages 155-163.

Català a Europa i a Amèrica, El / foreword Josep Massot i Muntaner. Barcelona: Publicacions de l'Abadia de Montserrat, 1982. 272 pages. (Estudis de llengua i literatura catalanes; 5).

Il contributo italiano agli studi catalani: 1945-1979: atti dei convegni dell'Associazione Italiana di Studi Catalani. Cosenza: Lerici, 1981. 115 pages.

NAVARRO DE ADRIAENSES, José María. «Lengua y cultura catalanas en Alemania». In *Arbor*. Madrid: Consejo Superior de Investigaciones Científicas. Tomo 99, nº 467-468 (sept.-oct. 1984). Pages 191-201.

PÖTTERS, Wilhelm. «Katalanische Forschungen der AILLC». In: Romanische Forschungen, 90 Band, 1978. Frankfurt am Main: Vittorio Klostermann, 1978, pages. 270-276.

Repertori de catalanòfils / Associació Internacional de Llengua i Literatura Catalanes... [et al.]. Barcelona: Publicacions de l'Abadia de Montserrat, 1983-1988. 3 vol. (Estudis de llengua i literatura catalanes; 7, 8, 17).

Zeitschrift für Katalanistik = Revista d'estudis catalans / ed. per Tilbert Dídac Stegmann... [et al.]. Vol. 1 (1988). Frankfurt am Main: Deutsch-Katalanische Gesellschaft, 1988. Yearly.

BIBLIOGRAPHIES ON CATALAN LANGUAGE

BADIA I MARGARIT, Antoni M.; et al. «Antoni M. Badia i Margarit». In *Anthropos: revista de documentación científica de la cultura*. Barcelona: Anthropos, 1981. Nº 81 (feb. 1988). Monographic issue.

BADIA I MARGARIT, Antoni M.; MASSOT I MUNTANER, Josep; MOLAS, Joaquim. «Situación actual de los estudios de lengua y literatura catalanas». 116 pages. In *Norte*. Amsterdam. Año 11, nº 1-2 (enero-abril 1970). 116 pages. Monographic issue.

Bibliographie linguistique des années 1939-1947 / publiée par le Comité International Permanent de Linguistes avec une subvention des Nations Unies pour l'Éducation, la Science et la Culture. Utrecht. Bruxelles: Spectrum, 1939.

CONCHEFF, Beatrice. *Bibliography of old Catalan texts*. Madison, WIS.: Hispanic Seminary of Medieval Studies, 1985. XI, 177 pages. (Bibliographical series; 5)

FABBRI, Maurizio. *A bibliograph of Hispanic dictionaries: Catalan, Galician, Spanish in Latin America and the Philippines. Appendix: a bibliography of Basque dictionaries*. Imola: Galeati, 1979. XIV, 381 pages.

GULSOY, Joseph. «Catalan». In *Trends in Romance linguistics and philology* / Rebecca Posner, John N. Green, eds. The Hague: Mouton, 1982. Vol. 3: Language and Philology in Romance Monographs 189-296. (Trends in Linguistics. Studies and Monographs; 14). Pages 189-296.

M.L.A. *International bibliography of books and articles on the modern languages and literatures*. New York: Modern Language Association, 1922. Yearly.

MOLL I CASASNOVAS, Francesc; BADIA I MARGARIT, Antoni M. «Francesc de B. Moll». In *Anthropos: Revista de información y documentación*. Barcelona: Anthropos, 1981. Nº 44 (dic. 1984). Monographic issue.

RIERA I SANS, Jaume; ROQUÉ I FIGULS, Jordi. «Gramàtics i filòlegs: repertori bibliogràfic». In *Butlletí interior* / Societat d'Onomàstica. Barcelona: Societat d'Onomàstica, 1980. Núm. 35 (març 1989). Pages 1-20.

SCHONBERGER, Axel; STEGMANN, Tilbert. «Katalanische und okzitanische Publikationen und Aktivitäten (1976-1983) aus dem deutschen Sprachbereich». In *Romanische Forschungen*. Tübingen. B. 96, Nr. 3 (1984). Pages 278-292.

SIEBENMANN, Gustav; CASETTI, Donatella. *Bibliographie der aus dem Spanischen, Portugiesischen und Katalanischen ins Deutsche übersetzten Literatur, 1945-1983*. Tübingen: Niemeyer, 1985. XX, 190 pages.

STEVENSON, John. *Catalán, gallego, vascuence: ensayo bibliográfico de estudios lingüísticos, publicados o realizados en España (1970-1986)*. Sidney: The University of New South Wales. School of Spanish and Latin American Studies, 1989. 235 pages.

TERRY, Arthur; RAFEL, Joaquim. *Introducción a la lengua y la literatura catalanas* / apéndice bibliográfico de Alberto Hauf y Enric Sullà. 2ª ed. Barcelona: Ariel, 1983. 327 pages. (Letras e ideas; 8).

Year's work in modern language studies, The / by a number of scholars; edited for the Modern Humanities Research Association by William J. Entwistle. Oxford: University Press, 1931.

ZUBATSKY, David S. «An annotated bibliography of 19th Century Catalan, Galician and Spanish author bibliographies». In *Hispania: a journal devoted to the teaching of Spanish and Portuguese*. Cincinnati, OH. Vol. 65, nº 2 (1982). Pages 212-224.

ZUBATSKY, David S. «An annotated bibliography of Twentieth-Century Catalan and Spanish author bibliographies». In *Hispania: a journal devoted to the interests of the teach-*

ing of Spanish and Portuguese. Cincinnati, OH. Vol. 61 (1978). Pages 654-679.

GENERAL ESSAYS AND ESSAYS ON LANGUAGE HISTORY

ARAMON I SERRA, Ramon. «Problèmes d'histoire de la langue catalane». In *La linguistique catalane: colloque international organisé par le Centre de Philologie et de Littérature Romanes de l'Université de Strasbourg du 23 au 27 avril 1968* / publiés par Antonio Badia Margarit et Georges Straka. Paris: Klincksieck, 1973. (Actes et colloques; 11). Pages 27-80.

BLASCO I FERRER, Eduard. *Grammatica storica del catalano e dei suoi dialetti, con speciale riguardo all'algherese*. Tübingen: Narr, 1984. xx, 410 pages. (Tübinger Beiträge zur Linguistik; 238).

BRUMMER, Rudolf. *Katalanische Sprache und Literatur: ein Abriss*. München: Fink, 1975. 86 pages.

COLON I DOMÈNECH, Germà. *El español y el catalán, juntos y en contraste*. Barcelona: Ariel, 1989. 352 pages. (Ariel lingüística).

COLON I DOMÈNECH, Germà. «Perfil lingüístico de Cataluña, Valencia y Mallorca». In *Mapa lingüístico de la España actual*. Madrid, 1986. N° 235. Pages 89-146.

EGERT, Gottfried. *Die sprachliche Stellung des Katalanischen auf Grund seiner Lautentwicklung: mit Berücksichtigung des Altlanguedokischen, Aragonesischen, Gaskognischen und Spanischen*. Frankfurt am Main: Haag und Herchen, 1985. 204 pages. (Mannheimer Studien zur Linguistik; 6).

LÜDTKE, Jens. *Katalanisch: eine einführende Sprachbeschreibung*. München: Max Hueber, 1984. 148 pages.

RÖNTGEN, Karl-Heinz. *Einführung in die katalanische Sprache*. Bonn: Romanistischer Verlag, 1987. 110 pages. (Bibliothek romanischer Sprachlehrwerke; 1).

RUSSELL-GEBBETT, Paul. *Mediaeval Catalan linguistic texts*. Oxford: The Dolphin Book, 1965. 312 pages.

SCHILLER, Eric. *Catalan*. Coraopolis, PA: Chess Enterprises, 1983. 100 pages.

VENY I CLAR, Joan. «Dialectologie catalane». In *La linguistique catalane: colloque international organisé par le Centre de Philologie et de Littérature Romanes de l'Université de Strasbourg du 23 au 27 avril 1968* / publiés par Antonio Badia Margarit et Georges Straka. Paris: Klincksieck, 1973. (Actes et colloques; 11). Pages 289-337.

WHEELER, Max W. «Catalan». In *The Romance languages* / by Martin Harris and Paul Vincent. London: Croom Helm, 1988. Pages 170-208.

GRAMMAR AND CATALAN LEARNING METHODS

BADIA I MARGARIT, Antoni Maria. *Gramática catalana*. Madrid: Gredos, 1985. 2 vol. (Biblioteca Románica Hispánica: Manuales; 10).

BADIA I MARGARIT, Antoni Maria. «Morphosyntaxe catalane». In *La linguistique catalane: colloque international organisé par le Centre de Philologie et de Littérature Romanes de l'Université de Strasbourg du 23 au 27 avril 1968* / publiés par Antonio Badia Margarit et Georges Straka. Paris: Klincksieck, 1973. (Actes et colloques; 11). Pages 181-273.

BADIA I MARGARIT, Antoni Maria. «Phonétique et phonologie catalanes». In *La linguistique catalane: colloque international organisé par le Centre de Philologie et de Littérature Romanes de l'Université de Strasbourg du 23 au 27 avril 1968* / publiés par Antonio Badia Margarit et Georges Straka. Paris: Klincksieck, 1973. (Actes et colloques; 11). Pages 115-179).

BLÀSCO I FERRER, Eduard. «La posizione linguistica del catalano nella Romania: studio di morfosintassi comparata». In *Zeitschrift für romanische Philologie*. Vol. 102 (1986). Pages 132-178.

COLON I DOMÈNECH, Germà. *El léxico catalán en la Romania*. Madrid: Gredos, 1976. 542 pages. (Biblioteca Románica Hispánica. Estudios y Ensayos; 245).

COLON I DOMÈNECH, Germà. «Quelques considérations sur le lexique catalan». In *La linguistique catalane: colloque international organisé par le Centre de Philologie et de Littérature Romanes de l'Université de Strasbourg du 23 au 27 avril 1968* / publiés par Antonio Badia Margarit et Georges Straka. Paris: Klincksieck, 1973. (Actes et colloques: 11). Pages 239-287.

GALLINA, Annamaria. *Grammatica della lingua catalana*. Barcelona: Barcino, 1969. 244 pages. (Manuals lingüístics i literaris Barcino, 5).

GILI, Joan. *Introductory Catalan grammar: with a brief outline of the language and literature, a selection from Catalan writers, and a Catalan-English and English-Catalan vocabulary*. 4th ed. with a new chapter on Pronunciation and Spelling by Max W. Wheeler. Oxford: The Dolphin Book, 1974. 251 pages.

LATORRE, Roser. *Primer curso de catalán*. 3ª ed. rev. Barcelona: Barcino, 1987. 238 pages. (Manuals lingüístics i literaris Barcino; 1).

LLOBERA I RAMON, J. *Prácticas de catalán básico*. 2ª ed. Barcelona: Teide, 1974. 216 pages.

QUINTANA, Artur. *Handbuch des Katalanischen*. Barcelona: Barcino, 1973. 310 pages. (Manuals lingüístics Barcino; 7).

SOLÀ I CORTASSA, Joan. «Ortographe et grammaire catalanes». In *La linguistique catalane: colloque international organisé par le Centre de Philologie et de Littérature Romanes de l'Université de Strasbourg du 23 au 27 avril 1968* / publiés par Antonio Badia Margarit et Georges Straka. Paris: Klincksieck, 1973. (Actes et colloques; 11). Pages 81-113.

VERDAGUER, Pere. *Cours de langue catalane*. Barcelona: Barcino, 1974. 258 pages. (Manuals lingüístics Barcino; 9).

WHEELER, Max W. *Phonology of Catalan*. Oxford: Basil Blackwell, 1979. xxiii, 330 pages. (Publications of the Philological Society; 28).

YATES, Alan. *Catalan*. London: Hodder and Stoughton, 1975. 381 pages. (Teach yourself books).

DICTIONARIES

ALBERTÍ, Santiago. *Diccionari Spanish-català i català-Spanish*. 15ª ed. Barcelona: Albertí, 1986. 1180 pages.

BATLLE, Lluís C. *Diccionari German-català*. Barcelona: Fundació Enciclopèdia Catalana, 1984. 659 pages.

CASTELLANOS I LLORENÇ, Carles; CASTELLANOS I LLORENÇ, Rafael. *Diccionari català-French*. Barcelona: Enciclopèdia Catalana, 1984. 627 pages.

CASTELLANOS I LLORENÇ, Carles; CASTELLANOS I LLORENÇ, Rafael. *Diccionari French-català*. Barcelona: Fundació Enciclopèdia Catalana, 1984. 619 pages.

Diccionari Spanish-català. Barcelona: Enciclopèdia Catalana, 1985. 1341 pages.

Diccionari català-Spanish. Barcelona: Enciclopèdia Catalana, 1987. 1300 pages.

FORNAS PRAT, Jordi. *Diccionari italià-català, català-italià*. 2ª ed. Barcelona: Pòrtic, 1985. 612 pages.

MESSNER, Dieter. «Dictionnaire chronologique catalan». In MESSNER, Dieter. *Dictionnaire chronologique des langues ibéro-romanes*. Heidelberg: Winter, 1979. Vol. 3.

OLIVA, Salvador; BUXTON, Angela. *Diccionari English-català*. 2ª ed. Barcelona: Enciclopèdia Catalana, 1986. 1107 pages.

OLIVA, Salvador; BUXTON, Angela. *Diccionari català-English*. Barcelona: Enciclopèdia Catalana, 1986. 842 pages.

SOCIOLINGUISTICS

AZEVEDO, Milton. «The reestablishment of Catalan as a language of culture». In *Hispa-*

nic linguistics. Vol. 1, no. 2 (1984). Pages 305-330.

BADIA I MARGARIT, Antoni Maria. «Le catalan aujourd'hui». In *La linguistique catalane: colloque international organisé par le Centre de Philologie et de Littérature Romanes de l'Université de Strasbourg du 23 au 27 avril 1968 /* publiés par Antonio Badia Margarit et Georges Straka. Paris: Klincksieck, 1973. (Actes et colloques, 11). Pages 379-451.

BADIA I MARGARIT, Antoni Maria. «Langue et société dans le domaine linguistique catalan, notamment à Barcelone». In *Revue de linguistique romane*. Strasbourg. No 36 (1972). Pages 263-304.

BADIA I MARGARIT, Antoni Maria. «Paralelismo entre normalización lingüística y nacionalismo en Cataluña (1901-1939)». In *Nation et nationalités en Espagne, XIXe et XXe s. Actes du Colloque International organisé du 28 au 31 mars 1984 à Paris.* Paris: Fondation Singer-Polignac, 1985. Pages 309-321.

BOYER, Henri. «Sociolinguistique et politique linguistique: l'exemple catalan». In *Études de linguistique appliquée.* No 65 (jan.-mars 1987). Pages 69-88.

CABRÉ I CASTELLVÍ, M. Teresa; MARTÍ I CASTELL, Joan. «Connaissance et usage du catalan écrit». In *Revue de linguistique romane*. Vol. 52 (1988). Pages 69-88.

ENTWISTLE, William J. *Las lenguas de España: castellano, catalán, vasco y gallego-portugués /* trad. Francisco Villar. 4ª ed. Madrid: Istmo, 1984. 443 pages. (Fundamentos; 30).

ESTEVA I FABREGAT, Claudi. «Aculturación lingüística de los inmigrantes en Barcelona». In *Ethnica.* Barcelona: Consejo Superior de Investigaciones Científicas. N° 8 (1974). Pages 73-120.

ESTEVA I FABREGAT, Claudi. «Ethnocentricity and bilingualism in Catalonia: the state and bilingualism». In *International journal of the sociology of language*. Bronx, NY. Vol. 47 (1984). Pages 43-57.

International journal of the sociology of language. Bronx, NY. Several articles on Catalan sociolinguistics published in the last few years.

KREMNITZ, Georg. «Démarche et particularités de la sociolinguistique catalane». In *Sociolinguistique*. Paris: Presses Universitaires de France, 1980. Pages 21-33.

KREMNITZ, Georg. Hrsg. *Sprachen im Konflikt: Theorie und Praxis der katalanischen Soziolinguisten: eine Textauswahl.* Tübingen: Gunter Narr, 1979. 233 pages. (Tübinger Beiträge zur Linguistik; 117).

LAITIN, David D. «Linguistic conflict in Catalonia». In *Language problems and language planning*. Potsdam, NY. V. 11, n° 2 (Summer 1987). Pages 129-147.

MARTÍ I CASTELL, Joan. *Gramática preceptiva y uso lingüístico: análisis de algunos aspectos en la comunidad lingüística catalana.* Roma: Bulzoni, 1979. Pages 577-603.

PÉREZ ALONSO, Jesús. «Catalan: an example of the current language struggle in Spain: sociopolitical and pedagogical implications». In *International journal of the sociology of language.* Bronx, NY. Vol. 21 (1979). Pages 109-125.

PRAT I SERRA, Montserrat. «Bibliografia bàsica: (Llengua catalana. Lingüística. Bilingüisme)». In *Miscel·lània Antoni M. Badia i Margarit.* Barcelona: Publicacions de l'Abadia de Montserrat, 1987. Vol. 7, pages. 278-293. (Estudis de llengua i literatura catalanes; 15).

SABATER, Ernest. «An approach to the situation of the Catalan language: social and educational use». In *International journal of the sociology of language.* Bronx, NY. Vol. 47 (1984). Pages 29-41.

SCHLIEBEN-LANGE, Brigitte. *Okzitanisch und Katalanisch: ein Beitrag zur Soziolinguistik zweier romanischer Sprachen.* 2. Auf. Tübingen: Gunter Narr, 1973. 62 pages.

STRUBELL I TRUETA, Miquel. «Catalan sociolinguistics: a brief review of research». In *International journal of the sociology of language.* Bronx, NY. Vol. 38. Pages 71-84.

STRUBELL I TRUETA, Miquel. «Language and Identity in Catalonia». In *International journal of the sociology of language*. Bronx, NY. Vol. 47 (1984). Pages 91-104.

TORRES, Joaquim. «Problems of linguistic normalization in the Països Catalans: from the Congress of Catalan Culture to the present day». In *International journal of the sociology of language*. Bronx, NY. Vol. 47 (1984). Pages 59-62.

VALLVERDÚ, Francesc. *El conflicto lingüístico en Cataluña: historia y presente*. Barcelona: Península, 1981. 175 pages. (Ediciones de bolsillo; 576).

VALLVERDÚ, Francesc. «A sociolinguistic history of Catalan». In *International journal of the sociology of language*. Bronx, NY. Vol. 47 (1984). Pages 13-28.

VALLVERDÚ, Francesc. *Sociología y lengua en la literatura catalana*. Madrid: Cuadernos para el Diálogo, 1971. 227 pages. (Ediciones de bolsillo; 148).

WOOLARD, Kathryn. «The politics of language status planning: normalization in Catalonia». In *Languages in the international perspective.* Norwood, NJ. Ablex, 1986. Pages 91-102.

INFORMATIVE BOOKLETS

Generalitat de Catalunya. Departament de Cultura. Direcció General de Política Lingüística. Barcelona. (Regularly publishes multilingual booklets on the state of Catalan language all over the world).

CATALAN LITERATURE

BIBLIOGRAPHY

BADIA, Lola. «Literatura catalana: bibliografía de la literatura catalana medieval publicada en 1987». In *Boletín Medieval*. Barcelona: PPU. Fasc. 1 (1987). (DL 1988). Pages 1-30.

BADIA, Lola. «Literatura catalana: bibliografía de la literatura catalana publicada el 1988 (i ocasionalment el 1987 o abans)». In *Boletín bibliográfico de la Asociación Hispánica de Literatura Medieval*. Barcelona: PPU. Fasc. 2 (1988). Pages 1-51.

BADIA I MARGARIT, Antoni M.; MASSOT I MUNTANER, Josep; MOLAS, Joaquim. «Situación actual de los estudios de lengua y literatura catalanas». In *Norte*. Amsterdam. Año 11, n° 1-2 (enero-abril 1970). 116 pages. Monographic issue.

MASSOT I MUNTANER, Josep. *Trenta anys d'estudis sobre la llengua i la literatura catalanes (1950-1980).* Barcelona: Publicacions de l'Abadia de Montserrat, 1980. (Biblioteca Serra d'Or; 5). Vol. 2 «La literatura: de l'Edat Mitjana a la Renaixença». 243 pages.

Catalan Literature Overseas; (Summary and coordination: Cinta Massip. Documentalist: Míriam Sort. - (Barcelona): Institució de les Lletres Catalanes, 1989. - 27 pages - (Frankfurt 1989) (Catalan literary text multilingual guidebook).

ESSAYS

BIHLER, Heinrich. «Zur Darstellung und Bedeutung der Themenkreise Katalonien und Spanien in der katalanischen Lyrik des 20. Jhs., unter besonderer Berücksichtigung von Gedichten Maragalls, Carners und Esprius». In *Romanische Literaturbeziehungen im 19. und 20. Jahrhundert: Festschrift für Franz Rauhut zum 85. Geburtstag.* Tübingen, 1985. Pages 41-55.

Catalan writing. Barcelona: Institució de les Lletres Catalanes, 1988.

COLON, Germán. *Literatura catalana*. Madrid: La Muralla, 1975. 47 pages.+slides.

COMAS, Antoni. «Literatura catalana». In *Historia de las literaturas hispánicas no castellanas /* planeada y coordinada por José María Díez Borque. Madrid: Taurus, 1980. Pages 427-620.

ESPADALER, Antoni M. *Literatura catalana.* Madrid: Taurus, 1988. 256 pages. (Historia crítica de la literatura hispánica).

Fuster Ortells, Joan. *Literatura catalana.* Madrid: Taurus, 1988. 256 pages. (Historia crítica de la literatura hispánica).

Fuster Ortells, Joan. *Literatura catalana contemporánea.* Madrid: Editora Nacional, 1975. 447 pages. (Prosa. Literatura).

Grilli, Giuseppe. *La letteratura catalana: la diversità culturale nella Spagna moderna.* Napoli: Guida Editori, 1979. 216 pages. (Esperienze; 49).

Hösle, Johannes. *Die katalanische Literatur von der Renaixença bis zur Gegenwart.* Tübingen: Max Niemeyer, 1982. x, 97 pages.

Iberomania. Tübingen: Niemeyer, 1979. Neue Folge, No. 9 (1979). 170 pages. Issue dedicated to Catalan literature.

«Littérature catalane, La». In *Europe: revue littéraire mensuelle.* Paris: Éditeurs Français Réunis. 59e année, no 621-622 (janvier-février 1981). 251 pages. Monographic issue.

Llinares, Armand. *Raymond Lulle.* Edit. Moll. Palma de Mallorca, 1983. 116 pages.

Molas, Joaquim. «Die katalanische Literatur». In *Handbücher der Auslandskunde: Spanien /* Hg. Günther Haensch, Paul Hartig. Frankfurt, etc.: Diesterweg, 1975. Pages 159-172.

Riquer, Martí de. *Literatura catalana medieval.* Barcelona: Ajuntament de Barcelona, 1972. 138 pages. (Publicaciones del Museo de Historia de la Ciudad; 25).

Riquer, Martí de; et al. «Martín de Riquer». In *Anthropos: revista de documentación científica de la cultura.* Barcelona: Anthropos, 1981. N° 92 (enero 1989). Monographic issue.

Roca-Pons, Josep. *Introduction to Catalan literature /* Catalan texts translated by Patricia Boehne. Bloomington, IN.: Indiana University, Heitor Martins, 1977. 144 pages. (Hispanic literature studies; 1).

Rubió i Balaguer, Jordi. «Literatura catalana». In *Historia general de las literaturas hispánicas /* dir. Guillermo Díaz Plaja. Barcelona: Barna, 1950-1958. Vol. 1, pages. 643-746; vol. 2, pages. 727-930; vol. 3, pages. 493-597; vol. 4, pages. 213-337.

Sugranyes de Franch, R. «Dipendenza e indipendenza della letteratura catalana». In *Rivista di letterature moderne e comparate.* Firenze. No 24 (1971). Pages 301-310.

Süss, Kurt. *Untersuchungen zum Gedichtwerk Salvador Esprius.* Nürnberg: Carl, 1978. 210 pages.

Terry, Arthur. *Catalan literature.* London: Ernest Benn, 1972. 136 pages.

Valentí Fiol, Eduard. *El primer Modernismo literario catalán y sus fundamentos ideológicos.* Barcelona: Ariel, 1973. 357 pages.

Verdaguer, Pere. *Histoire de la littérature catalane.* Barcelona; Barcino, 1981.379 pages. (Manuals lingüístics i literaris; 12).

Zubatsky, D.S. «An annotated bibliography of 19th Century Catalan, Galician and Spanish author bibliographies». In *Hispania: a journal devoted to the teaching of Spanish and Portuguese.* Vol. 65, n° 2 (1982). Pages 212-224.

ANTHOLOGIES

Anthology of Catalan lyric poetry / select. and introd. by Joan Triadú; ed. by Joan Gili. Oxford: The Dolphin Book, 1953. LXXX, 395 pages.

Cross-cultural review 1. «Four Postwar Catalan Poets». Compiled and Translated by David H. Rosenthal; Series editor Stanley H. Barkan. Merrick, New York: Cross-Cultural Communications, 1978. 48 pages; (Salvador Espriu. Joan Brossa. Vicent Andrés Estellés. Miquel Martí i Pol).

Écrivains de Catalogne: anthologie / présentés et traduits par Mathilde Bensoussan. Paris: Denoël, 1973. 279 pages. (Lettres nouvelles).

Katalanische Lyrik im zwanzigsten Jahrhundert: eine Anthologie / Johannes Hösle, Antoni Pous. Mainz: Hase und Koehler, 1970. 152 pages.

Modern Catalan poetry: an anthology / translated by David H. Rosenthal. Saint Paul, Min.: New Rivers Press, 1979.

Ocho siglos de poesía catalana; antología bilingüe / selección y prólogo de J.M. Castellet y Joaquim Molas; trad. José Batlló y José Corredor Matheos. Madrid: Alianza, 1969. 548 pages. (El libro de bolsillo; 216).

Poetas catalanes contemporáneos: Carner, Riba, Foix / selección y traducción por José Agustín Goytisolo. Barcelona: Seix Barral, 1968. 370 pages. (Biblioteca breve de bolsillo; 16).

Poeti catalani / testi e traduzioni a cura di Livio B. Wilcock; introduzione di J. Rodolfo Wilcock. Milano: Bompiani, 1962. 379 pages.

Rövenstrunck, Bernat. *Cançoner català = Katalanisches Liederbuch.* Hamburg; Berlin: Trekel, 1976. 91 pages.

Spiel von Spiegeln: katalanische Lyrik des 20. Jahrhunderts, Ein / ed. Tilbert D. Stegmann. Leipzig: Reclam, 1987. 225 pages. Bilingual edition. Other editions, München: Beck, 1987; Frankfurt am Main: Büchergilde Gutenberg, 1987.

Viera, David. *Medieval Catalan literature: prose and drama.* Twayne, 1988. 116 pages. (Twayne's World Authors Series; 802).

GEOGRAPHY

All Barcelona. 9th ed. Barcelona: Escudo de Oro, 1989. 94 pages. (All Spain; 2).

Atlas gráfico de Cataluña / Servicio de Estudios del Departamento Cartográfico de Aguilar. Madrid: Aguilar, 1977. 79 pages. (Atlas gráficos de España).

Barcelona. 3ª ed. Barcelona: Escudo de Oro, 1989. 160 pages. Text in Italian.

Barcelona / photographs Antonio Campañà, Juan Antonio Puig-Ferran. Barcelona: A. Campañà, D.L. 1978. 176 pages.

Barcelona: a pictorial book of Gaudí's city. Firenze: Bonechi, 1987. 96 pages.

Barcelona: die Stadt von Gaudí. Firenze: Bonechi, 1987. 96 pages.

Barcelona: tutta la città di Gaudí. Firenze: Bonechi, 1987. 96 pages.

Barcelona: la ville et les œuvres de Gaudí. Firenze: Bonechi, 1987. 96 pages.

Batlló, José. *Costa Brava.* León: Everest, 1982. 160 pages, 24 pages. (Guías Everest). Edition in German and French.

Bentley, James. *Otto città per un weekend.* Milano: Club Edizioni, 1990. 297 pages. (Le città).

Buyschaert, Martine; Rossetti, Alberto. *Barcellona e la Spagna orientale.* Verona: Futuro, 1989.

Calders, Pere. *Voir Barcelone /* photos sheet. Català Roca. 2ᵉ éd. Barcelona: Destino, 1987. 210 pages.

Capel, Horacio; et al. *Espaces péripheriques: études et enquêtes dans le midi de la France et en Catalogne.* Paris: Centre National de la Recherche Scientifique, 1978. 184 pages.

Capel, Horacio; Sánchez, J.E. «Wirtschaftsentwicklung und Struktur der spanischen Städte, 1950-1980». In *Stadtentwicklung, Weltmarkt, nationales Wirtschaftswachstum /* Hans Dieter Frieling, Jürgen Strassel, editors. Oldenburg: Bibliotheks und Informationssystem der Universität, 1986. Band 2, pages. 7-122.

Carreras i Verdaguer, Carles. *Geografía humana de Cataluña.* Vilassar de Mar: Oikos-Tau, 1985. 110 pages. (Opera geographica minora).

Carreras i Verdaguer, Carles; Martín-Vide, Javier. *La ciudad de Barcelona. La ville de Barcelona. The city of Barcelona.* Barcelona: Ajuntament de Barcelona, 1986. 55 pages.

Catalogne aujourd'hui, La. Barcelona: Generalitat de Catalunya. Departament de Comerç, Consum i Turisme, 1981. 48 pages.

Catalunya: imatges del temps = Catalunya: imágenes del tiempo = Catalogne: images du temps = Catalonia: images of time. Barcelona: Generalitat de Catalunya. Comissió del Mil·lenari, D.L. 1989. 117 pages. Text in Catalan, Spanish, French and English.

Cities: statistical, graphic and administrative information on the major urban areas of the world. Barcelona: Institut d'Estudis Metropolitans de Barcelona, 1988. 5 vol.

CORTÉS SOLÀ, J. *Barcelona*. Lloret de Mar: L'autor, 1989. 80 pages. Text in German.

CORTÉS SOLÀ, J. *Barcelona*. Lloret de Mar: L'autor, 1989. 80 pages. Text in French.

CORTÉS SOLÀ, J. *Barcelona*. Lloret de Mar: L'autor, 1989. 80 pages. Text in Dutch.

CORTÉS SOLÀ, J. *Barcelona*. Lloret de Mar: L'autor, 1989. 80 pages. Text in Italian.

Costa Brava: zona Costa Brava e provincia di Girona. Barcelona: Escudo de Oro, 1984. 160 pages.

Costa Brava, Catalogne, Baléares. Paris: Solar, 1985. 96 pages.

COURTOT, R.; FERRAS, R. *Les grandes villes du monde: Barcelone*. Paris: La Documentation Française, 1969. 67 pages.

CRASTRE, Victor. *Catalogne: des Corbières à l'Ebre*. Paris: Horizons de France, 1959. 153 pages.

CUADROS, Ignasi; DURÀ I GUIMERÀ, Antoni. «Josep Iglésies i Fort, 1902-1986». In *Geographers: biobibliographical studies*. London: Mansell. Vol. 12 (1988). Pages 107-111.

DEFFONTAINES, P. «Essai de description régionale de la Catalogne». In *Méditerranée*. 1962. Pages 3-50.

DEFFONTAINES, P. «L'immigration française en Catalogne et à Barcelona». In *Estudios geográficos*. Núm. 105 (nov. 1966). Pages 561-578.

DEFFONTAINES. Pierre. - *La Méditerranée catalane*.- Paris: Presses Universitaires de France, (1975). - 126 pages. (Que sais-je; 1609)

DURAZZO, Michelangelo. *Barcelone* / préface de Pierre Lartigue. Paris: Hatier, 1989. Multiple pagination.

FERRER I AIXALÀ, A.; NEL·LO COLOM, Oriol. «Barcelona: the transformation of an industrial city». In *The future of the industrial city* / ed. Lester Salamon. Baltimore, MD: John Hopkins University Press, 1990.

GARCIA-RAMON, M. Dolors; NOGUÉ, J. «Pau Vila i Dinarès, 1881-1980». In *Geographers: biobibliographical studies*. London: Mansell. In print.

«Grands établissements industriels dans le midi de la France et de la Catalogne, Les» / coordination de la recherche: Horacio Capel. In *Remica: Recerques Midi Catalunya*. Toulouse. 05 (1974).

Guía del viajero. Plaza & Janés: Cataluña. Esplugues de Llobregat: Plaza y Janés, 1990. 302 pages.

Guida del viaggiatore: Plaza & Janés: Catalogna 1990 / Departamento de creación editorial de Plaza & Janés, 1990. 316 pages, 3 sheets, 38 map pages.

Guide du voyageur: Plaza & Janés: Catalogne 1990 / Departamento de creación editorial de Plaza & Janés. Esplugues de Llobregat: Plaza & Janés, 1990. 316 pages, 3 sheets, 38 map pages.

Health spas in Catalonia. Barcelona: Generalitat de Catalunya. Departament de Comerç, Consum i Turisme, 1988. 36 pages.

IBÀÑEZ I ESCOFET, Manuel; et al. *Catalogna*. Barcelona: Generalitat de Catalunya. Departament de Comerç, Consum i Turisme, 1985. 94 pages.

IBÀÑEZ I ESCOFET, Manuel; et al. *Catalogne*. Barcelona: Generalitat de Catalunya. Departament de Comerç, Consum i Turisme, 1983. 94 pages.

IBÀÑEZ I ESCOFET, Manuel; et al. *Catalonia*. Barcelona: Generalitat de Catalunya. Departament de Comerç, Consum i Turisme, 1983. 94 pages.

IBÀÑEZ I ESCOFET, Manuel; et al. *Katalonien*. Barcelona: Generalitat de Catalunya. Departament de Comerç, Consum i Turisme, 1983. 94 pages.

KAMINSKI, Hanns-Erich. *Barcelona: ein Tag und seine Folgen*. Berlin: Tranvia, 1986. 208 pages.

Long distance footpaths. Barcelona: Generalitat de Catalunya. Departament de Comerç, Consum i Turisme, 1988. 32 pages.

MAISTERRA, Pascual. *Barcelona*. 8ª ed. León: Everest, 1988. 176 pages, 48 pages. (Guías Everest). Text in French.

Merian: Barcelona-Costa Brava / ed. H.M. Thomsen, T.D. Stegmann. Hamburg: Hoffmann und Campe, 1979. 130 pages.

NEL·LO I COLOM, Oriol. «Le grandi città spagnole: economia, pianificazione e struttura urbana: 1939-1987». In *Le aree metropolitane in Europa* / ed. Giorgio Piccinato. Milano: Franco Angeli, 1990.

PEFFER, R. «Spain's country within a country: Catalonia». In *National geographic*. Vol 165-nº 1 (January 1984) Pàg 95-127.

PLA I CASADEVALL, Josep. *Cataluña*. Barcelona: Destino, 1961. 631 pages, 6 folding maps. (Guías de España).

PLA I CASADEVALL, Josep; SARRAMON, Christian. *Seeing Catalonia*. 3rd ed. Barcelona: Destino, 1988. 175 pages.

PLA I CASADEVALL, Josep; SARRAMON, Christian. *Voir Catalogne*. 2e éd. Barcelona: Destino, 1988. 175 pages.

RACIONERO, Lluís. «Die Costa Brava wiederentdecken». In RACIONERO, Lluís. *Retrobar la Costa Brava* / fotografies: Sebastià Jordi Vidal i Andreu Masagué. Barcelona: Lunwerg, 1985. Pages 171-196.

RECASENS COMES, José María. *Tarragona*. 10ª ed. León: Everest, 1984. 160 pages, 24 pages. (Guías Everest). Text in English.

«Retrouver Barcelona». In SOBREQUÉS I CALLICÓ, Jaume; et al. In *Retrobar Barcelona*. Barcelona: Lunwerg, 1986. Pages 209-269.

RÜBESAMEN, H.E. *Barcelone* / trad. de l'allemand d'Evelyne Hegeler-Mahé, Martine Blondel. [S.l.]: MA, 1990. 126 pages. (MA guides).

SANMARTÍ, Josep-Maria. *Geografia de Catalunya*. Barcelona: Grup / Promotor: Santillana, 1981. 136 pages.

SARRAMON, Christian; PLA, Josep. *Catalogne*. Paris: DS, 1980. 176 pages.

«Schwerpunkt Mallorca». In *Hispanorama*. Nürnberg. 40 (1985).

Sentiers de grande randonnée. Barcelona: Generalitat deCatalunya. Departament de Comerç, Consum i Turisme, 1988. 32 pages.

Stations thermales en Catalogne. Barcelona: Generalitat de Catalunya. Department de Comerç, Consum i Turisme, 1988. 36 pages.

Terre catalane / volume dirigé par Jean-François Brousse. Paris: Eole, 1978. 485 pages.

THIRLMERE, R. *Letters from Catalonia and other parts of Spain*. London: Gordon Press, 1976. 2 vol.

Tout Barcelona. 8e éd. Barcelona: Escudo de Oro, 1989. 94 pages. (Toute l'Espagne; 2).

Traveller's Guide: Plaza & Janés: Catalonia 1990 / Departamento de creación editorial de Plaza & Janés. Esplugues de Llobregat: Plaza & Janés, 1990. 316 pages, 3 sheets, 38 map pages.

VILÀ I VALENTÍ, Joan. *La Péninsule ibérique* / trad. de l'espagnol par H. Leconte. Paris: Presses Universitaires de France, 1968. 296 pages, 22 maps. (Magellan; 13).

VILÀ I VALENTÍ, Joan. *La penisola Iberica*. Segrate, Milano: Il Saggiatore, 1982. 303 pages, 22 maps.

HISTORY

BIBLIOGRAPHY

Índice histórico español / fundado por Jaume Vicens Vives. Barcelona: Universidad de Barcelona. Centro de Estudios Históricos Internacionales, 1953. - Four-monthly. 80 issues released.

ESSAYS

ALBA, Víctor. *Catalonia: a profile.* London: C. Hurst and Company, 1975. IX, 258 pages.

AMELANG, James S. *La formación de una clase dirigente: Barcelona 1490-1714.* Barcelona: Ariel, 1986. 238 pages. (Ariel Historia).

AMELANG, James S. *Honored Citizens of Barcelona: patrician culture and class relations, 1490-1714.* Princeton, NJ.: Princeton University Press, 1986. XXVI, 259 pages.

BALCELLS, Albert. *Catalunya contemporánea.* Madrid: Siglo XXI, 1984. 2 vol.; (Estudios de historia contemporánea).

BISSON, Thomas N. *The medieval crown of Aragon: a short history.* Oxford: Clarendon Press, 1986. XII, 240 pages.

BONNASSIE, Pierre. *La Catalogne du milieu du Xe à la fin du XIe siècle: croissance et mutations d'une société.* Toulouse: Association des Publications de l'Université de Toulouse-Le Mirail, 1975-1976. 2 vol. (Publications de l'Université de Toulouse-Le Mirail. Série A; tome 23; 29).

BONNASSIE, Pierre. *Cataluña mil años atrás: siglos X-XI.* Madrid: Península, 1988. 444 pages. (Historia, ciencia, sociedad; 212).

CARR, Raymond; FUSI, Juan P. *Spain: dictatorship to democracy.* 2nd ed. London: George Allen & Unwin, 1981. 282 pages.

CARRERES I PÉRA. Joan. *Roots of Catalonia.* Girona: Bisbat de Girona. Delegació de Pastoral, 1987. 49 pages.

CUARTAS, Augusto. *Apellidos catalanes: heráldica de Cataluña.* Madrid: Paraninfo, 1987. VII, 336 pages.

ELLIOT, John H. *The revolt of the Catalans: a study in the decline of Spain (1598-1640).* Cambridge: University Press, 1963. XVI, 624 pages.

FILVER, Philippe W. *Nacionalismo y transición: Euskadi-Cataluña-Galicia* / Prólogo de Javier Sádaba. San Sebastián: Txertoa, 1988. 222 pages. (Askatasun Haizea, 9).

GARCÍA CÁRCEL, Ricardo. *Historia de Cataluña: siglos XVI-XVII.* Barcelona: Ariel, 1988. 2 vol. (Ariel historia).

GAROSCI, Aldo. *Gli intellettuali e la guerra di Spagna.* Milano: Giulio Einaudi, 1959. XIII, 482 pages. (Saggi; 254).

HANSEN, Edward C. *Rural Catalonia under the Franco Regime: the fate of regional culture since the Spanish Civil war.* Cambridge: Cambridge University Press, 1977. X, 182 pages.

HARRISON, Joseph. *An economic history of modern Spain.* Manchester: University of Mancherster, 1978. 187 pages.

Histoire de la Catalogne / [work supervised by] Joaquim Nadal Farreras, Philippe Wolff. Toulouse: Privat, 1982. 560 pages.

HOFFMANN, Léon-François. *La peste à Barcelone.* Paris: Presses Universitaires de France, 1964. 101 pages. (Que sais-je).

JONES, Norman L. «The Catalan question since the Civil War». In *Spain in crisis: the evolution and decline of the Franco regime* / ed. Paul Preston. London: The Harvester Press, 1976. Pages 234-267.

MCDONOUGH, Gary Wray. *Las buenas familias de Barcelona: historia social del poder en la era industrial.* Barcelona: Omega, 1989. 352 pages.

MCDONOUGH, Gary Wray. *Good families of Barcelona: a social history of power in the Industrial Era.* Princeton, NJ.: Princeton University Press, 1986. 288 pages.

MELO, Francisco de; TIÓ, Jaime. *Historia de los movimientos y separación de Cataluña y de la guerra entre la majestad católica de D. Felip el IV, rey de Castilla y de Aragón, y la diputación general de aquel Principado: crónicas* / [introducción de Elena Mampel]. Barcelona: Eds. Universidad, etc., 1981. XIV, 260 pages.

MUNTANER, Ramon; DESCLOT, Bernat. *Cronache catalane del secolo XIII e XIV* / traduzione di Filippo Moisè; introduzione di Leonardo Sciascia. Palermo: Sallerio, 1984. XII, 680 pages.

ORWELL, George. *Hommage à la Catalogne: 1936-1939.* Paris: Ledovici [Éditions Gérard], 1982. 296 pages.

PEERS, Edgar Allison. *Catalonia infelix.* Westport, Conn.: Greenwood Press, 1970. xxiv, 326 pages. Issue from 1938 edition.

PI-SUNYER, Oriol. *The stalled transformation: six years of the autonomy process in Catalonia.* Amherst, MA.: University of Massachusetts, 1986. 46 pages. (Program in Western European Studies. Occasional Papers Series; 3).

REGLÀ I CAMPISTOL, Joan. *Historia de Cataluña* / con un prólogo de Jesús Pabón. Madrid: Alianza, 1981. 223 pages. (El libro de bolsillo; 502).

RUDLOFF, Diether; GABRIEL, Ingrid. *Romanisches Katalonien: Kunst, Kultur, Geschichte.* Stuttgart: Urachhaus, 1980. 342 pages.

SANMARTÍ, Josep-María. *Història de Catalunya.* Barcelona: Grup Promotor-Santillana, 1979. 88 pages.

SEMPRÚN-MAURA, Carlos. *Révolution et contre-révolution en Catalogne (1936-1937).* Paris: Éd. d'aujord'hui, 1981. 307 pages. (Les introuvables).

SEMPRÚN-MAURA, Carlos. *Rivoluzione e contrarivoluzione in Catalogna.* Milano: Antistato, 1976. 328 pages.

SHNEIDMAN, J. Lee. *The rise of the Aragonese-Catalan empire: 1200-1350.* New York, NY.: University Press, 1970. 2 vol.

TOVAR, Antonio. *Iberische Landeskunde: 2. Teil, III Tarraconensis.* Baden-Baden: Koerner, 1989. 508 pages.

TRUETA I RASPALL, Josep. *Trueta: surgeon in war and peace: the memoirs of...* / translated by Meli and Michael Strubell; with a foreword by J.W. Goodfellow. London: Victor Gollancz, 1980. 288 pages.

ULLMAN, John Connelly. *The Tragic Week: a study of anticlericalism in Spain, 1875-1912.* Cambridge: Harvard University Press, 1968. 441 pages.

VALLS I TABERNER, Ferran; SOLDEVILA, Ferran. *Historia de Cataluña* / versión castellana de Núria Sales. Madrid: Alianza, 1982. 530 pages. (Alianza Universidad; 325).

VICENS I VIVES, Jaume. *Los catalanes en el siglo XIX* / introd. de E. Giralt i Raventós. Madrid: Alianza, 1986. 280 pages. (Biblioteca de Cultura Catalana; 3).

VICENS I VIVES, Jaume. *Noticia de Cataluña.* Barcelona: Destino, 1980. 150 pages. (Destinolibro; 104).

VICENS I VIVES, Jaume; NADAL I OLLER, Jordi. *An economic history of Spain* / translated by Francesc M. López-Morillas. Princeton, NJ.: Princeton University Press, 1969. 825 pages.

VILAR, Pierre. *La Catalogne dans l'Espagne moderne: recherches sur les fondements économiques des structures nationales.* Red. Paris, Le Sycomore, 1982. 3 vol.

WEINTRAUB, Stanley. *The last great cause: the intellectuals and the Spanish Civil War.* New York, NY.: Weybright and Talley, 1968. X, 340 map pages.

ESSENTIAL WORKS IN CATALAN

GENERAL WORKS

CATALAN CULTURE

Catalunya 77-78: societat, economia, política, cultura: un informe de la Fundació Jaume Bofill. Barcelona: La Magrana, 1989. 463 pages.

Gran enciclopèdia catalana / director: Joan Carreras i Martí. 2ª ed. Barcelona: Enciclopèdia Catalana, 1986-1989. 24 vol.

SOLDEVILA, Ferran. *Què cal saber de Catalunya.* 3ª ed. Barcelona: Club Editor, 1979. 248 pages. (El Pi de les Tres Branques; 1).

Terra nostra [col·lecció] / directors: Joaquim Castells i Josep M. Infiesta. Barcelona: Nou Art Thor, 1989. In the process of being published.

PRESS

Anuari de la premsa catalana 1986 / ed. Jaume Guillamet. Barcelona: Generalitat de Catalunya. Departament de Cultura, 1987. VII, 287 pages.

BALCELLS, Josep Maria. *Revistes dels catalans a les Amèriques: repertori de 230 publicacions des de 1831.* Barcelona: Comissió Catalana del Cinquè Centenari del Descobriment d'Amèrica, 1988. 142 pages.

Butllet í / Comissió Internacional de Difusió de la Cultura Catalana. Núm. 1 (maig 1988).- Barcelona (Rambla de Santa Mònica, 8): Generalitat de Catalunya. Departament de Cultura, 1988.

TORRENT, Joan; TASIS, Rafael. *Història de la premsa catalana* / foreword: Agustí Pedro Pons. Barcelona: Bruguera, 1966. 2 vol.

BIBLIOGRAPHIC PRODUCTION

Bibliografia nacional de Catalunya / Institut Català de Bibliografia. 1982, 1 / 2. - Barcelona: Generalitat de Catalunya. Departament de Cultura, 1983. Quarterly with some irregularity.

Llibres en català. Barcelona: Instituto Nacional del Libro Español, 1967. Yearly with some irregularity. From 1981 published by: Generalitat de Catalunya. Departament de Cultura.

RELIGION

VILANOVA, Evangelista. *Història de la teologia cristiana.* Barcelona: Facultat de Teologia; Herder, 1984-1989. 2 vol. (Colectània Sant Pacià).

SOCIAL SCIENCES

BIBLIOGRAPHY

GIRALT, Emili. *Bibliografia dels moviments socials a Catalunya, País Valencià i les Illes.* Barcelona: Lavínia, 1972. 848 pages.

ESSAYS

AMADES, Joan. *Costumari català: el curs de l'any.* 2ª ed. facsímil. Barcelona: Salvat: Edicions 62, 1982-1983. 5 vol.

Anuari estadístic. Barcelona: Consorci d'Informació i Documentació de Catalunya, 1985. Yearly.

ARTAL, Francesc; et al. *Ictineu: diccionari de les ciències de la societat als Països Catalans: segles XVIII-XX.* Barcelona: Edicions 62, 1979. 549 pages. (Cultura catalana contemporània).

BILBENY, Norbert. *La ideologia nacionalista a Catalunya.* Barcelona: Laia, 1988. 234 pages. (L'entrellat).

Calendari de festes de Catalunya, Andorra i la Franja: estudi antropològic, inventari i descripció de totes les celebracions populars... / Fundació Serveis de Cultura Popular. Barcelona: Alta Fulla, 1989. 630 pages.

COLOMER I CALSINA, Josep Maria. *Espanyolisme i catalanisme: la idea de nació en el pensament polític català (1939-1979).* Barcelona: L'Avenç, 1984. XVII, 428 pages. (Clio); 4).

CUCURULL, Fèlix. *Panoràmica del nacionalisme català.* París: Edicions catalanes de París, 1975. 6 vol.

Estatut d'Autonomia de Catalunya. 4ª ed. Barcelona: Generalitat de Catalunya. Entitat Autònoma del Diari Oficial i de Publicacions, 1988. 78 pages.

FÀBREGAS, Xavier. *El llibre de les bèsties: zoologia fantàstica catalana.* Barcelona: Edicions 62, 1983. 280 pages. (Vida i costums dels catalans).

Història econòmica de la Catalunya contemporània / direcció: Jordi Nadal i Oller... [et al.]. Barcelona: Enciclopèdia Catalana, 1988. Seran 6 vol.

Lleis polítiques de Catalunya / rapporteur: Joaquim Tornos i Mas. Barcelona: Bosch, 1984. 462 pages.

SCIENCES

Història natural dels Països Catalans / direction: Ramon Folch i Guillèn. Barcelona: Enciclopèdia Catalana, 1984-1989. 15 vol.

Enciclopèdia de medicina i salut / direction: Josep del Hoyo i Calduch. Barcelona: Enciclopèdia Catalana, 1989. There will be 10 volumes.

Natura ús o abús?: Llibre blanc de la gestió de la natura als Països Catalans / Ramon Folch i Guillèn, dir. 2ª ed. Barcelona: Barcino, 1989. 584 pages.

RIERA I TUÈBOLS, Santiago. *Síntesi d'història de la ciència catalana.* Barcelona: La Magrana, 1983. 345 pages. (La Magrana; 26).

ART AND MUSIC

Anuari del disseny a Catalunya. Barcelona: Fundació BCD, 1987. Yearly.

Catàleg de monuments i conjunts històrico-artístics de Catalunya. Barcelona: Generalitat de Catalunya. Departament de Cultura, 1990. 470 pages.

Catalunya romànica / direcció: Jordi Vigué. Barcelona: Enciclopèdia Catalana, 1984. There will be 24 vol.

CIRICI I PELLICER, Alexandre. *Museus d'art catalans.* Barcelona: Destino, 1982. 303 pages.

Història de l'art català / coord. de Francesc Miralles. Barcelona: Edicions 62, 1983-1986. 8 vol.

PADROL, Jordi. *Recull de la discografia catalana vigent.* [Barcelona: Jordi Padrol, 1984]. 2 vol.

PLADEVALL I FONT, Antoni. *Això és Catalunya: guia del patrimoni arquitectònic.* Generalitat de Catalunya. Departament de Cultura. Direcció General del Patrimoni Artístic. Barcelona: Plaza & Janés, 1987. 515 pages.

CATALAN LANGUAGE

DICTIONARIES

ALCOVER, Antoni M.; MOLL, Francesc de B. *Diccionari català-valencià-balear: inventari lexicogràfic i etimològic de la llengua catalana.* Palma de Mallorca: Moll, 1976-1978. 10 vol.

COROMINES, Joan. *Diccionari etimològic i complementari de la llengua catalana.* Barcelona: Curial: La Caixa, 1980. 9 vol.

COROMINES, Joan. *Onomasticon Cataloniae.* Barcelona: Curial: La Caixa, 1989.

Diccionari de la llengua catalana. Barcelona: Enciclopèdia Catalana, 1982. 1679 pages.

FABRA, Pompeu. *Diccionari general de la llengua catalana.* 19ª ed. Barcelona: EDHASA, 1984. XXX, 1786 pages.

ESSAYS ON PHILOLOGY AND LINGUISTICS

BONET, Sebastià; SOLÀ, Joan. *Sintaxi generativa catalana.* Barcelona: Enciclopèdia Catalana, 1986. 431 pages. (Biblioteca Universitària; 6. Manuals de llengua catalana).

BRUGUERA, Jordi. *Història del lèxic català;* presentació general de J. Solà. 2ª ed. Barcelona: Enciclopèdia Catalana, 1986. 147 pages. (Biblioteca Universitària; 1. Manuals de llengua catalana).

CABRÉ, Maria Teresa; RIGAU, Gemma. *Lexicologia i semàntica.* Barcelona: Enciclopèdia Catalana, 1986. 198 pages. (Biblioteca Universitària; 3. Manuals de llengua catalana).

COLON, Germà; SOBERANAS, Amadeu J. *Panorama de la lexicografia catalana. De les glosses medievals a Pompeu Fabra.* Barcelona: Enciclopèdia Catalana, 1986. 276 pages. (Biblioteca Universitària; 7. Manuals de llengua catalana).

MARTÍ I CASTELL, Joan. *Gramàtica catalana: curs superior.* Barcelona: Edhasa, Reimp. 1983. 209 pages. (El Punt).

MASCARÓ, Joan. *Morfologia.* Barcelona: Enciclopèdia Catalana, 1986; 148 pages. (Biblioteca Universitària; 5. Manuals de llengua catalana).

NADAL I FARRERAS, Josep M. *Història de la llengua catalana.* Barcelona: Edicions 62, 1982. En 3 vol. (Estudis i documents; 33) vol. 1. 1982. In print.

RAFEL I FONTANALS, Joaquim. *Gramàtica catalana, curs elemental.* 13ª reimp. Barcelona: Edhasa, 1985. 367 pages. (Col., El punt; 1).

SEGARRA, Mila. *Història de la normativa catalana.* Barcelona: Enciclopèdia Catalana, 1985. 222 pages. (Biblioteca Universitària; 2. Manuals de llengua catalana).

VENY, Joan. *Introducció a la dialectologia catalana.* 2ª ed. Barcelona: Enciclopèdia Catalana, 1986. 230 pages. (Biblioteca Universitària; 4. Manuals de la llengua catalana).

Documents d'història de la llengua catalana: dels orígens a Fabra. Joan Martí i Castell, Josep Moran. Barcelona: Empúries, 1986. 448 pages. (Les naus d'Empúries. Timó; 2)

CATALAN LITERATURE

Diccionari de la literatura catalana / director: Joaquim Molas and Josep Massot i Muntaner. Barcelona Edicions 62, 1979. 762 pages.

Història de la literatura catalana / director: Joan Manuel Prado and Francesc Vallverdú. Barcelona: Edicions 62: Orbis, 1985. 4 vol.

Història de la literatura catalana / director: Martí de Riquer. Barcelona: Ariel, 1982-1989. 11 vol.

GEOGRAPHY

Atlas universal català / technical director: J. Vilà i Valentí. Barcelona: Enciclopèdia Catalana, 1984. 462 pages.

CASASSAS I SIMÓ, Lluís; CLUSA, Joaquim. *L'organització territorial de Catalunya.* Barcelona: Fundació Jaume Bofill, 1981. 326 pages. (Temes bàsics).

GALERA I MONEGAL, Montserrat. «Bibliografia de Pau Vila». In *Miscel·lània Pau Vila: biografia, bibliografia, treballs d'homenatge.* Granollers: Montblanc-Martín, 1975. Pages 65-85.

GALERA I MONEGAL, Montserrat. *Bibliografía geográfica de la ciudad de Barcelona* / prólogo de J. Vilá Valentí. Barcelona: Ajuntament de Barcelona: Departamento de Geografía del CSIC, 1973. 2 vol.

GALERA I MONEGAL, Montserrat; ROCA, Francesc; TARRAGÓ, Salvador. *Atlas de Barcelona: [segles XVI-XX]* / introduction by Pau Vila. 2ª ed. [Barcelona]: Col·legi Oficial d'Arquitectes de Catalunya, 1982. XXVIII, 1067 pages: illus.

Gran geografia comarcal de Catalunya / direcció: Max Cahner. Barcelona: Enciclopèdia Catalana, 1981-1989. 19 vol.

Guia del viatger: Plaza & Janés: Catalunya 1990 / Departament de creació editorial de Plaza & Janés. Barcelona: Plaza & Janés, 1990. 316 pages; 38 map pages.

HISTORY

ESSAYS

GALERA I MONEGAL, Montserrat. «Barcelona vista pels viatgers del segle XVIII». In *Revista catalana de geografia.* Barcelona: Montblanc-Martín, 1978. Any 5, Vol. 5, núm. 17 (gener-març 1982). Pages 87-102.

Història de Catalunya / director: Pierre Vilar. Barcelona: Edicions 62, 1987-1989. 8 vol.

Història dels Països Catalans / director: Albert Balcells. 2ª ed. Barcelona: EDHASA, 1980-1982. 3 vol.

BIOGRAPHIES

200 catalans a les Amèriques: 1493-1987: mostra del diccionari de Catalunya i Amèrica / dir. Pere Grases i Pere Molas. Barcelona: Generalitat de Catalunya. Comissió Catalana del Cinquè Centenari del Descobriment d'Amèrica, 1988. 699 pages.

ALBERTÍ, Santiago. *Diccionari biogràfic.* Barcelona: Albertí, 1966-1970. 4 vol.

Gent nostra [col·lecció] / director: Josep M. Infiesta. Barcelona: Nou Art Thor, 1978.- In the process of being published.

TUDELA, Xavier. *Catalans de fora.* Barcelona: El Llamp, 1985. 2 vol. (Col·lecció La Rella).

BASIC CHRONOLOGY

This chronology outlines the historical, cultural, social and political events that have marked Catalonia's collective trajectory. At the same time, it points out some of the world-wide events that are considered decisive in universal history, in order to provide a frame of reference and a deeper understanding of those corresponding to Catalonia. The chronology begins in the fifth century BC, with the Greek foundation of two colonies on the Catalan coast, a key factor in the later opening-up of Catalonia to other cultures, and concludes with the year 1989, a year marked by far-reaching global events.

This chronology has been prepared by Josep M. Cadena in cooperation with Josep-Maria Puigjaner.

5th cent. BC The Greeks settle in Roses and Empúries.

218 BC Hannibal enters the territory that will in time become Catalonia, and crosses the Pyrenees.

1st cent. BC The Romans settle in the city of Barcelona.

2nd-3rd cent. AD Christianity is introduced to Catalonia.

415 The visigothic King Ataülf establishes his capital in Barcelona.

476 The fall of the Roman Empire.

655 The promulgation of the *Liber iudiciorum* which unifies the legislation of the Visigoths and the Hispanics. Around the year 1140, it is translated into Catalan.

717-718 The Saracens, who began to invade Spain in the year 710, take over Catalonia.

732 The Battle of Poitiers halts the Islamic advance towards Europe.

800 Charlemagne tries to reestablish the Western Roman Empire.

801 The conquest of Barcelona by the Franks and the foundation of the Spanish March.

848 The death of Sunifred I, the first count of the Catalonian dynasty, under the Frankish Empire.

897 Death of Count Wifred I, the founder of the monasteries of Ripoll (879) and Sant Joan de les Abadesses (887).

9th-10th cent. The beginning and the development of the group of constructions comprising the monastery of Sant Pere de Rodes, an impressive testimony to the Romanesque Catalan era and centre of medieval culture.

902 The Saracens invade the Balearic Islands.

985 The city of Barcelona is destroyed by Al Mansur.

988 Borrell II establishes the independence of the Catalan Earldom from the Franks.

c. 1025 Abbot Oliba, Bishop of Vic, transforms the small hermitage of Santa Maria into a monastery, thereby founding the Monastery of Montserrat.

1027 First assembly of "peace and truce" in Toluges (Rosselló), called by Abbot Oliba of Ripoll.

11thcent. The beginning of the Compilation of the *Usatges*, the base of Catalan civil law regulating feudalism.

12th cent. The Catalan knights returning from the Holy Land initiate in Catalonia the devotion for Saint George, who will later be the patron saint of the nation.

1112 The Earldom of Provence falls under Catalan rule through the marriage of Raymond Berenguer III with Dolça of Provence.

1137 The union of Catalonia and Aragon through the engagement of Raymond Berenguer IV of Barcelona to Petronila, the daughter of Ramiro II of Aragon.

1153 The expulsion of the Saracens from all Catalan territory. The foundation of the Cistercian Monastery of Santa Maria de Poblet.

1156 Treaty of Catalonia-Aragon with Castile-León, to fix the limits of the expansion of the respective kingdoms.

1162 The beginning of the writing of the *Gesta comitum Barcinonensium et regnum Aragoniae*, the first of the major chronicles.

1168 The establishment of the Cistercian monks at Santa Maria de Santes Creus, which in 1152 was already an abbey with the name Valldaura.

12th cent. The *Homilies d'Organyà*, the first Catalan literary text, are written, and are conserved to this day.

1204 Peter I of Catalonia-Aragon is crowned king in Rome by Pope Innocence III.

1212 Catalonia-Aragon, with Peter I, participates in the Battle of Las Navas de Tolosa, defeating the Muslims.

1213 Peter I dies in the Battle of Muret against the French, and Catalonia loses its influence in Occitania.

1218 The Order of Mercy is founded in Barcelona by Saint Pere Nolasc, with the mission of rescuing Christian captives.

1229 King James I of Catalonia-Aragon takes Majorca from the Saracens.

1230 Beginning of the writing of the *Llibre dels feits*, the great chronicle of the reign of James I.

1232-33 Ramon Llull (Raymond Lully), the philosopher and writer, is born in Majorca; he is the most universal Catalan of his century.

1232-38 King James I takes Valencia from the Muslims.

1258 Treaty of Corbeil between James I of Catalonia-Aragon and St. Louis IX of France, in which Catalonia renounced its claim to Languedoc, and France renounces to its claims of the Catalan territories.

1265 The Council of the Hundred (Consell de Cent), an advisory assembly of the municipal governement of Barcelona, is formed.

1266 James I conquers Murcia.

c. 1271 The fundamental work *Art abreujada de trobar la veritat* is written by Ramon Llull.

1274 *Summa contra gentiles*, is written by Saint Thomas of Aquino, at the request of Saint Raymond of Penyafort.

1276 Division of the Catalan Kingdom upon the death of James I, among his children: Peter (Catalonia, Aragon and Valencia) and James (the Balearic Islands, Rosselló or Roussillon and Montpellier).

1282 Peter II conquers Sicily. The *Consolat de Mar*, the first western code of maritime law, takes effect.

1285 Crusade of Pope Martin IV is waged against Peter II, King of Catalonia-Aragon.

1287 Completion of the first translation of the Bible into Catalan.

1288 *Llibre del rei En Pere*, or the chronicle of Bernat Desclot, the second great Catalan chronicle, is written.

1295 The Treaty of Anagni is signed, by which Catalonia makes peace with the Vatican, after the conflicts resulting from the Catalan conquest of Sicily.

1300 The *Estudi General de Lleida*, the first Catalan university, is established.

1305 Roger de Flor, head of the great Catalan Company in the Byzantine Empire, is murdered. The Catalan mercenaires avenge themselves, causing great destruction, and the expression "Catalan Vengeance" is introduced into the language.

1307 Dante Alighieri begins writing the *Divine Comedy*.

1323 The Catalans conquer the island of Sardinia under the Infant Alphonse, the son of James II of Catalonia-Aragon.

1325/1328 Ramon Muntaner writes his *Crònica*, a work of historic and literary interest that studies the period between 1207 and 1328.

1336 Peter III the Ceremonious, the King of Catalonia-Aragon and the architect of Catalan expansion into the Mediterranean, begins his long reign.

1337 The Hundred Years' War between France and England begins, and lasts until 1453.

1348 The Black Plague is declared in Catalonia, and causes the death of two thirds of the population.

1349 The Catalan-Aragonese Crown recaptures Majorca under the crown of Peter III the Ceremonious.

1350 By order of King Peter III, documents are dated according to the year of the Nativity, which begins on December 25. This norm is followed until the eighteenth century.

1356-1369 War breaks out between Peter III of Catalonia and Peter I the Cruel of Castile.

1359 Establishment of the Generalitat as a permanent institution, at the "Corts" of Cervera, which acts as a delegated organ of the Corts.

1360 *De consolatione philosophiae* by Boetius, is translated into Catalan.

1375 The beginning of the writing of the *Crònica* of Peter III the Ceremonious, covering the period from 1299-1387, that is, of the lives of King Peter, who ordered it written, and of his father, Alphonse the Good. The Majorcan school of cartography distinguishes itself. The *Atles català*, written by the Jewish Majorcans Cresques Abraham and Jafudà Creques, reflects the vision of the world as it is known at the time.

1378 The beginnings of the Western Schism, the division of the Christians, under two Popes at once.

1387/1410 With the death of John I and Martin I, the royal Catalan dynasty comes to an end.

1391 The Feast of the *Gaia Ciència*, precursor of the *Jocs Florals* of the *Renaixença*, is introduced in Catalonia.

1399 Bernat Metge writes *Lo Somni*, his masterpiece.

14th century *Els Pastorets*, a particular form of popular theatre, begins to appear.

1412 The Pledge of Casp causes the Catalan-Aragonese crown to pass to Ferdinand of Antequera of Castile-León. The Valencian Saint Vincent Ferrer, the Dominican and writer who devoted himself especially to the conversion of Jews and Saracens, takes the pulpit.

1417 The Council of Constance ends the Western Schism.

1435 An anonymous writer begins *Curial e Güelfa*, an outstaading Catalan novel of chivalry, in Valencia.

1450 The struggle ensues between the "Busca" and the "Biga", political groups whose conflicts in Barcelona stem from economic motives.

1453 The Turks take Constantinople and the Byzantine Empire falls.

1462 War breaks out between the Generalitat and King John II, representing a conflict between Catalan constitutionalism and monarchic authoritarianism.

1468 Isabella the Catholic is recognized as the Queen of Castile.

1472 The Agreement of Pedralbes is signed between John II and Barcelona.

1474 The *Trobes en llaor de la Verge Maria*, the first book printed in Catalan, is published in Valencia.

1478 The creation of the Inquisition in Castile results in an ecclesiastic organism charged with purifiying the faith, under the threat of punishment.
The first Bible printed in Catalan, translated by Friar Bonifaci Ferrer, is published in Valencia.

1479 Ferdinand II becomes the King of Catalonia-Aragon and Castile.

1485/1486 *Guerra dels Remences*, or War of the Serfs (the farmers versus the gentlemen) begins and is solved by the declaration of Guadalupe.

1487 The Inquisition is established in Catalonia.

1490 The first edition of *Tirant lo Blanc* by Joanot Martorell is published in Valencia; it is considered the first modern novel.

1492 Granada is taken from the Muslims. America is discovered.
The Jews are expelled from Spain.

1493 Catalonia is excluded from the partition of occupied lands in the conquest of America.
Rosselló and Sardinia are retaken by the Catalan-Aragonese Crown.

1494 Columbus, the discoverer of America, is received in Barcelona by the Catholic Monarchs.

1500 The "Italian Wars" begin between the Hispanics and the French for dominion of the peninsula.

1517 Luther proclaims the 95 Thesis of Wittenberg, marking the rupture with the Catholic Church.

1519 Hernán Cortés discovers and conquers Mexico.

1531 Francisco Pizarro discovers and conquers Peru.

1540 The Pope approves the founding statutes of the Society of Jesus.

1545 The Council of Trento begins, to be concluded in 1563.

1565 The revolution of the Low Countries is waged against Philip II, the King of Spain.

1571 The Hispanic fleet sent by the Catalan Lluís de Requesens neutralizes the Turkish threat in the Mediterranean in the Battle of Lepanto.

1573 Sevillian monopoly in Spain's commerce with America, excludes Catalonia.

1605 Cervantes publishes the first part of his work *Don Quijote de la Mancha.*

1609 Jeroni Pujades publishes the *Crònica Universal del Principat de Catalunya.*

1618 The Thirty Years' War begins, involving all of Europe, France and the Spanish monarchy.

1621 The reign of Philip IV begins, marked by the centralist ideas of his prime minister, the Conde Duque de Olivares.

1640 *Corpus de Sang* (Bloody Corpus) and *guerra dels Segadors* (Reapers's War), in which the Catalans confront King Philip IV.

1648 Peace of Westphalia and the congress establishing the principle of the independence of nations.

1649 Charles I is decapitated in Great Britain; Cromwell becomes the head of the English Republic.

1653 The Reapers' War ends. Philip IV, King of Spain, promises to respect the Constitutions of Catalonia.

1659 Treaty of the Pyrenees. The Spanish monarchy cedes the Earldom of Rosselló (Roussillon) and half Cerdanya (Cerdagne), at the expense of Catalonia.

1676 Llorenç Cendrós publishes the *Gramàtica Catalana.*

1683 *Fénix de Cataluña*, is published by Narcís Feliu de la Penya, a symbol of the beginning of the economic reactivation of Catalonia.

1700 Charles II dies; Philip V is named King of Spain and agrees to respect the Catalan Constitutions.

1701 The War of Succession to the Spanish Crown begins, and Catalonia takes the side of the Archduke Charles of Austria.

1705 Archduke Charles of Austria is recognized as King of Catalonia.

1708 The first performance of opera in Barcelona, in the Llotja de Mar, with music by the Venetian Antonio Caldara.

1714 Barcelona capitulates on September 11 to the French and Spanish troops of Philip V. The historic Catalan institutions are dissolved (Generalitat), and a period of strict repression follows.

1716 King Philip V imposes the *Nueva Planta* Decree, calling for a new juridic and political regime for Catalonia, with ultimate authority vested in the military.

1717 The University of Barcelona is moved to Cervera by order of Philip V, as a punitive measure.

1733 The families of the crowns of Spain and France sign their first pact to divide among them the kingdoms and dukedoms of Europe.

1736 The manufactures of calicos turn Barcelona into an industrial city.

1740 The War of Succession begins in Austria.

1745 The royal families of Spain and France (Philip V and Louis XIV) sign their second pact to divide among them areas of dominance.

1746 Ferdinand VI is crowned the King of Spain.

1748 The treaty of Aix-la-Chapelle, between France and Great Britain ends the War of Succession in Austria.

1749 Baldiri Reixac publishes *Instruccions per a l'ensenyament de minyons*, a new pedagogic system which defends the teaching in Catalan language.

1756 The Seven Years' War breaks out between Great Britain and Prussia against France, Austria and their allies.
Ferdinand VI authorizes the Commercial Company of Barcelona to trade in America.

1759 Charles III becomes the King of Spain.

1761 The royal families of Spain and France make their third pact.

1769 The Baron of Maldà begins to write his *Calaix de Sastre*, a record of events comprising 60 volumes.

1778 Charles III gives Catalans the right to partake in trade in America.

1779 *Memóricas historias*, the first economic historical text published in Europe, is written by Antoni de Capmany.

1789 The French Revolution begins.

1792 Proclamation of the First French Republic.
The *Diario de Barcelona*, one of the oldest newspapers in Europe, begins publication.

1804 Napoleon is proclaimed emperor.

1805 The Catalan Domènec Badia, "Alí-Bey", is the first European to travel to Mecca, and in 1814 he publishes *Voyage d'Ali-Bey* in Paris; it is later translated into several languages.

1808 War with France. Catalonia defends itself against Napolean.

1810 Napoleon unites France and Catalonia.

1812 The first Spanish Constitution is proclaimed in Cadiz.

1814 Ferdinand VII returns to Spain, the war with France having end-ed.

1815 The Battle of Waterloo, ends Napoleon's military power. The Congress of Vienna results in the creation of the Holy Alliance of the victorious European powers.
Gramàtica de la llengua catalana, by Josep Pau Ballot, is the first step in the Catalan *Renaixença.*

1824 The Battle of Ayachucho ends with the victory of General Sucre; the South American countries consummate their independence.

1832 The Industrial Revolution begins in Catalonia; the first factories operate with steam heat.

1833 Ferdinand VII dies; Isabella II is proclaimed queen.
The First Carlist War begins between the Isabellans and the Carlists, supporters of Charles of Bourbon.

1835 Revolution of July in Catalonia: the social radicalization of the urban proletariat.
Utopian socialism, based on the doctrines of Saint-Simon, Fourier, and Cabot, extends throughout Catalonia.

1836-1843 Uprisings and *bullangues*, or socio-political agitation. The workers begin to organize.

1837 Pep Ventura renews the *sardana*, the national dance of Catalonia.

1838 Coronation of Queen Victoria of England.
Mendizábal's *desamortización* decree confiscates the Church's possessions.

1840 The First Carlist War ends in Catalonia between the supporters of Charles of Bourbon, or the absolutists, and those of Isabella II, or the liberals.

The Association of Textile Workers, the first workers' union, is founded in Catalonia.

1841 Rubió i Ors publishes *Lo Gaiter del Llobregat*; this was also his pseudonym. *Lo Pare Arcàngel* appears; it is the first newspaper to be written entirely in Catalan.
The first gas lights are put into use in Barcelona.

1842 Catalan uprising against Espartero's free-trade policy. Barcelona is bombed.

1844 The Caja de Ahorros y Monte de Piedad (the Savings and Loan Bank) of Barcelona is founded.

1845 Josep Anselm Clavé creates his popular choral groups.

1847 The Gran Teatre del Liceu is inaugurated in Barcelona, dedicated to the performance of opera up to the present day. Opera was first performed in Barcelona as early as 1750 in the Teatre de la Santa Creu.

1848 The Second French Republic.
The *guerra dels Matiners*, or Second Carlist War, in which not only Carlists, but also progressives and Republicans participate.
Catecisme de la Doctrina Cristiana by Antoni M. Claret.
The first train is inaugurated, between Barcelona and Mataró.

1854-1855 Catalonia and Spain experience their first general strikes.

1858 Napoleon III is named Emperor of France.
Construction begins on the Eixample (Expansion) of Barcelona, according to the Cerdà Plan.

1859 General Prim and the Catalan volunteers fight valiently in the War of Africa.
Restoration in Barcelona of the *Jocs Florals* (literary competitions), a continuation of those created by King John I in 1393.

1860 The Catalan Narcís Monturiol demonstrates with his *Ictíneo* the possibility of underwater navigation.

1861 The War of Secession in the United States between the protectionist states of the North and the free-traders of the South.
Bismarck becomes Prime Minister of Prussia.

1863 Inauguration of the Romea Theatre, where Catalan actors and playwrights would develop their careers.

1864 The First International, a supernational organization devoted to defending workers' interests, is founded in London.

1868 The Revolution of September, the fall of Isabella II and the beginning of a period of liberties.

1870 The French defeat in the Franco-Prussian War results in the fall of Napoleon III.
The First Spanish Workers' Congress in Barcelona is held and attended by delegates from all over Spain.

1871 The Paris Commune, a revolutionary international movement with legislative and executive powers is founded.
The Second Reich begins under Bismarck's reunified Germany.
Amadeo of Savoy, King of Spain, is elected by the Cortes in 1870.

1872 The Third Carlist War begins.
The first tram lines are inaugurated in Barcelona.

1873 The First Spanish Republic is declared in Barcelona.

1875 Alphonse XII comes to Spain through the port at Barcelona. The Monarchy is restored.
La llumanera de Nova York, an illustrated magazine written in Catalan, begins publication in New York.
"La febre d'or" ("The gold fever)" is the name given to the period between 1875 and 1885; it is a time of great prosperity for the Catalan bourgeoisie.

1876 Pi i Maragall publishes the work *Las Nacionalidades*, an anti-centralist treatise on Spain.
The Catalan Scientific Excursionist Association is founded; it is the precursor of the Excursionistic Centre of Catalonia.

1878 The definitive edition of the epic poem *L'Atlàntida* by Jacint Verdaguer is published.

1879 *Diari Català* is founded by Valentí Almirall; it is the first newspaper to be written in Catalan.
The phylloxera, a disease affecting wine grapes, wreaks havoc in Catalonia.

1880 The Catalanist Congress, the first political platform for Catalanism, is established.

1882 Valentí Almirall founds the Centre Català, a pro-Catalan political organization.

1884 At the Conference of Berlin, promoted by France and Germany, commercial and colonialist interests in Arica are divided up.
Lighting at night is introduced to Barcelona.

1885 *"Memorial de greuges"* ("Record of Offences") is presented to the King of Spain in the first exclusively political action of Catalanism.
Serious outbreak of cholera in Barcelona.

1886 Valentí Almirall writes *Lo Catalanisme*, a masterpiece of political doctrine.

1888 The World Exhibition is held in Barcelona.
Àngel Guimerà debuts his theatrical work *Mar i Cel*.
The UGT is founded in Barcelona; the PSOE holds its first congress in Barcelona.

1891 Creation of the Catalan Choral Society (Orfeó Català).

1892 Unió Catalanist and *"Bases de Manresa"* proclaim the sovereingty of Catalonia's internal government.
Narcís Oller writes the novel *La febre d'or*.

1893 Anarchists plant a bomb in the Liceu Theatre, resulting in twenty-one deaths.

1896 A bomb explodes on Canvis Nous street. Trial at Montjuïc of several anarchists.

1897 Forty-six heads of Catalan companies send a message to the King of Greece, urging autonomy for the island of Crete.
The newspaper *La Renaixença* is outlawed.
The founding of "Els Quatre Gats", a cabaret and bar which serves as a meeting place for artists and intellectuals of the "modernist" era, including Picasso.
Terra Baixa, a theatrical work by Àngel Guimerà, makes its debut.

1898 The Spanish-American War with the United States, in which Spain loses its remaining colonies, including Cuba.
First Catalan automobile factory begins operations.

1899 "Locked cashboxes", or movement of protest by the industrialists of Barcelona in response to the central government's tax increase.
Codification of Catalan Civil Law.
First Catalan Congress of Cooperation.

1901 The presidents of the four Catalan provincial councils (diputaciones provinciales) are elected to posts in the Spanish house of Parliament.

The aerial cable car to Tibidabo is inaugurated; it is the first in Spain.

1902 Alphonse XIII, at the age of sixteen, is declared king.
General strike in Barcelona demanding a 9-hour work-day.
Jacint Verdaguer, national poet of Catalonia, dies.

1904 Russo-Japanese War: Japan gains control of Korea and Manchuria.
Founding of the Catalan childrens' magazine *En Patufet*.

1906 Several Catalan political parties converge to form the "Solidaritat Catalana" ("Catalan Solidarity") movement, in defence of Catalonia's identity.
Eugeni D'Ors promotes *noucentisme*, a cultural movement with a political agenda.
The Costa Brava begins to develop as a tourist area.

1907 The Institut d'Estudis Catalans is created.

1909 *"Setmana Tràgica"* ("the Tragic Week") in Barcelona, the name given to the popular antimilitary and anticlerical movement.

1911 First aviation tests take place in Barcelona.
The CNT (National Workers' Council), an anarchist union, is founded.

1912 *Història dels moviments nacionalistes* is written by Antoni Rovira i Virgili.
Introduction of the boy-scout movement in Catalonia.

1914 The First World War begins, and will last until the year 1918.
Creation of the Mancomunitat de Catalunya, under the presidency of Enric Prat de la Riba; it is the first attempt at self-government.

1915 Creation of the Official Stock Exchange of Barcelona.

1916 Great electoral victory of Lliga Catalana. Cambó requests that the Spanish Parliament grant Catalonia autonomy.

1917 October Revolution in Russia gives rise to the Bolshevick party.
Assembly of MPs — deputies and senators — in a number of non-official meetings in Barcelona.
Diccionari Ortogràfic by Pompeu Fabra, which complemented the *Normes Ortogràfiques* ("Orthographic Rules") published in 1913.

1918 The Mancomunitat de Catalunya and the Catalan MP again request autonomy for Catalonia in Madrid.
The *Gramàtica catalana*, by Pompeu Fabra, is published; it is an essential tool in the normalization of the language.

1919 The Mancomunitat de Catalunya holds an assembly to approve a Statute of Autonomy.
Threats are made against the lives of union leaders.
Strike of La Canadiense.
Catalan employers "lock-out" workers.

1920 First Sample Fair in Barcelona.

1922 Antoni Rovira Virgili begins to publish the *Història nacional de Catalunya*.
The Metro Transversal (Underground railway) is inaugurated in Barcelona.
Regular air service begins between Madrid and Barcelona.

1923 Coup d'état and subsequent dictatorship of General Primo de Rivera, which will last until 1930.

1924 Breton publishes his *Manifeste du Surréalisme*.
The publications *Revista de Catalunya* and the *Gaseta de les Arts* are born.
Ràdio Barcelona, the first radio station, begins to broadcast.

1929 Crisis of the New York Stock Exchange, with repercussions the world over.
International Exhibition is held in Barcelona.

1930 The Dictatorship of Primo de Rivera falls.

1931 The Monarchy falls and the Spanish Republic is proclaimed. Francesc Macià wins the municipal elections in Barcelona, representing Esquerra Republicana de Catalunya. In Barcelona, the Catalan Republic is declared, within the Federation of Iberian Republics, which will later be the Generalitat of Catalonia.

1932 The Catalan Statute of Autonomy and constitution of the Catalan Parliament are approved.
The Institut Escola for the education of Catalan professors is created.
Revolutionary general strike is held in the industrial basins of Llobregat and Cardener.

1933 Hitler is named Chancellor of Germany.
Francesc Macià dies, and is succeeded by Lluís Companys as President of the Generalitat.

1934 "Events of October 6" culminate in the proclamation of the Catalan State within the Spanish Republic: Lluís Companys and the Government of the Generalitat are sentenced and jailed.

1936 The Leftist Front experiences an electoral victory.
Lluís Companys resumes the presidency of the Generalitat.
Military uprising of General Franco sets off the Spanish Civil War.

1937 "Events of May": the Generalitat's peace-keeping forces and anarchist groups face each other in armed confrontations.

1939 Second World War begins.
The Republic loses the Civil War; the Generalitat dissolves and the Catalan Statut is suppressed. Concentration camps, prisons, executions and exile affect thousands.

1940 Lluís Companys is executed by Franco's dictatorial regime after a brief military trial.

1941 Alphonse XIII dies.

1944 The maquis, Republican anti-Franco guerillas, invade the Aran Valley.
Clandestine Catalan classes begin.
The publishing house Selecta resumes publications in Catalan.

1945 Atomic bombs are exploded over Hiroshima and Nagasaki.
The UN condemns Franco's regime.

1946 Foreign countries withdraw their diplomats from Spain.
Nuremberg Trial passes sentences on Nazi leaders.

1947 India and Pakistan gain their independence.
Referendum and Law of Spanish Succession result in the perpetuation of Franco's regime.
The "Joanot Martorell" prize for novel is established in order to promote Catalan literature.

1948 The State of Israel is born.
Within the closed post-war atmosphere, a group of innovative artists form the group "Dau al Set" and publish a magazine of the same name.

1949 NATO is established.

1950 Foreign diplomatics return to Spain.
Korean War.

1951 Tram strike in Barcelona; it is the first major strike against Franco's regime.

1952 International Eucharistic Conference is held in Barcelona.

1953 Spain and the United States make military agreements.

Stalin dies.
Spain joins UNESCO.
Spain reaches an agreement with the Holy See.

1954 President Tarradellas is elected president of the Catalan Parliament by exiled deputies in Mexico.

1955 Spain joins the UN.

1956 Hungarian Revolution: Catholics, youths and intellectuals oppose the presence of Soviet troops.

1957 First free assembly of students of the University of Barcelona requests democratic liberties.

1958 The first "Sputnik", in the series of satellites of the same name is launched by the Soviet Union.

1959 Socialist revolution in Cuba brings Fidel Castro to power.
The magazine *Serra d'Or*, an important Catalan cultural platform, begins publication.

1961 Second Vatican Council is held.
Massive American intervention begins in Vietnam.
The Berlin Wall is raised.
Òmnium Cultural, an entity dedicated to the promotion of Catalan culture, is founded.
The *"Nova cançó"* movement begins, restoring traditional Catalan music.

1962 Pope John XXIII writes his encyclical *Peace on Earth*.

1963 President John F. Kennedy is assassinated.
The Picasso Museum is created in Barcelona.

1964 Commissions Obreres trade union is founded in Catalonia.

1966 Referendum is held on the Organic Law of the Spanish State, which is passed by the Francoist Parliament.
Democratic Students' Syndicate of the University of Barcelona passes its constitution.
Democratic Group of Journalists is formed.

1967 The "Six Days' War": Israel invades Syria and Egypt without warning.

1968 Leftist students agitate in Paris during the month of May.
Russia invades Czechoslovakia.

1969 Man makes his first trip to the moon.
The *Gran Enciclopèdia Catalana* is published.

1970 ETA members are tried in Burgos and 300 Catalan intellectuals are confined in Montserrat.

1971 The Catalan Assembly, a unitarian anti-Francoist platform of political forces, unions and Catalan civic groups joins under the slogan "Liberty, Amnesty, Statute of Autonomy".

1973 The Vietnam War ends.
Picasso and Pau Casals die.
Admiral Carrero Blanco, Vice-President of the Spanish Government, dies in an attack by ETA.

1975 The Council of Political Forces of Catalonia is set up.
Franco dies. Juan Carlos I becomes King of Spain.
The Miró Foundation is inaugurated in Barcelona.
The Congress of Catalan Culture at the initiative of the Bar Association of Barcelona.

1976 Referendum is held on Spanish political reform.
Avui, the first Catalan newspaper since 1939, begins to publish.

1977 Democratic elections send deputies and senators to the Parliament in Madrid.
Popular demonstration on September 11 requests democratic liberties and political power for Catalonia.
The Generalitat is re-estabalished under the presidency of Josep Tarradellas.

1979 Formation of the first European Parliament.
Approval by referendum of the Catalan Statute of Autonomy.

1980 First elections to the Catalan Parliament since the Dictatorship.
The Parliament of Catalonia elects Jordi Pujol President of the Generalitat and leader of its government.
Joan Coromines begins the publication of the *Diccionari etimològic i complementari de la llengua catalana*.

1981 "Events of February 23": A coup d'état against the democratic government fails.

1983 Televisió de Catalunya (TV3) begins to broadcast in Catalan.

1986 Barcelona is appointed as host city of the 1992 Olympic Games.
The Second International Congress of the Catalan Language is held.

1987 The poet J.V. Foix, a preeminent figure in the literary Catalan vanguard, dies.
Frederic Montpou, one of the most important pianists and composers of the century, dies.

1988 Gorbachev becomes head of State of the Soviet Union.
Bush is elected President of the United States.
Catalonia celebrates its millennium.
The President of the Generalitat, Josep Tarradellas, dies.
The Convergència i Unió coalition wins its third victory in the Parliament elections of Catalonia, under the leadership of Jordi Pujol.

1989 Salvador Dalí, a major figure in surrealism and pictoric art of the twentieth century, dies.
Chinese army slaughters protesters in Tiananmen Square in Peking.
The Berlin Wall falls.
Democratic reforms begin in the socialist countries of Europe.
Queen Elizabeth II of England is received by President Pujol in the Palace of the Generalitat.
The Ist International Catalonia Prize is awarded to the Austrian philosopher Karl Popper.

1990 Inauguration of the new Pompeu Fabra University.
The European Parliament aknowledges Catalan as an official language.
Death of Miquel Coll i Alentorn, ex-President of the Parliament of Catalonia.
The IInd International Catalonia Prize is awarded to the Pakistani physic Abdús Salam.

1991 Inauguration of the Ramon Llull University, the first private university in Catalonia.
The IIIrd International Catalonia Prize is awarded to the oceanogapher Jacques-Yves Cousteau.
War in the Persian Gulf due to the annexation of Kuwait by Irak.

1992 The XXV Olympic Games of the modern era are held in Barcelona.
Jordi Pujol is elected President of the Generalitat of Catalonia for the fourth consecutive time.
The IVth International Catalonia Prize is awarded to the Russian cellist Mstislav Rostropovich.
Death of Joan Fuster, essayist, Catalan Literature Honour Prize-winner.

GRAPHIC DOCUMENTATION

Photography

EADOP Archives, Jordi Gumí, Municipal Historical Institute of Barcelona, AGE Fotostock, Firo-Foto, Alfa Omega, Montserrat Sagarra, Biblioteca de Catalunya, AISA, Eugeni Bofill, TAVISA, Montserrat Manent, Pere Rotger, COOB 92, Europa Press, Joan Bordas, Català Roca, Gasull, Banús March, EFE, Ros Ribas, Brangulí Archives, Barceló, Figueras Foundation, Diocesan Archives of La Seu d'Urgell, Robert Ramos, Fototeca Stone, Francesc Tur, Mas Archives, Aragon Crown Archives, Francesc Bedmar, Library of the Abbey of Montserrat, Public Episcopal Library of the Seminary of Barcelona, Eduard Cànovas, Toni Catany, Centelles, Colita, Fototeca Stone, Church Museum of Santa Maria at Terrassa, Eugenio, Museum of the Cathedral of Segorbe, Historical Museum of the City of Barcelona, Paisajes Españoles, Umberto Rivas, Robert, Gabriel Roman, Ferran Sendra, Serra d'Or, Xavier Trepat, Francis Vernhet

Cover photograph

Joan Garrigosa

The editor would like to express his appreciation to the following people and organizations for their collaboration in the collection of graphic material

Andrés Andreu, AUTEMA, Newspaper *Avui*, Ricard Badia, BCD, "Cantiga" Choir, "Càrmina" Choir, Carles Caballé, Càtedra Gaudí, High Standard Sports Study Centre, Generalitat Drama Centre, Centre of Contemporary History of Catalonia, Barraquer Centre of Ophthalmology, Col·legi Públic La Granja, Comediants, Commission of the Exhibition "Catalunya, la Fàbrica d'Espanya", Comissions Obreres, Confederació General del Treball, Confederació Sindical de Catalunya, Confederación Hidrográfica del Ebro, Promotional Consortium on Tourism, Convergència i Unió, Xavier Corberó, Càmping Cypsela, General Directorate for Linguistic Policy, General Directorate for Commerce, General Directorate for Public Security, Lluís Domènech i Girbau/Roser Amadó i Cercós, Edicions de l'Eixample, Edicions de Nou Art Thor, Enciclopèdia Catalana, Police Academy of Catalonia, Magazine *Espais*, Esquerra Republicana de Catalunya, FAD, Núria Feliu, Ferrocarrils de la Generalitat de Catalunya, Fair of Barcelona, Advisory Council of the Department of Agriculture, Livestock and Fisheries, Gabinete Uribe, Giralt Miracle, Grau Garriga, Montserrat Gudiol, Hospital de la Santa Creu i Sant Pau, IDIADA, IMPUSA, INEFC, Iniciativa per Catalunya, Catalan Literature Institution, Catalan Health Institute, Catalan Institute for Services to Young People, IRTA, ITEC, General Tests and Research Laboratory, Mariette Llorens, Marcel Martí, Molas Batalla, El Molino, Museum of Science and Technology of Terrassa, Olimpíada Cultural, Partit Popular, Partit Socialista de Catalunya, Catalan Pro Europa Board, Càmping Pirineos, Poliorama, Protocol of the Parliament of Catalonia, Publitempo, Ricard Bofill Taller d'Arquitectura, Saló Internacional del Còmic de Barcelona, Sarsanedas-Azcunce, Enric Satué, Joan Manuel Serrat, Plastic Arts Service of the Department of Culture, Agricultural Training Centre of the Department of Agriculture, Livestock and Fisheries, Administrative Organization and Documentation Service of the Departament of Justice, Publications Service of the Department of Culture, Publications Service of the Parliament of Catalonia, Síndic de Greuges, General Subdirectorate for Interdepartmental Activities, General Subdirectorate for Mass Media, General Subdirectorate for Works and Patrimony of the Department of Justice, Tocs Bookstore, Avel·lí Trinxet, Montserrat Trueta, TV3, Unió General de Treballadors, Xavier Vivanco

Els Segadors

sempre f